The Private Pilot's Licence Course

Question and Answer Simplifier

The Private Pilot's Licence Course

Question and Answer Simplifier

ISBN 978 1 906559 07 6

Published by

Airplan Flight Equipment Ltd

This book is intended to be a study aid to the written examination element of the PPL course. It does not in any way replace or overrule the instruction you will receive from a flight instructor at a flying training organisation (FTO) or registered facility (RF). No part of this book overrules or supersedes the Air Navigation Order (ANO), Aeronautical Information Publication (AIP), Aeronautical Information Circulars (AICs), Joint Aviation Requirements (JAR) and other documents published by a competent authority; the flight manual/pilot's operating handbook for the aircraft being flown; the pilot order book/flying training organisation or registered facility syllabus; and the general provisions of good airmanship and safe flying practice.

Originally published as The Questions and Answers Book for the Private Pilots Licence

First Edition 1993

Second Edition 1994

Reprinted with revisions 1997

Republished as Questions & Answers for the PPL Course

Third Edition 1999

Reprinted with revisions 2003

Reprinted with revisions 2004

Reprinted with revisions 2006

This 4th Edition 2008

Copyright © 2008 Airplan Flight Equipment Ltd

**The Private Pilot's Licence Course
Question and Answer Simplifier**

ISBN 978 1 906559 07 6

Airplan Flight Equipment Ltd
1a Ringway Trading Estate, Shadowmoss Road, Manchester M22 5LH
Tel: 0161 499 0023   Fax: 0161 499 0298
email: enquiries@afeonline.com
www.afeonline.com

Contents

Introduction
    Studying for the PPL theoretical knowledge
       examinations 6-9
Air Law and Operational Procedures...................11-61
    Essential Revision 13-22
    Question Paper 1...23-30
    Question Paper 2...31-37
    Question Paper 3 38-44
    Answers and Explanations 45-61
Meteorology 63-101
    Essential Revision 65-69
    Question Paper 1...72-77
    Question Paper 2...78-83
    Question Paper 3...84-89
    Answers and Explanations...........................90-101
Navigation 103-161
    Essential Revision 105-109
    Question Paper 1...112-118
    Question Paper 2 119-125
    Question Paper 3 126-132
    Answers and Explanations..........................133-161
Communications 163-196
    Essential Revision 165-168
    Question Paper 1...170-174
    Question Paper 2 175-179
    Question Paper 3 180-184
    Answers and Explanations..........................185-196

Flight Performance and Planning.....................197-235
    Essential Revision 199-201
    Question Paper 1..204-209
    Question Paper 2..210-214
    Question Paper 3 215-220
    Answers and Explanations 221-235
Aircraft General & Principles of Flight...........237-297
    Essential Revision 239-243
    Question Paper 1...246-254
    Question Paper 2...255-263
    Question Paper 3...264-272
    Answers and Explanations 273-297
Human Performance and Limitations 299-327
    Essential Revision 301-303
    Question Paper 1...306-309
    Question Paper 2...310-313
    Question Paper 3...314-317
    Answers and Explanations.........................318-327
Answers...329-341
    Air Law and Operational Procedures 331-333
    Meteorology...334
    Navigation 335
    Communications 336
    Flight Performance and Planning 337
    Aircraft General & Principles of Flight......338-340
    Human Performance and Limitations 341
    Answer sheets 353-363

Contributors & Acknowledgments

Rod Brown

Rod has been involved in aviation since 1956 when he became an RAF engineer. He gained his PPL in 1959 and his Commercial licence and ratings in 1985. Rod has been the CFI of various flying establishments within the London area for the past 20 years. He joined Cabair in 1996 and has been the CFI of Denham School of Flying since 1998.

John Dale

Formerly an Air Traffic Control Officer at Manchester International Airport working tower and approach sectors with 35 years experience. He gained his PPL in 1984 and now holds a Commercial licence, Instructor and Examiner ratings. John established JD Aviation in 2002 specialising in Commercial flight training, based at Manchester International Airport. He flies all types of aircraft up to business jets.

James Murphy

Gained his PPL in 1996, instructor and examiner rating in 1998. James has over 3000 flying hours instructing. He is the ground and flight examiner at Manchester School of Flying, and has been CFI at various flying schools in the North West of England. When not instructing he flies business jets from Manchester and Liverpool airports.

Ian Sixsmith

Ian has been flying since the age of 16 years, he gained his PPL in 1962. After gaining his instructor rating he became CFI of Comed Aviation at Blackpool, followed by Leicester Aero Club and Manchester School of Flying. Latterly he was a Director of Operations and CFI at Aviation Manchester at Woodford. He is a qualified ground instructor and examiner, currently running his own ground school within the North West of England.

As always this book would not have been possible without the invaluable assistance of many people and organisations including:

Louise Southern

Robert Taylor, GDi studio

Cabair Group

JD Aviation

Manchester School of Flying

Claire Hardman

Simon Hayes

Gill Tumley

Roger Gilles

Doug Patton

Studying for the PPL theoretical knowledge examinations

It's probably fair to say that anybody embarking on a Private Pilot Licence (PPL) course is far more enthusiastic about the flying ahead of them than the prospect of studying for and passing seven written examinations of theoretical knowledge. Whilst this is understandable, it is also a shame because (if approached properly), gaining the theoretical knowledge to pass the PPL written examinations is in itself potentially fascinating and rewarding.

The theoretical knowledge element of the PPL course is also essential. It is no use being able to fly the perfect short-field approach and landing if you don't know how to calculate aircraft performance, and consequently attempt to land on a runway far too short for the aircraft. There's little to be gained by being well-practiced in simulated forced-landings if you don't know enough about the engine and aircraft systems to avoid engine trouble in the first place. You will be a danger to yourself and your passengers if you don't know how to interpret aviation weather reports and forecasts. Visual navigation skills are of little use if you don't know what the symbols on the map mean. If you don't understand ATC and airspace rules and procedures, you'll always be needlessly frightened by controlled airspace. And so on.

The point is that the theoretical knowledge required of a PPL holder is an integral part of the pilot's make-up. It allows a pilot to make sound, well-informed decisions, exercise good judgement and operate legally and safely. You are urged not to treat the PPL theoretical knowledge requirement as an impediment to getting your PPL, or something to be dispensed with as quickly as possible. Instead, if you treat the process of learning and understanding the theoretical knowledge part of the PPL course with the same effort that you will surely apply to the flying training, you'll be a better pilot as a result.

It is common in PPL training for the student to be expected to 'self study' a substantial element of the theoretical knowledge requirement, backed-up possibly with group lectures and one-on-one instruction from a flying instructor. As the publisher of the 'Private Pilot's Licence Course' series of books we, naturally, recommend these books as study guides for the PPL course. The seven theoretical knowledge subjects are tackled in this series as follows:

Air Law and Operational Procedures Communications
PPL 2 (Air Law, Operational Procedures and Communications)

Meteorology Navigation
PPL 3 (Navigation & Meteorology)

Principles of Flight, Aircraft General Knowledge, Flight Performance and Planning
PPL 4 (Principles of Flight, Aircraft General Knowledge, Flight Performance and Planning)

Human Performance and Limitations
PPL 5 (Human Factors & Flight Safety)

We also recommend the UK Aeronautical Information Manual (AIM) which includes comprehensive information on aviation rules and procedures, as well as extensive safety advice and recommendations and other invaluable guidance. The UK AIM has a section listing the recommended sections to be read by someone studying for a PPL.

When tackling one of the theoretical knowledge subjects, the first step is to read the relevant PPL Course series publication a chapter at a time. A first reading should be enough to establish the basics of each subject, but expect to need to make at least a second or third reading of each chapter for the knowledge to accumulate into the longer term memory by the process of rehearsal. When you think you have grasped the chapter subject, attempt the revision questions at the end of the chapter. Do not expect to get every question right, but aim for around an 80% pass rate. Do also make the effort to relate the theoretical knowledge you are acquiring to the practical business of flying aircraft. Although there is no mandatory order or schedule in which to pass the written examinations, our recommendation to help you integrate your theoretical training with the flying training is to tackle the examinations (and so arrange your studying) as below:

Air Law and Operational Procedures – it is often recommended that this examination is passed before first solo flight, and so this is the subject that virtually all PPL students tackle first.

Meteorology

Navigation

Communications – these are often expected to be passed before undertaking solo cross-country flight

Flight Performance and Planning

Aircraft General and Principles of Flight

Human Performance and Limitations – these should be completed before taking the 'Skill Test' at the end of the PPL course.

Your training organisation may wish you to tackle these subjects in a different order, and will be happy to advise you.

All the theoretical knowledge examinations must have been completed before taking the Skill Test at the end of the PPL course.

The same examinations – and so the same knowledge requirement – applies to both the National PPL (NNPL) and Joint Aviation Requirements PPL (JAR PPL) for aeroplanes. All the examinations are multiple choice and in the UK are written by the UK Civil Aviation Authority (CAA). They also share the characteristic that your best chance of passing the written examination comes with one important step: before you take the exam – know the subject!

How to use the PPL Q & A simplifier

We have designed the 'Question and Answer Simplifier' as a comprehensive study and revision guide for the PPL theoretical knowledge subjects, and we recommend that you use this guide as follows:

1. Tackle one subject at a time. The subjects in the 'Simplifier' are presented in the same order as the recommended exam schedule, but you can tackle the subjects in a different order if you wish. Having chosen a subject, start by reviewing the 'Essential Revision' chapter at the beginning of the subject section. If you are properly prepared, the information in this section should not be new to you – the aim is to focus on the most important aspects of each subject.

2. Read the notes at the beginning of the sample examinations, then tackle the first practice paper, marking your chosen answer on the tear-out answer sheet provided at the back of this guide. Make sure you are able to work through the exam undisturbed and observe the time limit given. The exam time limits normally allow plenty of time to complete the papers so 'pace yourself' and build up your concentration stamina. If you really cannot make a confident attempt at a question it's worth making an educated guess (a process of elimination might lead you to the most likely answer). Where you have to make a guess like this, make a mark against the answer (eg 'G' for 'guess') for later reference.

3. Mark your answers by reference to the answer paper, and establish the percentage of questions answered correctly. In all the practice papers the pass mark is 75%. Marks are not deducted for incorrect answers, no credit is given for unanswered questions.

4. Review those questions you failed and those you were not confident in answering (even if you were lucky enough to get the correct answer). The 'Explanation' section of each subject not only confirms the correct answer, but explains how that answer was arrived at. Each explanation is coded as overleaf:

EHFP1Q1 Answer C

    E Explanation

    H Human Factors and Performance

    P1 Paper 1

    Q1 Question 1

Work through the answer explanation:

At the end a 'Further Reference' gives a reference back to the PPL Course series in the following format:
Further Reference: PPL5 » Human Factors » The Functions of the Mind (Basic Psychology) » Spatial Disorientation and Visual Illusions

Book: PPL5

Section: Human Factors

Chapter: The Functions of the Mind (Basic Psychology)

Sub-chapter: Spatial Disoriention and Visual Illusions

EHFP1Q1   **Answer C**

It is not uncommon for pilots – even those with considerable flying experience – to receive conflicting signals about the aircraft's attitude when flying in poor or zero flight visibility. In these circumstances, the recommended response is to rely on, and trust, the aircraft instruments, as in the absence of a visual horizon these are far more likely to be giving an accurate representation of the aircraft's attitude and performance than the balance senses.
Further Reference: PPL5 » Human Factors » The Functions of the Mind (Basic Psychology) » Spatial Disorientation and Visual Illusions

If necessary, revise the whole of the sub-chapter to ensure that you now fully understand how the correct answer was arrived at. Noting the further references for those questions you failed or had to guess will allow you to identify areas of weakness or particular gaps in your knowledge.

5.   If necessary revise areas of weakness in the PPL Course series books and review the Essential Revision section before attempting the second practice paper in the subject. When you have marked this paper, review those questions guessed or answered incorrectly as before.

6.   Repeat the process for the third paper. If you have followed these steps, you should be achieving a comfortable pass mark no later than the third practice paper.

Above all, use this publication to deepen and reinforce your knowledge of the subject area. Do not attempt to learn set answers to set questions – the papers are written to cancel out such tactics – but instead use the practice papers to try-out your exam technique, assess your knowledge and identify potential weaknesses and problem areas before you take the actual written exam.

And remember, to have the best chance of a pass – know the subject!

Taking the PPL theoretical knowledge examinations

It is normal to sit the examination at the Registered Facility (RF) or Flight Training Organisation (FTO) where you are carrying out your training, and it may be necessary to arrange an appointment to be sure that an examination room will be available. Your instructor will not recommend you to take the exam before you are ready, but be prepared to postpone the exam if you are not happy with the results you have achieved with these practice papers.

The exam will be invigilated either by an authorised examiner or by a responsible person appointed by the examiner. The security of the examination paper and the conduct of the examination are taken very seriously by the Civil Aviation Authority and before the exam starts you should be cautioned that any infringement of the examination rules may result in disqualification. There are certain items which are permitted, and some that are prohibited, in the exam room:

Permitted	Prohibited
Writing Equipment	Reference material
Drawing Equipment (ruler, protractor etc)	Notes
'Mechanical' Flight computer (eg ARC-1)	Programmable electronic calculator
Map (for the navigation exam)	Mobile phone

The exam invigilator will ensure that strict silence and discipline is maintained throughout the exam and is not permitted to enter into any discussion about the content or interpretation of any question. You should note the exam duration and will be told when the exam is about to start. Make a note of the finish time.

Start by taking a minute or two to look through the exam paper to get a feel for the questions. In the case of the navigation paper, you will need to start by completing the flight plan form – take time to do this carefully as many of the questions in the navigation exam directly refer to the specified route and flight plan. Remember too in the navigation exam that questions about map symbols can be answered by reference to the map key.

In all the exams, work through the question methodically, reading each question carefully to make sure that you fully understand it. Try to answer the question without direct reference to the answer choices – looking at those only when you have formed a view as to the correct answer. Be wary of an answer choice that simply 'looks right' if you have not worked out the answer – some of the answer choices may be based on a common misconception or a common calculation mistake. If you do become stuck on a question, leave it for later reference and continue working through those questions you are more confident of answering.

If you reach the end of the paper with time to spare (which is quite usual), return to any questions you passed over. Read the question again, carefully, and review the answer choices. If you absolutely cannot decide on the correct answer, it's worth taking a guess after ruling out answer choices that you believe to be incorrect. Incorrect answers are not deducted from the exam marks and there is no credit for unanswered questions, so there is nothing to be gained by leaving a question unanswered. If you still have time left, go back through the paper reviewing your answers – even for those questions you were confident in answering. Once again, check that you have read the question correctly and have given the answer you believe to be correct. Keep an eye on the time, but you may be given a five minute warning before the end of the permitted time anyway, so you should not be caught out by the exam finishing suddenly.

After the exam

When the exam finishes, your answer paper will be passed to the examiner for marking. In the event of a pass – well done! The examiner cannot discuss specific answers to specific questions, but can indicate any general areas of weakness.

In the event of a fail you will be given a 'notice of failure'. Again, the examiner cannot discuss specific answers to specific questions, but can indicate general areas of weakness. Each subject has three CAA exam papers, and as it is not permitted to take the same paper again you can make three attempts at each subject. In the event that you fail all three exams, your training organisation should assist you to undertake further training as necessary before sitting a fourth exam at a CAA regional centre.

All the theoretical knowledge examinations must be passed within an 18 month period and the passes are valid for the issue of a PPL for 24 months after completing all of the exams.

And that's it – but not quite. In all the areas of theoretical knowledge, there **will** be changes and updates over the course of your flying career. Just as you should expect your flying skills to expand and develop with increasing experience, so you should keep developing, increasing and updating your theoretical knowledge. You will never know everything but as even the most experienced pilots will confirm, you should never stop learning.

Air Law and Operational Procedures

Air Law Essential Revision

▶ Legislation

According to ICAO's 'Chicago' convention every state has complete and exclusive **sovereignty** over airspace above its territory. The **territory** of a state is the land areas and adjacent territorial waters under the sovereignty, protection or mandate of the state. A state may require arriving, crossing and departing aircraft to route via a **designated customs airport**. Every aircraft flying over a state's territory, and every aircraft carrying a territory's nationality mark – wherever it is – must comply with that territory's **rules of the air**. Every aircraft engaged in international navigation must have a valid **Certificate of Airworthiness** issued by the state in which it is registered. The pilot and crew of every aircraft engaged in international navigation must have **certificates of competency and licences** issued or validated by the state in which the aircraft is registered. No aircraft or personnel with **endorsed licences or certificates** will engage in international navigation except with the permission of the state or states whose territory is entered. An endorsed licence or certificate will state why the aircraft or pilot does not meet international standards.

▶ Rules of the Air

Where aircraft are **converging in the air,** the aircraft on the right has right of way: "On the right, in the right". An aircraft which has right of way should maintain course and speed.

Rule of Precedence in the air:

 1. Balloons

 2. Gliders

 3. Airships

 4. Flying Machines (aeroplanes, helicopters etc.)

Powered aircraft give way to aircraft towing gliders or objects

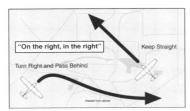

Converging aircraft: The aircraft giving way turns right to pass behind the other

Head On: Both aircraft turn to the right

Overtaking   The overtaking aircraft turns to the right. Overtaking exists while the overtaking aircraft is within 70° of the centreline of the overtaken aircraft

Where landings and take-offs are **not** confined to a runway, an aircraft taking-off must leave on its left an aircraft which has taken off or is about to take-off and an aircraft landing must leave on its left an aircraft which has landed.

An aircraft in flight following a **line feature** must keep to the right of that feature.

Rule of Precedence **on the ground:**

 1. Aircraft taking off and landing

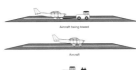 2. Aircraft being towed

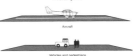 3. Aircraft

4. Vehicles & people

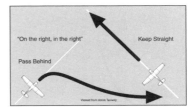

Converging aircraft: The aircraft giving way turns right to pass behind the other

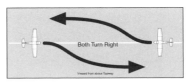

Head On: Both aircraft turn to the right

Overtaking   The overtaking aircraft turns to the left

If an aircraft is to fly in **simulated instrument-flight** conditions

– the aircraft must be fitted with dual controls.

– a safety pilot must be carried in the second control seat.

– if the safety pilot does not have a complete field of vision, a 'competent observer' must also be carried.

The **low flying** rules:

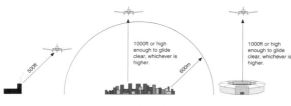

Emergencies can be 'distress' or 'urgency'. A **Distress** situation, where the aircraft is threatened by grave and imminent danger and requires immediate assistance, is indicated by the spoken word "**Mayday**". An **urgency** situation regarding the aircraft itself, or something or somebody in sight of the aircraft is indicated by the spoken words "**Pan Pan**".

The emergency transponder codes are:

7700   *Distress*

7600   *Radio communications failure*

7500   *Unlawful interference*

Except airfields which do not accept non-radio aircraft, the following **ground-air visual signals** may be used:

There may be **runway lights** to mark the useable portion of the runway

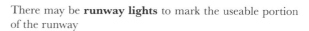
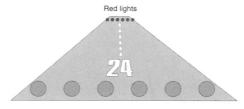

Runway markings are white

(a) Threshold, centre line and runway direction in tens of degrees magnetic

(b) A displaced threshold, the area of the arrows cannot be used for landing

(c) A displaced threshold, the area of the crosses is unfit for any movement of aircraft

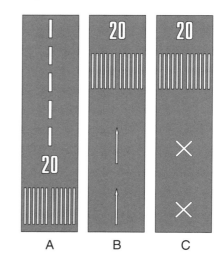

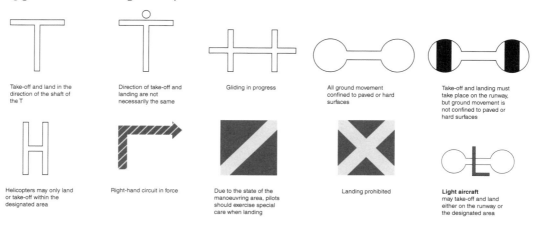

Runway distances can be defined in a number of ways:

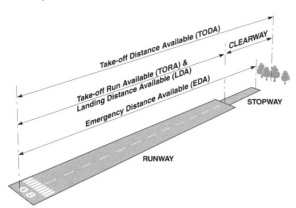

Runway condition can be defined in a number of ways:

Description	Runway condition
Dry	The surface is not affected by water, slush, snow or ice
Damp	The surface shows a change of colour due to moisture
Wet	The surface is soaked but no significant patches of standing water are visible
Water Patches	Significant patches of standing water are visible
Flooded	Extensive standing water is visible

JAR definition: A runway that has water patches or is flooded is considered to be *contaminated*.

Light signals can be made from aircraft to ATSU and vice versa:

Taxiway markings are yellow:

A holding point

Surface signals:

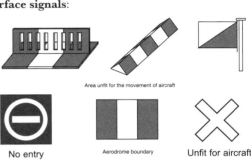

Area unfit for the movement of aircraft

No entry   Aerodrome boundary   Unfit for aircraft

An aircraft must not move on the **apron or manoeuvring** area of an aerodrome without permission:

Aircraft stand – a designated area of an apron used for the parking of an aircraft.

Apron – the part of an aerodrome where aircraft can load and unload, refuel and park.

Landing area – the part of the movement area for the take-off or landing of aircraft.

Manoeuvring area – the part of the aerodrome provided for the take-off and landing and movement of aircraft, excluding the apron and any maintenance area.

Movement area – the part of an aerodrome used by aircraft taking-off, landing and taxying, including the apron (this is not the same as the manoeuvring area).

Light Signal	FROM AN AERODROME	
	to Aircraft in Flight	to Aircraft on Ground
STEADY RED	Give way to other aircraft and continue circling	Stop
RED PYROTECHNIC LIGHT OR RED FLARE	Do not land; wait for permission	–
RED FLASHES	Do not land; aerodrome not available for landing	Move clear of landing area
GREEN FLASHES	Return to aerodrome; wait for permission to land	To an aircraft: You may move on the manoeuvring area & apron. To a vehicle: you may move on the manoeuvring area
STEADY GREEN	You may land	You may take-off
WHITE FLASHES	Land at this aerodrome after receiving continuous green light & then, after receiving green flashes, proceed to apron	Return to starting point on the aerodrome

Light Signal	FROM AN AIRCRAFT IN FLIGHT TO AN ATSU
RED PYROTECHNIC LIGHT OR RED FLARE	Immediate assistance is requested
STEADY GREEN OR GREEN FLASHES OR GREEN PYROTECHNIC LIGHT OR GREEN FLARE	By night: May I land? By day: May I land in a direction different from that indicated from the landing T?
WHITE FLASHES OR WHITE PYROTECHNIC LIGHT OR SWITCHING ON AND OFF LANDING LIGHTS OR IRREGULAR FLASHING OF THE NAVIGATION LIGHTS	I am compelled to land

Marshalling signals (from a marshaller to an aircraft)

By day signals are given by hand or by circular bats and by night by torches or illuminated wands.

Meaning of signal	In Daylight
Wingwalker/guide This signal provides an indication by a person positioned a the aircraft wing tip, to the pilot/marshaller/push back operator, that the aircraft movement on/off a parking position would be unobstructed.	
Identify gate	
Proceed to next signalman or as directed by tower/ground control.	
Straight ahead	
Turn left (from pilot's point of view).	
Turn right (from pilot's point of view)	
Normal stop	
Emergency stop	

Meaning of signal	In Daylight
Set brakes	
Release brakes	
Chocks inserted	
Chocks removed	
Start engine(s)	
Cut engines(s)	
Slow down	
Slow down engine(s) on indicated side	
Move back	

Helicopter signals (from a marshaller to a helicopter)

By day signals are given by hand or by circular bats and by night by torches or illuminated wands.

Meaning of signal	In Daylight
Turns while backing (for tail to starboard)	
Turns while backing (for tail to port)	
Affirmative/all clear	
Fire	ENGINE FIRE / BRAKE FIRE
Hold position/stand by	
Dispatch aircraft	

Meaning of signal	In Daylight
Hover	
Move upwards	
Move downwards	
Move horizontally left (from pilot's point of view)	
Move horizontally right (from pilot's point of view)	
Land	

Marshalling signals (from a pilot to a marshaller)

An aircraft must not enter an **Aerodrome Traffic Zone** (**ATZ**) without permission of an ATC unit or without having contacted the AFIS or AGCS unit. An ATZ has the following dimensions:

Airfield Type	ATZ Active
Government aerodrome	During the notified hours
Aerodrome with an ATC or AFIS unit	During the notified hours of watch of the unit
Licensed aerodrome with air/ground communications service	During the notified hours of watch of the AGCS

AERODROME TRAFFIC ZONE (ATZ)

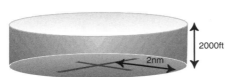

* If the runway is more than 1850m long, the ATZ has a radius of 2.5nm

▶ Division of Airspace and Air Traffic Services

To fly in accordance with **Visual Flight Rules** (**VFR**) an aircraft must be in **Visual Metrological Conditions** (**VMC**). VMC minima are:

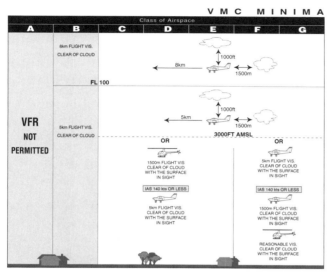

If weather conditions are worse than VMC, then they are IMC – **Instrument Meteorological Conditions**. In IMC, an aircraft must fly in accordance with **Instrument Flight Rules** (IFR). When flying IFR outside controlled airspace, the cruising Flight Level (FL) should be chosen in compliance with the **quadrantal rule.** The quadrantal rule is based on magnetic track.

When operating under a **Special VFR** (**SVFR**) clearance the pilot is absolved from the '1000ft' provision of the low flying rules, but not the 'land clear' requirement – compliance is the pilot's responsibility. The pilot must comply with ATC instructions, ATC is responsible for separating the SVFR flight from IFR flights.

The following rules apply to flight in various **airspace classifications**:

Controlled airspace = Classes A, B, C, D and E;

Uncontrolled airspace = Classes F and G.

Airspace Classification	Flight Rules	Notes
Class A	IFR flight only	All flights subject to ATC service and separated from each other
Class B	IFR & VFR flight	All flights subject to ATC service and separated from each other
Class C	IFR & VFR flight	All flights subject to ATC service. IFR flights separated from all other IFR flights and receive traffic information about VFR flights. VFR flights separated from IFR flights and receive traffic information about other VFR flights
Class D	IFR & VFR flight	All flights subject to ATC service. IFR flights separated from all other IFR flights and receive traffic information about VFR flights. VFR flights receive traffic information about other VFR flights
Class E	IFR & VFR flight	IFR flights subject to ATC service and separated from all other IFR flight. All flights receive traffic information as far as is practical
Class F	IFR & VFR flight	Participating IFR flights receive an air traffic advisory service. All flights receive flight information service if requested
Class G	IFR & VFR flight	All flights receive flight information service if requested

▶ Rules of the Air and Air Traffic Services

A **full flight plan** should be filed at the departure airfield ATSU at least 60 minutes before anticipated start/taxying time. If there is no ATSU at the departure airfield, the flight plan should be filed with a 'parent ATSU'. Once a flight plan has been submitted, if a departure delay of more than 30 minutes occurs, a new flight plan should be submitted and the old one cancelled. If the flight lands at an airfield other than the destination specified in the flight plan, the pilot *must* inform the specified destination within 30 minutes of the ETA there.

The three main **altimeter settings** in the UK are:

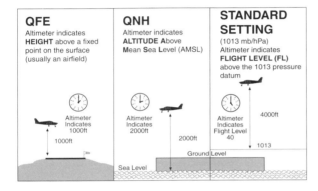

The **transition altitude** is the altitude above which the altimeter can be set to the Standard Setting (1013mb) so that the altimeter indicates Flight Level. The **transition level** is the lowest useable flight level above the transition altitude. The **transition layer** is the layer between the transition altitude and transition level.

As a general rule, a VFR flight can use any desired **altimeter setting,** although when flying within or beneath controlled airspace such as a TMA or CTA, the QNH of an airfield under that TMA or CTA should be used. IFR flights usually use QNH when flying beneath the transition altitude, and Standard Setting (1013) when flying above the transition altitude, except when descending from a Flight Level to an altitude.

The following **wake turbulence** minimum separations are recommended for light aircraft in the UK:

Departure

Leading aircraft category	Departure point	Time
Heavy or medium	Same	2 minutes
Heavy or medium	Intermediate	3 minutes

Landing

Leading aircraft category	Distance/Time
Heavy	8nm/4 minutes
Medium	6nm/3 minutes
Small	4nm/2 minutes

Some **ATC definitions:**

Aerodrome Control Service	– an air traffic control service for aerodrome traffic
Air Traffic	– all aircraft in flight or operating on the manoeuvring area of an aerodrome
Alerting Service	– a service provided to notify appropriate organisations regarding aircraft in need of search and rescue aid, and assist such organisations as required
Approach Control Service	– an air traffic control service for arriving and departing controlled flights
Area Control Service	– an Air Traffic Control service for controlled flights in control areas
Flight Information Service	– a service provided for the purpose of giving advice and information useful for the safe and efficient conduct of flights
Radar Approach	– an approach where the final approach phase is conducted under the direction of a radar controller
Radar Vectoring	– the provision of navigational guidance to aircraft, in the form of specific headings, based on the use of radar

▶ Aircraft Registration

The state of registry is the state on whose register an aircraft is entered. According to ICAO recommendations the **Certificate of Registration** should be carried in the aircraft at all times. An aircraft should also carry a fireproof metal **identification plate**.

▶ Airworthiness of Aircraft

A **Certificate of Airworthiness** may be invalidated if an aircraft is repaired or modified in some way which is not approved, if the aircraft is operated outside the operating limits prescribed in the Pilot's Operating Handbook/Flight Manual (POH/FM), and also found in markings and placards, or if the aircraft is not maintained in accordance with an approved maintenance schedule. An aircraft's C of A is normally required to be carried on board an aircraft making an international flight. In the UK an aircraft with a C of A must also have a **weight schedule**. A new weight schedule will be prepared after a significant repair or modification to an aircraft, in which case, the original weight schedule must be preserved for at least six months after the new weight schedule has been prepared.

▶ JAA Regulations

The **minimum age** for a student pilot to fly solo is 16, the minimum age to hold a PPL is 17. The **JAA PPL course** consists of at least 45 flight hours, including at least 10 hours of solo flight. A **JAA licence** is issued for a maximum of five years. A JAR PPL holder is required to hold at least JAR-FCL Class 1 or Class 2 **medical certificate**. A medical certificate holder must seek advice upon becoming aware of:

– a hospital or clinic admission for more than 12 hours;

– a surgical operation or invasive procedure;

– the regular use of medication; or

– the need to regularly use correcting lenses.

and must inform the authority in writing of any significant personal injury involving incapacity to function as a member of a flight crew, or of becoming pregnant. In the case of an illness throughout a period of 21 days or more, the authority must be informed in writing as soon as the period of 21 days has elapsed. The medical certificate will then be considered as suspended.

Flight time to be credited for a licence or rating must be flown in the same category of aircraft for which the licence or rating is sought. An applicant for a licence or rating is credited in full with all solo, dual instruction or Pilot-In-Command (PIC) flight time towards the total flight time needed for the relevant licence or rating. An applicant applies for **licence issue** to the Authority of the state under whose Authority the training and testing for the licence were carried out. A licence holder may transfer a licence to another JAA Member State if employment or normal residency is established in that state.

To act as PIC whilst **carrying passengers**, a PPL (A) holder must have made three take-offs and three landings as the sole manipulator of the controls, in an aeroplane of the same type or class, within the preceding 90 days. The PPL does not enable the holder to fly for 'valuable consideration', with a few exceptions such as **aerial work** involving glider towing, parachute dropping, air racing and charitable flights. PPL privileges and limitations are set-out in **schedule 8** of the Air Navigation Order (ANO). The Air Navigation Order (ANO) defines **night** as the period from half an hour after sunset until half an hour before sunrise. The ICAO definition of night is the hours between the end of evening civil twilight and the beginning of morning civil twilight.

The **JAR PPL weather minima** are:

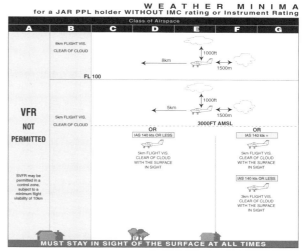

Type ratings and **multi-engine class ratings** are valid for one year. To retain validity the holder must pass a proficiency check within the three months immediately preceding the expiry of the rating; <u>AND</u> during the period of validity of the rating undertake at least ten route sectors as pilot of the relevant class or type, or one route sector with an examiner.

Single-pilot, single-engine class ratings are valid for two years. To retain validity the holder must pass a proficiency check within the three months immediately preceding the expiry of the rating; <u>OR</u> **w**ithin 12 months preceding rating expiry complete 12 hours of flight time, including six hours PIC time and 12 take-offs and landings and also complete a training flight of at least one hour with a flight instructor within the 12 months preceding the expiry of the rating. This training flight may be replaced by any other proficiency check or skill test for a class or type rating.

The **IMC Rating** is a special purpose, UK-only rating, it has no validity outside the UK.

►Operation of Aircraft

The ultimate responsibility for the operation of an aircraft and the safe conduct of the flight lies with the **pilot in command** (PIC) also known as the aircraft commander.

The **lights to be displayed** by flying machines at night are:

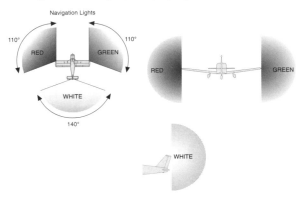

The **lights to be displayed** by other aircraft are:

Gliders	As for flying machines **or** a steady red light showing in all directions.
Free Balloons	A steady red light showing in all directions, suspended between 5 and 10 metres under the basket.
Airships	In addition to the standard navigation lights, a white nose-light showing through 110° either side of straight ahead, and an anti-collision light.

►Search and Rescue

Definitions:

Alert phase	– a situation where apprehension exists regarding the safety of an aircraft and its occupants.
Distress phase	– a situation where there is reasonable certainty that an aircraft and its occupants are threatened by grave and imminent danger or require immediate assistance.
Ditching	– the forced landing of an aircraft on water.
Uncertainty phase	– a situation where uncertainty exists regarding the safety of an aircraft and its occupants.

During the uncertainty phase, the Rescue Co-ordination Centre will co-operate with other agencies and services to evaluate incoming reports. When the alert phase occurs the Rescue Co-ordination Centre will alert the search and rescue units.

An aircraft that observes an aircraft or surface craft in distress must, first and foremost, keep it in sight for as long as necessary.

The following **search and rescue ground signals** may be made by survivors:

Message	Code Symbol
Require assistance	V
Require medical assistance	X
No or Negative	N
Yes or Affirmative	Y
Proceeding in this direction	↑

To acknowledge that it has understood these signals, an aircraft may rock its wings (by day) or switch the landing light on and off twice (by night).

►Accident and Incident Investigation

A **reportable accident** occurs between the time when any person boards the aircraft with the intention of flight and when all persons have left the aircraft after flight when:

1. A person is killed or seriously injured while in, on, or in direct contact with, the aircraft.

2. The aircraft incurs damage or structural failure affecting its structural strength, performance or flight characteristics and will require major repair or replacement.

3. The aircraft is missing or completely inaccessible.

A 'reportable' accident must be notified to the Air Accident Investigation Branch (AAIB) and the local Police Authority. Notification is the duty of the aircraft commander, or the aircraft operator if the commander is unable to do so.

JAA Private Pilot Licence – Aeroplanes
Air Law and Operational Procedures

Time allowed: 60 minutes

No. of questions: 40

Total Marks: 100

Instructions:

The paper consists of 40 multiple choice questions, each carries 2.5 marks. The pass mark is 75% (i.e. 30 questions or more must be answered correctly). Marks are not deducted for incorrect answers.

Be sure to carefully read each question and ensure that you understand it before considering the answer choices. Only one of the answers is complete and correct; the others are either incomplete, incorrect or based on a misconception.

You should indicate the correct answer by placing a cross in the appropriate box of the answer sheet. If you decide to change an answer, you should erase the original choice and put a cross in the box representing your new selection.

Each question has an average answer time of 1.5 minutes. No credit is given for unanswered questions.

1. According to the 'Chicago Convention', the authorities of a state have the right to search the aircraft of another state on landing or departure:

    (a) Without unreasonable delay

    (b) Only with the permission of the state of registry

    (c) Only with the permission of the Pilot In Command

    (d) Only with the permission of the aircraft operator

2. If a pilot's licence is 'endorsed' to state that it does not meet minimum international standards, the pilot's licence:

    (a) Is invalid in the state or registry

    (b) Is only valid if the holder is accompanies by another pilot

    (c) Must have attached or endorsed on it information regarding why the licence does not satisfy international standards

    (d) May not be used for international air navigation under any circumstances

3. Under the Chicago Convention, which state is responsible for ensuring that an aircraft in flight complies with rules and regulations?

    (a) Only the state whose territory is being over-flown

    (b) The contracting state

    (c) The ICAO governing state

    (d) None of the above

4. By ICAO definition, the person responsible for the operation and safety of an aircraft during flight is:

    (a) The Air Traffic Controller

    (b) The aircraft operator

    (c) The pilot operating the flight controls at any given moment

    (d) The pilot-in-command

5. In order for the altimeter to indicate altitude, the subscale setting should be:

    (a) QNH

    (b) QFE

    (c) QNE

    (d) QFF

6. Which aircraft are permitted to fly at night displaying only a single red light?

    (a) A glider or free balloon

    (b) A glider, free balloon or airship

    (c) A helicopter or free balloon

    (d) A microlight or airship

7. A line of red lights across the runway width indicate:

    (a) A displaced threshold

    (b) An exit

    (c) The 'stop' end of the runway

    (d) That the runway is unavailable for use

8. A runway condition where the surface shows a change of colour due to moisture can be described as being:

    (a) Flooded

    (b) Damp

    (c) Contaminated

    (d) Cleaned

9. By ICAO recommendation, an alerting service is provided to:

    (a) Only an aircraft that has specifically requested it

    (b) All aircraft receiving an ATC service

    (c) Only to aircraft that have filed a flight plan

    (d) Only aircraft engaged in scheduled international air transport

10. A Control Area (CTA), where several routes merge in the vicinity of several airfields, is most likely to be:

    (a) An Advisory Route (ADR)

    (b) A Control Zone (CTR)

    (c) A Terminal Control Area (TMA)

    (d) A Terminal Manoeuvring Region (TMR)

11. An air traffic control service for arriving and departing controlled flights is an:

    (a) Approach Control Service

    (b) Area Control Service

    (c) Airspace Control Service

    (d) Airfield Control Service

12. A pilot who encounters a significant en-route meteorological hazard (SIGMET), such as severe mountain wave activity, is recommended to:

    (a) Complete a CAA SIGMET REP form within 7 days of the flight

    (b) Make a report to the area met. office within 45 minutes of landing at the destination

    (c) Make a special air report

    (d) Make an open broadcast on 123.45MHz

13. A runway's Emergency Distance Available (EDA) is defined as:

    (a) The TODA minus the stopway

    (b) The TORA plus any stopway

    (c) Never being greater than the TORA

    (d) The TORA plus any clearway

14. Where a national rating, such as a UK IMC rating, is added to a JAR PPL:

(a) It may be used outside of the state of origin if the issuing state so authorises

(b) Approval from individual member states is required before it may be used in their airspace

(c) It will automatically be accepted in all JAR member states

(d) It will automatically be accepted in all ICAO member states

15. JAR-FCL 3 states that should a pilot suffer an incapacitating injury, the pilot's medical certificate:

(a) Should be considered as suspended, subject to arrangements made by the authority

(b) Should be considered as suspended, the holder may 're-certify' when fit

(c) Should be considered as valid unless the authority states otherwise

(d) Is permanently invalidated

16. The holder of a PPL(A) intends to make a flight carrying passengers; which of the following is true?

(a) The pilot must then complete 3 take-offs and 3 landings within the next 90 days in an aircraft of the same class or type

(b) The pilot must have made 3 take-offs or 3 landings with an instructor in the preceding 90 days in an aircraft of any class or type

(c) The pilot must have made 3 take-offs and 3 landings as sole manipulator of the controls in the preceding 90 days in an aircraft of the same class or type

(d) The pilot must have made 3 take-offs and 3 landings as sole manipulator of the controls in the preceding 90 days in an aircraft of any class or type

17. A JAR PPL without instrument qualifications is given a clearance that will take the aircraft into IMC. The pilot should:

(a) Accept the clearance

(b) Maintain the existing level and heading and request revised instructions

(c) Follow the clearance as far as possible without entering IMC

(d) Follow the clearance while requesting revised instructions

18. In order to operate an aircraft radio over the territory of another state:

(a) Both the radio and the radio operator must be licenced by the state over whose territory the aircraft is being flown

(b) The radio (but not the radio operator) must be licenced by the state over whose territory the aircraft is being flown

(c) The radio (but not the radio operator) must be licenced by the state of registry of the aircraft

(d) The radio and the radio operator must be licenced by the state of registry of the aircraft

19. Which of the following does NOT invalidate a Certificate of Airworthiness?

(a) An unauthorised repair or modification

(b) Change of ownership not notified within 7 days

(c) Operating outside the limits stated on placards in the cockpit

(d) Use of a material not approved by the CAA

20. All aircraft which are known by the air traffic services to be operating within a Flight Information Region (FIR) are provided with at least:

(a) An Air Traffic Advisory Service

(b) A Flight Information Service

(c) A Radar Advisory Service

(d) An Alerting Service

21. Which of the following would be classified as a reportable accident?

(a) An aircraft is destroyed by fire during maintenance work in a hangar

(b) An aircraft in flight suffers an engine failure, but damage is limited to the engine and no further damage occurs during the forced landing

(c) A person suffers a broken leg after being struck by the aircraft undercarriage during 'push back' prior to departure

(d) During a crosswind landing the aircraft's wing tip is damaged and requires replacement.

22. If an aircraft is being flown in simulated instrument flight conditions:

(a) A safety pilot must be carried in a second control seat

(b) At least a 'competent observer' must be carried in a second control seat

(c) At least a Flight Instructor must occupy the second control seat

(d) The aircraft must remain inside controlled airspace

23. In relation to aircraft of different classes converging in flight, which of the following statements is true?

(a) Gliders must give way to airships and balloons

(b) Balloons must give way to airships

(c) Airships must give way to gliders and balloons

(d) Gliders must give way to aircraft towing other aircraft

24. A white T in the signal area means:

(a) Aeroplanes and gliders taking-off or landing must do so parallel to the shaft of the T and towards the cross arm

(b) The aerodrome has technical facilities for aircraft engineering

(c) Approach and take-off is particularly susceptible to turbulence

(d) Direction of take-off and landing may differ

25. In class D airspace, to remain within VMC minima at between 3000ft AMSL and FL100, the minimum flight visibility required is:

(a) 8km

(b) 5nm

(c) 5km

(d) 8nm

26. The transition level is defined as:

(a) The altitude above which the altimeter can be set to the Standard Setting (1013)

(b) The Flight Level below which the altimeter can be set to the Standard Setting (1013)

(c) The layer between the transition altitude and transition level

(d) The lowest available Flight Level above the transition altitude

27. With regard to an aircraft's Certificate of Registration:

(a) It is not required for aircraft of less than 5700kg MTWA

(b) It need not show the name and address of the registered owner

(c) By ICAO recommendation it should be carried on all flights

(d) It contains the limitations of the Flight Manual/Pilot's Operating Handbook

28. Responsibility for notifying the appropriate search and rescue units during an alert phase rests with:

(a) The Rescue Co-ordination Centre

(b) The departure ATSU

(c) The aircraft commander

(d) The aircraft operator

29. The first action and overriding priority of a pilot who observes another aircraft or surface vehicle in distress is to:

(a) Make a PAN PAN call

(b) Keep the craft in distress in sight

(c) Note the location to be passed on in a post-flight report

(d) Record the craft's identification details

30. In relation to ground markings painted on runways and taxiways, ICAO recommend that:

(a) Runway and taxiway markings should be white

(b) Runway markings should be yellow and taxiway markings should be white

(c) Runway markings should be white and taxiway markings should be yellow

(d) Runway and taxiway markings should be yellow

31. The signal by an aircraft meaning that a ground search and rescue signal has been understood is to:

(a) Rock the wings

(b) Open and close the throttle or change propeller pitch

(c) Circle the signal once clockwise

(d) Circle the signal once anti– clockwise

32. The best definition of the title 'Pilot In Command' is:

(a) Whichever pilot in the aircraft has the superior licence, or the more experienced pilot if both hold the same licence

(b) The Pilot Flying (PF) at any time

(c) The pilot occupying the left-hand seat

(d) The pilot responsible of the operation and safety of the aircraft during flight

33. ICAO recommend that single-engine aircraft flying more than 100nm from land should carry:

(a) Liferafts instead of lifejackets

(b) Liferafts in addition to lifejackets

(c) Liferafts or lifejackets

(d) None of the above

34. When operating under a special VFR clearance the responsibility for
(i) remaining clear of ground obstructions and;
(ii) separation from other SVFR or IFR traffic;
rests with:

	(i)	(ii)
(a)	The aircraft commander	Air Traffic Control
(b)	The aircraft commander	The aircraft commander
(c)	Air Traffic Control	Air Traffic Control

(d) Responsibility for both is jointly shared by the aircraft commander and Air traffic Control

35. When take-offs and landings are not confined to a runway, the commander of an aeroplane that is taking off shall position:

(a) To the right of an aircraft ahead, leaving it clear to the left

(b) To the left of an aircraft ahead, leaving it clear to the right

(c) Directly behind the aircraft ahead

(d) Either side, at the following pilot's discretion

36. An aircraft with a valid Certificate of Airworthiness also has a weight schedule produced. If the aircraft is re-weighed in June 2006 and a new schedule produced, the old one:

(a) Must be kept until at least December 2006

(b) Must be kept until at least July 2008

(c) Must be kept until any subsequent weighing

(d) Must be destroyed immediately

37. At night, a flying machine in flight is intending to overtake another flying machine. An overtaking situation is considered to exist until:

(a) The pilot of the overtaking flying machine can no longer see the white rear navigation light of the other flying machine

(b) The pilot of the overtaking flying machine can see both the red and green navigation lights of the other flying machine

(c) The overtaking flying machine passes abeam the red or green navigation lights of the other flying machine

(d) The pilot of the overtaking flying machine can no longer see any navigation lights of the other flying machine

38. From the age of 16 years a pilot can:

(a) Obtain a Private Pilot Licence (PPL)

(b) Fly solo

(c) Obtain a Commercial Pilot Licence (CPL)

(d) Obtain a Student Pilot Licence (SPL)

39. The period validity of a single-engine piston aeroplane (land) – SE piston (land) – class rating for a single pilot aeroplane is:

(a) 13 months

(b) One year

(c) 60 months

(d) Two years

40. Where two aircraft of the same class are converging in flight, the aircraft that has right of way will:

(a) Orbit to its right immediately

(b) Maintain its height and reduce speed

(c) Maintain its height and speed

(d) Maintain its course and speed

1. In accordance with the Convention on International Civil Aviation (Chicago Convention), aircraft entering or departing a state's territory:

   (a) Will be required to do so at a designated customs airport

   (b) May be required to do so at a designated customs airport

   (c) Can only be required to do so at a designated customs airport in an emergency

   (d) Can do so at any airport at the commander's discretion

2. According to the Convention on International Civil Aviation (also known as the Chicago Convention):

   (a) Scheduled international air services may make flight across the territory of other states without obtaining prior permission

   (b) Flights other than scheduled international air services may make flight across the territory of other states without obtaining prior permission

   (c) All flights across the territory of other states are required to obtain prior permission

   (d) Non-scheduled flights across the territory of other states are required to obtain prior permission

3. The Chicago Convention (Convention on International Civil Aviation) permits the following items to be admitted temporarily exempt from customs duty when flying to, from or across the territory of a state:

   (a) Alcohol and tobacco carried on board only

   (b) The aircraft itself and fuel, oil and spare parts remaining on board

   (c) Electrical equipment only

   (d) None of the above

4. According to Chicago Convention (Convention on International Civil Aviation), which of the following is required to be carried on an international flight?

   (a) Certificate of Airworthiness; Certificate of Registration and Certificate of Maintenance Review

   (b) Certificate of Airworthiness and Certificate of Registration

   (c) Crew logbooks and passports

   (d) Journey logbook, crew licences and noise certificate

5. An aircraft is flying at 2500ft amsl and 100kts IAS in uncontrolled airspace. In order to comply with VMC minima the required conditions are:

   (a) 5km flight visibility, 1500m horizontally and 1000ft vertically clear of cloud

   (b) 1·5nm flight visibility, clear of cloud, in sight of the surface

   (c) 5km flight visibility, clear of cloud

   (d) 1500m flight visibility, clear of cloud and in sight of the surface

6. The relevant Joint Aviation Requirements for (i) Aeroplanes and (ii) Medical are published in which documents?

	(i)	(ii)
(a)	JAR-FCL 4	JAR-FCL 5
(b)	JAR-FCL 3	JAR-FCL 2
(c)	JAR-FCL 2	JAR-FCL 4
(d)	JAR-FCL 1	JAR-FCL 3

7. During a night landing you see a line of fixed unidirectional lights across the runway centreline, showing green in the direction of approach. You should aim to land:

   (a) Using these lights for glideslope reference

   (b) Before these lights, they mark the stop end of the runway

   (c) Beyond these lights, they mark the runway threshold

   (d) On another runway, this runway is closed

8. By ICAO definition, Visual Meteorological Conditions (VMC) minima are determined by reference to:

   (a) Flight visibility only

   (b) Runway Visual Range only

   (c) Distance from cloud only

   (d) Flight visibility, distance from cloud and cloud ceiling

9. An air traffic service which supplies information and advice useful to the safe and efficient conduct of a flight is a/an:

   (a) Flight Information Service

   (b) Air Traffic Advisory Service

   (c) Alerting Service

   (d) Air Traffic Control Service

10. For a JAR PPL (Aeroplane) holder without instrument qualification, the weather minima when operating at or below 3000ft amsl, at or below 140 knots IAS outside controlled airspace, is:

    (a) 3nm flight visibility, clear of cloud

    (b) 1800m flight visibility, in sight of the surface

    (c) 1500m flight visibility, clear of cloud

    (d) 3km flight visibility, clear of cloud, in sight of the surface

11. Aircraft operating procedures, limitations and restrictions essential to aircraft airworthiness are specified in:

    (a) The aircraft's Certificate of Registration

    (b) The CAA website

    (c) The aircraft type information handbook

    (d) The aircraft's Flight Manual/Pilot's Operating Handbook (POH/FM) and cockpit placards

12. In order to file a full flight plan before departure at an aerodrome that does not have an Air Traffic Service Unit (ATSU), the aircraft commander should:

    (a) File the flight plan with the Parent Unit designated to cover the departure aerodrome

    (b) File the flight plan with any nominated responsible person at the aerodrome of departure

    (c) File the flight plan with any aerodrome ATSU

    (d) File the flight plan once airborne

13. The holder of a UK-issued JAR-FCL Private Pilot's Licence (Aeroplane) is permitted to undertake aerial work which consists of:

(a) Glider towing and dropping of parachutists only

(b) Banner towing and glider towing only

(c) Dropping of parachutists and remunerated instruction in flying only

(d) Dropping of parachutists and aerial photography only

14. A radar service available in the UK to aircraft outside controlled airspace, at up to FL95 and 30nm from the participating ATSU, is most likely to be:

(a) An Aerodrome Traffic Zone

(b) A Lower Airspace Radar Service (LARS)

(c) An Alerting Service

(d) A Military Aerodrome Traffic Zone (MATZ)

15. A class D control zone around an airfield extends:

(a) From a specified altitude to a specified Flight Level

(b) From ground level to a specified altitude or Flight Level

(c) From 1000ft above airfield elevation to 2500ft AMSL

(d) From ground level to 2000ft Above Aerodrome Level (AAL)

16. If an aeroplane inbound to an airfield has fuel reserves approaching a critical level and so requires priority handling, the commander should:

(a) Declare a 'Fuel Emergency'

(b) Use the RTF phrase 'Minimum Fuel'

(c) Make an emergency radio call prefixed by 'Mayday' or 'Pan Pan' as appropriate

(d) Request ATC handling priority as the aircraft is 'Fuel Priority'

17. The designated part of an aerodrome apron to be used for the parking of an aircraft has the ICAO name of:

(a) Landing Area

(b) Movement Area

(c) Manoeuvring area

(d) Aircraft stand

18. In accordance with JAR-FCL3 (Medical), a licence holder must seek advice from the authority or an Authorised Medical Examiner (AME) <u>without delay</u> if:

(a) They become aware of the need for a surgical operation

(b) They decide to become a blood or bone marrow donor

(c) They make any out-patient appointment with a hospital or clinic

(d) They contract an illness that reduced their fitness to fly

19. In order to exercise the privileges of a JAR pilot licence, the holder must hold a valid:

(a) Class rating; plus any one type rating

(b) Type rating for any aircraft, regardless of the type or class to be flown

(c) Appropriate class rating or type rating

(d) Type rating for any multi-engine aircraft

20. An applicant for a JAR-FCL PPL (Aeroplanes) must have completed at least:

(a) 32 hours flight time, including 5 hours solo

(b) 40 hours flight time, including 15 hours solo

(c) 45 hours flight time, including 10 hours solo

(d) 50 hours flight time, including 10 hours solo

21. The apron and part of the airfield used for take-off, landing and taxying, is known as:

(a) The mandatory area

(b) The manoeuvring area

(c) The movement area

(d) The aircraft stand

22. According to ICAO Annex six, and subject to any additional equipment prescribed by the relevant authority, the minimum aircraft instrumentation for VFR flight is best represented by which of the following options:
(i) A magnetic compass.
(ii) An accurate timepiece.
(iii) A sensitive pressure altimeter.
(iv) An airspeed indicator
(v) An attitude indicator
(vi) A turn coordinator

(a) (i), (ii) and (vi)

(b) (i), (ii), (iii) and (iv)

(c) (i), (iii), (iv) and (v)

(d) (i), (iv), (v) and (vi)

23. You are the pilot of an 'aeroplane'. If you are converging with other aircraft in flight, which of the following statements is true?

(a) You must give way to helicopters and balloons

(b) You must give way to helicopters only

(c) Helicopters must give way to you

(d) You and helicopters must give way to an aircraft towing a banner

24. The Secondary Surveillance Radar (SSR) transponder code 7700 is used to indicate:

(a) An aircraft carrying out aerobatics

(b) A communications failure

(c) A practice or real emergency

(d) An emergency

25. A ground-to-air Search and Rescue signal by survivors, in the form of a single arrow, has the meaning:

(a) This is North

(b) Aircraft wreckage in this direction

(c) Proceeding in this direction

(d) What is in this direction?

26. An aircraft is approaching another aircraft 'head on' and there is a danger of collision. The appropriate response is which of the following?

(a) The smaller aircraft should alter course to the right

(b) Each aircraft must alter course to the right

(c) Each aircraft should alter course to the left (if on the ground)

(d) The larger aircraft should start a maximum rate descent

27. An aircraft that has been intercepted should attempt to contact the intercepting aircraft on which radio frequency?

(a) The radio frequency currently in use

(b) The 'FIS' frequency for the FIR within which the aircraft are flying

(c) The VHF emergency frequency – 121.5MHz

(d) The frequency of the closest military airfield

28. An aircraft will normally express vertical position in terms of 'altitude' when operating:

(a) At or above the transition altitude

(b) At or above the transition level

(c) Within the transition layer only

(d) At or below the transition altitude

29. Take Off Distance Available (TODA) of a runway is defined as:

(a) The length of the runway plus stopway

(b) The length of the runway plus any clearway

(c) The length of the runway only

(d) The length of the runway minus any stopway

30. A flight has been cleared to taxy to the holding point for the active runway. There are several sets of markings on the taxiway. Which of the following is the holding point?

(a) A solid white line across the taxiway

(b) Two or more white crosses on the taxiway

(c) Two continuous and two broken yellow lines across the taxiway

(d) None of the above

31. Two or more large white diagonal crosses displayed on a runway or taxiway mean that:

(a) The runway or taxiway should be used in an emergency only

(b) The runway or taxiway is unfit for the movement of aircraft

(c) The runway or taxiway may be used with caution

(d) The runway or taxiway may be used only with ATC permission

32. Runway markings are normally painted in:

(a) Solid white colour

(b) A white outline only

(c) Solid green colour

(d) Red

33. The minimum medical standard required by for the holder of a JAR-FCL private pilot licence (Aeroplanes) is:

(a) A medical declaration

(b) A class 1 medical, as defined in JAR-FCL2

(c) A certificate of medical competence

(d) A class 2 medical, as defined in JAR-FCL3

34. The holder of a medical certificate must consider the medical certificate to be suspended if:

(a) The holder donates blood

(b) The holder receives an out-patient appointment

(c) The holder has an illness making them unable to act as the member of a flight crew for a period of 14 days

(d) The holder suffers an injury making them unable to act as the member of a flight crew

35. For administrative convenience licence holders may transfer a licence from one JAA member state (state A) to another JAA member state (state B):

(a) Provided a dwelling in state B is owned by the licence holder

(b) Provided residency is maintained for more that 180 days per year in state A.

(c) Provided employment or normal residency is established in state B

(d) Provided both state A and state B are ICAO states

36. You are the PIC of a light aircraft, waiting to take off behind a heavy category aircraft from the same starting point on the runway. If the heavy aircraft is airborne at 14:02.30, for minimum wake turbulence separation you should be airborne no sooner than:

(a) 14:04.30

(b) 14:05.30

(c) 14:06.30

(d) 14:03.30

37. In flight by night you see only the red navigation light of another aircraft flying at approximately the same level as your aircraft, and on a constant relative bearing of 060°:

(a) There is no collision risk

(b) There is a collision risk, you should avoid passing over, under or ahead of the other aircraft. Prepare to alter course to right to pass behind the other aircraft

(c) You have right of way. Maintain course and speed but be prepared to take avoiding action

(d) Increase speed to pass ahead of the other aircraft. As you are overtaking, you have right of way

38. An accident must be reported if:

(a) A person is killed on board an aircraft at any time

(b) A part falling from an aircraft seriously injures a person on the ground

(c) The commander of the aircraft becomes ill

(d) An aircraft is damaged whilst being positioned for maintenance within a hangar

39. By ICAO definition, the person responsible for the safe conduct of flight is:

(a) The safety officer of the aircraft operator

(b) Any ATC controller in continuous radio contact with the flight

(c) The aircraft operator as a corporate body

(d) The aircraft commander

40. A 'distress' phase is defined as a situation where:

(a) An aircraft and its occupants are threatened by grave and imminent danger and require immediate assistance

(b) Uncertainty exists regarding the safety of an aircraft and its occupants

(c) Apprehension exists regarding the safety of an aircraft and its occupants

(d) An aircraft is compelled to land, but does not require immediate assistance

1. Under the terms of the Chicago Convention:

   (a) Every state has complete sovereignty within airspace up to FL245 above its territory

   (b) Every ICAO state has complete sovereignty over all airspace

   (c) Every state has complete and exclusive sovereignty over airspace above its territory

   (d) Only states that operate under JAR-OPS have sovereignty over their airspace

2. A pilot engaged in international air navigation:

   (a) Must hold a licence validated by the state to be visited or over-flown

   (b) Must hold a licence issued or validated by the state in which the aircraft is registered

   (c) Must seek approval for the flight from the national licensing authority

   (d) Must hold a JAR licence

3. At night you see the red navigation light of a flying machine on a constant relative bearing of 080°. Which of the following statements is correct?

   (a) There is no collision risk, you have right of way

   (b) There is a collision risk, you have right of way and should maintain course and speed

   (c) There is no collision risk, although you do not have right of way

   (d) There is a collision risk, you should turn right to pass behind the other aircraft

4. In accordance with Article 5 of the Chicago Convention, when an aircraft of one state is required to be flown over another state on a non-scheduled flight:

   (a) Prior permission is required from the state being overflown, although a landing is not required

   (b) Prior permission is not required from the state being overflown, although a landing may be required

   (c) Prior permission is only required if not planning a landing in that state

   (d) Prior permission is only required if the state is not a JAA state

5. Which of the following most accurately describes documents that ICAO regulations require every aircraft engaged in international air navigation to carry?

   (a) Certificate of Registration, Certificate of Airworthiness, Crew licences, Journey Log, Radio Licence, list of passenger details

   (b) Certificate of Registration, Certificate of Airworthiness, Certificate of Maintenance Review, Crew licences, Radio Licence

   (c) Certificate of Registration, Certificate of Airworthiness, Weight schedule, Interception procedure guide

   (d) Certificate of Airworthiness, Certificate of Maintenance Review, Crew licences, Radio Licence, Crew passports

6. Rules and regulations regarding entry and departure from a state for international flights should be those of:

   (a) The Chicago Convention

   (b) ICAO

   (c) The state whose territory is involved

   (d) Any JAA state

7. VFR flight in class D airspace below FL100 in the UK requires minimum radio equipment of:

   (a) A VHF communications radio

   (b) A VHF communications radio, a transponder and one VOR

   (c) A VHF communications radio and a transponder

   (d) A VHF communications radio, a VOR and a DME

8. When 'transiting' controlled airspace under a Special VFR clearance:

   (a) The aircraft commander must obey the 1000ft and 500ft rules at all times

   (b) The aircraft commander is absolved from the 1000ft rule

   (c) The responsibility of keeping the aircraft clear of built up areas rests solely with ATC

   (d) The aircraft commander is absolved from the 1000ft and 'land clear' rules

9. When flying 'en-route' below the transition altitude, an aircraft's vertical distance above mean sea level is usually referred to in terms of (i) and the appropriate altimeter subscale setting is (ii)

	(i)	(ii)
(a)	Altitude	QNH
(b)	Height	QFE
(c)	Height	QNH
(d)	Altitude	QFE

10. Airspace where IFR & VFR flight is permitted and participating IFR flights receive an air traffic advisory service whose instructions are mandatory, is:

   (a) Class D airspace

   (b) Class G airspace

   (c) Class F airspace

   (d) Class A airspace

11. Choose which of the following combinations best describes the objectives of Air Traffic Services as defined by ICAO:
   (i)   Prevent collisions between aircraft
   (ii)   Prevent collisions between aircraft on the manoeuvring area and obstructions on that area
   (iii) Expedite and maintain an orderly flow of air traffic
   (iv)   Provide advice and information of the safe and efficient conduct of flights
   (v)   Notify organisations of aircraft in need of search and rescue aid, and assist such organisations

   (a) (i), (ii) and (v)

   (b) (ii), (iii) and (iv)

   (c) (i), (ii) and (iv)

   (d) (i), (ii), (iii), (iv) and (v)

12. 'Air Traffic', as defined by ICAO, consists of all aircraft in flight and aircraft:

   (a) Taking-off and landing

   (b) Receiving an ATC service

   (c) Operating anywhere on an airfield

   (d) Operating on the manoeuvring area of an airfield

13. An airfield-based light beacon, red in colour and flashing a two-letter morse code identification is:

    (a) An Identification Beacon at a military airfield

    (b) An aerodrome Beacon at a civil airfield

    (c) An obstruction light

    (d) A runway lead in light (rabbit)

14. By ICAO definition a Control Area extends:

    (a) From the surface to a specified upper level

    (b) From a specified lower level to a specified upper level

    (c) At least 10nm either side of its centre point and has specified upper and lower levels

    (d) From the surface to 2000ft AGL

15. The length of unobstructed runway that will support the aircraft during take-off is known as:

    (a) Take-off Distance Available (TODA)

    (b) Accelerate Run Available (ARA)

    (c) Take-off Run Available (TORA)

    (d) Emergency Distance Available (EDA)

16. A runway condition where significant patches of standing water are visible is described as:

    (a) Wet

    (b) Flooded

    (c) Water Patches

    (d) Damp

17. If you are given an ATC clearance you consider unsuitable you should:

    (a) Carry-out the clearance and file a report on landing

    (b) Amend the clearance as necessary on reading it back to ATC

    (c) Request and try to obtain an amended clearance

    (d) Disregard the clearance

18. The transponder code 7600 indicates:

    (a) A radio communications failure

    (b) That the aircraft is performing aerobatics

    (c) The VFR conspicuity code

    (d) The aerobatics conspicuity code

19. Under what circumstances does the weather minima for VFR flight in class F airspace include a minimum flight visibility of 8km?

    (a) If flying at an Indicated Air Speed of more than140 knots

    (b) If flying at or above Flight Level 100

    (c) If flying with passengers

    (d) If flying at or above 3000ft AGL

20. All flight time to be credited for the grant of a licence or rating must be flown:

(a) In the same category of aircraft for which the licence or rating is sought

(b) In an aeroplane fitted with dual controls

(c) With a qualified instructor

(d) In any aircraft defined as a flying machine

21. Under the Air Navigation Order, a lifejacket should be carried for each occupant of an aircraft in what circumstances?

(a) If flying over any body of water

(b) When flying within 10nm of the coast

(c) For all flights

(d) When flying over water beyond gliding distance of land

22. An aviation accident within the UK must be reported to:

(a) The Civil Aviation Authority

(b) Air Traffic Control and the police

(c) The Air Accidents Investigation Branch and the police

(d) The aircraft operator and the police

23. The marking within an airfield's 'signal square' to indicate that landing is prohibited is:

(a) A red square with a single diagonal yellow stripe

(b) A red and yellow striped arrow, pointing to the right

(c) A red 'L' over a white 'dumbbell'

(d) A red square overlaid with a yellow cross

24. An area of taxiway or runway that is unfit for the movement of aircraft may be marked by:

(a) Yellow crosses painted on the surface

(b) Yellow 'ladder' markings across the taxiway or runway

(c) Two continuous and broken lines across the taxiway or runway

(d) Two or more white crosses painted onto the surface of the taxiway or runway

25. The pre-flight preparation for a flight, for example checking and assessing the weather, is the responsibility of:

(a) The registered aircraft owner or operator

(b) The aircraft commander (pilot in command)

(c) Any person designated by the operator

(d) The CFI or chief pilot

26. A certificate of airworthiness issued by an ICAO state (i), will be recognised as valid by other ICAO states (ii) provided:

(a) State (i) and state (ii) have investigated each other's standards

(b) State (i) is an ICAO council member

(c) The certificate of airworthiness cannot be recognised by state (ii)

(d) The requirements of issue of the certificate in state (i) is equal to or above the minimum standards established by the Convention on International Civil Aviation (Chicago Convention)

27. An aircraft must be flown no closer to any vehicle, vessel, person or structure than:

(a) 700ft

(b) 1000ft

(c) 500ft

(d) 1500ft

28. Revalidation of a single-engine piston aeroplane (land) – SE piston (land) – class rating for a single pilot aeroplane can be done by:

(a) Flying 5 hours in the 13 months preceding rating expiry

(b) At any time within the period of validity of the rating

(c) Flying 6 hours in the 6 months prior to expiry of the rating and making a dual flight with a flying instructor within the 12 months prior to the expiry date of the rating

(d) Flying 12 hours, of which 6 must be Pilot in Command, in the 12 months prior to expiry of the rating and making a dual flight with a flying instructor within the 12 months prior to the expiry date of the rating

29. A fire-proof metal plate, affixed to an aircraft and giving the registration and nationality, is most likely to be:

(a) The registration markings

(b) The notification of ownership placard

(c) An identification plate

(d) The lien of an aircraft mortgagee

30. Taxying out from an apron, when you see an aircraft being towed, converging with you from your left-hand side. Who has right of way?

(a) You

(b) The aircraft being towed

(c) Both have equal claim to right of way

(d) The faster aircraft

31. A continuous red light directed to an aircraft on the ground means:

(a) Return to your starting point on the airfield

(b) Stop

(c) Stop until conflicting traffic has passed

(d) Give way to traffic merging, then continue

32. By ICAO definition, within class D airspace:

(a) IFR flights are separated from other IFR and VFR flights

(b) IFR flights are separated from other IFR flights and are given information about VFR flights

(c) VFR flights are separated from other VFR and IFR flights

(d) Only IFR flight is permitted

---

33. In relation to the Transition Layer:

(a) It is the lowest available Flight Level

(b) It is the altitude above which vertical position is controlled by reference to altitude

(c) It is the airspace between the Transition Altitude and the Transition Level

(d) It is the altitude below which vertical position is controlled by reference to altitude

---

34. An aerodrome to which an aircraft may proceed when it becomes impossible or inadvisable to continue to, or land at, the intended destination is the:

(a) Alternative Aerodrome

(b) Alternate Aerodrome

(c) Standby Aerodrome

(d) Optional Aerodrome

---

35. Definitive information regarding an aircraft's safe operation and operating limits will be found in:

(a) The reverse side of the Certificate of Airworthiness

(b) The Pilot's Operating Handbook/Flight Manual (POH/FM) and markings and cockpit placards

(c) The operator's flying order book or operations manual

(d) Aeronautical Information Circulars

---

36. A JAR-FCL PPL is issued in June 2006. Medical and rating considerations apart, this licence is valid until:

(a) July 2009

(b) June 2010

(c) June 2011

(d) June 2008

---

37. The holder of a JAR PPL(A) may act as pilot in command or co-pilot of an aeroplane:

(a) Whilst on a non-revenue flight

(b) Whilst on a remunerated flight

(c) Whilst on a flight where 'valuable consideration' is given

(d) Provided the remuneration is declared for tax purposes

---

38. By ICAO definition, the hours between the end of evening civil twilight and the beginning of morning civil twilight are:

(a) Nautical twilight

(b) Daylight

(c) Night

(d) Nominal twilight

39. Before carrying out a flight on which it is planned to carry passengers, a pilot must ensure that:

(a) 3 take-offs and landings have been completed as sole manipulator of the controls of any aeroplane in the preceding 90 days

(b) A 'club' check ride has been undertaken

(c) 3 take-offs and landings as sole manipulator of the controls in the same type or class of aeroplane have been completed in the preceding 90 days

(d) 1 take-off and 1 landing have been made in the preceding 90 days under the supervision of a flight instructor

40. A ground air visual signal in the shape of the letter V means:

(a) Assistance is required

(b) Medical assistance is required

(c) Proceed in the direction indicated by the point of the V

(d) There are five survivors

Paper 1 Answers and Explanations

EALP1Q1 — Answer A

Article 16 (Search of Aircraft) of the Convention on International Civil Aviation – the Chicago Convention – states that "The authorities of each state shall have the right to search the aircraft of other states on landing or departure, without unreasonable delay…"

Further Reference: PPL2 Air Law » Legislation » Basis of Aviation Law

EALP1Q2 — Answer C

Article 40 of the Convention on International Civil Aviation (also known as the Chicago Convention) deals with endorsed certificates and licences. It states that "No aircraft or personnel with endorsed licences or certificates will engage in international navigation except with the permission of the state or states whose territory is entered. Any licence holder who does not satisfy international standards relating to that licence or certificate shall have attached to or endorsed on that licence information regarding the particulars in which he does not satisfy those standards."

Further Reference: PPL2 Air Law » Legislation » Basis of Aviation Law

EALP1Q3 — Answer B

Article 12 of the Convention on International Civil Aviation (also known as the Chicago Convention) states in part that "Each state shall keep its own rules of the air as uniform as possible with those established under the convention, the duty to ensure compliance with these rules rests with the contracting state."

Further Reference: PPL2 Air Law » Legislation » Basis of Aviation Law

EALP1Q4 — Answer D

It can't be said enough times – it is the pilot in command who is the person ultimately responsible for the safe operation of an aircraft in flight – and this responsibility extends from the pre-flight actions (such as flight planning, loading and checking of the aircraft) all the way through to when the last of the passengers and crew have left the aircraft at the end of the flight and all the paperwork has been completed.

Further Reference: PPL2 Operational Procedures » Operation of Aircraft » Operation of Aircraft

EALP1Q5 — Answer A

QNH is the code for the altimeter sub-scale setting which will allow the altimeter to indicate Altitude – this is the 'default' altimeter setting when flying below the Transition Altitude.

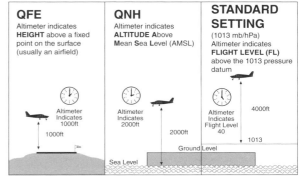

Further Reference: UK AIM » Aeronautical Information Publication » ENR 1.7

PPL2 Air Law » Rules of the Air and Air Traffic Services » Altimeter Pressure Settings

EALP1Q6 — Answer A

The lights to be displayed by a flying machine are set-out in the rules of the air, rules 8 through 15.

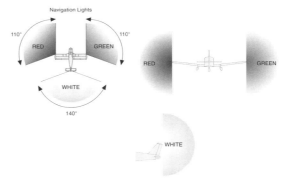

Gliders should display the same navigation lights as a flying machine, or a steady red light showing in all directions.

Free Balloons should display a steady red light showing in all directions, suspended between 5 and 10 metres under the basket.

Airships should display the same navigation lights as a flying machine, plus a white nose-light showing through 110° either side of straight ahead, and also an anti-collision light.

Further Reference: UK AIM » Air Navigation Order – The Rules of the Air » Rule 9

PPL2 Operational Procedures » Operation of Aircraft » Lights to be Displayed by Aircraft

EALP1Q7   Answer C

Runway 'end' lights are as shown in the diagram below:

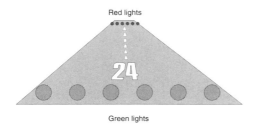

Red lights

24

Green lights

Further Reference: PPL2 Air Law » Rules of the Air » Aerodrome Lighting

EALP1Q8   Answer B

The presence of surface water on a runway is reported by radio using the following descriptions:

Description	Runway condition
Dry	The surface is not affected by water, slush, snow or ice
Damp	The surface shows a change of colour due to moisture
Wet	The surface is soaked but no significant patches of standing water are visible
Water Patches	Significant patches of standing water are visible
Flooded	Extensive standing water is visible

> JAR definition: A runway that has water patches or is flooded is considered to be *contaminated*.

Further Reference: UK AIM » Aeronautical Information Publication » AD1.1.1 (para.15)
PPL2 Air Law » Rules of the Air » Runways

EALP1Q9   Answer B

In general terms, any aircraft whose details are known to the Air Traffic Services is, by default, receiving an alerting service. The last Air Traffic Services Unit (ATSU) to have been in contact with the aircraft is responsible for initiating action if the aircraft is known or believed to be overdue, missing or in an emergency state.

Further Reference: UK AIM » Aeronautical Information Service » GEN 3.6.6 (para. 2)
PPL2 Air Law » Division of Airspace and Air Traffic Services » Air Traffic Services

EALP1Q10   Answer C

ICAO doc 4444 (Rules of the Air and Air Traffic Services) defines various elements of controlled and advisory airspace as below:

Airway	– a control area in the form of a corridor equipped with radio navigation aids.
Advisory airspace	– airspace of defined dimensions, or a designated route, within which an air traffic advisory service is available.
Control Area	– controlled airspace extending upwards from a specified limit above the earth.
Control Zone	– controlled airspace extending upwards from the surface of the earth to a specified upper limit.
Terminal Control Area	– a control area usually established at the confluence of air traffic routes in the vicinity of one or more major aerodromes.

Further Reference: PPL2 Air Law » Division of Airspace and Air Traffic Services » Airspace Classifications

EALP1Q11   Answer A

ICAO Doc 4444 (Rules of the Air and Air Traffic Services) contains the following definitions:

Aerodrome Control Service	– an air traffic control service for aerodrome traffic.
Approach Control Service	– an air traffic control service for arriving and departing controlled flights.
Area Control Service	– an Air Traffic Control service for controlled flights in control areas.

Further Reference: UK AIM » Aeronautical Information Publication » GEN 3.3.3 (para. 3)

PPL2 Air Law » Rules of the Air and Air Traffic Services » Approach Control Service

EALP1Q12 **Answer C**

The criteria for making a Special Aircraft Observation are set-out in the UK AIP, but include such hazards as:

■ severe turbulence

■ severe icing

■ hail

■ cumulonimbus clouds

■ other conditions which might effect the safety of other aircraft operations.

These weather conditions would give rise to a SIGMET message (also defined in the UK AIP). The Rules of the Air also place an obligation on the commander of an aircraft to report hazardous conditions, as soon as possible, to the appropriate Air Traffic Control Unit.

Further Reference: UK AIM » Aeronautical Information Publication » GEN 3.5.6 and GEN 3.5.8 and Air Navigation Order – the Rules of the Air » Rule 4

PPL2 Air Law » Rules of the Air and Air Traffic Services » Air Reports (AIREP)

EALP1Q13 **Answer B**

The definitions of the various runway 'declared distances' are summarised in the diagram below:

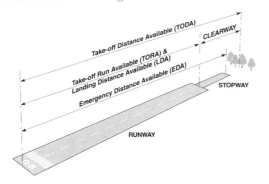

Take-Off Distance Available (TODA)

Take-Off Run Available (TORA)

Landing Distance Available (LDA)

Emergency Distance Available (EDA)

Further Reference: UK AIM » Aeronautical Information Publication » AD1.1.1 para.9

PPL2 Air Law » Rules of the Air » Runways

EALP1Q14 **Answer B**

A special purpose rating (such as the IMC rating in the UK) is not automatically valid outside the state of origin, and each member state must approve it before it can be used within their airspace.

Further Reference: UK AIM » Air Navigation Order » Schedule 8 Part B – ratings

PPL2 Air Law » JAA Regulations » Private Pilot Licence (Aeroplane) – PPL (A)

EALP1Q15 **Answer A**

The Air Navigation Order follows the JAR-FCL recommendation closely in this respect, stating that in the case of illness exceeding 21 days or more, or injury, either of which involves incapacity to undertake flight crew functions, or pregnancy:

"The medical certificate shall be deemed to be suspended upon the occurrence of such injury or the expiry of such period of illness or the confirmation of the pregnancy; and:

(a) in the case of injury or illness the suspension shall cease upon the holder being medically examined under arrangements made by the CAA and pronounced fit to resume his functions as a member of the flight crew or upon the CAA exempting, subject to such conditions as it thinks fit, the holder from the requirement of a medical examination; and

(b) in the case of pregnancy, the suspension may be lifted by the CAA for such period and subject to such conditions as it thinks fit and shall cease upon the holder being medically examined under arrangements made by the CAA after the pregnancy has ended and pronounced fit to resume her functions as a member of the flight crew."

Further Reference: UK AIM » Air Navigation Order » Article 32

PPL2 Air Law » JAA Regulations » JAA Regulations – General

EALP1Q16 **Answer C**

Schedule 8 of the Air Navigation Order states that the holder of a PPL (A) "… shall not fly as pilot in command of such an aeroplane carrying passengers unless within the preceding 90 days he has made three take-offs and three landings as the sole manipulator of the controls of an aeroplane of the same type or class and if such a flight is to be carried out at night and his licence does not include an instrument rating (aeroplane) at least one of those take-offs and landings shall have been at night.

Further Reference: UK AIM » Air Navigation Order » Schedule 8

PPL2 Air Law » JAA Regulations » Private Pilot Licence (Aeroplane) – PPL(A)

EALP1Q17   Answer B

ICAO document 4444 (Rules of the Air and Air Traffic Services) states that if an air traffic control clearance is not suitable to the pilot-in-command of an aircraft, that pilot may request, and if practical obtain, an amended clearance. During this time the pilot should maintain the existing level and heading, but not to the extent of entering conditions for which he or she is not qualified.

Further Reference: PPL2 Air Law » Rules of the Air and Air Traffic Services » Area Control Service

EALP1Q18   Answer D

Article 30 of the Convention on International Civil Aviation (also known as the Chicago Convention) deals with aircraft radio equipment. According to article 30, aircraft of a state flying in or over the territory of another state shall only carry radios licensed and used in accordance with the regulations of the state in which the aircraft is registered. The radio(s) may only be used by members of the flight crew suitably licenced by the state in which the aircraft is registered.

Further Reference: PPL2 Air Law » Legislation » Basis of Aviation Law

EALP1Q19   Answer B

The Air Navigation Order stipulates that a certificate of airworthiness will cease to be in force if the aircraft, or such of its equipment as is necessary for the airworthiness of the aircraft, is overhauled, repaired or modified, or if any part of the aircraft or of such equipment is removed or is replaced, otherwise than in a manner and with material of a type approved by the CAA either generally or in relation to a class of aircraft or to the particular aircraft. Certain of the operating limits contained in the approved Pilot's Operating Handbook/Flight Manual (which forms part of the Certificate of Airworthiness) may be displayed in the cockpit in the form of placards – usually those relating to limiting airspeeds. Operating outside these limits invalidates the Certificate of Airworthiness. Failure to notify a change of ownership (within 28 days) is an offence in relation to the Certificate of Registration, but not the Certificate of Airworthiness.

Further Reference: UK AIM » Air Navigation Order » Article 10
PPL2 Air Law » PPL2 Air Law » Airworthiness of Aircraft » Airworthiness of Aircraft and Aircraft Limits and Information

EALP1Q20   Answer D

An alerting service is the most basic air traffic service, always available when an aircraft's flight details are known to an Air Traffic Service Unit (ATSU).

Further Reference: UK AIM » Aeronautical Information Publication » GEN 3.6.6 para. 2.1
PPL2 Air Law » Division of Airspace and Air Traffic Services » Air Traffic Services

EALP1Q21   Answer C

The definition of a reportable accident is that of one of three possible instances occurring between the time when any person boards the aircraft with the intention of flight and when all persons have left the aircraft after flight:

(1) A person is killed or seriously injured while in, on, or in direct contact with, the aircraft. Also included is death or serious injury caused by jet blast or by parts that have become detached from the aircraft. Natural causes, or self-inflicted injuries, are excluded.

(2) The aircraft incurs damage or structural failure affecting its structural strength, performance or flight characteristics and will require major repair or replacement. Exceptions are engine failures or damage limited to the engine or cowlings; damage limited to propellers, wingtips, antenna, tyres, brakes, fairings; and small holes or dents in the aircraft skin.

(3) The aircraft is missing or completely inaccessible.

Further Reference: PPL2 Operational Procedures » Accident and Incident Investigation » Definitions

EALP1Q22   Answer A

Rule 6 of the rules of the air deals with simulated instrument flight:

(1) An aircraft shall not be flown in simulated instrument flight conditions unless:

    (a) the aircraft is fitted with dual controls which are functioning properly;

    (b) an additional pilot (in this rule called a "safety pilot") is carried in a second control seat of the aircraft for the purpose of rendering such assistance as may be necessary to the pilot flying the aircraft; and

    (c) if the safety pilot's field of vision is not adequate both forward and to each side of the aircraft, a third person, being a competent observer, occupies a position in the aircraft from which his field of vision makes good the deficiencies in that of the safety pilot, and from which he can readily communicate with the safety pilot.

(2) For the purposes of this rule the expression "simulated instrument flight" means a flight during which mechanical or optical devices are used in order to reduce the field of vision or the range of visibility from the cockpit of the aircraft.

Further Reference: UK AIM » Air Navigation Order – Rules of the Air » Rule 6
PPL2 Air Law » Rules of the Air » Simulated Instrument Flight

EALP1Q23   Answer C

Rule 17 of the Rules of the Air deals with the order of precedence, which is:

Flying machines shall give way to airships, gliders and balloons;

Airships shall give way to gliders and balloons;

Gliders shall give way to balloons;

Mechanically driven aircraft shall give way to aircraft which are towing other aircraft or objects.

 1. Balloons

 2. Gliders

3. Airships

4. Flying Machines (aeroplanes, helicopters etc.)

 Powered aircraft give way to aircraft towing gliders or objects

Further Reference: UK AIM » Air Navigation Order – The Rules of the Air » Rule 17

PPL2 Air Law » Rules of the Air » Rights of Way in Flight

EALP1Q24   Answer A

Rule 42 of the Rules of the Air deals with ground signals, and all pilots should be thoroughly familiar with the contents of this rule. The 'white landing T' described in this question signifies that:

"… aeroplanes and gliders taking-off or landing shall do so in a direction parallel with the shaft of the T and towards the cross arm, unless otherwise authorised by the appropriate air traffic control unit"

Furthermore:

"A white disc 60 centimetres in diameter displayed alongside the cross arm of the T and in line with the shaft of the T signifies that the direction of landing and take-off do not necessarily coincide."

Further Reference: UK AIM » Air Navigation Order – The Rules of the Air » Rule 42

PPL2 Air Law » Rules of the Air » Ground-to-Air Visual Signals

EALP1Q25   Answer C

The VMC minima are summarised below. These minima must be learnt.

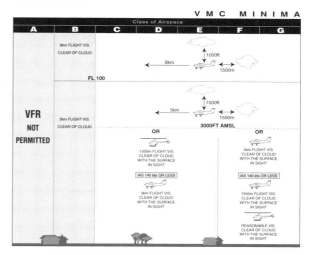

Further Reference: UK AIM » Air Navigation Order – the Rules of the Air » Rule 24-27

PPL2 Air Law » Division of Airspace and Air Traffic Services » Visual Meteorological Conditions (VMC) and Instrument Meteorological Conditions (IMC)

EALP1Q26   Answer D

In terms of the 'changeover' between reporting altitude and reporting Flight Level, the following definitions apply:

Transition altitude The altitude above which the altimeter can be set to Standard Setting (1013) to read Flight Levels.

Transition level The lowest available Flight Level above the transition altitude.

Transition layer The layer between the transition altitude and the transition level.

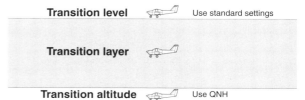

Further Reference: UK AIM » Aeronautical Information Publication » ENR 1.7

PPL2 Air Law » Rules of the Air and Air Traffic Services » Transition Level

EALP1Q27   Answer C

ICAO Annex 7 (Aircraft Nationality and Registration Marks) recommends that the certificate of registration should be carried in the aircraft at all times, although there is no such stipulation in UK law as promulgated in the Air Navigation Order. The Air Navigation Order does stipulate the particulars to be shown on a Certificate of Registration, including the nationality mark and registration, the aircraft constructor and designation, the serial number of the aircraft and the name and address of the registered owner(s).
Further Reference: UK AIM » Air Navigation Order » Article 4
PPL2 Air Law » Aircraft Registration » Aircraft Registration

EALP1Q28   Answer A

ICAO Annex 12 (Search and Rescue) outlines operating procedures for rescue co-ordination centres during emergency phases, including the following recommendations:

Uncertainty Phase During the uncertainty phase, the Rescue Co-ordination Centre will co-operate with air traffic service units and other agencies and services so that incoming reports may be speedily evaluated.

Alert Phase When the alert phase occurs the Rescue Co-ordination Centre will immediately alert the appropriate search and rescue units and initiate any necessary action.

Further Reference: PPL2 Operational Procedures » Search and Rescue » Alerting Phases

EALP1Q29   Answer B

A pilot who sees another aircraft or surface vehicle in distress shall, unless unable to assist or if it is unreasonable or unpractical to do so;

■ Keep the craft in distress in sight.

■ Determine the position if not already known.

■ Report to an ATSU details such as the type and identification of the craft in distress, its position and the number and situation of any survivors spotted.

■ Act as instructed by the ATSU or RCC

Further Reference: PPL2 Operational Procedures » Search and Rescue » Procedures for the Pilot in Command

EALP1Q30   Answer C

ICAO Annex 14 (Aerodromes) states that runway markings shall be white, and taxiway and aircraft stand markings shall be yellow.
Further Reference: PPL2 Air Law » Rules of the Air » Runways and Taxiway Signals and Markings

EALP1Q31   Answer A

The signals from an aircraft to indicate that ground signals have been understood are:

By Day To rock the aircraft wings.

By Night To flash the aircraft's landing light on and off twice, or to switch the navigation lights on and off twice.

The absence of these signals indicates that the ground signals have not been understood.
Further Reference: UK AIM » Aeronautical Information Publication » GEN 3.6.6.12
PPL2 Operational Procedures » Search and Rescue » Procedures for the Pilot in Command

EALP1Q32   Answer D

By ICAO definition, the Pilot In Command is the person in command and charged with the safe conduct of the flight. This is not necessarily the pilot flying the aircraft, nor the pilot occupying the left-hand seat (for example, during a dual training flight the Flight Instructor, occupying the right-hand seat and probably not actually flying the aircraft, is normally the PIC). Nor is it necessarily the most experienced or best-qualified pilot on board. For this reason it is important that when two pilots fly together, there is a clear understanding over which one is the 'pilot in command'.
Further Reference: PPL2 Air Law » Operation of Aircraft » Operation of Aircraft

EALP1Q33   Answer B

ICAO Annex 6 (Operation of Aircraft) recommends that an aeroplane flying more than 100nm/185km (single-engined aircraft) or 200nm/370km (multi-engined aircraft) should have onboard liferafts to carry all persons carried, plus lifejackets and equipment for making pyrotechnic distress signals.
Further Reference: PPL2 Operational Procedures » Operation of Aircraft » Instruments and Equipment

EALP1Q34   Answer A

The rules for Special VFR flight are set-out in the UK AIP. In part, this states:

"When operating on a Special VFR clearance, the pilot must comply with ATC instructions and remain at all times in conditions which enable him to determine his flight path and to keep clear of obstacles."

It is therefore implicit that when operating on a special VFR clearance terrain clearance is the responsibility of the pilot in command or aircraft commander.

Permission for SVFR flight is only granted by ATC when traffic conditions permit. Whilst operating on an SVFR clearance, the pilot *must* comply with ATC instructions. ATC will provide separation between Special VFR flights and IFR traffic.
Further Reference: UK AIM » Aeronautical Information Publication » ENR1.2
PPL2 Air Law » Division of Airspace and Air Traffic Services » Special VFR

EALP1Q35 — Answer A

Rule 17 of the Rules of the Air deals with this situation as follows:

"Where take-offs and landings are not confined to a runway:

(i) a flying machine or glider when landing shall leave clear on its left any aircraft which has landed or is already landing or about to take off; if such a flying machine or glider is about to turn it shall turn to the left after the commander of the aircraft has satisfied himself that such action will not interfere with other traffic movements; and

(ii) a flying machine about to take off shall take up position and manoeuvre in such a way as to leave clear on its left any aircraft which has already taken off or is about to take off."

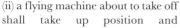

Further Reference: UK AIM » Air Navigation Order – The Rules of the Air » Rule 17
PPL2 Air Law » Rules of the Air » Landing and Take-off

EALP1Q36 — Answer A

Article 23 (Aircraft weight schedule) of the Air Navigation Order states in part "...the weight schedule shall be preserved by the operator of the aircraft until the expiration of a period of six months following the next occasion on which the aircraft is weighed...". Therefore, 6 months forward from June 2006 is December 2006.

Further Reference: UK AIM » Air Navigation Order » Article 23
PPL2 Air Law » Airworthiness of Aircraft » Weight Schedule

EALP1Q37 — Answer A

By ICAO recommendation, an overtaking situation is deemed to exist when the overtaking aircraft is within an angle of less than 70° from the extended centreline of the aircraft being overtaken.

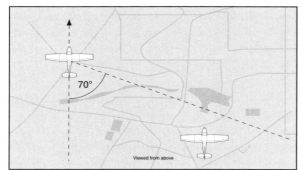

The rear navigation light of a flying machine is white, and visible 70° either side of the extended centreline of the aircraft.

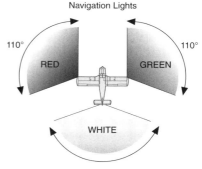

Navigation Lights

Therefore, in accordance with the ICAO recommendation on overtaking, once the overtaking machine can no longer see the white light of the other aircraft, the overtaking situation has ceased to exist.

Further Reference: PPL2 Air Law » Rules of the Air » Rights of Way in Flight
PPL2 Operational Procedures » Operation of Aircraft » Lights to be Displayed by Aircraft

EALP1Q38 — Answer B

Student pilots must be at least 16 years old before first solo flight. The minimum age for an applicant for a PPL is 17 years old.

Further Reference: UK AIM » Air Navigation Order » Article 26
UK AIM » Air Navigation Order » Schedule 8 Part A
PPL2 Air Law » JAA Regulations » Student Pilots (Aeroplanes) and Private Pilot Licence (Aeroplane)

EALP1Q39 — Answer D

The periods of validity of class and type ratings are:

Type ratings and multi-engine class ratings – One year

Single-pilot, single-engine class ratings (including touring motor gliders) – Two years

Further Reference: UK AIM » Air Navigation Order » Schedule 8 Part A
PPL2 Air Law » JAA Regulations » Type and Class Ratings (Aeroplane)

EALP1Q40 — Answer D

Under the Rules of the Air an aircraft which has right of way "... shall maintain its course and speed."

Further Reference: UK AIM » Air Navigation Order » Rules of the Air Rule 17
PPL2 Air Law » Rules of the Air » Rules for Avoiding Collisions

Paper 2 Answers and Explanations

EALP2Q1   Answer B

Article 10 of the Convention on International Civil Aviation (also known as the Chicago Convention) deals with landing at customs airports. According to article 10, the state <u>can</u> require that landing to be at a designated customs airport and similarly departure from the territory <u>can</u> be required to be from a designated customs airport.

Further Reference: PPL2 Air Law » Legislation » Basis of Aviation Law

EALP2Q2   Answer B

Article 5 (Non-Scheduled Flights Over State's Territory) of the Convention on International Civil Aviation (also known as the Chicago Convention) states "The aircraft of states, other than scheduled international air services, have the right to make flights across state's territories and to make stops without obtaining prior permission..."

Further Reference: PPL2 Air Law » Legislation » Basis of Aviation Law

EALP2Q3   Answer B

Article 24 (Customs Duty) of the Convention on International Civil Aviation (also known as the Chicago Convention) states that aircraft flying to, from or across, the territory of a state shall be admitted temporarily free of duty. Fuel, oil, spare parts, regular equipment and aircraft stores retained on board are also exempt customs duty, inspection fees or similar charges.

Further Reference: PPL2 Air Law » Legislation » Basis of Aviation Law

EALP2Q4   Answer B

Article 29 of the Convention on International Civil Aviation (also known as the Chicago Convention) states that before an international flight, the pilot in command must ensure that the aircraft is airworthy, duly registered and that the relevant certificates are on board the aircraft. The required documents are:

- Its Certificate of Registration
- Its Certificate of Airworthiness
- Crew licences
- Journey logbook
- Radio licence
- A list of passenger names, places of embarkation and destination
- A cargo manifest

Further Reference: PPL2 Air Law » Legislation » Basis of Aviation Law

EALP2Q5   Answer D

The VMC minima are summarised at the explanation EALP1Q25. These minima must be learnt.

Further Reference: UK AIM, Air Navigation Order – the Rules of the Air, Rule 25 & 26

PPL2 Air Law, Division of Airspace and Air Traffic Services, Visual Meteorological Conditions (VMC) and Instrument Meteorological Conditions (IMC)

EALP2Q6   Answer D

The relevant publications of JAR-FCL are:

JAR-FCL 1	Aeroplane
JAR-FCL 2	Helicopter
JAR-FCL 3	Medical

Further Reference: PPL2 Air Law, JAA Regulations, JAA Regulations – General

EALP2Q7   Answer C

Runway 'end' lights are as shown in explanation EALP1Q7

Further Reference: PPL2 Air Law » Rules of the Air » Aerodrome Lighting

EALP2Q8   Answer D

ICAO defines Visual Meteorological Conditions (VMC) as 'Meteorological conditions expressed in terms of visibility, distance from cloud, and ceiling, equal to or better than specified minima'.

In the UK, VMC minima are specified in terms of visibility and distance from cloud, but a cloud ceiling is not specified.

Further Reference: PPL2 Air Law » Rules of the Air » Visual Flight Rules (VFR)

EALP2Q9   Answer A

A Flight Information Service is a service provided for the purpose of giving advice and information useful for the safe and efficient conduct of flights.

Further Reference: PPL2 Air Law » Division of Airspace and Air Traffic Services » Air Traffic Services

EALP2Q10 — Answer D

The weather minima for a JAR PPL (Aeroplane) holder is summarised in the table below. In essence, outside controlled airspace (ie Class F & G) the licence holder must remain VMC, subject to an absolute minimum flight visibility of 3km when at or below 3000ft amsl, at or below 140 knots IAS. The JAR PPL must also remain in sight of the surface at all times.

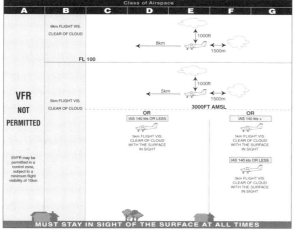

WEATHER MINIMA
for a JAR PPL holder WITHOUT IMC rating or Instrument Rating

Further Reference: UK AIM » Air Navigation Order » Schedule 8 Part 1
UK AIM » Air Navigation Order » Rules of the Air (Rules 24-27)
PPL2 Air Law » JAA Regulations » Private Pilot Licence (Aeroplane)

EALP2Q11 — Answer D

Each individual aircraft with a C of A will have its own individual copy of the POH/FM. The C of A will refer to the aircraft's POH/FM. *For the C of A to remain valid, all the limitations, procedures and restrictions in the POH/FM must be complied with.*

Certain key limitations and information from the POH/FM may be displayed in the cockpit in the form of placards.
Further Reference: PPL2 Air Law » Airworthiness of Aircraft » Aircraft Limits and Information

EALP2Q12 — Answer A

Procedures for filing a full flight plan are set out in the Aeronautical Information Publication (AIP) at ENR1.10 (Flight Planning). This states in part that "… a pilot intending to make a flight shall inform the Air Traffic Service Unit (ATSU) at the aerodrome of departure…In the absence of an ATSU at the departure aerodrome, the pilot may submit his flight plan through the Parent Unit…"
Further Reference: UK AIM » Aeronautical Information Publication » ENR1.10 (in particular paragraphs 1.5, 1.7 and 2.5)
PPL2 Air Law » Rules of the Air and Air Traffic Services » Flight Plans

EALP2Q13 — Answer A

The privileges of the UK Private Pilot's Licence (Aeroplane) are set out in Schedule 8 of the Air Navigation Order. This states in part that a licence holder "…may fly such an aeroplane for the purpose of aerial work which consists of:
(a) towing a glider in flight; or
(b) a flight for the purpose of dropping of persons by parachute"
Further Reference: UK AIM » Air Navigation Order » Schedule 8 section 1
PPL2 Air Law » JAA Regulations » Private Pilot Licence (Aeroplane) – PPL (A)

EALP2Q14 — Answer B

LARS is a radar service available in the UK in Class F and G airspace, up to FL95, from participating units. A LARS unit will normally be able to offer a Radar Advisory Service (RAS) or Radar Information Service (RIS) within 30nm of the unit.
Further Reference: UK AIM » Aeronautical Information Publication » ENR 1.6.3
PPL2 Communications » En Route Procedures » Lower Airspace Radar Service (LARS)

EALP2Q15 — Answer B

See the definitions listed at explanation EALP1Q10. Further, ICAO document 4444 (Rules of the Air and Air Traffic Services) defines a control zone as "Controlled Airspace extending upwards from the surface of the earth to a specified upper limit". The Air Navigation Order also defines a control zones as "…controlled airspace which has been further notified as a control zone and which extends upwards from the surface.". It is an ICAO recommendation that a control zone should extend at least 5nm from the centre of the airfield in the direction from which approaches may be made.
Further Reference: UK AIM » Air Navigation Order » Article 155
PPL2 Air Law » Division of Airspace and Air Traffic Services » Airspace Classifications

EALP2Q16 — Answer C

Advice from the CAA states "Pilots should be aware that although every effort will be made to expedite their arrival, a call such as 'Fuel Emergency' has no status in the UK and ATC cannot give priority to an aircraft with a shortage of fuel unless an emergency is declared. A radio call prefixed by MAYDAY for distress or PAN PAN for urgency will ensure priority handling…"
Further Reference: PPL2 Air Law » Rules of the Air and Air Traffic Services » Approach Control Service

EALP2Q17   **Answer D**

ICAO Annex 14 (Aerodromes) contains the following definitions:

Aircraft stand – a designated area on an apron intended to be used for parking an aircraft.

Landing Area – that part of a movement area intended for the take-off or landing of aircraft.

Movement Area – that part of an aerodrome to be used for the take-off, landing and taxying of aircraft, consisting of the manoeuvring area and the apron.

The apron and manoeuvring area are defined as follows:

Apron – the part of an aerodrome where aircraft can be stationed for the embarkation and disembarkation of passengers, for loading and unloading cargo, fuelling, maintenance and parking.

Manoeuvring area – the part of the aerodrome provided for the take-off and landing and movement of aircraft, excluding the apron and any maintenance area.

Further Reference: UK AIM » Air Navigation Order » Schedule 155
PPL2 Air Law, Rules of the Air, Movements at Aerodromes

EALP2Q18   **Answer A**

JAR-FCL 1.04 (Decrease in Medical Fitness) states in part that holders of medical certificates shall, without undue delay, seek the advice of the authority or an AME when becoming aware of:

(1) hospital or clinic admission for more than 12 hours; or

(2) surgical operation or invasive procedure; or

(3) the regular use of medication; or

(4) the need for regular use of correcting lenses.

Further Reference: PPL2 Air Law » JAA Regulations » JAA Requirements – General

---

EALP2Q19   **Answer C**

Schedule 8 of the Air Navigation Order states that the holder of a Private Pilot Licence (Aeroplanes) can act as pilot in command or co-pilot of any aeroplane specified in a class or type rating included in their licence.

Further Reference: UK AIM » Air Navigation Order » Schedule 8 Section 2
PPL2 Air Law » JAA Regulations » Type and Class Ratings (Aeroplanes)

EALP2Q20   **Answer C**

An applicant for a JAR PPL (Aeroplane) must have completed at least 45 hours of flight time, including not less than 25 hours of dual instruction and not less than 10 hours solo flight time.

Further Reference: PPL2 Air Law » JAA Regulations » Private Pilot Licence (Aeroplane)

EALP2Q21   **Answer C**

A Movement Area is defined as that part of an aerodrome to be used for the take-off, landing and taxying of aircraft, consisting of the manoeuvring area and the apron.

Further Reference: PPL2 Air Law » Rules of the Air » Movements at Aerodromes

---

EALP2Q22   **Answer B**

ICAO Annex six sets out recommended minimum equipment for aircraft, including instrumentation. According to Annex six aircraft on a VFR flight should be equipped with at least:

A magnetic compass.

An accurate timepiece.

A sensitive pressure altimeter.

An airspeed indicator.

Any additional instrument prescribed by the relevant authority.

Further Reference: PPL2 Air Law » Operation of Aircraft » Instruments and Equipment

---

EALP2Q23   **Answer D**

Where aircraft are converging in the air, the following order of precedence applies:

1. Balloons
2. Gliders
3. Airships
4. Flying Machines (ie heavier than air powered aircraft – aeroplanes, helicopters, gyroplanes etc).

Additionally, powered aircraft must give way to aircraft towing gliders or objects.

Because helicopters and aeroplanes are of the same class, no rule of precedence applies between them.

Further Reference: UK AIM » Air Navigation Order » The Rules of the Air – Rule 17 (2)
PPL2 Air Law » Rules of the Air » Rights of Way in Flight

EALP2Q24   **Answer D**

The standard emergency transponder codes are as follows:

7700 Distress

7600 Radio communications failure

7500 Unlawful interference

Further Reference: UK AIM » Aeronautical Information Publication » ENR 1.6.2 para.2
PPL2 Air Law » Rules of the Air » Distress, Difficulty and Urgency Signals

EALP2Q25   **Answer C**

The Ground-Air visual signal code for use by survivors is set out below:

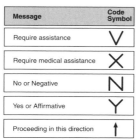

Message	Code Symbol
Require assistance	V
Require medical assistance	X
No or Negative	N
Yes or Affirmative	Y
Proceeding in this direction	↑

Further Reference: UK AIM » Aeronautical Information Publication » GEN3.6.6

PPL2 Air Law » Search and Rescue » Search and Rescue Signals

EALP2Q26   **Answer B**

Where two aircraft are converging 'head on', and there is a risk of collision, each must alter heading to the right.

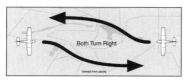

Further Reference: UK AIM » Air Navigation Order » The Rules of the Air – Rule 17

PPL2 Air Law » Rules of the Air » Rights of Way in Flight and Rights of Way on the Ground

EALP2Q27   **Answer C**

The following initial actions are recommended to the pilot of an aircraft which has been intercepted:

(1) Stay calm and comply immediately with the instructions or signals of the intercepting aircraft.

(2) Notify the ATSU with which you are in contact.

(3) Attempt to establish communication with the interceptor on the emergency frequency of 121.5, giving callsign and flight details.

(4) Set the distress code – 7700 Mode C – on the transponder, unless instructed otherwise by an ATSU.

Further Reference: UK AIM » Aeronautical Information Publication » ENR 1.12

PPL2 Air Law » Rules of the Air » Rights of Way in Flight and Rights of Way on the Ground

EALP2Q28   **Answer D**

When operating en-route, at or below the transition altitude, vertical positioning of an aircraft is normally expressed in terms of 'altitude' – that is the altimeter reading with the relevant QNH set, in other words the vertical distance above mean sea level (amsl).

Further Reference: UK AIM » AIP ENR 1.7

PPL2 Air Law » Rules of the Air and Air Traffic Services » Altimeter Setting Procedures

EALP2Q29   **Answer B**

ICAO Annex 14 (Aerodromes) sets out the definitions of the various runway distances (sometimes referred to as 'declared distances'), and these definition are summarised at explanation EALP1Q13.

Further Reference: PPL2 Air Law » Rules of the Air » Runways

EALP3Q30   **Answer C**

Rule 43 (Markings for paved runways and taxiways) of the Rules of the Air states that the holding position closest to the runway is marked by two yellow broken lines and two continuous lines (the broken lines are on the runway side of the marking).

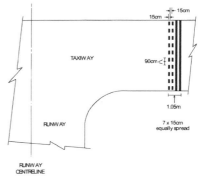

No part of an aircraft or vehicle may project further than these markings in the direction of the runway beyond with permission from ATC.

Further Reference: UK AIM » Air Navigation Order – The Rules of the Air » Rule 43

PPL2 Air Law » Rules of the Air » Taxiway Signals and Markings

EALP2Q31   **Answer B**

Rule 43 (Markings for paved runways and taxiways) of the Rules of the Air states that two or more white crosses, with the arms of the cross at 45° to the runway or taxiway centreline, denote a section not fit for the movement of aircraft. You should be familiar with the contents of Rule 43.

Further Reference: UK AIM » Air Navigation Order – The Rules of the Air » Rule 43

PPL2 Air Law » Rules of the Air » Ground-to-Air Visual Signals

EALP2Q32   **Answer A**

ICAO Annex 14 (Aerodromes) states that runway markings shall be solid white, although this white may be outlined in black for clarity.

Further Reference: PPL2 Air Law » Rules of the Air » Runways

EALP2Q33   **Answer D**

JAR-FCL 1.105 (Medical Fitness) states that the applicant for a PPL(A) shall hold a valid Class1 or Class 2 medical certificate. Class 2 is to a lower standard than Class 1.

Further Reference: PPL2 Air Law » JAA Regulations » JAA Regulations – General

EALP2Q34   Answer D

The holder of a medical certificate issued in accordance with JAR-FCL3 must inform the authority in writing of;

■ any significant personal injury involving incapacity to function as a member of a flight crew,

■ becoming pregnant,

■ Illness involving incapacity to function as a member of flight crew throughout a period of 21 days or more (the authority must be informed in writing as soon as the period of 21 days has elapsed).

In all cases the medical certificate will then be considered as suspended; this suspension shall cease or be lifted subject to a medical examination under arrangements made by the authority. The authority may exempt the holder from a medical examination, or impose conditions to the lifting of the suspension, as it sees fit.

Further Reference: UK AIM » Air Navigation Order » Article 26
PPL2 Air Law » Airworthiness of Aircraft » Aircraft Limits and Information

EALP2Q35   Answer C

JAR-FCL 1.065 (State of Licence Issue) provides for a licence holder to transfer a licence issued by the State of licence issue to another JAA member state provided that employment or normal residency is established in that state.
Further Reference: PPL2 Air Law » JAA Regulations » JAA Regulations – General

EALP2Q36   Answer A

The subject of Wake Turbulence is usually covered in detail in a pink AIC (AIC17/1999 Pink 188 at the time of writing). Using the diagram below:

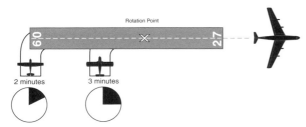

For the situation outlined in the question (light aircraft departing from the same point behind a heavy aircraft) the minimum spacing based on airborne time is 2 minutes. Therefore, if the leading 'heavy' aircraft is airborne at 14:02 and 30 seconds, the following light aircraft should be airborne no earlier than 14:04 and 30 seconds.
Further Reference: UK AIM » Aeronautical Information Circulars » AIC 17/1999
PPL2 Air Law » Rules of the Air and Air Traffic Services » Wake Turbulence

EALP2Q37   Answer B

The question assumes that both the aircraft are 'flying machines' – that is heavier-than-air, power-driven aircraft. The fact that you can see a red light infers that it is on the port (left) wingtip of the other flying machine, and the relative bearing of the other flying machine puts it on your right-hand side – therefore it has right of way (**on the right, in the right**). Further, the fact that the bearing is constant means that the aircraft are almost certainly converging and there is a risk of a collision. Therefore you should avoid passing over, under or ahead of the other machine, and prepare to alter course to starboard (right) to pass clear behind it.

Further Reference: UK AIM » Air Navigation Order – the Rules of the Air » Section III
PPL2 Operational Procedures » Operation of Aircraft » Lights to be Displayed by Aircraft
Air Law » Rules of the Air » Rules for Avoiding Collisions and Rights of Way in Flight

EALP2Q38   Answer B

The definition of an accident is contained within the Civil Aviation (Investigation of Air Accidents and Incidents) Regulations. The key points are that the occurrence takes place between the time that any person boards the aircraft with the intention of flight, until all such persons have disembarked. An accident can include a situation where a person is killed or injured either in or on the aircraft, or by direct contact with the aircraft, including parts which have become detached from an aircraft. Therefore, for example, a death on an aircraft that occurs while it is in a hanger with no intention of being flown is not reportable under these regulations, but a broken foot caused by something falling off an aircraft as it is pushed-back for departure would be.
Further Reference: PPL2 Operational Procedures » Accident and Incident Investigation » Definitions

EALP2Q39   Answer D

By ICAO definition the pilot in command (also sometimes known as the 'Commander' in the UK) is the person in command and charged with the safe conduct of the flight. That's where the buck stops!
Further Reference: PPL2 Operational Procedures » Operation of Aircraft » Pre-flight Actions

EALP2Q40   Answer A

'Distress' is classified as a state of emergency where an aircraft is threatened by serious and imminent danger and is in need of immediate assistance.
Further Reference: UK AIM » Aeronautical Information Circulars » AIC 93/2004 Pink 68
PPL2 Air Law » Rules of the Air » Distress Difficulty and Urgency Signals

Paper 3 Answers and Explanations

EALP3Q1   Answer C

Article 1 of the Chicago Convention (also known as the Convention on International Civil Aviation) states simply that every state has complete and exclusive sovereignty over airspace above its territory.

Further Reference: PPL2 Air Law » Legislation » Basis of Aviation Law

EALP3Q2   Answer B

Article 32 (Licences of Personnel) of the Chicago Convention (Convention on International Civil Aviation) states in part "The pilot and crew of every aircraft engaged in international navigation must have certificates of competency and licences issued or validated by the state in which the aircraft is registered."

Further Reference: PPL2 Air Law » Legislation » Basis of Aviation Law

EALP3Q3   Answer D

See EALP2Q37

In assessing collision risk the golden rule is:

"Constant Bearing, Constant Danger"

Therefore there IS a risk of collision.

The other flying machine is to your right. Therefore it has right of way:

"On the right, in the right"

Where a flying machine has right of way, the other should give way by, if safe, turning right to pass behind the other aircraft.

Further Reference: UK AIM » Air Navigation Order – the Rules of the Air » Rule 17

PPL2 Air Law » Rules of the Air » Rights of Way in Flight

EALP3Q4   Answer B

Article 5 (Non-Scheduled Flights Over State's Territory) of the Convention on International Civil Aviation (also known as the Chicago Convention) states "The aircraft of states, other than scheduled international air services, have the right to make flights across state's territories and to make stops without obtaining prior permission, although the state may require the aircraft to make a landing".

Further Reference: PPL2 Air Law » Legislation » Basis of Aviation Law

EALP3Q5   Answer A

Article 29 of the Chicago Convention (Convention on International Civil Aviation) recommends that aircraft engaged in international navigation should carry the following documents:

- Its Certificate of Registration
- Its Certificate of Airworthiness
- Crew licences
- Journey logbook
- Radio licence
- A list of passenger names, places of embarkation and destination
- A cargo manifest

Further Reference: PPL2 Air Law » Legislation » Basis of Aviation Law

EALP3Q6   Answer C

Article 13 (Entry and Clearance Regulations) of the Chicago Convention (Convention on International Civil Aviation) recommends that "A state's laws and regulations regarding the admission and departure of passengers, crew or cargo from aircraft shall be complied with on arrival, upon departure and whilst within the territory of that state."

Further Reference: PPL2 Air Law » Legislation » Basis of Aviation Law

EALP3Q7   Answer A

The minimum scales of radio equipment for flight in various circumstances is set out in schedule 5 of the Air Navigation Order. In this situation scale A is required, which is "Radio equipment capable of maintaining direct two-way communication with the appropriate aeronautical radio stations."

Further Reference: UK AIM » Air Navigation Order » Schedule 5
PPL2 Operational Procedures » Operation of Aircraft » Instruments and Equipment

EALP3Q8   Answer B

An aircraft on a Special VFR clearance is not required to observe the '1000ft rule' element of Rule 5 (low flying). However, such a flight is not absolved from the other provisions of rule 5, including in particular the requirement to fly over a congested area at such a height as to be able to land clear in the event of an engine failure.

Further Reference: UK AIM » Aeronautical Information Publication » ENR 1.2 (para2) and Air Navigation Order – the Rules of the Air » Rule 5

PPL2 Air Law » Division of Airspace and Air Traffic Services » Special VFR

EALP3Q9   Answer A

See the illustration given at explanation EALP1Q5.

Further Reference: UK AIM » Aeronautical Information Publication » ENR1.7

PPL2 Air Law » Rules of the Air and Air Traffic Services » Altimeter Pressure Settings

EALP3Q10   Answer C

In class A airspace, VFR flight is not permitted. Within controlled airspace (Classes A – E) all IFR flights receive an Air Traffic Control Service. In Class G airspace, aircraft are *expected* to comply with clearances and instructions, however a pilot can advise otherwise. This effectively leaves only Class F 'Advisory' airspace from the answer choices.

Further Reference: UK AIM » Aeronautical Information Publication » ENR 1.4

PPL2 Air Law » Division of Airspace and Air Traffic Services » Airspace Summary

EALP3Q11   Answer D

The objectives of air traffic services are defined as being to:
- Prevent collisions between aircraft
- Prevent collisions between aircraft on the manoeuvring area and obstructions on that area
- Expedite and maintain an orderly flow of air traffic
- Provide advice and information of the safe and efficient conduct of flights
- Notify organisations of aircraft in need of search and rescue aid, and assist such organisations

Further Reference: PPL2 Air Law » Division of Airspace and Air Traffic Services » Air Traffic Services

EALP3Q12   Answer D

According to an ICAO definition, 'Air Traffic' is all aircraft in flight or operating on the manoeuvring area of an aerodrome.

Further Reference: PPL2 Air Law » Rules of the Air and Air Traffic Services » Flight Information Service and Alerting Service

EALP3Q13   Answer A

An Identification Beacon (IBn) is a light flashing a two-letter morse code at an aerodrome. It is coloured red at a military aerodrome, green at a civilian aerodrome.

Further Reference: PPL2 Air Law » Rules of the Air » Aerodrome Lighting

EALP3Q14   Answer B

See the definitions at explanation EALP1Q10. By ICAO definition (also further notified in the Air Navigation Order) a control area extends upwards from a specified limit above the earth.

Further Reference: UK AIM » Air Navigation Order » Articles Part B
PPL2 Air Law » Division of Airspace and Air Traffic Services » Airspace Classifications

EALP3Q15   Answer C

The definitions of the various runway 'declared distances' are summarised in explanation EALP1Q13.

Further Reference: UK AIM » Aeronautical Information Publication » AD1.1.1
PPL2 Air Law » Rules of the Air » Runways

EALP3Q16   Answer C

The presence of surface water on a runway is reported by radio using the descriptions listed at explanation EALP1Q8.

Further Reference: UK AIM » Aeronautical Information Publication » AD1.1.1
PPL2 Air Law » Rules of the Air » Runways

EALP3Q17   Answer C

ICAO document 4444 (Rules of the Air and Air Traffic Services) states that if an air traffic control clearance is not suitable to the pilot-in-command of an aircraft, that pilot may request, and if practical obtain, an amended clearance.

Further Reference: PPL2 Air Law » Rules of the Air and Air Traffic Services » Area Control Service

EALP3Q18   Answer A

The 'special purpose' transponder codes are summarised below:

7700 Emergency condition

7600 Radio failure

7500 Unlawful interference

Further Reference: UK AIM » Aeronautical Information Publication » ENR 1.6.2
PPL2 Air Law » Rules of the Air » Distress Difficulty and Urgency Signals

EALP3Q19   Answer B

See the table at EALP1Q25 which summarises the weather minima for VFR flight. To fly VFR, the aircraft must be in Visual Meteorological Conditions (VMC). Note that class F airspace is uncontrolled airspace. It is important to appreciate that VMC minima are not the same as licence minima, and not at all affected by licences and ratings held, pilot experience, etc.

Further Reference: UK AIM » Air Navigation Order – the Rules of the Air » Rule 24-27
PPL2 Air Law » Division of Airspace and Air Traffic Services » Visual Meteorological Conditions (VMC) and Instrument Meteorological Conditions (IMC)

EALP3Q20   Answer A

JAR-FCL 1.05 (Crediting of flight time) states that, unless otherwise specified, flight time to be credited for a licence or rating shall have been flown in the same category of aircraft for which the licence or rating is sought.

Further Reference: PPL2 Air Law » JAA Regulations » JAA Regulations – General

EALP3Q21   Answer D

Schedule 4 of the Air Navigation Order covers required equipment of aircraft, and in certain circumstances it requires that, when flying over water beyond gliding distance from land, lifejackets must be carried for each person on board (each lifejacket be equipped with a whistle and light).

Further Reference: UK AIM » Air Navigation Order » Schedule 4
PPL2 Operational Procedures » Operation of Aircraft » Instruments and Equipment

EALP3Q22 Answer C

In legal terms an accident or serious incident must be reported to the Chief Inspector of Air Accidents, which in practice means the Air Accidents Investigation Branch (AAIB) of the Department of Transport. Where the accident occurs in or over the UK, the police must also be informed.

Further Reference: UK AIM » Civil Aviation Investigation of Accidents Regulations Article 5

Aeronautical Information Publication » GEN 1.1

PPL2 Operational Procedures » Accident and Incident Investigation » National Procedures

EALP3Q23 Answer D

A red square overlaid with a yellow cross in the signal area indicates that landing is prohibited. The Ground-Air signals must be learnt.

Further Reference: UK AIM » Air Navigation Order » Rules of the Air – Rule 42

PPL2 Air Law » Rules of the Air » Ground-to-Air Visual Signals

EALP3Q24 Answer D

Two or more white crosses displayed on a runway or taxiway, with each arm at an angle of 45° to the runway or taxiway centre line, signify a section of taxiway or runway unfit for the movement of aircraft

Further Reference: UK AIM » Air Navigation Order » Rules of the Air – Rule 43

PPL2 Air Law » Rules of the Air » Runways

EALP3Q25 Answer B

In general terms, you can assume that any practical pre-flight action is the responsibility of the aircraft commander/pilot in command, even if he/she does not undertake the action in person. In this respect there is no differentiation between a private flight, a public transport flight or whatever, the principle applies equally to the pilot of a C150 as it does to the commander of a 747.

Further Reference: UK AIM » Air Navigation Order » Article 52-53

PPL2 Operational Procedures » Operation of Aircraft » Pre-flight Actions

EALP3Q26 Answer D

Article 33 (Recognition of Certificates and Licences) of the Chicago Convention (Convention on International Civil Aviation) recommends that "Certificates of Airworthiness, certificates of competency and licences issued or validated by the state in which the aircraft is registered, shall be recognised as valid by other states. The requirements for issue of those Certificates of Airworthiness, certificates of competency and licences must be equal to or above the minimum standards established by the Convention."

Further Reference: PPL2 Air Law » Legislation » Basis of Aviation Law

EALP3Q27 Answer C

The low flying rules state that "An aircraft shall not fly closer than 500 feet to any person, vessel, vehicle or structure." As you might expect there are certain exceptions to this rule (such as during take-off and landing). The fundamental nature of this rule is such that every pilot should know its contents thoroughly.

Further Reference: UK AIM » Air Navigation Order – Rules of the Air » Rule 5

PPL2 Air Law » Rules of the Air » The Low Flying Rules

EALP3Q28 Answer D

The full requirements for the revalidation of an SEP (land) rating are not simple. For revalidation of single-pilot single-engine piston aeroplane (land) class ratings and/or touring motor glider class ratings the applicant shall satisfy the following requirements:

■ Within the three months preceding the expiry date of the rating, either pass a proficiency check with an authorised examiner on either a single-engine piston aeroplane (land) or a touring motor glider;

or within 12 months preceding the expiry of the rating:

■ complete 12 hours of flight time in the class including 6 hours of pilot-in-command time and 12 take-offs and landings;

■ complete a training flight of at least 1 hours duration with a flight instructor. This flight may be replaced by any other proficiency check or skill test for a class or type rating.

Further Reference: PPL2 Air Law » JAA Regulations » Type and Class Ratings (Aeroplane)

EALP3Q29 Answer C

ICAO Annex 7 (Aircraft Nationality and Registration Marks) recommends that aircraft carry an identification plate inscribed with its registration (although this plate normally also states the exact aircraft type and model, serial number and sometimes the registered owner too). This identification plate should be made of "…fire-proof metal or other fireproof material of suitable physical properties…"

Further Reference: PPL2 Air Law » Aircraft Registration » Aircraft Registration

EALP3Q30 Answer B

The order of precedence on the ground is set-out in rule 37 of the Rules of the Air:

(a) Flying machines and vehicles shall give way to aircraft which are taking off or landing.

(b) Vehicles, and flying machines which are not taking off or landing, shall give way to vehicles towing aircraft.

(c) Vehicles which are not towing aircraft shall give way to aircraft.

Further Reference: UK AIM » Air Navigation Order – Rules of the Air » Rule 37

PPL2 Air Law » Rules of the Air » Rights of Way on the Ground

EALP3Q31   Answer B

The table of light signals to aircraft is reproduced below:

Rule 46: Lights and pyrotechnic signals for control of aerodrome traffic

Each signal described in the first column of Table A, when directed from an aerodrome to an aircraft or to a vehicle, or from an aircraft, shall have the meanings respectively appearing in the second, third and fourth columns of that Table opposite the description of the signal.

Table A – Meaning of lights and pyrotechnic signals

Characteristic and colour of light Beam or pyrotechnic	From an aerodrome — To an aircraft in flight	From an aerodrome — To an aircraft or vehicle on the aerodrome	From an aircraft in flight to an aerodrome
(a) Continuous red light	Give way to other aircraft and continue circling	Stop	–
(b) Red pyrotechnic light, or red flare	Do not land; wait for permission	–	Immediate assistance is requested
(c) Red flashes	Do not land; aerodrome not available	Move clear of landing area	–
(d) Green flashes	Return to aerodrome; wait for permission to land	To an aircraft; you may move on the manoeuvring area and apron. To a vehicle, you may move on the Manoeuvring area	–
(e) Continuous green light	You may land	You may take-off (not applicable to a vehicle)	–
(f) Continuous green light, or green Flashes, or green pyrotechnic light	–	–	By night; may I land? By day; may I land in direction different
(g) White flashes	Land at this aerodrome after receiving continuous green light, and then after receiving green flashes, proceed to the apron	Return to starting point on the aerodrome	I am compelled to land
(h) White pyrotechnic lights switching on and off the navigation lights. Switching on and off the landing lights	–	–	I am compelled to land

Further Reference: UK AIM » Air Navigation Order – Rules of the Air » Rule 46

PPL2 Air Law » Rules of the Air » Light Signals

EALP3Q32   Answer B

Actual separation of IFR and VFR flights only takes place in Class B airspace. The UK AIP contains more detailed information, but is closely based on ICAO procedures.

Further Reference: UK AIM » Aeronautical Information Publication » ENR 1.4

PPL2 Air Law » Division of Airspace and Air Traffic Services » Airspace Summary

EALP3Q33   Answer C

ICAO Doc 4444 (Rules of the Air and Air Traffic Services) defines Transition Layer as "…the airspace between the transition altitude and the transition level". See also EALP1Q26

Further Reference: UK AIM » Aeronautical Information Publication » ENR1.7 (in particular paragraphs 3.4)

PPL2 Air Law » Rules of the Air and Air Traffic Services » Transition Level & Altimeter Setting Procedures

EALP3Q34   Answer B

ICAO Doc 4444 (Rules of the Air and Air Traffic Services) defines an alternate aerodrome as an aerodrome to which an aircraft may proceed when it becomes either impossible or inadvisable to proceed to or land at the aerodrome of intended landing. Alternate aerodromes can be further classified as take-off, en-route or destination alternate.

Further Reference: PPL2 Operational Procedures » Operation of Aircraft » Operation of Aircraft

EALP3Q35   Answer B

An individual aircraft's Pilot's Operating Handbook/Flight Manual (POH/FM) is the definitive document regarding the safe operation of an aircraft, its limits, operating techniques etc. Information from the POH/FM is often displayed on the aircraft, its controls and its instruments in the form of markings and placards.

Further Reference: PPL2 Air Law » Airworthiness of Aircraft » Aircraft Limits and Information

EALP3Q36   Answer C

A private pilot's licence issued in accordance with JAR-FCL has a maximum period of validity of 5 years. Therefore, a licence issued in June 2006 will be valid for five years, ie to June 2011

Further Reference: UK AIM » Air Navigation Order » Schedule 8 (section 2 – JAR-FCL licences)

PPL2 Air Law » JAA Regulations » JAA Regulations – General

EALP3Q37   Answer A

Schedule 8 of the Air Navigation Order sets-out the privileges of both UK and JAR licences, and in relation to the JAR PPL it states that the basic privileges of a PPL (A) are "… to act, but not for remuneration, as pilot in command or co-pilot of any aeroplane specified in a class or type rating included in Part XII of the licence engaged in non-revenue flights."

Further Reference: UK AIM » Air Navigation Order » Schedule 8 (Section 2 – JAR-FCL Licences)

PPL2 Air Law » JAA Regulations » Private Pilot Licence (Aeroplane) – PPL(A)

EALP3Q38   Answer C

ICAO defines 'night' as the hours between the end of evening civil twilight and the beginning of morning civil twilight, or such other period between sunset and sunrise as may be prescribed by the appropriate authority.

Civil twilight ends in the evening when the centre of the sun's disc is six degrees below the horizon and begins in the morning when the centre of the sun's disc is six degrees below the horizon.

You should note that within the UK, the definition of night is different to this ICAO recommendation.

Further Reference: PPL2 Air Law » JAA Regulations » Private Pilot Licence (Aeroplane) – PPL(A)

EALP3Q39   Answer C

Schedule 8 of the Air Navigation Order states that the holder of a PPL (A) "…shall not fly as pilot in command of such an aeroplane carrying passengers unless within the preceding 90 days he has made three take-offs and three landings as the sole manipulator of the controls of an aeroplane of the same type or class and if such a flight is to be carried out at night and his licence does not include an instrument rating (aeroplane) at least one of those take-offs and landings shall have been at night. Note that answer A is not correct because the take-offs and landings must have been made in an aircraft "…of the same type or class…".

Further Reference: UK AIM » Air Navigation Order » Schedule 8
PPL2 Air Law » JAA Regulations » Private Pilot Licence (Aeroplane) – PPL(A)

EALP3Q40   Answer A

The table of search and rescue signals for use by survivors is reproduced at EALP2Q25.

Further Reference: UK AIM » Aeronautical Information Publication » GEN 3.6.6
PPL2 Operational Procedures » Search and Rescue » Search and Rescue Signals

Meteorology

geostrophic wind   parallel isobars

gradient wind   curved istobar

fog

Advection fog

Frontal fog

Radiation fog

FRONTS & FRONTAL WEATHER

Meteorology Essential Revision

▶ Properties of the Atmosphere

Most 'weather' occurs in the **troposphere**, the layer of the atmosphere in contact with the earth.

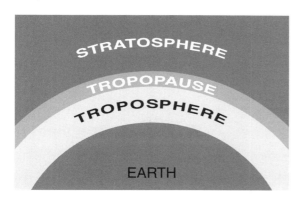

▶ The Motion of the Atmosphere

Air flows from high pressure to low pressure as a consequence of **pressure gradient force**. Moving air is deflected to the right (in the northern hemisphere) by **Coriolis Force**.

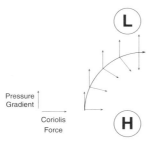

If the pressure gradient and Coriolis forces balance, the resulting air flow tends to be parallel to isobars.

A **sea breeze** is caused by unequal heating of land and sea, leading to higher pressure over a cool sea than over warm land. This causes low-level air flow from sea to land, which initially flows at right-angles (90°) to the coastline.

Buys Ballot's Law states that in the northern hemisphere, if you stand with your back to the wind, the low-pressure area is on your left.

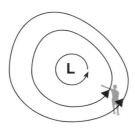

Buys Ballot's Law

▶ Pressure and Altimetry

Altitude	QNH is set on the altimeter sub-scale, altitude above mean sea level is indicated.
Height	QFE is set on the altimeter sub-scale, height above a set datum is indicated.
Flight Level	1013mb/hPa is set on the altimeter sub-scale, Flight Level above this pressure level is indicated.

If an aircraft flies from high-pressure to low-pressure without updating the altimeter setting, the altimeter will over-read (indicating that the aircraft is higher than it actually is): "**high to low, down you go**".

▶ Humidity and Stability

Warm air can hold more water vapour than cold air. As air temperature decreases, relative humidity increases. When the air reaches its dewpoint temperature, the air is saturated, any further reduction in temperature causes the water vapour to condense into water droplets – cloud.

When water changes state, an exchange of heat energy takes place:

Solid – (*Melting*) – **Liquid** – (*Evaporation*) – **Gas** (heat energy is absorbed)

Gas – (*Condensation*) – **Liquid** – (*Freezing*) – **Solid** (heat energy is released)

Stable air resists vertical motion, **unstable air** does not resist vertical motion.

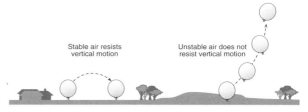

▶The International Standard Atmosphere

Temperature	+15°C.
Pressure	1013·25 mb/hPa (29·92inHg or 760mmHg).
Temperature Lapse Rate	1·98°C/1000ft. The temperature decreases at this rate until 36,090ft, above which it remains at a constant -56·5°C.

▶Clouds and Precipitation

To find the height at which **convective cloud** will form, find the difference (in °C) between the surface temperature and the dew point, and multiply by 400. Unstable air encourages vertical clouds to develop, which may give short-lived, intense precipitation. Stable air tends to contain layered clouds, which may give long-lasting, gentle precipitation.

▶Visibility

Advection fog is a widespread sheet of fog produced when warm moist air flows over a cooler surface. Advection fog forming over the sea can persist even in strong winds and does not vary between day and night. **Radiation fog** forms only over land and is caused by surface cooling at night. The three principal factors for the formation of radiation fog are:
– Little or no cloud at night and cooling by radiation.
– High relative humidity.
– Light winds, ideally 2-8 knots.

Frontal fog can form in the prolonged precipitation ahead of a slow-moving warm or occluded front.

▶Air Masses

Air Mass	Characteristics
Tropical maritime	Warm and humid. In winter tends to bring low stratus cloud, poor visibility and advection fog.
Tropical continental	Hot and dry, visibility is often poor in haze and dust.
Polar continental	Cold and dry, usually brings clear skies and good visibility.
Polar maritime	Moist and unstable, often containing big showers but good visibility otherwise.

▶Low Pressure Systems

A **warm front** brings warm air to replace cold air. A **cold front** brings cold air to replace warmer air.

A warm front has a frontal slope of around 1:150, cloud is layer type and precipitation tends to reach the ground 100-200nm ahead of the surface front.

A cold front has a frontal slope of around 1:50, cloud is vertical type and heavy precipitation is common.

At the passage of a 'typical' warm and cold front, the following changes take place:

	Warm Front	Cold Front
Cloud	May persist	May clear quickly
Visibility	May remain poor	Improves
Precipitation	Lessens, but may persist	Ceases or becomes sporadic
Temperature	Rises	Falls
Pressure	Stops falling	Rises
Wind	Veers	Veers (in the Northern hemisphere) and wind speed increases, possibly becoming more gusty

The warm front moves at two-thirds the speed of the cold front. When the cold front overtakes the warm they combine as an **occluded fronts**. An occlusion has all the cloud and precipitation of the two fronts, often there is little change of wind velocity across the occlusion.

▶High Pressure Systems

An **anticyclone** generally has light winds and little cloud. A summer anticyclone in Europe often brings 'heatwave' weather. In spring and autumn, the slack winds and clear skies within an anticyclone can encourage the formation of radiation fog. In winter a persistent anticyclone can develop widespread low cloud and poor visibility – 'anticyclonic gloom'.

▶Icing

The classic environment for **rain ice** is the area just ahead of a warm front in winter.

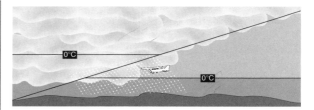

The dominant factor in **carburettor icing** is the moisture content of the air: the more humid the air, the higher the risk of carburettor icing. Carburettor icing is a particular danger at low power settings. **Hoar frost** can occur on the ground or if an aircraft descends from above the freezing level into warmer air. **Rime ice** and **clear ice** generally only occur if an aircraft is flown in cloud above the freezing level.

▶ Thunderstorms

The three factors for **thunderstorm development** are:
- An **unstable atmosphere**, with the instability reaching to the upper layers.
- A supply of **moist air**.
- Some form of **lifting action** to trigger-off the thunderstorm.

The three stages of a thunderstorm's life cycle are:
- The **cumulus stage**, a period of rapid vertical growth, leading to 'towering cumulus'.
- The **mature stage** is marked by precipitation beginning to fall from the cloud. This is the most active phase of the storm.
- The **dissipating stage** when the top of the cloud spreads out in the characteristic anvil shape.

▶ Flight Over Mountainous Areas and Other Weather Hazards

Strong airflow across a mountain range can create **mountain waves**. Where the waves turn down on the downwind or 'lee' side of the mountains the mass of descending air can force aircraft to descend, even at full power and best climb airspeed. Saucer-shaped **lenticular** clouds can form at the crests of the mountain waves.

▶ Aviation Weather Reports and Forecasts

A **TAF** is a fixed-period forecast of expected weather for a specific airfield. A **METAR** is an actual observation of the weather at an airfield. **VOLMET** is a recorded broadcast giving the METARs for around ten airfields in an area.

▶ Meteorology Symbols

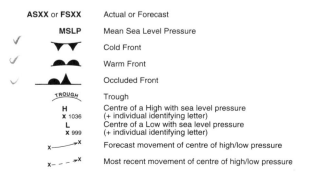

ASXX or **FSXX**	Actual or Forecast
MSLP	Mean Sea Level Pressure
	Cold Front
	Warm Front
	Occluded Front
TROUGH	Trough
H x 1036	Centre of a High with sea level pressure (+ individual identifying letter)
L x 999	Centre of a Low with sea level pressure (+ individual identifying letter)
x——→x	Forecast movement of centre of high/low pressure
x– – –→x	Most recent movement of centre of high/low pressure

Pressure Systems, Fronts and Convergence Zones

▲▲	Cold front at surface
●●	Warm front at surface
▲●▲●	Occluded front at surface
▲●▲●	Quasi-stationary front at surface
—▼—▼—	Convergence line
	Intertropical convergence zone
L x 999	Centre of low pressure area (with indication of pressure at centre)
H ○ 1020	Centre of high pressure area (with indication of pressure at centre)
10	Speed of movement
—→	Direction of movement
SLW	Slow
STNR	Stationary

Zone Boundaries

∿∿∿	Boundary of area of significant weather
—————|	Boundary of area of Clear Air Turbulence (CAT)

Significant Weather Symbols

/// /// /// ///	Rain *
,	Drizzle *
★	Snow *
▽	Shower *
▲	Hail *
ꙍ	Light Icing *
=	Widespread Mist *
≡	Widespread Fog *
≝	Freezing Fog *
∿	Widespread Smoke *
∼	Freezing Rain
ꙍ	Moderate Icing
ꙍ	Severe Icing
⦿ꙍ	Freezing Precipitation
∧	Moderate Turbulence
⩓	Severe Turbulence
⑀	Severe Sand or Dust Haze
⑀⑀	Widespread Sandstorm or Duststorm
∞	Widespread Haze
CAT	Clear Air Turbulence
⌁	Severe Line Squall
⟨	Thunderstorm
⬯	Marked Mountain Waves
⚲	Tropical Cyclone

* these symbols are not used at high altitude

Temperature and Tropopause

Tropopause 'High' centre and altitude (FL 400)

Tropopause 'Low' centre and altitude (FL 340)

Freezing level (in thousands of feet as a Flight Level)

Temperature and Flight Level of the tropopause

Wind & Temperature at Altitude Charts

L   Centre of a low-pressure system

H   Centre of a high-pressure system

Temperature

0°C   In degrees Celsius

Wind

Arrow shaft marks wind direction

Each long feather equals 10 knots

Each half feather equals 5 knots

Each solid triangle equals 50 knots

0   Calm

Flight level of jetstream

ADJ   Adjacent

BEC   Becoming

BLW   Below

CLD   Cloud

EMBD   Embedded

FRQ   Frequent

GEN   Generally

MOD   Moderate

MTW   Mountain Wave

NIL   None

SEV   Severe

SFC   Surface

TURB   Turbulence

VSP   Vertical speed

WDSPR   Widespread

WKN   Weakening

METAR & TAF CODES:

METAR   Aviation Routine Weather Report

TAF   Terminal Aerodrome Forecast

AUTO   Automated METAR

SURFACE WIND

00000	Wind Calm
G	Wind Gust
KMH	Kilometres per hour
KT	Knots
MPS	Metres Per Second
V	Variation in wind direction
VRB	Variable Wind Direction

VISIBILITY

9999	Visibility 10km or more
0000	Visibility less than 50m
R	RVR Runway Visual Range
NDV	No Directional Variation
N	North
NE	North East
E	East
SE	South East
S	South
SW	South West
W	West
NW	North West

WEATHER

Description:

BC	Patches
BL	Blowing
DR	Drifting
FZ	Freezing
MI	Shallow
SH	Shower(s)
TS	Thunderstorm
VCTS	Thunderstorm in the vicinity

Precipitation:

DZ	Drizzle
GR	Hail
GS	Small Hail
IC	Ice Crystals (diamond dust)
PL	Ice Pellets
RA	Rain
SG	Snow Grains
SN	Snow
UP	Unidentified Precipitation
-	Light
+	Heavy

Visibility Factor:

BR	Mist
DU	Dust
FG	Fog
FU	Smoke
HZ	Haze
PRFG	Partial Fog (fog banks)
SA	Sand
VA	Volcanic Ash

Other:

DS	Dust Storm
FC	Funnel Cloud(s) – tornado or water-spout
NSW	No Significant Weather
PO	Dust Devils
SQ	Squall(s)
SS	Sandstorm
VC	in the Vicinity

CLOUD

BKN	Broken, 5-7 oktas
FEW	Few, 1-2 oktas
OVC	Overcast, 8 oktas
SCT	Scattered, 3-4 oktas
CB	Cumulonimbus
TCU	Towering Cumulus
NCD	No Cloud Detected
NSC	No Significant Cloud
SKC	Sky Clear
VV	Sky obscured
VV///	Sky obscured, vertical visibility cannot be assessed.
CAVOK	Ceiling And Visibility OK

(i) Visibility: 10km or more.

(ii) Cloud: no cloud below 5000ft or below highest Minimum Sector Altitude, whichever is greater, and no CB at any height.

(iii) No significant weather phenomena at, or in the vicinity of, the aerodrome.

AIR TEMPERATURE/DEW POINT

M	Minus

PRESSURE

Q	QNH

SUPPLEMENTARY INFORMATION

/////	information not available
BECMG	Becoming
DENEB	Fog dispersal operations in progress
NOSIG	No Significant changes forecast
PROB 30	30% Probability
PROB 40	40% Probability
RE	Recent weather
TEMPO	Temporary
TREND	Trend indicator
WS	Windshear

JAA Private Pilot Licence – Aeroplanes & Helicopters

Meteorology

Time allowed:	60 minutes
No. of questions:	20
Total Marks:	100

Instructions:

The paper consists of 20 multiple choice questions, each carries 5 marks. The pass mark is 75% (i.e. 15 questions or more must be answered correctly). Marks are not deducted for incorrect answers.

Be sure to carefully read each question and ensure that you understand it before considering the answer choices. Only one of the answers is complete and correct; the others are either incomplete, incorrect or based on a misconception.

You should indicate the correct answer by placing a cross in the appropriate box of the answer sheet. If you decide to change an answer, you should erase the original choice and put a cross in the box representing your new selection.

Each question has an average answer time of 3 minutes. No credit is given for unanswered questions.

1. When a strong wind is blowing across a mountain ridge, where is the strongest turbulence in 'rotor' conditions most likely to be found?

   (a) Approximately 10,000ft directly above the ridge

   (b) Upwind of the ridge

   (c) On the valley floor

   (d) Downwind of the ridge

2. A parcel of air has a relative humidity of 85%. If this parcel of air is cooled, the relative humidity can be expected to:

   (a) Decrease

   (b) Increase

   (c) Move further away from saturation

   (d) Remain unchanged

3. If the wind at 2000ft altitude is 240/35, the most likely surface wind at an inland airfield is:

   (a) 270/20

   (b) 250/40

   (c) 220/40

   (d) 220/20

4. Lenticular clouds (that is, clouds of the 'Lenticularis' species) are most likely to form:

   (a) In a layer of fog over the sea

   (b) In calm conditions

   (c) In orographic lift or mountain waves

   (d) Over lakes and open water on a calm winter night

5. Which of the following is the correct definition of 'Flight Visibility'?

   (a) The visibility forward from the flight deck of an aircraft in flight

   (b) The lowest visibility that can be viewed from the flight deck of an aircraft

   (c) The visibility forward from the flight deck of an aircraft at any time it is moving under its own power

   (d) The visibility forecast or observed by a qualified met observer at the appropriate flight level

6. What is the meaning of the following significant weather symbol?

   ≩

   (a) Freezing Fog

   (b) Hail

   (c) Thunderstorms

   (d) Marked Mountain waves

7. If weather conditions are reported as 'CAVOK', which of the following could **not** be present?

   (a) 10km visibility, gales

   (b) 10nm visibility, freezing level below 1000ft

   (c) 10km visibility, overcast cloud at 5100ft

   (d) 20km visibility, FEW CB at 9000ft

8. The great majority of 'weather' is found in the lowest level of the atmosphere, which is known as:

   (a) The ozonesphere

   (b) The tropopause

   (c) The troposphere

   (d) The stratosphere

9. Flight close to or within a thunderstorm should be avoided at all times. Nevertheless, where within a cumulonimbus cloud would you expect to find the most severe airframe icing?

   (a) Where the temperature range is between 0°c and -30°c

   (b) Only above 10,000ft

   (c) At the base of the cloud

   (d) Only below 10,000ft

10. Within a depression two air masses meet so that a warm front is formed. In relation to a 'typical' warm front:

    (a) Warm air will be replaced by cold air, the frontal slope will be around 1:150

    (b) Cold air will be replaced by warm air, the frontal slope will be around 1:150

    (c) Warm air will be replaced by cold air, the frontal slope will be around 1:50

    (d) Cold air will be replaced by warm air, the frontal slope will be around 1:50

11. You are flying in rain ahead of a warm front in winter. The outside air temperature is -2°C. Which of the following meteorological phenomena is most likely to affect the aircraft?

    (a) Tornadoes

    (b) Hail

    (c) Rain ice

    (d) Radiation fog

12. An unstable air mass is forced to rise over a mountain range, which of the following is most likely?

    (a) Extensive stratus cloud

    (b) Radiation Fog

    (c) Scattered cirrus cloud

    (d) Cumuloform cloud

13. The cloud sequence that could be expected during the passage of a 'typical' warm front would be:

(a) CI, AS, CB, CU

(b) AS, NS, CI, CS, CB,

(c) CI, CS, AS, NS, ST

(d) CB, AS

14. In the UK, an unstable air mass bringing extensive convective cloud, heavy showers and possibly thunderstorms is most likely to be a:

(a) Polar Maritime air mass

(b) Polar Continental air mass

(c) Tropical Continental air mass

(d) Tropical Maritime air mass

Turn to the METFORM 214 at appendix A

15. Which of the following most closely represents the forecast wind velocity (i) and temperature (ii) at 2000ft at position 50N 00E/W:

	(i)	(ii)
(a)	280/15	+11°C
(b)	270/18	+13°C
(c)	260/20	+14°C
(d)	270/20	+11°C

Turn to the METFORM 215 at appendix B to answer the following questions:

16. The freezing level (where 0°C occurs) over the South coast is:

(a) 8000ft amsl

(b) 800ft amsl

(c) 800ft agl

(d) 5000ft amsl

17. In Area A 'SURFACE VIS ANDWX' what does the following mean: "**ISOL 4000M +SHRA/+TSGR MON N 56N**"

(a) Occasional areas of 40.00mm of precipitation heavy showers of rain or thunderstorms with hail, over mountains north of latitude 56°N

(b) Isolated areas of 4000 metres visibility, additionally showers of rain, snow or hail anywhere above FL56 over mountains

(c) Isolated areas of 4000 metres visibility in heavy showers of rain or heavy thunderstorms with hail, above or covering mountains north of latitude 56°N in area A

(d) Isolated areas may experience 40.00mm of precipitation in heavy showers of rain or thunderstorms with hail, over mountains north of latitude 56°N

18. What is the feature identified as (i) in the lower third of the forecast chart?

(a) A warm front

(b) A cold front

(c) A jet stream

(d) A cold occlusion

19. In Area A 'CLOUD' what does the following mean: "**BKN CB 008 – XXX** ⩊ ⩕ "?

(a) Broken (5-7 oktas) Cumulonimbus cloud, base 800ft above ground level, upper limit unknown, moderate icing, moderate turbulence

(b) Broken (5-6 oktas) Cumulus cloud, base 8000ft above ground level, upper limit unknown, moderate icing, severe turbulence

(c) Broken (5-7 oktas) Cumulonimbus cloud, base 800ft above mean sea level, extending to above chart upper limit, severe icing, severe turbulence

(d) Broken (5-7 oktas) Cumulonimbus cloud, base 800ft above mean ground level, extending to information missing, severe icing, severe turbulence

---

20. Disregard airspace along the stated route for the purposes of answering this question.

A flight is planned from Coventry (A) to Newcastle (B) with alternate Durham Tees Valley (C), routing outside controlled airspace where possible and avoiding high ground.

The aircraft cannot fly in known icing conditions.

The pilot holds a PPL without instrument qualification, so the flight must be conducted under VFR.

The minimum en-route altitude will be 1000ft agl, VMC minima require that the aircraft remains clear of cloud, in sight of the surface and in a minimum flight visibility of 5km.

The estimated time of departure is 1400Z, the time en-route is two hours.

The METAR for the departure airfield 'A' at 1350Z is:

27016KT 9999 SCT020 15/8 Q1001

The TAF for the destination airfield 'B' is:

031322 29015KT 9999 BKN022 TEMPO1622 9000 SHRA BKN012

Considering this information, and METFORM 215 (appendix B), choose the most reasonable course of action:

(a) Cancel the flight, the forecasts indicate that the weather will be below limits with en-route visibility down to 800m in fog and cloud base down to 200ft.

(b) Delay the departure by two hours. Although the departure conditions are suitable, the destination aerodrome forecast indicates that conditions will get better after 1600, although before that the cloud base will be down to 220ft.

(c) The conditions at the departure airfield and en-route forecast are generally suitable, although there may be occasional showers en-route. The destination airfield forecast indicates that showers may occur starting at around the ETA, proceed with caution.

(d) The departure conditions indicate scattered cloud down to 200ft. Delay the departure until this cloud has cleared. Conditions at the destination are also forecast to improve after 1600 so delaying departure will allow arrival into better conditions.

Appendix A: UK Low-Level Spot Wind Chart (Form 214)

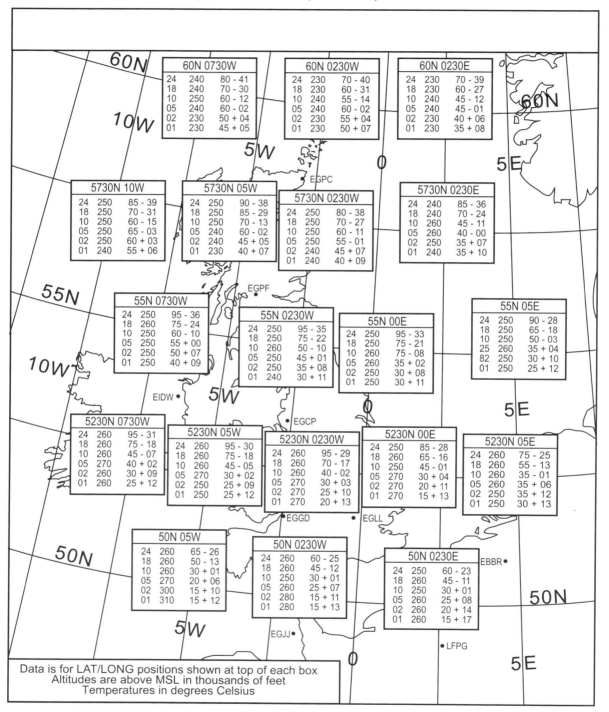

60N 0730W		
24	240	80 - 41
18	240	70 - 30
10	250	60 - 12
05	240	60 - 02
02	230	50 + 04
01	230	45 + 05

60N 0230W		
24	230	70 - 40
18	230	60 - 31
10	240	55 - 14
05	240	60 - 02
02	230	55 + 04
01	230	50 + 07

60N 0230E		
24	230	70 - 39
18	230	60 - 27
10	240	45 - 12
05	240	45 - 01
02	230	40 + 06
01	230	35 + 08

5730N 10W		
24	250	85 - 39
18	250	70 - 31
10	250	60 - 15
05	250	65 - 03
02	250	60 + 03
01	240	55 + 06

5730N 05W		
24	250	90 - 38
18	250	85 - 29
10	250	70 - 13
05	240	60 - 02
02	240	45 + 05
01	230	40 + 07

5730N 0230W		
24	250	80 - 38
18	250	70 - 27
10	250	60 - 11
05	250	55 - 01
02	240	45 + 07
01	240	40 + 09

5730N 0230E		
24	240	85 - 36
18	240	70 - 24
10	260	45 - 11
05	260	40 - 00
02	260	35 + 07
01	240	35 + 10

55N 0730W		
24	250	95 - 36
18	260	75 - 24
10	250	60 - 10
05	250	55 + 00
02	250	50 + 07
01	250	40 + 09

55N 0230W		
24	250	95 - 35
18	250	75 - 22
10	260	50 - 10
05	250	45 + 01
02	250	35 + 08
01	240	30 + 11

55N 00E		
24	250	95 - 33
18	250	75 - 21
10	260	75 - 08
05	260	35 + 02
02	250	30 + 08
01	250	30 + 11

55N 05E		
24	250	90 - 28
18	250	65 - 18
10	250	50 - 03
25	260	35 + 04
82	250	30 + 10
01	250	25 + 12

5230N 0730W		
24	260	95 - 31
18	260	75 - 18
10	260	45 - 07
05	270	40 + 02
02	260	30 + 09
01	260	25 + 12

5230N 05W		
24	260	95 - 30
18	260	75 - 18
10	260	45 - 05
05	270	30 + 02
02	250	25 + 09
01	250	25 + 12

5230N 0230W		
24	260	95 - 29
18	260	70 - 17
10	260	40 - 02
05	270	30 + 03
02	270	25 + 10
01	270	20 + 13

5230N 00E		
24	250	85 - 28
18	260	65 - 16
10	250	45 - 01
05	270	30 + 04
02	270	20 + 11
01	270	15 + 13

5230N 05E		
24	260	75 - 25
18	260	55 - 13
10	260	35 - 01
05	260	35 + 06
02	250	35 + 12
01	250	30 + 13

50N 05W		
24	260	65 - 26
18	260	50 - 13
10	260	30 + 01
05	270	20 + 06
02	300	15 + 10
01	310	15 + 12

50N 0230W		
24	260	60 - 25
18	260	45 - 12
10	250	30 + 01
05	260	25 + 07
02	280	15 + 11
01	280	15 + 13

50N 0230E		
24	250	60 - 23
18	260	45 - 11
10	250	30 + 01
05	260	25 + 08
02	260	20 + 14
01	260	15 + 17

Data is for LAT/LONG positions shown at top of each box
Altitudes are above MSL in thousands of feet
Temperatures in degrees Celsius

Appendix B: UK Forecast Weather

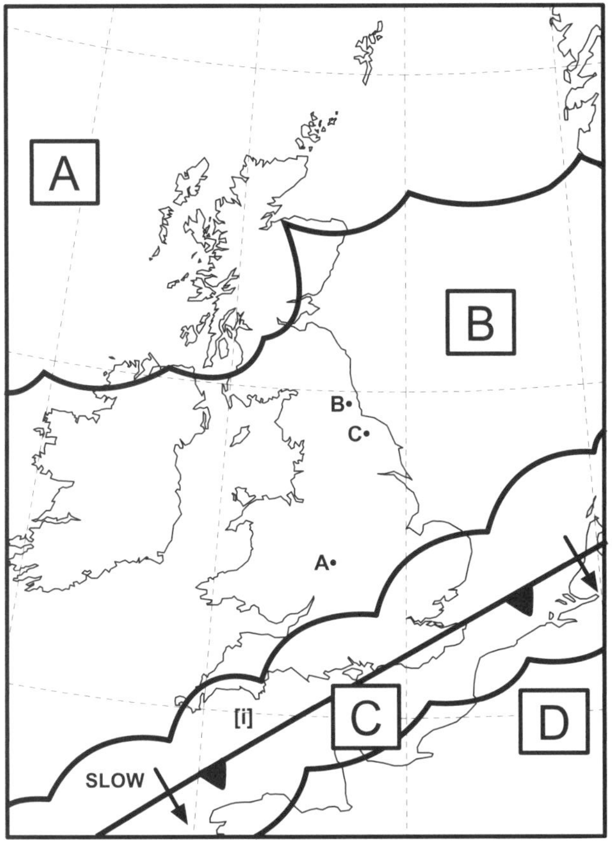

Forecast Weather

Valid 030800 to 031700 Z

Fronts/zones valid at 1200 Z

AREA	SURFACE VIS AND WX	CLOUD	0 C
A	30KM NIL FRQ 8KM SHRA ISOL 4000M +SHRA/ +TSGR MON N 56N	BKN CU SC 020 - 080 BKN CU 012 – XXX ⅏ ⋏ BKN CB 008 - XXX ⅏ ⋏	040
B	30KM NIL OCNL 10KM RA SH	SCT/BKN CU 025-060 BKN ST SC 015 – 100	050 - 080
C	10KM NIL/RA OCNL 3500M RA/DZ OCNL 800M FG/DZ	BKN ST 012-015 OVC NS 006-100 SCT/BKN SC 002 – 050	080
D	20KM NIL/RA	NIL/FEW SC 035-060	100

Outlook Until:

Similar

All heights in 100's of feet above mean sea level
XXX means above chart upper limit
Cloud amount (Oktas)
FEW : 1-2 SCT: 3-4
BKN: 5-7 OVC: 8

MOD / SEV ICE ⅏/⅏
MOD / SEV TURB ⌄/⋏
TS / CB implies GR /⅏/⋏

Speed of movement in KT
Temperatures in DEG C
Hill FG implies VIS <200 M

F215

This forecast may be amended at any time.

1. The following symbol means: _⋀_
   ^
   (a) Moderate turbulence
   (b) Moderate icing
   (c) Severe line squall
   (d) Freezing rain

2. When flying at night in cloudless (clear) conditions and with a full moon, in which direction is the greatest flight visibility most likely to be found?
   (a) Directly away from the moon
   (b) Flight visibility is the same regardless of direction
   (c) At an angle of about 10° to the moon
   (d) Directly towards the moon

3. Heating of the atmosphere is mostly achieved via:
   (a) Evaporation of water in the atmosphere
   (b) Carbon Dioxide emissions
   (c) Heating of the earth's surface by the sun's radiation
   (d) Direct heating by the sun's radiation

4. The wind along straight parallel isobars can be referred to as the ....(i).... wind and the wind around curved parallel isobars can be referred to as the ....(ii).... wind:

	(i)	(ii)
(a)	Geostrophic	Gradient
(b)	Pressure	Isobaric
(c)	Cyclonic	Irrigonic
(d)	Coriolis	Friction

5. The layer of the atmosphere closest to the earth's surface and containing most 'weather' is commonly known as the:
   (a) Tropopause
   (b) Troposphere
   (c) Stratosphere
   (d) Mesosphere

6. You are flying at a constant indicated altitude of 2000ft with a QNH set of 1015mb. After a long flight with constant starboard drift and without up-dating the pressure setting, a new QNH of 998mb is passed. Before the updated QNH is applied (i.e. while 1015 is still set on the altimeter), will the aircraft be:
   (a) Lower than indicated, the altimeter is over-reading
   (b) Higher than indicated, the altimeter is under-reading
   (c) At the altitude shown by the altimeter
   (d) It depends on the temperature

7. Lenticular clouds are most likely to form in which particular conditions?

   (a) Unstable air with strong convective currents

   (b) Zero wind, air cooled at the surface

   (c) Light winds over oceans

   (d) Stable air rising over a mountain range

8. Which of the following best defines 'water vapour'?

   (a) Water droplets held in suspension in the atmosphere and appearing in the form of cloud

   (b) A liquid component of the atmosphere

   (c) A gas present only in the stratosphere

   (d) A gas which makes up a large proportion of the lower atmosphere

9. Polar maritime air reaching the UK is generally:

   (a) Cold, moist, stable

   (b) Cold, dry, unstable

   (c) Warm, moist, stable

   (d) Cold, moist, unstable

10. Which of the following situations is most likely to cause an aircraft to encounter 'Rain Ice'?

    (a) Descending in a cloudless sky from above the freezing level to below to freezing level

    (b) Flight above the freezing level ahead of a warm front in winter

    (c) Flight below the freezing level ahead of a warm front in winter

    (d) Flight in high humidity condition with an air temperature of +10°C

11. Select which of the following meteorological situations is most likely to lead to carburettor icing if all other factors are equal:

    (a) Flight above cloud, air temperature -20°C

    (b) Flight close below cloud in rain, air temperature +5°C

    (c) Flight in clear sky, air temperature +30°C

    (d) Flight in clear sky, air temperature -30°C

12. A METAR reads:

EGSX 160950Z 16005KT 0650E DZ MIFG VV/// 06/05 Q1012 NOSIG=

Select the correct decode for this METAR:

(a) Observation timed at 0950 UTC on the 16th; surface wind 160°T 5 knots; minimum visibility 650 metres looking East; moderate Drizzle; Shallow Fog; vertical visibility cannot be assessed; air temperature +6°C, dew point +5°C; QNH1012mb/hPa; No Significant Changes expected in the next two hours

(b) Observation timed at 0950 UTC on the 16th; surface wind 160°M 5 knots; minimum visibility 650 metres looking East; light Drizzle; Drifting Fog; vertical visibility cannot be assessed; air temperature +6°C, dew point +5°C; QNH1012mb/hPa; No Significant Changes expected this day

(c) Observation timed at 0950 local on the 16th; surface wind 160°T 5 knots; maximum visibility 650 metres looking East; moderate Drizzle; Shallow Fog; vertical visibility varying; air temperature +6°C, dew point +5°C; QNH1012mb/hPa; No Ground Signals

(d) Observation timed at 0950 UTC on the 16th; surface wind 160°M 5 knots; minimum visibility 650 metres looking East; light Drizzle; Shallow Fog; vertical visibility cannot be assessed; air temperature +6°C, dew point +5°C; QNH1012mb/hPa; No Signal on ILS

---

13. At what stage of its development does precipitation start to fall from a thunderstorm and vertical currents are at their most intense?

(a) The cumulus stage

(b) The mature stage

(c) The dissipating stage

(d) The cell stage

---

14. A VOLMET broadcast is:

(a) A recorded broadcast of the METAR for a specific airfield

(b) A special ATC broadcast, to all aircraft on frequency, of a significant change in weather conditions

(c) A voluntary met. report

(d) A recorded broadcast of about 10 METARs for airfields mostly in a specific region

---

15. The air behind a cold front in a 'typical' depression is part of the depression's 'cold sector'. The most likely flying conditions in this area will be:

(a) Poor visibility and continuous precipitation beneath overcast high stratus cloud

(b) Moderate visibility beneath overcast layers of low cloud

(c) Increasing temperature, wind backing

(d) Good visibility and scattered cumulus-type cloud

Turn to the METFORM 214 at appendix A

---

16. Which of the following most closely represents the forecast wind velocity (i) and temperature (ii) at 5000ft at position 5230N 0230E:

	(i)	(ii)
(a)	170/20	+04°C
(b)	170/20	+7°C
(c)	185/27	+03°C
(d)	190/30	+03°C

Turn to the METFORM 215 at appendix B to answer the following questions:

17. The freezing level (where 0°C occurs) at about 54N 0E/W (approximately the centre of the chart) is:

    (a) 6000m amsl

    (b) 600ft amsl

    (c) 6000ft agl

    (d) 6000ft amsl

18. The feature identified as (i) on the left-hand side of the forecast for 1500Z is:

    (a) A warm front moving at around 7 knots

    (b) An occluding front at around 7 knots

    (c) An occluding front moving at around 12 knots

    (d) A quasi stationary front

19. In Area B 'SURFACE VIS AND WX' what does the following mean: "**ISOL 2000M RA/DZ COT FM 10 Z**"?

    (a) Isolated above 2000 meters, visibility reduced in rain and/or drizzle, clear orographic turbulence, from 10:00 LOCAL

    (b) Isolated 2000 meters visibility in rain and/or drizzle, on coasts, from 10:00 UTC

    (c) Isolated 2000 meters visibility in rain and/or drizzle, on coasts, from 10:00 LOCAL

    (d) Isolated 2000 meters visibility in rain and/or drizzle, clear orographic turbulence, from 10:00 UTC

20. Disregard airspace along the stated route for the purposes of answering this question.
    A flight is planned from Biggin Hill (A) to Bembridge Isle of White (B) with alternate Southampton (C), routing outside controlled airspace where possible.
    The aircraft cannot fly in known icing conditions.
    The pilot holds a PPL without instrument qualification, so the flight must be conducted under VFR.
    The minimum en-route altitude will be 1000ft agl, the average ground level en-route is 500ft. VMC minima require that the aircraft remains clear of cloud, in sight of the surface and in a minimum flight visibility of 5km.
    The estimated time of departure is 1600Z, the time en-route is 1 hour 30 minutes.
    The METAR for the departure airfield 'A' at 1550Z is:
    26010KT 9999 SCT025 11/3 Q1003
    The TAF for the destination airfield 'B' is:
    291601 27015KT 9999 SCT025 BECMG 1701 8000 RA BKN009 TEMPO 1901 5000 RA BKN005
    Considering this information, and METFORM 215 (appendix B), choose the most reasonable course of action:

    (a) Conditions at the airfield 'A' are suitable for departure. Departure should be made as soon as possible to avoid the forecast weather deterioration. The aerodrome forecast for airfield 'B' show the cloud temporarily dropping to 900ft amsl between 1700 and 0001, otherwise conditions in Zone 3 (which covers the whole of the flight) are suitable for VFR flight in all respects

    (b) Delaying the departure by two hours will allow the front to clear the area, and the zone 1 conditions behind indicate good visibility and isolated rain showers

    (c) The conditions at the departure airfield are generally suitable. However at ETA (1730) at airfield 'B' the aerodrome forecast is for visibility to be falling to 8000m and the cloud base to 900ft. As Zone 2 conditions move to cover the destination there is increased risk of low cloud, rain and reduced visibility. Further, the Zone 3 forecast mentions isolated areas of reduced visibility and low cloud. Cancel the flight.

    (d) The departure conditions indicate scattered cloud down to 250ft. Delay the departure until this cloud has cleared. According to the destination aerodrome forecast, conditions there will improve after 1700 so delaying departure will allow arrival into better conditions.

Appendix A: UK Low-Level Spot Wind Chart (Form 214)

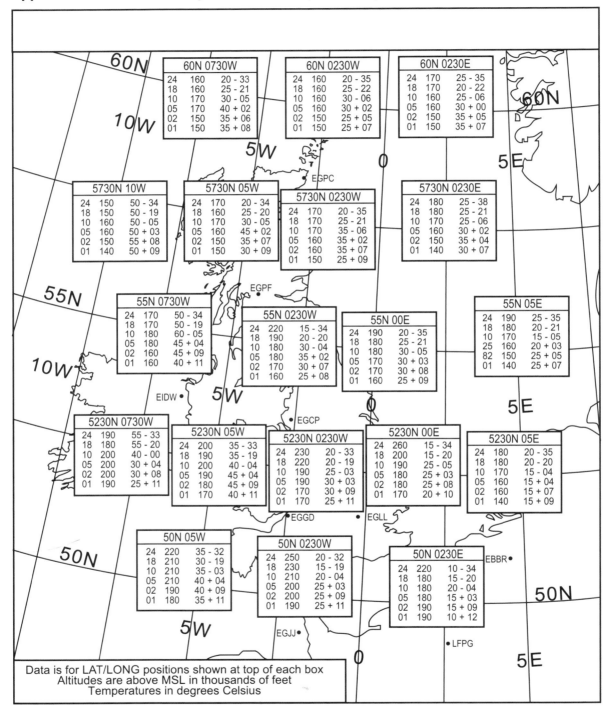

60N 0730W		
24	160	20 - 33
18	160	25 - 21
10	160	30 - 05
05	170	40 + 02
02	150	35 + 06
01	150	35 + 08

60N 0230W		
24	160	20 - 35
18	160	25 - 22
10	160	30 - 06
05	160	30 + 02
02	150	25 + 05
01	150	25 + 07

60N 0230E		
24	170	25 - 35
18	170	20 - 22
10	160	25 - 06
05	160	30 + 00
02	150	35 + 05
01	150	35 + 07

EGPC

5730N 10W		
24	150	50 - 34
18	150	50 - 19
10	160	50 - 05
05	160	50 + 03
02	150	55 + 08
01	140	50 + 09

5730N 05W		
24	170	20 - 34
18	160	25 - 20
10	170	30 - 05
05	160	45 + 02
02	150	35 + 07
01	150	30 + 09

5730N 0230W		
24	170	20 - 35
18	170	25 - 21
10	170	35 - 06
05	160	35 + 02
02	160	35 + 07
01	150	25 + 09

5730N 0230E		
24	180	25 - 38
18	180	25 - 21
10	170	25 - 06
05	160	30 + 02
02	150	35 + 04
01	140	30 + 07

EGPF

55N 0730W		
24	170	50 - 34
18	170	50 - 19
10	180	60 - 05
05	180	45 + 04
02	160	45 + 09
01	160	40 + 11

55N 0230W		
24	220	15 - 34
18	190	20 - 20
10	180	30 - 04
05	180	35 + 02
02	170	30 + 07
01	160	25 + 08

55N 00E		
24	190	20 - 35
18	180	25 - 21
10	180	30 - 05
05	170	30 + 03
02	170	30 + 08
01	160	25 + 09

55N 05E		
24	190	25 - 35
18	180	20 - 21
10	170	15 - 05
25	160	20 + 03
82	150	25 + 05
01	140	25 + 07

EIDW

5230N 0730W		
24	190	55 - 33
18	180	55 - 20
10	200	40 - 00
05	200	30 + 04
02	200	30 + 08
01	190	25 + 11

EGCP

5230N 05W		
24	200	35 - 33
18	190	35 - 19
10	200	40 - 04
05	190	45 + 04
02	180	45 + 09
01	170	40 + 11

5230N 0230W		
24	230	20 - 33
18	220	20 - 19
10	190	25 - 03
05	190	30 + 03
02	170	30 + 09
01	170	25 + 11

5230N 00E		
24	260	15 - 34
18	200	15 - 20
10	190	25 - 05
05	180	25 + 03
02	180	25 + 08
01	170	20 + 10

5230N 05E		
24	180	20 - 35
18	180	20 - 20
10	170	15 - 04
05	160	15 + 04
02	160	15 + 07
01	140	15 + 09

EGGD • EGLL

50N 05W		
24	220	35 - 32
18	210	30 - 19
10	210	35 - 03
05	210	40 + 04
02	190	40 + 09
01	180	35 + 11

50N 0230W		
24	250	20 - 32
18	230	15 - 19
10	210	20 - 04
05	200	25 + 03
02	200	25 + 09
01	190	25 + 11

50N 0230E		
24	220	10 - 34
18	180	15 - 20
10	180	20 - 04
05	180	15 + 03
02	190	15 + 09
01	190	10 + 12

EBBR •

EGJJ •

• LFPG

Data is for LAT/LONG positions shown at top of each box
Altitudes are above MSL in thousands of feet
Temperatures in degrees Celsius

Appendix B: Forecast Weather

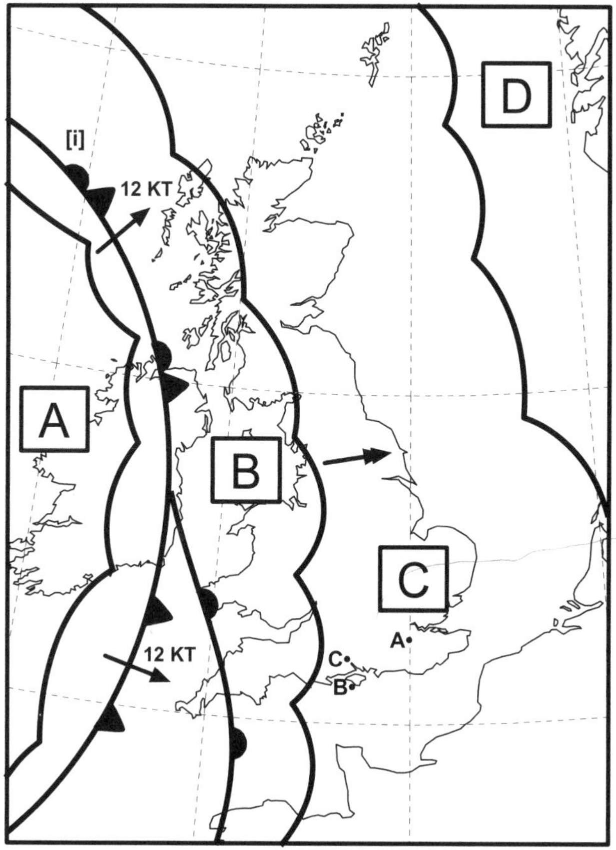

Forecast Weather

Valid 290800 to 291700 Z   Fronts/zones valid at   1200 Z

AREA	SURFACE VIS AND WX	CLOUD	0 C
A	30KM NIL OCNL 8KM SHRA	BKN CU SC 020 - 080 BKN CU SC 015 – XXX	030
B	14KM NIL/RA OCNL 8KM RA ISOL 5000M +RA NEAR FRONT ISOL 2000M RA/DZ COT FM 10 Z	BKN SC 015-060 BKN ST SC 008 – 015 OVC ST005-XXX OVC ST 003-060	070
C	15KM NIL OCNL 6KM NIL ISOL 2500M BR/DZ ISOL 8KM SHRA SW	BKN CU SC 030-060 BKN ST SC 010-070 OVC SC 005 – 070 BKN CU SC 020 – 100	060
D	20KM NIL	FEW SC 025-060	060

Outlook Until:

Similar

All heights in 100's of feet above mean sea level
XXX means above chart upper limit
Cloud amount (Oktas)   MOD / SEV ICE   Speed of movement in KT
FEW : 1-2   SCT: 3-4   MOD / SEV TURB   Temperatures in DEG C
BKN: 5-7   OVC: 8   TS / CB implies GR   Hill FG implies VIS <200 M

This forecast may be amended at any time.

F215

1. Which of the following thunderstorm scenarios is likely to present the greatest hazard to aircraft?

   (a) Dissipating thunderstorms

   (b) Nocturnal thunderstorms

   (c) Well-separated convective thunderstorms in clear air

   (d) Thunderstorms embedded in the extensive stratus cloud of an occluded front

2. A mountain range runs north-south and a strong wind is blowing from the west. Based on this information what meteorological phenomenon is most likely and where will it be at its most dangerous?

   (a) Radiation fog; in the valleys

   (b) Mountain wave activity; to the west of the mountains

   (c) Hoar frost, in the valleys

   (d) Mountain wave activity; to the east of the mountains

3. Which of the following situations is most likely to lead to serious carburettor icing?

   (a) Summer, warm air mass, Descent power

   (b) Summer, warm air mass, Cruise power

   (c) Winter, cold air mass, Descent power

   (d) Winter, cold air mass, Cruise power

4. If standard pre-flight meteorological self-briefing material cannot be obtained, or is inadequate, for a planned flight, a Special Forecast may be requested. This Special Forecast should be requested from ....(i).... and for a flight of 300nm the minimum prior notification before collection is ....(ii)....:

	(i)	(ii)
(a)	A Forecast Office	4 hours
(b)	An ATSU	3 hours
(c)	The CAA	3 hours
(d)	A Forecast Office	2 hours

5. What is the correct decode for the following METAR?
   EGZZ 231320Z 05005KT 020V080 8000 FEW015 BKN017 02/M01 Q1023 NOSIG

   (a) Actual weather report observed at 1320 UTC on the 25th day of the month. Surface wind from 050° (Magnetic) speed five knots. Wind direction variable from 020° to 080° (Magnetic). Horizontal visibility 8000 metres. Cloud 1 – 2 oktas base 1500ft above airfield level, cloud 5 – 7 oktas base 1700ft above airfield level. Air temperature 2°C, dewpoint -1°C. QNH 1023 millibars/hectopascals. No significant changes are forecast during the current TAF period.

   (b) Actual weather report observed at 2312 UTC on the 20th day of the month. Surface wind from 050° (True) speed five knots. Wind direction variable from 020° to 080° (True). Horizontal visibility 8000 metres. Cloud 1 – 2 oktas base 1500ft above airfield level, cloud 5 – 7 oktas base 1700ft above airfield level. Air temperature 2°C, dewpoint -1°C. QNH 1023 millibars/hectopascals. No significant changes are forecast during the next 30 minutes.

   (c) Actual weather report observed at 1320 UTC on the 23rd day of the month. Surface wind from 050° (True) speed five knots. Wind direction variable from 020° to 080° (True). Horizontal visibility 8000 metres. Cloud 1 – 2 oktas base 1500ft above airfield level, cloud 5 – 7 oktas base 1700ft above airfield level. Air temperature 2°C, dewpoint -1°C. QNH 1023 millibars/hectopascals. No significant changes are forecast during the two hours after observation time.

   (d) Actual weather report observed at 1320 UTC on the 23rd day of the month. Surface wind from 050° (True) speed five knots. Wind direction variable from 020° to 080° (True). Horizontal visibility 8000 metres. Cloud 1 – 2 oktas base 1500ft above airfield level, cloud 5 – 7 oktas base 1700ft above airfield level. Air temperature 2°C, dewpoint -1°C. QNH 1023 millibars/hectopascals. No significant changes are forecast during the four hours after observation time.

6. You depart an airfield (A) where the QNH is 1015mb/hPa. After a long flight towards a low pressure area you land at an airfield (B) which has an elevation of 500ft. The QNH at airfield B is 995mb/hPa. Once on the ground at airfield B, if the QNH of airfield A is reset on the altimeter, and assuming that 1mb/hPa = 30 feet, the indicated altitude will be:

   (a) 700ft

   (b) 500ft

   (c) -100ft

   (d) 1100ft

7. Fog that forms just ahead of a warm or occluded front is most likely to be:

   (a) Radiation fog

   (b) Frontal fog

   (c) Steaming Fog

   (d) Isobaric fog

8. Which of the following types of icing can occur when flying outside cloud?
   (i)   carburettor icing
   (ii)   rain ice
   (iii)   hoar frost
   (iv)   rime ice
   (v)   clear ice

   (a) (i), (iii) and (v)

   (b) (i), (ii) and (iv)

   (c) (iii), (iv) and (v)

   (d) (i), (ii) and (iii)

9. A METFORM 215 (Low Level Weather Chart) has a valid time of 0300 UTC. What will the valid time of the next METFORM to be issued and for how long is it valid?

   (a) 0300 UTC the next day, 24 hours

   (b) 0600 UTC, 3 hours

   (c) 0900 UTC, 6 hours

   (d) 1100 UTC, 8 hours

10. The force that causes air to start moving from an area of high pressure to an area of low pressure is called:

    (a) The Geostrophic force

    (b) The Coriolis force

    (c) The Pressure Gradient Force

    (d) The Isothermic force

11. Which of the following is most likely to occur after several days of a prolonged winter anticyclone in the UK?

(a) Isolated showers with good visibility outside precipitation

(b) Clear, unstable air

(c) Creation of an inversion with cloud and poor visibility beneath

(d) Extensive cumulus or cumulonimbus clouds

---

12. A cold and dry air mass with clear skies and good visibility, reaching the UK from the east, but possibly bringing snow showers to the eastern coast in winter, is most likely to be:

(a) A tropical maritime air mass

(b) A tropical continental air mass

(c) A polar continental air mass

(d) A polar maritime air mass

---

13. What does the following SIGWX chart symbol mean?

(a) Severe Turbulence

(b) Moderate icing

(c) Widespread Fog

(d) Hail

---

14. An aircraft is flying on a constant track and a constant indicated altitude and is experiencing consistent starboard drift. If the altimeter setting is not updated, which of the following statements is most likely to be correct:

(a) The aircraft is flying towards an area of high pressure, the aircraft is higher than the level indicated on the altimeter

(b) The aircraft is flying towards an area of low pressure, the aircraft is higher than the level indicated on the altimeter

(c) The aircraft is flying towards an area of low pressure, the aircraft is at the level indicated on the altimeter

(d) The aircraft is flying towards an area of low pressure, the aircraft is lower than the level indicated on the altimeter

Turn to the METFORM 214 at appendix A

---

15. Which of the following most closely represents the forecast wind velocity (i) and temperature (ii) at 5000ft at position 55N 0230E?

	(i)	(ii)
(a)	285/20	+01°C
(b)	270/20	0°C
(c)	285/18	+01°C
(d)	285/10	-01°C

Turn to the METFORM 215 at appendix B to answer the following questions

---

16. The lowest forecast freezing level (where 0°C occurs) at about 60N 05W (approximately the top centre of the chart) is:

    (a) 4000m amsl

    (b) 4000ft amsl

    (c) FL40

    (d) 400m amsl

---

17. The weather feature identified as (i) crossing Wales on the forecast chart is:

    (a) A warm front moving east at around 7 knots

    (b) A warm front moving west at around 7 knots

    (c) A warm front moving east at around 15 knots

    (d) A warm front not moving

---

18. In which zone would the following METAR be typical of a sea level aerodrome?
    EGZZ 211420Z 20005KT 130V230 0400 -RA FG VV/// 11/11 Q1023

    (a) Zone A

    (b) Zone B

    (c) Zone C

    (d) Zone D

---

19. The lowest forecast visibility in the METFORM 215 forecast is:

    (a) 8 kilometres in rain in Zone B

    (b) Occasionally 2,500 metres in mist and drizzle on the sea and coasts in Zone A

    (c) Occasionally 500 metres in rain, mist and/or drizzle in Zone C

    (d) Isolated 500 metres in fog and drizzle behind the front in Zone B

---

20. Disregard airspace considerations for the purposes of answering this question.
    A navigation exercise is planned in the north East Anglia area, routing outside controlled airspace.
    The aircraft cannot fly in known icing conditions.
    The pilot holds a PPL without instrument qualification, so the flight must be conducted under VFR.
    The minimum en-route altitude will be 1000ft agl, the average ground level en-route is 250ft. VMC minima require that the aircraft remains clear of cloud, in sight of the surface and in a minimum flight visibility of 5km.
    The estimated time of departure is 1300Z, the exercise will last for around 1 hour 30 minutes. Flight authorisation is based on maintaining an in-flight visibility of not less than 10km.
    Considering the METFORM 215 (appendix B), choose the most reasonable course of action:

    (a) Conditions are likely to be no better than 8km visibility in rain, with occasional patches of 5000m in rain/drizzle and cloud base 800ft. Cancel the flight.

    (b) Occasional conditions of 2500m visibility in mist/drizzle and cloud down to 500ft amsl are forecast for the area. Cancel the flight.

    (c) Based on the METFORM 215, conditions are suitable for the planned flight and it should be able to proceed as planned.

    (d) The departure should be delayed to allow conditions to improve as zone 3 moves into the region after 1700.

Appendix A: UK Low-Level Spot Wind Chart (Form 214)

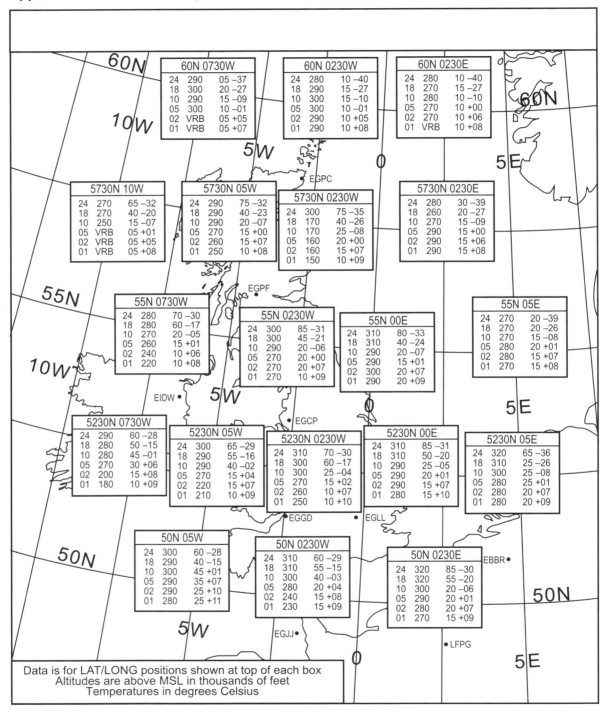

60N 0730W
24	290	05 −37
18	300	20 −27
10	290	15 −09
05	300	10 −01
02	VRB	05 +05
01	VRB	05 +07

60N 0230W
24	280	10 −40
18	290	15 −27
10	300	15 −10
05	300	10 −01
02	290	10 +05
01	290	10 +08

60N 0230E
24	280	10 −40
18	270	15 −27
10	280	10 −10
05	270	10 +00
02	270	10 +06
01	VRB	10 +08

5730N 10W
24	270	65 −32
18	270	40 −20
10	250	15 −07
05	VRB	05 +01
02	VRB	05 +05
01	VRB	05 +08

5730N 05W
24	290	75 −32
18	290	40 −23
10	290	20 −07
05	270	15 +00
02	260	15 +07
01	250	10 +08

5730N 0230W
24	300	75 −35
18	170	40 −26
10	170	25 −08
05	160	20 +00
02	160	15 +07
01	150	10 +09

5730N 0230E
24	280	30 −39
18	260	20 −27
10	270	15 −09
05	290	15 +00
02	290	15 +06
01	290	15 +08

55N 0730W
24	280	70 −30
18	280	60 −17
10	270	20 −05
05	260	15 +01
02	240	10 +06
01	220	10 +08

55N 0230W
24	300	85 −31
18	300	45 −21
10	290	20 −06
05	270	20 +00
02	270	20 +07
01	270	10 +09

55N 00E
24	310	80 −33
18	310	40 −24
10	290	20 −07
05	290	15 +01
02	300	20 +07
01	290	20 +09

55N 05E
24	270	20 −39
18	270	20 −26
10	270	15 −08
05	280	20 +01
02	280	15 +07
01	270	15 +08

5230N 0730W
24	290	60 −28
18	280	50 −15
10	280	45 −01
05	270	30 +06
02	200	15 +08
01	180	10 +09

5230N 05W
24	300	65 −29
18	290	55 −16
10	290	40 −02
05	270	15 +04
02	220	15 +07
01	210	10 +09

5230N 0230W
24	310	70 −30
18	300	60 −17
10	300	25 −04
05	270	15 +02
02	260	10 +07
01	250	10 +10

5230N 00E
24	310	85 −31
18	310	50 −20
10	290	25 −05
05	290	20 +01
02	290	15 +07
01	280	15 +10

5230N 05E
24	320	65 −36
18	310	25 −26
10	300	25 −08
05	280	25 +01
02	280	20 +07
01	280	20 +09

50N 05W
24	300	60 −28
18	290	40 −15
10	300	45 +01
05	290	35 +07
02	290	25 +10
01	280	25 +11

50N 0230W
24	310	60 −29
18	310	55 −15
10	300	40 −03
05	280	20 +04
02	240	15 +08
01	230	15 +09

50N 0230E
24	320	85 −30
18	320	55 −20
10	300	20 −06
05	290	20 +01
02	280	20 +07
01	270	15 +09

Data is for LAT/LONG positions shown at top of each box
Altitudes are above MSL in thousands of feet
Temperatures in degrees Celsius

Appendix B: Forecast Weather

Forecast Weather

Valid 211400 to 212300 Z

Fronts/zones valid at 1800Z

AREA	SURFACE VIS AND WX	CLOUD	0 C
A	25KM NIL OCNL 2500M BR/DZ SEA/COT ISOL 10KM SHRA LAND ISOL 7KM SHRA LAND N	BKN CU SC 025 – 060 BKN ST 005 – 015 BKN CU SC 020 – 080 BKN CU AC 016 – XXX Ψ ⋏	040 – 060
B	8KM RA OCNL 5000M RA/RADZ ISOL 500M FG DZ W OF FRONT ISOL 15KM NIL	BKN SC 020-070 BKN ST SC 008 – 070 OVC 000-5000 FEW/BKN SC 020-050	070 – 100
C	12KM NIL OCNL 5000M BR/RADZ OCNL 20KM NIL MAINLY SW	SCT/BKN ST SC 010-050 BKN ST SC 005-060 SCT/BKN SC 015 – 050	100

Outlook Until:

Showers in East dying out

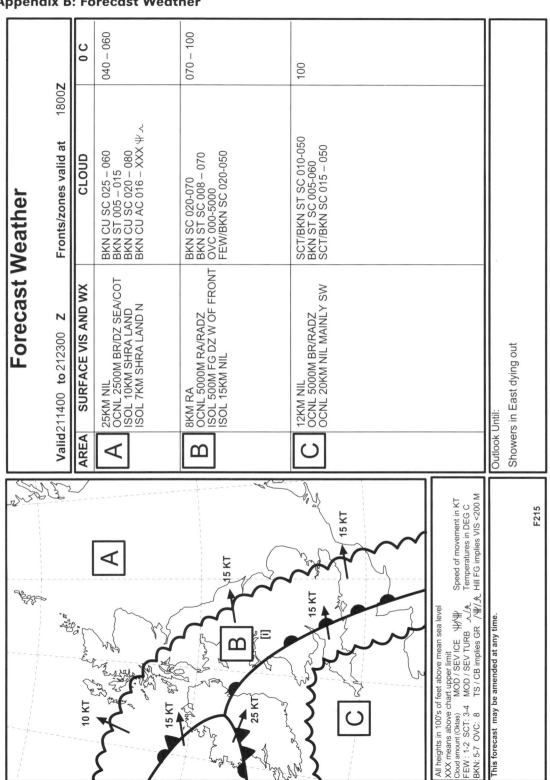

All heights in 100's of feet above mean sea level
XXX means above chart upper limit   Speed of movement in KT
Cloud amount (Oktas)   MOD / SEV ICE Ψ/Ψ   Temperatures in DEG C
FEW : 1-2 SCT: 3-4   MOD / SEV TURB ⋏/⋏
BKN: 5-7 OVC: 8   TS / CB implies GR /Ψ/⋏ Hill FG implies VIS <200 M

F215

This forecast may be amended at any time.

Meteorology Practice – Answers and Explanation Section

Paper 1 Answers and Explanations

EMP1Q1   Answer D

'Rotor' is an area of dangerous turbulence that can form just downwind of a ridge when a wind is blowing across it. It is occasionally marked by an area of 'roll' or 'rotor' cloud.

Further Reference: PPL3 » Meteorology » Flight over Mountainous Areas and Other Weather Hazards » Mountain Waves

EMP1Q2   Answer B

Relative humidity is the percentage of water vapour a parcel of air is holding, compared to the amount it could hold before becoming saturated. A parcel of air containing half the water vapour it could hold before becoming saturated has a relative humidity (RH) of 50%. A relative humidity of 100% means that the air is saturated, it is holding all the water vapour it can before condensation will occur and visible water droplets (eg cloud) form.

As the temperature of air decreases it is able to hold less water vapour before becoming saturated. So, even though its water content may remain the same, as air is cooled its relative humidity will increase until, at the dew point temperature, it reaches saturation.

Further Reference: PPL3 » Meteorology » Humidity and Stability » Humidity

EMP1Q3   Answer D

Over the land, surface friction means that typically the 2000ft wind is slowed by around 50% and backed by up to 30° at the surface. A 'backing' in direction means that the direction as expressed in degrees reduces (move backwards). Given a 2000ft wind of 240/35, the closest fit to this modification is answer D, with reduction in speed of a backing about 40% and a backing in direction of 20°.

Further Reference: PPL3 » Meteorology » The Motion of the Atmosphere » Variation of Wind Velocity with Altitude

EMP1Q4   Answer C

The wind blowing over a mountain range can create large-scale disturbances in the atmosphere. These disturbances are usually referred to as *mountain waves*. Mountains cause the air flow to undulate, like waves in the ocean. Where mountain waves rise up (also known as orographic uplift), gliders have reached great heights with their assistance. However, where the waves turn down they can force aircraft to descend, even at full power and best climb airspeed. This can continue right down to ground level.

When cloud forms in a mountain wave, it will often be of the "lenticular" variety. This is smooth and elongated cloud - not unlike an almond in appearance - and actually remains stationary at the 'crest' of the wave, the cloud forming at the leading edge and dissipating at the trailing edge. In favourable conditions for orographic uplift there may be lenticular clouds at the crest of each wave, and even several such clouds piled on top of one another.

Further Reference: PPL3 » Meteorology » Flight over Mountainous Areas and Other Weather Hazards » Mountain Waves

EMP1Q5   Answer A

Flight Visibility is defined as "The visibility forward from the flight deck of an aircraft in flight".

Further Reference: PPL3 » Meteorology » Visibility » Definitions and Measurement
UK AIM » Air Navigation Order (ANO) » Article 155 Interpretation

EMP1Q6   Answer A

The significant weather symbols are used in a number of meteorological charts and need to be learnt. They are listed in the 'Essential Revision' section.

Further Reference: PPL3 » Meteorology » Aviation Weather Reports and Forecasts » Specific Forecast and Actual Formats

EMP1Q7   Answer D

CAVOK – meaning Ceiling And Visibility OK, can be used if the following conditions exist or are forecast:

  (a) Visibility: 10km or more

  (b) Cloud: no cloud below 5000ft or below the highest Minimum Sector Altitude, whichever is greater, <u>and no CB at any height</u>

  (c) No significant weather phenomena at, or in the vicinity of, the aerodrome

Therefore, 'CAVOK' cannot be reported with CB (cumulonimbus) cloud at any level.

Further Reference: PPL3 » Meteorology » Aviation Weather Reports and Forecasts » Specific Forecast and Actual Formats
UK AIM » Aeronautical Information Publication » GEN 3.5.10

EMP1Q8   Answer C

The troposphere is the layer of atmosphere in contact with the surface, and this is where virtually all 'weather' occurs. The troposphere is capped by an effective 'lid' on the weather in the form of a temperature inversion known as the tropopause. The level of the tropopause varies from around 20,000ft over the poles to 60,000ft over the tropics. Above the tropopause, the thin, dry and cold air of the stratosphere makes any weather (e.g. clouds and precipitation) quite rare.

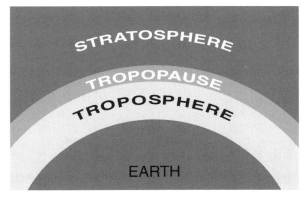

Further Reference: PPL3 » Meteorology » Properties of the Atmosphere » Composition and Structure

EMP1Q9   Answer A

The general advice to pilots is that airframe icing can be expected anywhere within a thunderstorm cloud. Nevertheless, in accordance with normal icing theory, the most severe icing is likely to be encountered where the air temperature is between 0°c and -30°c.

Further Reference: PPL3 » Meteorology » Thunderstorms » Hazards for Aircraft

EMP1Q10   Answer B

By simple definition, a warm front brings warm air to replace colder air – it marks the boundary between cold and warm air masses. By this classification, the choice is narrowed down to two possible answers. The assumption the average slope of a 'typical' warm front is very much an idealised theoretical principle, although the figure of 1:150 is that most often quoted in meteorological textbooks.

Further Reference: PPL3 » Meteorology » Low Pressure Systems – Depressions » Definition of a Front & The Warm Front

EMP1Q11   Answer C

Flying ahead of a warm front in winter is a 'classic' situation in which to encounter rain ice – potentially a very hazardous situation.

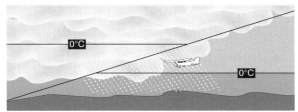

As the air temperature is -2°C (i.e. below freezing), it is safe to assume that the surface of the aircraft itself (especially a metal surface) will also be below freezing. Precipitation may fall as liquid rain through the warm front (possible because of the higher freezing level in the warm air behind the warm front) can freeze on contact with the cold aircraft skin, leading to small lumps of ice forming all over the upper surfaces of the aircraft which are very difficult to remove. The weight and drag caused by this rain ice has very serious implications for the performance and handling characteristics of the afflicted aircraft.

Further Reference: PPL3 » Meteorology » Icing » Rain Ice

EMP1Q12   Answer D

The key word in the question is that referring to an 'unstable' air mass. If unstable air is forced to rise (in this case by a mountain range – orographic lifting), the result is most often cloud of mostly vertical extent – namely cumulus-type or 'Cumuloform' clouds.

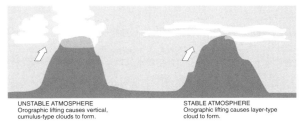

UNSTABLE ATMOSPHERE
Orographic lifting causes vertical, cumulus-type clouds to form.

STABLE ATMOSPHERE
Orographic lifting causes layer-type cloud to form.

Further Reference: PPL3 » Meteorology » Clouds and Precipitation » Formation of Clouds

EMP1Q13   Answer C

To answer this question, you first need to know what types of cloud the abbreviations are referring to. In summary, the cloud-type abbreviations are:

High Level Cloud	CI	Cirrus
	CS	Cirrostratus
	CC	Cirrocumulus
Medium Level Cloud	AS	Altostratus
	AC	Altocumulus
Low Level Cloud	ST	Stratus
	CU	Cumulus
	SC	Stratocumulus
	NS	Nimbostratus
Cloud that may exist through all levels	CB	Cumulonimbus
	TCU	Towering Cumulus

Next you need to know that a 'typical' warm front (a situation found more in text books than in real-life), brings with it mostly layered type clouds, starting with high-level Cirrus (CI) at the top of the warm front slope, gradually thickening – Cirrostratus (CS), and descending – Altostratus (AS), as the front approaches with low Stratus (ST) and Nimbostratus (NS) at the passage of the front.

Answer C is the only sequence that describes this idealised 'typical' warm front cloud progression.

Further Reference: PPL3 » Meteorology » Low Pressure Systems – Depressions » The Warm Front

EMP1Q14   Answer A

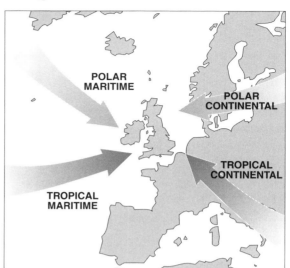

The four main air masses that affect the UK can be broadly characterised as follows:

Air Mass	Stability	Visibility	Cloud Types
Tropical Maritime	Stable	Poor	Extensive stratus-type
Tropical Continental	Stable	Becoming Poor	Little cloud
Polar Continental	Stable	Good	Little cloud
Polar Maritime	Unstable	Good	Frequent showers

Further Reference: PPL3 » Meteorology » Air Masses » Characteristics of Air Masses

EMP1Q15   Answer B

At the position given (50N 00E/W) there is no data box. Therefore it is necessary to interpolate between the closest data boxes – namely those at 50N 0230W and 50N 0230E. It happens that the position given is half-way between each box.

The 2000ft wind at 50N 0230W is 280° at 15 knots, at 50N 0230E it is 260° at 20 knots.

To interpolate mathematically between these figures, they can be added together and divided by two;

i.e.

260 + 280 ÷2 = **270** (although it is clear even without a formulae that 270 is half way between 260 and 280).

In the same way;

15 + 20 ÷2 = 17·5, which is rounded up to **18**,

The temperature is interpolated in the same way:

11 + 14 ÷2 = 12·5, which is rounded up to **+13**

Remember, if your calculation gives a slightly different answer to any of the given options, you should select the one which is closest to your answer.

Further Reference: PPL3 » Meteorology » Aviation Weather Reports and Forecasts » Specific Forecast and Actual Formats

EMP1Q16   Answer A

The 0°C isotherm (in other words, the freezing level) is given as a figure representing thousands of feet above mean sea level (amsl) – see the text explanation on the left-hand side of the charts.

Further Reference: PPL3 » Meteorology » Aviation Weather Reports and Forecasts » Specific Forecast and Actual Formats
UK AIM » Aeronautical Information Publication » Gen 3.2.4.3

EMP1Q17   Answer C

"ISOL" = Isolated

"4000M" = 4000 metres visibility

"+SHRA" = heavy shower of rain

"+TSGR" = heavy thunderstorm with hail

"MON" = Mountain

"N 56N" = North of latitude 56°N

Further Reference: PPL3 » Meteorology » Aviation Weather Reports and Forecasts » Specific Forecast and Actual Formats

EMP1Q18   Answer B

For a full list of met. symbols, see the essential revision section.

Further Reference: PPL3 » Meteorology » Aviation Weather Reports and Forecasts » Specific Forecast and Actual Formats

EMP1Q19   Answer C

"BKN" = Broken (5-7 oktas) cloud cover

"CB" = Cumulonimbus cloud type

"008" = 800ft above mean sea level (amsl)

"XXX" = Above chart upper limit

" ⩊ " = Severe icing

" _⋀_ " = Severe turbulence

Further Reference: PPL3 » Meteorology » Aviation Weather Reports and Forecasts » Specific Forecast and Actual Formats

EMP1Q20   Answer C

Consideration of the departure METAR, arrival TAF and Zone B condition on the METFORM 215 give a view of generally good in-flight visibility, with a cloud base at around 2500ft amsl. There may be showers en-route, and these also may occur temporarily at the destination airfield, but only after 1600 (i.e. about the arrival ETA). In the good visibility, it should be possible to see and avoid and showers in good time. It is reasonable to proceed with the planned flight, exercising caution to avoid any showers.

All the other answer options are based on a mis-reading of the METAR, TAF or METFORM 215 information.

Further Reference: PPL3 » Meteorology » Aviation Weather Reports and Forecasts » Specific Forecast and Actual Formats

Paper 2 Answers and Explanations

EMP2Q1   Answer A

The most common significant weather symbols used on (SIGWX) charts are found in the essential revision section: they should be learnt.

Further Reference: PPL3 » Meteorology » Aviation Weather Reports and Forecasts » Specific Forecast and Actual Formats

EMP2Q2   Answer D

Although the debate is mostly subjective, rather than scientifically measured, many experienced pilots believe that at night, visibility is best when looking directly towards the moon that in any other direction.

Further Reference: PPL3 » Meteorology » Visibility » Haze, Smoke, Dust and Sand

EMP2Q3   Answer C

The atmosphere itself acquires virtually no heat energy directly from the sun – it is essentially transparent to solar radiation. Radiation from the sun heats up the earth's surface, and the atmosphere is then warmed from below. In effect, the sun's energy (heat) only heats the atmosphere by re-radiation from the surface. The differing surfaces of the earth (land, sea, snow cover etc.), the shape of the earth and the fact that the earth is tilted on its axis means that surface heating is not uniform across the globe, leading to the movement of air around the planet.

Further Reference: PPL3 » Meteorology » The Motion of the Atmosphere » Heating of the Atmosphere

EMP2Q4   Answer A

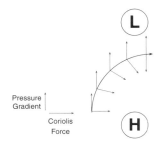

Air first begins to move under the influence of pressure gradient force – air moves from high pressure towards low pressure. Once air is in motion, it is acted upon by the Coriolis force which deflects air to the right in the northern hemisphere (and to the left in the southern hemisphere).

At some point, a balance will be reached between the effect of the pressure gradient force and the Coriolis force. Where the resulting balanced wind is following straight, parallel isobars, the resulting wind is sometimes referred to as the Geostrophic wind. When the balanced wind is following curved isobars it can be referred to as the gradient wind. This second definition takes into account the effect of centrifugal force in addition to the pressure gradient force and Coriolis force that define the Geostrophic wind.

Further Reference: PPL3 » Meteorology » The Motion of the Atmosphere » Coriolis Force, Geostrophic Wind

EMP2Q5   Answer B

The layer of the atmosphere closest to the earth and of most interest to the light-aircraft pilot is the troposphere. The troposphere extends from the surface upwards to a region known as the tropopause. Because the troposphere contains virtually all the water in the atmosphere, this is where most 'weather' – clouds, fog, mist, rain, snow etc. – is found. The height of the top of the troposphere is 36,000ft in the International Standard Atmosphere.

Further Reference: PPL3 » Meteorology » Properties of the Atmosphere » Composition and Structure

EMP2Q6 Answer A

Firstly:

   Starboard = Right

   Port = Left

One way of remembering this is that 'Port' and 'Left' have the same number of letters. Not very catchy, but it is true.

The fact that the aircraft is flying with a constant starboard drift indicates that the wind is blowing from the left. According to Buys Ballot's law, in the northern hemisphere if you stand with your back to the wind, the low pressure area is on your left. Transposed onto the situation in the question, this indicates that the aircraft is flying towards an area of low pressure.

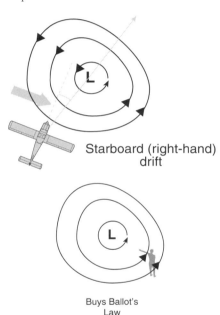

Starboard (right-hand) drift

Buys Ballot's Law

This presumption is confirmed by the fact that when the altimeter pressure setting is updated, the new QNH is lower than before.

If an aircraft flies towards a low pressure area without updating the sub-scale setting, the altimeter will **over-read** – the aircraft is lower than the altimeter reading.

Hence the saying; "**high to low, down you go**".

Although the question does not ask for the exact magnitude of the error, based on 1mb = 30ft you can calculate that before changing setting the altimeter was <u>over-reading</u> by 510ft (i.e. the mb difference of 17mb x 30ft). Therefore the altimeter was indicating that the aircraft was 510ft higher than it really was: the indicated altitude of 2000ft equates to an actual altitude of 1490ft (2000ft – 510ft).

Further Reference: PPL3 » Meteorology » The Motion of the Atmosphere » Depressions and Anticyclones

PPL3 » Meteorology » Pressure and Altimetry » Altimetry

EMP2Q7 Answer D

When air is forced to rise by terrain (such as a mountain or mountain range) it can be said to be undergoing 'orographic lifting', and where stable air flows over a mountain or a range of mountains, particularly in strong wind conditions, this lifting action can lead to the formation of mountain waves, also known as 'standing waves' or 'lee waves'. These waves are sought out by glider pilots who can use the orographic uplift to reach spectacular altitudes, although the downdraughts where the waves turn down can be equally spectacular in the opposite sense.

Lenticular clouds are stationary saucer-shaped clouds that sometimes form at the crests of these waves. Due to their shape, lack of movement and exceptionally smooth contours lenticular clouds have been mistaken for UFOs in the past! To a meteorologist, lenticular clouds belong to the 'lenticularis species' (clouds formed in the lee wave parallel to a mountain ridge) and can be classified by meteorologists as altocumulus lenticularis, stratocumulus lenticularis or cirrocumulus lenticularis.

Further Reference: PPL3 » Meteorology » Flight Over Mountainous Areas and Other Weather Hazards » Mountain Waves

UK AIM » Aeronautical Information Circular » AIC 6/2003 (Pink 48) Flight Over and in the Vicinity of High Ground

EMP2Q8   **Answer D**

Water vapour is a gas, put simply it is water in its gas state and as such it is invisible. Water in the atmosphere only becomes visible when water vapour changes state either by condensing into liquid water droplets (eg cloud, fog, steam) or sublimating into solid water – ice – (eg frost). Virtually all water vapour is found in the troposphere (the lowest level of the atmosphere) and it is responsible for the formation of clouds, fog, precipitation etc. The proportion of water vapour in the lower atmosphere varies but it is generally considered to be the third largest component of the lower atmosphere after nitrogen and oxygen.

Further Reference: PPL3 » Meteorology » Properties of the Atmosphere » Composition and Structure

EMP2Q9   **Answer D**

The fact that the air is coming from a polar region, and that it is a maritime airflow, indicates that it is cold and moist. Because the air is being warmed from beneath as it travels southwards, it tends to become unstable – as a rule air masses become unstable if heat energy is put into them.

Further Reference: PPL3 » Meteorology » Air Masses » Characteristics of Air Masses

EMP2Q10   **Answer B**

The 'classic' situation for rain ice to occur is ahead of a warm front in winter. Rain falls from the warm air of the warm front into the cold air ahead of it. If this rain hits an object that is below freezing (for example, an aircraft flying above the freezing level), there is a good chance that the rain will freeze into it instantly, causing 'rain' or 'clear' ice to form.

Suffice to say such ice is very difficult to remove and hence very dangerous.

Further Reference: PPL3 » Meteorology » Icing » Rain Ice

EMP2Q11   **Answer B**

The dominant factor in carburettor icing is humidity – the more humid the air, the more likely carburettor icing. The temperature fall within the carburettor can be as much as 25°C, so temperatures below freezing, or above +30°C make carburettor icing far less likely. Of the options listed, the flight near cloud, in rain is clearly the most humid situation, with an air temperature (+5°C) which is within the range where carburettor icing can be considered likely.

Further Reference: PPL3 » Meteorology » Icing » Piston Engine Icing
UK AIM » CAA Safety Sense Leaflets 14 » Piston Engine Icing

EMP2Q12   **Answer A**

The full METAR and TAF decode must be learnt. Some further key points to remember:
■ All times are in UTC
■ Wind directions are in degrees True unless otherwise specified.
■ The direction of the minimum visibility is only given if there is a significant variation in visibility when looking in different directions.
■ The symbol '//' is used to denote missing information

Further Reference: PPL3 » Meteorology » Aviation Weather Reports and Forecasts » Specific Forecast and Actual Formats
UK AIM » Aeronautical Information Publication » GEN 3.5.10

EMP2Q13   **Answer B**

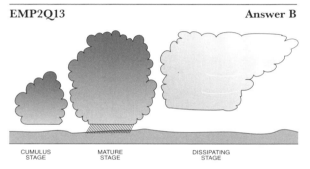

CUMULUS STAGE   MATURE STAGE   DISSIPATING STAGE

The mature stage of a thunderstorm is marked by precipitation beginning to fall from the base of the cumulonimbus cloud. It is generally at this stage that many of the hazards associated with thunderstorms (heavy precipitation including hail, vertical gusts and windshear, turbulence, gale-force winds) are at their most intense. Lightning and even tornadoes are also associated with the mature stage.

Whilst the mature stage is probably the time at which the thunderstorm is at its most dangerous, it should be fully understood that a rapidly growing cumulus (cumulus stage) or dispersing (dissipating stage) thunderstorm must also be avoided.

Further Reference: PPL3 » Meteorology » Thunderstorm » The Formation and Life-Cycle of Thunderstorms
UK AIM » Aeronautical Information Circulars » AIC81/2004 (pink 66) The Effect of Thunderstorms and Associated Turbulence on Aircraft Operations

EMP2Q14   **Answer D**

A VOLMET service is an automatic broadcast of recorded METARs for a number of airfields (usually around 10-12), grouped mostly in the same area. The name of the VOLMET broadcast will normally be the FIR name, plus a more precise region – e.g. 'London Volmet North', 'Paris Volmet' etc. Full details of VOLMET broadcasts including frequency, airfields covered etc. will be found in the appropriate AIPs and also commercial flight guides.

Further Reference: PPL3 » Meteorology » Aviation Weather Reports and Forecasts » Obtaining Met. Information In-Flight
UK AIM » Aeronautical Information Publication » GEN 3.5.6.4

EMP2Q15 Answer D

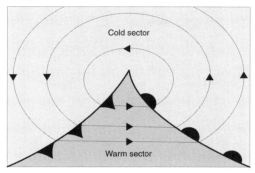

In the cold sector behind a cold front in a 'typical' North Atlantic depression, the pilot will often find a quick clearance of cloud and precipitation leading to good visibility and either clear skies, or scattered cumulus type clouds. In general the expression 'cold sector' is rarely used in real life, as it can be used to refer to any part of the depression outside the 'warm sector' which exists between the warm and cold fronts.

In a 'typical' North Atlantic depression crossing the UK, the warm sector is air drawn from the tropical maritime air mass, and the cold sector behind the cold front is the polar maritime air mass.

Further Reference: PPL3 » Meteorology » Low Pressure Systems – Depressions » The Cold Front

EMP2Q16 Answer A

At the position given (5230N 0230E) there is no data box. Check that again – the position given is 0230 <u>EAST</u> not 0230 <u>WEST</u>. Because there is no data box at the position given it is necessary to interpolate between the closest data boxes – namely those at 5230N 00E and 5230N 05E. The position given is half-way between each box.

The 5000ft wind at 5230N 00E is 180° at 25 knots, at 5230N 05E it is 160° at 15 knots.

Interpolating between these figures is fairly simple, giving a mid-point of 170° at 20 knots.

The temperature is interpolated in the same way, and rounded up to +4°C.

Remember, if your calculation gives a slightly different answer to any of the answer options, you should select the option which is closest to your calculation.

Further Reference: PPL3 » Meteorology » Aviation Weather Reports and Forecasts » Specific Forecast and Actual Formats

EMP2Q17 Answer D

The 0°C isotherm (in other words, the freezing level) is given as a figure representing thousands of feet above mean sea level (amsl) – see the text explanation on the left-hand side of the charts.

Further Reference: PPL3 » Meteorology » Aviation Weather Reports and Forecasts » Specific Forecast and Actual Formats
UK AIM » Aeronautical Information Publication » GEN 3.5.4.3

EMP2Q18 Answer C

For a full list of met. symbols, see the essential revision section. The speed of movement of the front is given on the 'arrow' that crosses the front.

Further Reference: PPL3 » Meteorology » Aviation Weather Reports and Forecasts » Specific Forecast and Actual Formats

EMP2Q19 Answer B

ISOL = Isolated

2000M = 2000m visibility

RA/DZ = rain and/or drizzle

COT = Coast

FM 10 Z = from 10:00 Zulu (UTC)
Further Reference: PPL3 » Meteorology » Aviation Weather Reports and Forecasts » Specific Forecast and Actual Formats

EMP2Q20 Answer C

Consideration of the departure METAR, arrival TAF and Zone 3 conditions on the METFORM 215 gives a view of a generally deteriorating weather situation, with the aircraft flying almost directly into the worsening weather of the occluding front. The conditions of Zone 2 (the occluding front) will begin to arrive at the destination around the ETA. Moreover, even in Zone 3 areas of mist and drizzle, with visibility down to 2500m and cloud base effectively down to ground level, are forecast. This combination of marginal en-route weather and the forecast deterioration at the destination make safe VFR flight unlikely.

All the other answer options are based on a mis-reading of the METAR, TAF or METFORM 215 information, or a failure to appreciate that Zone 2 conditions will move to cover the destination airfield.

Further Reference: PPL3 » Meteorology » Aviation Weather Reports and Forecasts » Specific Forecast and Actual Formats

Paper 3 Answers and Explanations

EMP3Q1   Answer D

All thunderstorms are hazardous to aircraft, and the universal advice is that all aircraft and pilots should avoid all thunderstorms.

Where thunderstorms occur in clear conditions and are well-separated, avoidance is not usually a problem – they are easy to see and avoid. At night, the lightning from an active thunderstorm may be visible from hundred of miles away to an aircraft in flight – again avoidance should not be a problem in these circumstances.

On the other hand, thunderstorms that are embedded inside extensive cloud – for example the layered cloud of a warm or occluded front – present a particular hazard precisely because they cannot be seen: they are masked by the frontal cloud. Thus it is possible for a pilot flying in cloud to blunder straight into a thunderstorm that could have easily been avoided if it was in clear air. Many pilots regard embedded thunderstorms as one of the greatest aviation weather hazards.

Further Reference: PPL3 » Meteorology » Thunderstorms » Practical Advice for Thunderstorm Avoidance

UK AIM » Aeronautical Information Circulars » AIC81/2004 (pink 66) The Effect of Thunderstorms and Associated Turbulence on Aircraft Operations

EMP3Q2   Answer D

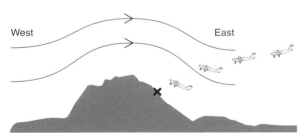

West   East

Strong airflow across a mountain range can create large-scale disturbances in the atmosphere known as *mountain waves* (or "standing waves" or "lee waves"). Where the waves turn down (as will happen on the downwind or 'lee' side of the mountains) the mass of descending air can force aircraft to descend, even at full power and best climb airspeed. The wind is blowing from the west, so it is to the east of the mountains – the downwind side – where hazardous mountain wave activity is most likely

Further Reference: PPL3 » Meteorology » Flight Over Mountainous Areas and Other Weather Hazards » Mountain Waves

UK AIM » Aeronautical Information Circular » AIC 6/2003 (Pink 48) Flight Over and in the Vicinity of High Ground

EMP3Q3   Answer A

Contrary to what might seem common sense, carburettor icing is if anything more likely to occur in summer – for the simple reason that warm air can hold more moisture (which in turn is converted into more ice) than cold air. The higher the moisture content of the air, the more likely carburettor icing.

The temperature drop within the carburettor can be anything up to 25°C, so even on at hot summer day (air temperature say +25°C), the air inside the carburettor venturi may be below freezing. Ironically during the winter (air temperature say 0°C), the further temperature drop within the carburettor means that any moisture in the air tends to turn into ice crystals which pass through the carburettor rather than sticking and blocking it.

Under any set of conditions, a low power setting (such as that used during a descent) makes carburettor icing more likely.

Further Reference: PPL3 » Meteorology » Icing » Piston Engine Icing
UK AIM » CAA Safety Sense Leaflets 14 » Piston Engine Icing

EMP3Q4   Answer D

A Special Forecast must be requested from a forecast office. The minimum notice prior to collection is 2 hours for a flight of up to 500nm, and 4 hours for a longer flight.

Further Reference: PPL3 » Meteorology » Aviation Weather Reports and Forecasts » Special Forecasts
UK AIM » Aeronautical Information Publication » Gen 3.5.5

EMP3Q5   Answer C

The TAF and METAR decodes are used worldwide and need to be learnt thoroughly – not just for exam purposes.

Note that the correct definition of NO SIG when used in a METAR is that **NO SIG**nificant changes are forecast to occur during the trend forecast period. The trend forecast period is the two hours after the observation time.

Further Reference: PPL3 » Meteorology » Aviation Weather Reports and Forecasts » Specific Forecast and Actual Formats
UK AIM » Aeronautical Information Publication » GEN 3.5.10

EMP3Q6   Answer D

This problem is best solved in stages.

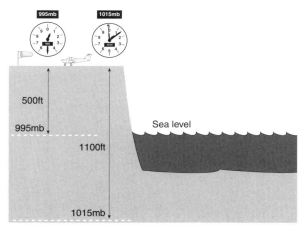

The QNH at airfield is 1015; the QNH at airfield B is 995. The different between the two is (1015 – 995) = 20.

20mb x 30ft = 600ft.

The aircraft has flown from high pressure to low pressure. When the 'old' QNH of 1015 is re-set at airfield B, the altimeter will over-read – it will indicate that the aircraft is higher than it really is.

If the amount of over-reading (600ft) is added to the actual altitude (500ft) – elevation is really only another word for altitude – the altimeter indication will be 1100ft.

This illustrates the absolute necessity of keeping the altimeter setting updated at all times.

Further Reference: PPL3 » Meteorology » Pressure and Altimetry » Altimetry

EMP3Q7   Answer B

Frontal fog occasionally forms just ahead of a warm or occluded front as at the surface, air becomes saturated by continuous rain. Rain falling from warm air above the front evaporates at or near the surface in the colder air ahead of the front. This cools the air whilst adding to the air's moisture content until the air becomes saturated and condensation (visible water droplets) occurs. Frontal fog (sometimes called precipitation fog) is most common in the vicinity of a slow moving or stationary warm or occluded front, the key factors include light winds and continuous precipitation.

Further Reference: PPL3 » Meteorology » Visibility » Fog and Mist

EMP3Q8   Answer D

The main types of icing can be summarised as follows:

Type of Ice	Characteristics
Carburettor icing	Icing inside the carburettor caused by the temperature drop within the venturi, can occur in clear air conditions
Rain ice	Rare form of icing that can occur ahead of a warm front in winter. Liquid precipitation falls into colder air and freezes on contact with a surface below freezing (eg an aircraft)
Hoar frost	Water vapour in the atmosphere freezes directly onto a surface below freezing
Rime ice	A brittle layer of ice that forms on leading edges, probes etc. when an aircraft flies through cloud containing supercooled water droplets above the freezing level.
Clear ice	A sheet of ice that forms on surfaces when an aircraft flies through cloud containing supercooled water droplets above the freezing level.

Further Reference: PPL3 » Meteorology » Icing »

EMP3Q9   Answer C

The Metform 214 (UK spot wind forecast chart) and Metform 215 (UK Low-level forecast chart) are issued every six hours, and are valid for six hours. Therefore if a chart has a valid time of 0300 UTC, the next valid date will be issued at 0900 UTC.

Please note that during 2006, the Metform format and periods of validity are expected to change, please check for the latest information.

Further Reference: PPL3 » Meteorology » Aviation Weather Reports and Forecasts » Specific Forecast and Actual Formats
UK AIM » Aeronautical Information Publication » Gen 3.5.4.3

EMP3Q10   Answer C

If you think of high pressure as being like a high mountain, and low pressure as being like a low valley, it is clear that air will want to flow from high to low. Pressure Gradient Force is a measure of the pressure differential over a fixed distance and the greater the pressure differential, the greater the pressure gradient force and so the faster the movement of air. The pressure gradient just like a surface gradient, you can consider isobars as being equivalent to contour lines on a map – the steeper the gradient, the closer together the lines and the quicker something will slide down it.

Further Reference: PPL3 » Meteorology » The Motion of the Atmosphere » Pressure Gradient

EMP3Q11   Answer C

An anticyclone is an area of 'subsiding' – that is descending – air, hence the high pressure that defines it. As the air subsides it is compressed and warmed, which can lead to a layer of warmer air above a layer of cold air next to the surface. This is a temperature inversion – a situation where temperature remains constant or even increases with increasing height, the opposite (or inverse) of the usual situation were temperature reduces with increasing height. This is especially common in winter, when the air in the lower atmosphere is cooled by contact with the cold earth's surface.

Water, smoke and dust particles tend to become trapped below a temperature inversion, leading to a reduction in visibility over a period of days or weeks. Particularly in winter, a solid overcast of unbroken cloud may form around the inversion layer. The lack of sunlight and 'gloomy' conditions with poor visibility beneath this cloud bring around so-called 'anti-cyclonic' gloom, which may persist for several weeks during the winter in northern Europe.

Further Reference: PPL3 » Meteorology » High Pressure Systems – Anticyclones and Ridges » Anticyclones

EMP3Q12   Answer C

A polar continental air mass usually arrives in the UK from Russia or Scandinavia. It is essentially cold and dry and usually brings clear skies and excellent visibility. As polar continental air crosses the North Sea during winter, it can pick up enough moisture from the relatively warm sea to trigger off convective clouds and showers on eastern coasts of the UK

Further Reference: PPL3 » Meteorology » Air Masses » Characteristics of Air Masses

EMP3Q13   Answer B

The most common significant weather symbols used on (SIGWX) charts are found in the essential revision section: they need to be learnt.

Further Reference: PPL3 » Meteorology » Aviation Weather Reports and Forecasts » Specific Forecast and Actual Formats

EMP3Q14   Answer D

If the aircraft has starboard (right-hand) drift, the wind must be coming from port (left-hand). According to Buys Ballot's law, in the northern hemisphere if you stand with your back to the wind, the low pressure area is on your left. Transposed onto the situation described in the question, this indicates that the aircraft is flying towards an area of low pressure.

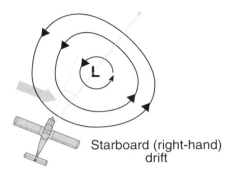

Starboard (right-hand) drift

If flying from high pressure to low pressure, without updating the altimeter setting, the aircraft will follow a constant pressure level which is, in fact, getting closer to the ground. Although the altimeter is showing a constant reading, the aircraft is in fact lower than the level indicated on the altimeter. Hence:

High to Low, down you go

High pressure   Low pressure

Please note that the concept of flying any distance without updating the altimeter setting is a very dangerous one, and is emphatically <u>not</u> recommended.

Further Reference: PPL3 » Meteorology » Pressure and Altimetry » Altimetry

EMP3Q15   Answer C

At the position given (55N 0230E) there is no data box – remember, this is 0230<u>E</u> not 0230<u>W</u>. Therefore it is necessary to interpolate between the closest data boxes – namely those at 55N 00E and 55N 05E. The position given is half-way between each box.

The 5000ft wind at 55N 00E is 290° at 15 knots, at 55N 05E it is 280° at 20 knots. Interpolating between these figures is fairly simple, giving a mid-point of 285° at 18 knots (rounded up to the nearest knot).

There is no need to interpolate the temperature as both boxes give a figure of +01°C at 5000ft.

Remember, if your calculation gives a slightly different answer to any of the answer options, you should select the option which is closest to your calculation.

Further Reference: PPL3 » Meteorology » Aviation Weather Reports and Forecasts » Specific Forecast and Actual Formats

EMP3Q16   Answer B

The 0°C level (in other words, the freezing level) is given as a figure representing thousands of feet above mean sea level (amsl) – see the text explanation on the left-hand side of the charts.

Further Reference: PPL3 » Meteorology » Aviation Weather Reports and Forecasts » Specific Forecast and Actual Formats
UK AIM » Aeronautical Information Publication » Gen 3.2.4.3

EMP3Q17   Answer C

For a full list of met. symbols, see the essential revision section.

Further Reference: PPL3 » Meteorology » Aviation Weather Reports and Forecasts » Specific Forecast and Actual Formats

EMP3Q18   Answer B

For a full list of met. symbols and METAR decode see the essential revision section.

The third line of the 'SURFACE VIS AND WX' section of area B states:

ISOL 500M FG DZ W OF FRONT – in other words isolated areas of 500m visibility in fog and drizzle west of front.

These forecast conditions closely fit the METAR report of fog and light rain.

Further Reference: PPL3 » Meteorology » Aviation Weather Reports and Forecasts » Specific Forecast and Actual Formats

EMP3Q19   Answer D

For a full list of met. abbreviations, see the essential revision. Note that the front is moving to the east, so the area to the west of the front is behind it.

Further Reference: PPL3 » Meteorology » Aviation Weather Reports and Forecasts » Specific Forecast and Actual Formats

EMP3Q20   Answer C

The estimated time of departure (1300Z) is within the forecast period (1200 – 1800), but two hours before the situation depicted on the 1500 chart. This means that the warm front and associated conditions will be a further 30 miles away from the area of the navigation exercise. The conditions forecast in the exercise area are generally good visibility (25km), nil weather and broken cloud base 2500ft amsl. The reference to 2500m in mist and drizzle refers to sea and coastal areas in the N and NE of zone A – e.g. the coast of Scotland or northern England. Even in the possible isolated rain showers visibility is forecast to be no less than 10km and cloud base 2000ft amsl, which is still well within VMC limits.

All the other answer options are based on a mis-reading of METFORM 215 information, for example a failure to appreciate that Zone B conditions will not move to cover the navigation exercise area until after the planned flight has been completed.

In real life, it would be very unwise to rely solely on an area weather forecast for making flight planning decisions. At the very least a METAR for the departure and destination airfields, and/or airfields close to the planned route, should be obtained together with any relevant aerodrome forecasts (TAF).

Further Reference: PPL3 » Meteorology » Aviation Weather Reports and Forecasts » Specific Forecast and Actual Formats

Navigation

Navigation Essential Revision

▶ The Earth

Degrees of **latitude** are measured north and south of the equator. Degrees of **longitude** are measured east or west from 0° longitude.

True north is the direction to the actual north pole. **Magnetic north** is the direction to the magnetic north pole. **Compass north** is the direction of north as measured by a compass.

▶ Aeronautical Maps

True direction corrected for **variation** gives **magnetic direction**. Correcting this for **deviation** gives **compass direction**.

True ± Variation = Magnetic ± Deviation = Compass

T   V   M   D   C

Westerly variation and deviation is added

Easterly variation and deviation is subtracted

Depiction of airfields and aeronautical information:

Aerodrome - Civil	○
Aerodrome - Civil, limited or no facilities	○
Heliport - Civil	Ⓗ
Aerodrome - Government, available for Civil use	⊙
Aerodrome - Government	⊙
Heliport - Government	Ⓗ
Aerodrome - Disused or Abandoned	⊗
Aerodrome Traffic Zone Regulated Airspace from the surface to 2000ft above the level of the aerodrome within a circle centred on the notified mid-point of the longest runway, radius 2NM (RW<1850m) or 2·5NM (RW>1850m).	◯
Aerodrome Elevation Numerals adjacent to aerodrome indicate elevation of aerodrome in feet Above Mean Sea Level	250
Customs Aerodromes Distinguished by a pecked line around the aerodrome name	
Glider Launching Site Primary activity at locations Additional activity at locations cables indicate winch launch	cables Ⓖ cables
Winch Launch Activity (Hang Gliding & Parascending Parachute) Primary activity at locations Additional activity at locations cables indicate winch launch	cables cables
Foot Launch Site	
Microlight Flying Site	Ⓜ
Free Fall Parachuting Site with DZ circle	
Aeronautical Ground Light	☆
Marine Light	•
Lightship	
VHF Omnidirectional Radio Range .... VOR	⊙
Distance Measuring Equipment .... DME	▫
Co-located VOR and DME .... VOR/DME	▣
UHF Tactical Air Navigational Aid .... TACAN	▽
Non-directional Radio Beacon .... NDB and NDB(L)	◎
Radio Marker Beacon or other Navigational Aid	⊙
VOR with compass Rose Orientated on Magnetic North	

Ⓐ	B3 Ⓐ FL45+
Ⓓ	CTR Ⓓ SFC-2000'ALT CTA Ⓓ 2500'-3500'ALT
Ⓔ	TMA Ⓔ 2000'-6000'ALT
Ⓕ	N571D Ⓕ FL55-FL235
Ⓖ	.....All airspace not covered by classes A-F.....
Low Level Corridor or Special Route	750'-2500'ALT
Radar Advisory Service Zone or Area	
Air Traffic Services Unit (ATSU) Area	
Altimeter Setting Region Boundary (ASR)	↔ ↔↔ ↔↔ ↔↔
Military Aerodrome Traffic Zone (MATZ)	(Showing two stubs)
Reporting Point	△
Special Access Lane Entry/Exit	E/E LIVERPOOL
Instrument Approach Procedure (IAP) outside Regulated Airspace	
Visual Reference Point (VRP) Notified in UK AIP	VRP SANDBACH ⊕
Airspace Restrictions Prohibited - 'P', Restricted - 'R' and Danger Area - 'D'. Danger Areas activated by NOTAM are shown with broken boundary line	
High Intensity Radio Transmission Area (HIRTA)	
Bird Sanctuary or GVS	
Area of Intense Air Activity (AIAA) and Aerial Tactics Area (ATA)	
Exceptionally High Obstacle (Lighted) 1000' AGL or more Single, Multiple	1978 (1031) 2297 (1050)
Single Obstacle (Unlighted)	825 (350) Λ
Multiple Obstacle (Lighted)	1614 (505)
Numerals in italics indicate elevation of top of obstacle Above Mean Sea Level. Numerals in brackets indicate height of top of obstacle above local Ground Level	
Cable Joining obstacles	
Spot Elevation	• 1525
Highest Elevation on chart	• 2595
Isogonic Line or Isogonal	5·5°W

▶Navigation Principles: The Triangle of Velocities

Calculation of heading and groundspeed: wind up method:

Example, given a true airspeed of 100 knots, a wind velocity of 230° at 20 knots (W/V 230/20) and a track of 170° (all directions are true), find the required true heading to maintain track and the resulting groundspeed.

Wind up method

Step 1   Place the wind direction under the 'INDEX', place the centre dot on the wind speed on the wind grid, make a mark at the top of the wind grid.

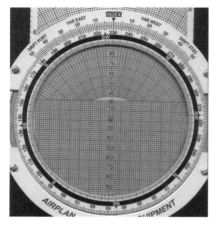

Step 2   Place the track direction under the 'INDEX', place the wind mark on the true airspeed. The wind mark is 10° right of the centre line. 10° right of the index mark indicates a required heading to maintain track – 180° (170 + 10). The centre dot represents the resulting ground speed – 89 knots.

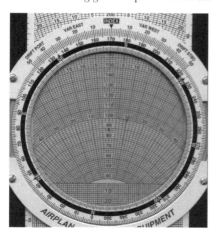

Calculation of heading and groundspeed: wind down method:

Example, given a true airspeed of 100 knots, a wind velocity of 230° at 20 knots (W/V 230/20) and a track of 170° (all directions are true), find the required true heading to maintain track and the resulting groundspeed.

Wind down method

Step 1   Place the wind direction under the 'INDEX', place the centre dot at the top of the wind grid, make a mark below it at the wind speed.

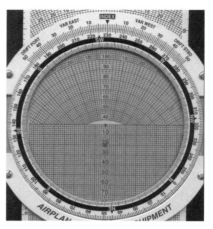

Step 2   Place the track direction under the 'INDEX', place the centre dot on the true airspeed. The wind mark is 11° left of the centre line.

Step 3   Rotate the plotting disc 11° to the left – bringing the wind mark down. The heading at the INDEX mark (181) is now 11° different to the track, but the wind mark is now only 10° to the left of the centre line. Move the plotting disc back 1° so that the difference in degrees between track and heading is the same both at the 'INDEX' mark and between the wind mark and the centre line.

At the 'INDEX' mark read-off the required heading (180°). At the wind mark read-off the resulting groundspeed (89 knots).

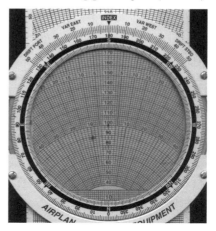

▶ Navigation Principles: Airspeed, Groundspeed, Time and Distance

The circular slide rule side of the flight computer is used for time/speed/distance calculations. The inner scale represents *time*, and the outer scale represents *distance*. On the inner scale there is a 'time index' which represents 60 minutes (i.e. one hour).

▶ Vertical Navigation

AIR NAVIGATION OBSTACLES
Exceptionally High Obstacle (Lighted)
1000ft or more AGL.. 1978 (1031)

Single Obstacle (Unlighted) 825 (350)
Multiple Obstacle (Lighted) 1614 (505)
Cable joining Obstacles .... cables

Numerals in italics indicate elevation of top of obstacle above Mean Sea Level. Numerals in brackets indicate height of top of obstacle above local Ground Level. Obstacles annotated 'flarestack' burn off high pressure gas. The flame, which may not be visible in bright sunlight, can extend up to 600ft above the installation.

> KNOWN LAND SITED OBSTACLES ABOVE 300ft AGL ARE SHOWN ON THIS CHART.
> A SMALL NUMBER OF OBSTACLES BELOW 300ft AGL ARE SHOWN FOR LANDMARK
> PURPOSES. PERMANENT OFF-SHORE OBSTACLES ARE SHOWN REGARDLESS OF
> HEIGHT CATEGORY. See UK AIP ENR 1-1.
> WARNING: INFORMATION IS TAKEN FROM BEST AVAILABLE SOURCES BUT IS NOT
> GUARANTEED COMPLETE.

Maximum Elevation Figures represents the maximum possible elevation of an obstruction within a box bounded by half a degree of latitude and longitude. It is **NOT** a safety altitude.

QNH – when QNH is set on the altimeter sub-scale, **altitude above mean sea level** is indicated.

QFE – when QFE is set on the altimeter sub-scale, **height above a set datum (usually an airfield)** is indicated.

Flight Level – when the standard pressure setting (1013mb/hPa) is set on the altimeter sub-scale, **flight level above the 1013 pressure level** is indicated.

Outside controlled airspace at or below the transition altitude, any desired **pressure setting** may be used. Regional QNH is the usual setting except in a MATZ, where QFE is normally used. When flying under a TMA or CTA, the QNH of an airfield beneath that airspace should be used.

When flying above the transition altitude outside controlled airspace, it is recommended (for a VFR flight, mandatory for an IFR flight) to fly at the appropriate flight level in accordance with the **quadrantal** rule.

Magnetic track	Flight level
000° to 089°	Odd Thousands
090° to 179°	Odd Thousands + 500
180° to 269°	Even Thousands
270° to 359°	Even Thousands + 500

A Flight Level can be converted to an altitude by taking the difference in millibars between 1013 and the actual QNH and multiplying by 30. If QNH is less than 1013, the difference is deducted from the FL to give altitude. If QNH is more than 1013, the difference is added to the FL to give altitude.

▶ Practical Navigation: Off-Track Calculations and Track Marking

$$\frac{\text{Distance off-track (in nm)}}{\text{Distance travelled (in nm)}} \text{ x } 60 = \textbf{track error} \text{ (in degrees)}$$

$$\frac{\text{Distance off-track (in nm)}}{\text{Distance to go (in nm)}} \text{ x } 60 = \text{closing angle (in degrees)}$$

▶ Fuel Planning

On the conversions side of the flight computer, given the flight time and the fuel consumption, fuel is read on the outer scale and time on the inner scale.

To find fuel weight (mass) given a volume and **specific gravity**, on the conversions side of the flight computer, set volume under the appropriate mark for the units being used (ie litres, imperial gallons or US gallons), and under the specific gravity (either in Lbs or Kg) read-off fuel weight (mass).

Example, to find the weight of 100 imperial gallons of AVGAS given a specific gravity of 0.72:

Step 1 Place 100 o the inner scale under 'IMP GAL' on the outer scale

Step 2 Under '72' on the Sp G. lbs scale, locate 72lbs on the innder scale

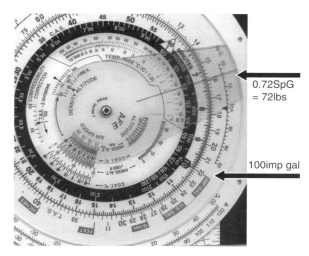

0.72SpG = 72lbs

100imp gal

►Crosswind Component

To find crosswind component on the flight computer:

Example: the surface wind direction is 240° at 15 knots and a pilot has a maximum allowable crosswind component for landing of 10 knots. What is the maximum angle by which the runway direction can differ to this surface w/v before this limit is reached?

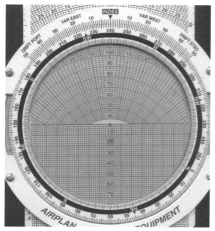

Step 1 Place the wind direction under the 'INDEX' mark. With the centre dot at the top of the wind grid, mark the wind speed.

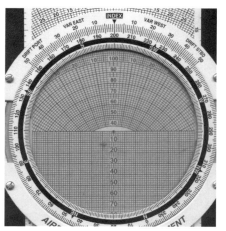

Step 2 Rotate the plotting disc to the right until the wind mark reaches the 10 knots maximum allowable crosswind component – this will occur with a direction of around 200°.

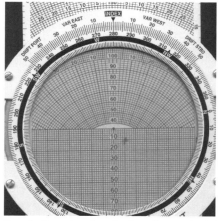

Step 3 Rotating the plotting disc to the left, the 10 knot crosswind limit is reached at 280°.

Therefore, in the stated surface wind the maximum allowable difference between wind direction and runway direction is 40°, namely runway directions 20 to 28.

▶ Radio Navigation

QDM	The aircraft's **magnetic track to** the station – the magnetic heading, if there was no wind, to take the aircraft to the station
QDR	The aircraft's **magnetic track from** the station
QUJ	The aircraft's **true track to** the station.
QTE	The aircraft's **true track from** the station.

The accuracy of VDF bearings:

Class A	Accuracy ±2°
Class B	Accuracy ±5°
Class C	Accuracy ±10°
Class D	Accuracy worse than class C

Radar operates at high radio frequencies and follows the 'line of sight' principle. An object over the horizon, or very close to the ground, may not reflect an echo back to the radar station. The range of radar can be increased by placing it on a high point, and a high-flying aircraft can be 'seen' by radar at a greater range than a low-flying one. **Secondary Surveillance Radar** (SSR) can usually detect an aircraft at lower altitudes and greater range than a 'primary' radar unit in the same location. SSR requires a transponder in the aircraft as well as a plan position indicator on the ground.

Low frequency (LF) or medium frequency (MF) signals from a **Non-Directional Beacon** (**NDB**) are received by an aircraft receiver called an **Automatic Direction Finder** (**ADF**). The needle of the associated **Relative Bearing Indicator** (**RBI**) points directly to the beacon, showing its direction relative to the aircraft's heading. To convert the RBI direction into a QDM or QDR, the relative bearing must be added or subtracted from the aircraft's magnetic heading.

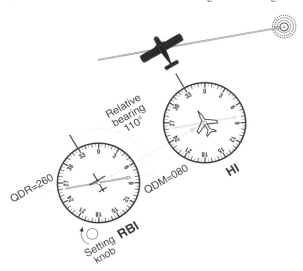

The promulgated **range of an NDB** is valid by day only. LF and MF radio waves can be subject to errors such as coastal refraction, thunderstorm effect and night effect.

VHF signals from a **VHF Omni-directional Range** (**VOR**) station are receiver at the aircraft's OR receiver and most often displayed on an **Omni Bearing Selector** (**OBS**). When the **Course Deviation Indicator** (**CDI**) needle is centred, the OBS is displaying either the QDM to, or QDR from the VOR station. The 'To/From' ambiguity is resolved by the 'To/From' flag.

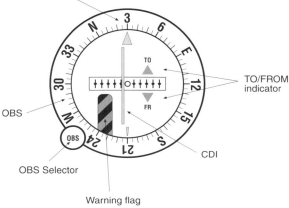

VOR

The OBS display is not affected by aircraft heading.

VHF transmission accuracy and range can be affected by site and propagation error, the height of the transmitting station and the altitude and distance of the receiving station.

Distance Measuring Equipment (**DME**) measures and displays the direct distance between the aircraft and the DME station – known as 'slant' range. The Time To Station (TTS) function of DME is only reliable when the aircraft is flying directly towards a DME.

JAA Private Pilot Licence – Aeroplanes

Navigation

Time allowed: 90 minutes

No. of questions: 25

Total Marks: 100

Instructions:

The paper consists of 25 multiple choice questions, each carries 4 marks. The pass mark is 75% (i.e. 19 questions or more must be answered correctly). Marks are not deducted for incorrect answers.

Be sure to carefully read each question and ensure that you understand it before considering the answer choices. Only one of the answers is complete and correct; the others are either incomplete, incorrect or based on a misconception.

You should indicate the correct answer by placing a cross in the appropriate box of the answer sheet. If you decide to change an answer, you should erase the original choice and put a cross in the box representing your new selection.

Each question has an average answer time of 3 minutes 36 seconds. No credit is given for unanswered questions.

Navigation Practice – Paper 1

It is planned to carry out a VFR flight from Chichester/ Goodwood (N5051.57 W00045.55) to Shobdon (N5214.50 W00252.88) via a turning point over the disused airfield at Grove (N5136.28 W00126.09). The destination alternate is Woonton (N5209.72 W00256.74).

Complete the attached flight plan using a CAA 1:500,000 chart and answer questions 1 to 20 below.

---

1. The magnetic heading from Chichester/Goodwood to Grove is:

(a) 337°

(b) 316°

(c) 327°

(d) 322°

---

2. The groundspeed from Chichester/Goodwood to Grove is:

(a) 89kts

(b) 80kts

(c) 71kts

(d) 93kts

---

3. The magnetic heading from Grove to Shobdon is:

(a) 330°

(b) 303°

(c) 297°

(d) 318°

---

4. The total distance from Chichester/Goodwood to Shobdon is:

(a) 113 nautical miles

(b) 116 nautical miles

(c) 117 statute miles

(d) 121 nautical miles

---

5. The magnetic heading from Shobdon to Woonton is:

(a) 205°

(b) 211°

(c) 216°

(d) 229°

6. Given:

– an allowance of 2 imperial gallons for start, taxy, power checks and take-off;

– flight plan time of 1 hour 30 minutes, additionally a diversion of 10 minutes to the destination alternate; at a fuel consumption of 9 imperial gallons per hour;

– an allowance of 2 imperial gallons for approach, landing and/or missed approach; and

– a reserve required of 5 imperial gallons when overhead the destination alternate,

Select the answer which gives the minimum fuel required for this flight (rounded up to the nearest gallon), in imperial gallons:

(a) 21

(b) 28

(c) 30

(d) 24

7. Based on the following information, what is the maximum payload (i.e. passengers, baggage etc.) that can be carried?

Basic (empty) weight	1200lbs
Pilot	180lbs
Fuel 42 imperial gallons (specific gravity 0.72)	
Maximum Total Weight Authorised (MTWA)	2400lbs

(a) 718lbs

(b) 1318lbs

(c) 848lbs

(d) 988lbs

8. An aircraft has a maximum crosswind component of 15kts. If the surface wind speed is 25kts, select the maximum angle (in degrees) by which the wind can differ from the runway direction before the maximum crosswind component is reached:

(a) 55°

(b) 25°

(c) 35°

(d) 45°

9. On a CAA 1:500,000 aeronautical chart, within quadrangles bounded by lines for every half degree of latitude and longitude, there are two-digit numbers in blue. This number represents:

(a) A safety altitude, in thousands and hundreds of feet agl, within that area

(b) The magnetic variation, in degrees (large number) and tenths of a degree (small number) within that area

(c) The bearing, to the nearest ten degrees, of the nearest diversion airfield within that area

(d) A Maximum Elevation Figure, the altitude in thousands (large number) and hundreds (small number) of feet amsl representing the highest known terrain and obstacle within that area

Airborne time is 1300 UTC. Heading is set over Chichester/Goodwood at 1305 UTC.

10. Approaching Alton you are unable to contact Farnborough for Odiham MATZ crossing although the time is within published hours of watch of the Farnborough ATSU. The best course of action is to:

    (a) Continue on course, it is not a legal requirement to obtain permission to cross a MATZ

    (b) Alter heading to the left to avoid Odiham MATZ

    (c) Alter heading to the right to avoid Odiham MATZ

    (d) Descend to 2,000ft amsl and route directly over Odiham airfield

11. On the CAA 1:500,000 aeronautical chart, what is located at 5118·3N 00114·5W?

    (a) Greenham Common disused airfield

    (b) A motorway service area

    (c) An obstacle (lighted), elevation 1247ft

    (d) A racecourse

12. On the leg from Grove to Shobdon, having held your planned heading, you establish your position as overhead Windrush airfield (N5148 W00144). Assuming no further change of wind velocity, what heading alteration is needed to fly to Shobdon?

    (a) 12° Port

    (b) 12° Starboard

    (c) 15° Port

    (d) 10° Port

13. Due to weather you plan to route significantly to the north of your planned route, and notice that your new routing will take you into the vicinity of Restricted area R204 (approximately 15nm North East of Cheltenham). Are you required to avoid this area:

    (a) Only if you are flying a helicopter or microlight

    (b) Only if you are flying above 2200ft AGL

    (c) Only if you are flying a glider or microlight

    (d) Only if you have munitions of war on board

14. In transit through the Oxford AIAA, aircraft should:

    (a) Maintain contact with Oxford Approach on 125.325MHz

    (b) Maintain contact with London FIS on 124.75MHz

    (c) Maintain contact with Brize Radar on 124.275MHz

    (d) Maintain contact with Brize Zone on 120.90kHz

15. You are overhead Grove at 1345 UTC and the remaining fuel is 18 imperial gallons. Assuming flight plan time from Grove to Shobdon, with a consumption of 5 imperial gallons/hour, what will be the remaining endurance (allowing a reserve of 5 imperial gallons) on arrival overhead Shobdon?

(a) 1 hour 18 minutes

(b) 1 hour 41 minutes

(c) 1 hour 58 minutes

(d) 1 hour 30 minutes

16. Your time overhead Grove was 13:45. At 14:21 you confirm your position as overhead the airfield at Berrow (approx. 9nm north west of Gloucestershire airfield). Using your groundspeed to this point, what is your revised ETA for Shobdon?

(a) 14:29

(b) 14:33

(c) 14:38

(d) 14:42

17. Your route passes overhead the town of Cheltenham. What would be the most suitable minimum altitude for over-flying Cheltenham?

(a) 500ft QNH

(b) 1000ft QNH

(c) 2500ft QNH

(d) 1500ft QNH

18. You will be passing just north of Gloucestershire airport (N5153.65 W00210.03) at 2,700ft. Which of the following courses of action is most appropriate?

(a) You are strongly recommended to contact Gloucestershire at least 10nm before reaching their overhead

(b) There is no need to contact Gloucestershire as you will be just above their ATZ

(c) You may cross the Gloucestershire ATZ without making contact as it is class G airspace

(d) If you cannot contact Gloucestershire, you may assume the ATZ is inactive

19. What is the elevation of Shobdon airfield?

(a) 123·5ft QNH

(b) 426ft QNH

(c) 317ft QNH

(d) 123·5ft QFE

20. Approximately nine miles SSE of Shobdon is a red circle centred on Credenhill, and denoted:

D216/2.3

OCNL/FL10.0

This area is best described as:

(a) A demilitarised zone, effective from 2300ft amsl to FL10

(b) A denied area, effective from 216ft to 2300ft agl

(c) A danger area, designator 216, with a radius of 2.3nm and active to 10,000ft amsl

(d) A danger area, designator 216, normally active from surface to 2300ft amsl, occasionally (with NOTAM notification) active to 10,000ft amsl

21. Which of the following radio navigation aids operate in the VHF band?

(a) VOR

(b) DME

(c) GPS

(d) NDB

22. An aircraft is located on the 165° radial from a VOR station. In order to track towards the VOR station, with the Course Deviation Indicator (CDI) operating in the natural sense, the Omni Bearing Selector (OBS) should be set to:

(a) 165°, TO flag

(b) 165°, FROM flag

(c) 345°, TO flag

(d) 345°, FROM flag

23. Which of the following effects will degrade the accuracy and range of a VHF transmission:

(i) Site and propagation error caused by terrain and buildings

(ii) Coastal refraction

(iii) Height of the VHF ground station

(iv) Night effect

(v) Thunderstorm effect

(vi) Altitude and distance of the receiving station

(a) All of the above

(b) (i), (iii) and (vi)

(c) (i), (ii), (iii) and (vi)

(d) (i), (ii), (v) and (vi)

24. If the antenna of a primary radar is set higher above surrounding terrain and obstacles, the principle effect will be to:

(a) Decrease atmospheric interference

(b) Increase the radar range

(c) Allow secondary radar information to be received

(d) Reduce the radar range

25. Secondary Surveillance Radar (SSR) equipment includes a ….(i)…. in the aircraft and a ….(ii)….. on the ground:

	(i)	(ii)
(a)	Transponder	Plan Position Indicator
(b)	DME	Transponder
(c)	Transponder	DME station
(d)	ADF	Transponder

From	To	FL/Alt	MSA	TAS	W/V	Trk (T)	Drift	Hdg (T)	Varn.	Hdg (M)	G/S	DIST	Time
Goodwood	Grove	3000	2300	85	250/20				3°W				
Grove	Shobdon	3500	2700	85	270/15				3°W				

Alternate

| Shobdon | Woonton | As req | 2700 | 85 | 270/15 | | | | 3°W | | | | |

Navigation Practice – Paper 2

It is planned to carry out a VFR flight from Shoreham (N5050.13 W00017.83) to Stapleford (N5139.15 E00009.35) via a turning point at Canterbury (N5116.73 E00104.73).

The destination alternate is North Weald (N5143.30 E000009.25).

Complete the attached flight plan using a CAA 1:500,000 chart and answer questions 1 to 20 below.

---

1. The magnetic heading from Shoreham to Canterbury is:

(a) 065°

(b) 071°

(c) 067°

(d) 074°

---

2. The groundspeed from Shoreham to Canterbury is:

(a) 89kts

(b) 85kts

(c) 95kts

(d) 82kts

---

3. The magnetic heading from Canterbury to Stapleford is:

(a) 300°

(b) 305°

(c) 293°

(d) 298°

---

4. The total flight time from Shoreham to Stapleford is:

(a) 57 minutes

(b) 1 hour 2 minutes

(c) 1 hour 7 minutes

(d) 1 hour 10 minutes

---

5. The magnetic heading from Stapleford to North Weald is:

(a) 010°

(b) 007°

(c) 358°

(d) 001°

6. Given:
– an allowance of 3 US gallons for start, taxy, power checks and take-off;
– flight plan time of 1 hour 50 minutes, additionally a diversion of 15 minutes to the destination alternate; at a fuel consumption of 9 US gallons per hour;
– an allowance of 2 US gallons for approach, landing and/or missed approach; and
– a reserve required of 7 US gallons when overhead the destination alternate,
Select the answer which gives the minimum fuel required for this flight (rounded up to the nearest gallon), in US gallons:

(a) 27

(b) 33

(c) 29

(d) 31

---

7. Based on the following information, what is the maximum payload (i.e. passengers, baggage etc.) that can be carried?

Basic (empty) weight	1300lbs
Pilot	170lbs
Fuel 40 US gallons (specific gravity 0.72)	
Maximum Total Weight Authorised (MTWA)	2300lbs

(a) 650lbs

(b) 590lbs

(c) 630lbs

(d) 570lbs

---

8. What activity takes place at position 5052·3N 00013·0W?

(a) Hang/Para gliding, with winch launching up to 2700ft amsl

(b) Parham gliding site, with winch launching up to 2200ft amsl

(c) Parham gliding site, gliding up to 2200ft amsl

(d) Deanland civil aerodrome, with limited or no facilities

---

9. The symbols at Shoreham airfield on the CAA 1:500,000 chart indicate that:

(a) It is a military aerodrome with a Military Aerodrome Traffic Zone (MATZ)

(b) It is a civil aerodrome with an elevation of 289ft

(c) It is a civil aerodrome with an Aerodrome Traffic Zone (ATZ) and customs facilities

(d) It is a military aerodrome limited to 7 civilian movements per day

Airborne time is 1100 UTC, and heading is set overhead Shoreham at 1105 UTC
Assume that Challock gliding site is inactive for the purposes of this flight.

10. For that part of the flight that routes between Uckfield (N5058.31 E00005.95) and Mayfield (N5101 E00015.85), flight can be carried out, avoiding controlled airspace, at:

    (a) 2400ft Shoreham QNH

    (b) 2400ft Gatwick QNH

    (c) 3400ft Gatwick QNH

    (d) 2400ft Gatwick QFE

11. For that section of the first leg between Challock and Canterbury, if the QNH is 1000mb, what is the lowest available flight level that complies with the quadrantal rule?

    (a) FL30

    (b) FL50

    (c) FL35

    (d) FL55

12. Approaching Lashenden/Headcorn airfield (N5109.42 E00038.50) you are unable to make contact with the Air/Ground Communication Service (AGCS), although you are within the notified hours of watch of the AGCS radio station. The best course of action is to:

    (a) Continue on track, climbing to 3500ft, maintain radio silence

    (b) Turn left towards Maidstone, climb to FL55, contact Gatwick Approach 126.825MHz

    (c) Turn right towards Ashford, remain not above 3400ft amsl, contact London FIS on 124.6MHz

    (d) Continue on track at any level up to 3500ft amsl.

13. If Challock gliding site (N5112.50 E00049.75) was active, up to what maximum altitude could you expect to encounter winch launching?

    (a) 260ft

    (b) 600ft

    (c) 597ft

    (d) 2600ft

14. On a CAA 1:500 000 aeronautical chart, the symbol at position N5128.50 E00036.00 represents:

    (a) Stoke microlight airfield

    (b) A Visual Reference Point, pilots can report position in relation to this point

    (c) An obstruction (power station) with an elevation of 654ft

    (d) A large industrial area

15. Overhead Canterbury the aircraft has 74 litres of fuel remaining on board. Based on a consumption of 30 litres per hour, and allowing flight plan time plus a ten minute diversion to the alternate, what will be the remaining endurance (allowing for a reserve of 25 litres) on arrival at the alternate:

(a) 58 minutes

(b) 1 hour and 12 minutes

(c) 1 hour and 2 minutes

(d) 1 hour and 6 minutes

16. On the leg from Canterbury to Stapleford, after flying 20nm you locate your position as overhead the power station 2.5nm south west of Stoke microlight site (with the obstruction top 654ft amsl). What course correction is required to fly directly to Stapleford?

(a) 9° port

(b) 9° starboard

(c) 17° starboard

(d) 15° port

17. You are now in the vicinity of Danger area D146. Which of the following statements is true in relation to this Danger area?

(a) It applies only to helicopters and microlights

(b) A Danger Area Crossing Service (DACS) is available from Southend Approach on 130.775

(c) A Danger Area Activity Information Service (DAAIS) is available

(d) If unable to contact the nominated ATSU, you may assume the Danger area is inactive

18. You are over head St Marys Marsh VRP at 3300ft, on track towards Stapleford, and you wish to descend to be level at 2200ft 3nm before reaching the boundary of the London TMA where the base drops to 2500ft. The groundspeed in the descent will be 105 knots

What minimum rate of descent is required to achieve this descent profile?

(a) 115ft/min

(b) 275ft/min

(c) 245ft/min

(d) 195ft/min

Refer to the Aeronautical Information Publication extract at Appendix A (page 125) and answer questions 19 and 20

19. The Stapleford ATS contact frequency and callsign is:

(a) 122·8; Stapleford ATZ

(b) 122·8; Stapleford Information

(c) 0900-1800; Stapleford radio

(d) 122·8; Stapleford Radio

20. What are the correct dimensions of the Stapleford Aerodrome Traffic Zone (ATZ)?

(a) 2nm radius, surface to 2000ft above mean sea level

(b) 2km radius, surface to 2000ft above mean sea level

(c) 2nm diameter, surface to 2000ft above aerodrome level

(d) 2nm radius, surface to 2000ft above aerodrome level

21. The particular item of aircraft radio navigation equipment which measures the phase difference between two signals from a ground station is a:

(a) Secondary Surveillance Radar (SSR)

(b) VHF Omni-directional Range (VOR)

(c) Distance Measuring Equipment (DME)

(d) Global Positioning System (GPS)

22. VOR operates in the ....(i).... band and its transmissions are subject to ....(ii)....

	(i)	(ii)
(a)	VHF	Night effect
(b)	LF	Site and propagation error
(c)	EHF	Thunderstorm effect
(d)	VHF	Site and propagation error

23. An aircraft is tracking directly away from an NDB on a QDR of 290° and experiencing 10° of port drift. The relative bearing of the NDB as indicated by the needle of the Relative Bearing Indicator (RBI) is:

(a) 170°

(b) 190°

(c) 290°

(d) 280°

24. An aircraft is located on the 150° radial of a VOR. If the pilot wishes to track directly towards the VOR, for the Course Deviation Indicator (CDI) to give indications in the correct sense, it should be set to:

(a) 150° FROM

(b) 150° TO

(c) 330° TO

(d) 330° FROM

25. When a pilot selects a Secondary Surveillance Radar (SSR) code on the aircraft's transponder, this information:

(a) Is displayed on all radar screens covering the area

(b) Can be displayed only to the controller communicating with the aircraft

(c) Appears at a suitably equipped ATSU, on the Plan Position Indicator next to the aircraft's 'primary' radar return

(d) Appears at all ATSUs within VHF range, on the Cathode Ray Tube also used for displaying VDF information

From	To	FL/Alt	MSA	TAS	W/V	Trk (T)	Drift	Hdg (T)	Varn.	Hdg (M)	G/S	DIST	Time
Shoreham	Canterbury	2400	2200	85	175/15				2°W				
Canterbury	Stapleford	2400	1900	85	190/20				2°W				

Alternate

Stapleford	North Weald	1400	1800	85	190/20				2°W				

Appendix A: UK AIP, Stapleford

UK AIP	STAPLEFORD	(20 Dec 07) AD 2-EGSG-1-3

EGSG AD 2.17 – ATS AIRSPACE

Designation and lateral limits	Vertical limits	Airspace Classification
1	2	3
Stapleford Aerodrome Traffic Zone (ATZ) Circle radius 2 nm centred on longest notified runway (04R/22L) 513909N 0000922E.	2000 ft aal SFC	G †

4	ATS unit callsign: Language:	Stapleford Radio. English.
6	Remarks:	ATZ Hours: See AD 2.18. † Refer to Section ENR 1.4 for Notifications.

EGSG AD 2.18 – ATS COMMUNICATION FACILITIES

Service Designation	Callsign	Frequency MHz	Hours of Operation Winter	Summer	Remarks
1	2	3	4		5
A/G	Stapleford Radio	122.800	0900-1800	0800-1700	ATZ hours co-incident with A/G hours.

EGSG AD 2.19 – RADIO NAVIGATION AND LANDING AIDS

VOR/DME LAM see ENR 4.1 for details.

EGSG AD 2.20 – LOCAL TRAFFIC REGULATIONS

4   **Warnings**

a Caution is necessary when operating from Runway 04/22 because of a radio mast 295 ft aal Southwest of the aerodrome and 1 nm from Runway 04R threshold.

b Caution is necessary as the aerodrome is used heavily for flying training.

c Not all taxiways are available for use. Pilots are warned that departure from the marked movement area can be hazardous.

EGSG AD 2.21 – NOISE ABATEMENT PROCEDURES

Pilots of aircraft are requested to avoid overflying the villages of Abridge and Lambourne below 1000 ft agl.

EGSG AD 2.22 – FLIGHT PROCEDURES

a Circuits normally LH.

b Runway 28 departures. Aircraft should maintain the runway heading until passing 1000 ft agl.

c Runway 22 departures. Right turnout on request.

Navigation Practice – Paper 3

It is planned to carry out a VFR flight from Gloucestershire airport (N5153.65 W00210.03) to Cambridge (N5212.30 E00010.50) via a turning point at Northampton Sywell (N5218.32 W00047.57).

The destination alternate is Duxford (N5205.45 E00007.92)

Complete the attached flight plan using a CAA 1:500,000 chart and answer questions 1 to 20 below.

---

1. The magnetic heading from Gloucestershire to Northampton Sywell is:

(a) 076°

(b) 079°

(c) 064°

(d) 103°

---

2. The groundspeed from Gloucestershire to Northampton Sywell is:

(a) 103kts

(b) 81kts

(c) 92kts

(d) 99kts

---

3. The magnetic heading from Northampton Sywell to Cambridge is:

(a) 099°

(b) 110°

(c) 113°

(d) 102°

---

4. The flight time from Gloucestershire to Cambridge is:

(a) 58 minutes

(b) 1 hour 4 minutes

(c) 1 hour 7 minutes

(d) 1 hour 32 minutes

---

5. The flight plan distance from Gloucestershire to Cambridge is:

(a) 99nm

(b) 88nm

(c) 58nm

(d) 92nm

6. Given:
   – an allowance of 10 litres for start, taxy, power checks and take-off;
   – flight plan time of 1 hour 40 minutes, additionally a diversion of 10 minutes to the destination alternate; at a fuel consumption of 28 litres per hour;
   – an allowance of 8 litres for approach, landing and/or missed approach; and
   – a reserve required of 25 litres when overhead the destination alternate,
   Select the answer which gives the minimum fuel required for this flight (rounded up to the nearest litre), in litres:

   (a) 99

   (b) 91

   (c) 86

   (d) 95

7. Based on the following information, what is the maximum payload (i.e. passengers, baggage etc.) that can be carried?

Basic (empty) weight	1150lbs
Pilot	175lbs
Fuel 35 US gallons (specific gravity 0.72)	
Maximum Total Weight Authorised (MTWA)	2200lbs

   (a) 650lbs

   (b) 665lbs

   (c) 630lbs

   (d) 705lbs

8. An aircraft has a maximum crosswind component of 12kts. If the surface wind speed is 20kts, select the maximum angle (in degrees) by which the wind can differ from the runway direction before the maximum crosswind component is reached:

   (a) 55°

   (b) 25°

   (c) 35°

   (d) 45°

9. On a CAA 1:500,000 aeronautical chart, within each quadrangles bound by lines for every half degree of latitude and longitude, there is a two-digit number in blue. This number represents:

   (a) A Mean Elevation Figure, the altitude in thousands (large number) and hundreds (small number) of feet amsl representing the average terrain and obstacle elevation within that area

   (b) A Minimum Elevation Figure, the altitude in thousands (large number) and hundreds (small number) of feet amsl representing the lowest known terrain and obstacle within that area

   (c) A Maximum Elevation Figure, the altitude in thousands (large number) and hundreds (small number) of feet amsl representing the safety altitude within that area

   (d) A Maximum Elevation Figure, the altitude in thousands (large number) and hundreds (small number) of feet amsl representing the highest known terrain and obstacle within that area

10. If the leg from Gloucestershire to Northampton/Sywell is to be conducted at the highest available quadrantal level (without entering controlled airspace), and the QNH is 1021, that correct level will be:

(a) FL35

(b) FL30

(c) FL50

(d) FL40

11. On the first leg, you establish your position as overhead Long Marston (N5208.44 W00145.18). How much and in what direction would you alter heading to regain track at Northampton/Sywell?

(a) 17° right

(b) 26° right

(c) 20° left

(d) 22° right

12. The meaning of the symbol on the CAA 1:500,000 aeronautical chart centred at around 5221.30N 00038.5W is:

(a) A military helipad

(b) The Windfarm airfield ATZ

(c) A windfarm with 617 turbines, maximum elevation 328ft

(d) A windfarm (turbines), with a maximum elevation of 617ft

13. Overhead Northampton Sywell fuel remaining is 70 litres. Assuming fuel consumption of 30 litres per hour, flight plan time to Cambridge, plus 10 minutes diversion to the alternate and a reserve of 25 litres, what will be the remaining endurance at the alternate?

(a) 1 hour 45 minutes

(b) 1 hour 8 minutes

(c) 43 minutes

(d) 55 minutes

14. You are overhead Northampton Sywell at 11·13. You fix your position as overhead the mast 1nm north east of Little Staughton airfield at 11·27. What is your ETA for Cambridge?

(a) 11·39

(b) 11·43

(c) 11·49

(d) 11·53

15. 18nm from Cambridge (i.e. when crossing the A1(M)) the aircraft is at 5000ft amsl. In order to descend to 2000ft amsl before crossing the M11 (4nm from Cambridge), what is the minimum rate of decent required? The groundspeed in the decent will be 105 knots.

(a) 375 feet per minute

(b) 225 feet per minute

(c) 445 feet per minute

(d) 270 feet per minute

16. Approximately 10 miles to the north-east of Cambridge is a large area of airspace with a blue dotted boundary and blue shading. This airspace is:

(a) An enlarged civilian Aerodrome Traffic Zone, contact frequency 115.9

(b) A Civil/Military Aerodrome Traffic Zone with a contact frequency of 128.9

(c) A Combined Military Aerodrome Traffic Zone with a contact frequency of 128.9

(d) The Ely Area of Intense Aerial Activity Zone, with a contact frequency of 128.9

17. Just to the south of track, approximately 3nm south west of Bourn airfield is the gliding site of Gransden Lodge. The maximum level of winch launching at this site is:

(a) 330ft agl

(b) 3300ft agl

(c) 3300ft amsl

(d) 2540ft amsl

Refer to the Aeronautical Information Publication extract at Appendix B (page 132) and answer questions 18 to 20

18. Because of recent heavy rain, aircraft requires a hard runway to land on. Which runway options are available?

(a) Runway 05

(b) Runway 10

(c) Runway 05/23

(d) None

19. What is the threshold elevation of hard runway 23?

(a) 35ft

(b) 151ft

(c) 47ft

(d) 47m

From overhead Cambridge at 3000ft QNH it is decided to divert to Duxford

20. Which of the Cambridge runways have displaced thresholds?

(a) Hard runway 05

(b) Grass runway 28

(c) Hard runway 23, grass runway 28

(d) Hard runways 05 and 23

21. A QUJ [i] and a QDM [ii] are best described as follows:

    [i]   [ii]

(a) A true track to a station   A true track from a station

(b) A true track from a station   A true track to a station

(c) A magnetic track to a station   A magnetic track from a station

(d) A true track to a station   A magnetic track to a station

---

22. An aircraft is tracking directly away from a Non Directional Beacon (NDB) maintaining a track of 050°, whilst experiencing 10° starboard drift. Under these circumstances, the nose of the needle of a Relative Bearing Indicator (RBI) will indicate a relative bearing to the NDB of:

(a) 190°

(b) 170°

(c) 240°

(d) 220°

---

23. An aircraft's transponder transmits:

(a) The aircraft's range and bearing from the ATSU it is in communication with

(b) Secondary Surveillance Radar (SSR) information, which is displayed on a radar screen

(c) The aircraft's range and bearing from the ATSU which gave the transponder code

(d) The aircraft's flight plan details

---

24. An aircraft's DME measures the:

(a) Ground distance to a DME station

(b) Route track to a DME station

(c) 'Slant' distance to a DME station

(d) Horizontal distance to a DME station

---

25. Which of the following radio navigation aids operate in the VHF band?

(a) VDF and VOR

(b) SSR and DME

(c) NDB and GPS

(d) NDB and VOR

From	To	FL/Alt	MSA	TAS	W/V	Trk (T)	Drift	Hdg (T)	Varn.	Hdg (M)	G/S	DIST	Time
Gloucestershire	Northampton Sywell	3000	2400	92	190/22				3°W				
Northampton Sywell	Cambridge	3000	1800	90	180/18				3°W				

Alternate

| Cambridge | Duxford | 2200 | 1800 | 90 | 180/18 | | | | 3°W | | | | |

Appendix B: UK AIP, Cambridge

AD 2-EGSC-1-4 (5 Jun 08)	CAMBRIDGE	UK AIP

EGSC AD 2.11 – METEOROLOGICAL INFORMATION PROVIDED

1	Associated MET Office:	Exeter.
2	Hours of service: MET Office outside hours:	H24.
3	Office responsible for TAF preparation: Periods of validity:	MET Office Exeter. 9 Hours.
4	Trend forecast: Interval of issuance:	
5	Briefing/consultation provided:	Self-briefing/Telephone.
6	Flight documentation: Language(s) used:	Charts, abbreviated plain language text. TAFs/METARs. English.
7	Charts and other information available for briefing or consultation:	
8	Supplementary equipment available for providing information:	
9	ATS units provided with information:	Cambridge.
10	Additional Information (limitation of service etc):	

EGSC AD 2.12 – RUNWAY PHYSICAL CHARACTERISTICS

Designations RWY Number	True bearing	Dimensions of RWY (m)	Strength (PCN) and surface of RWY and stopway	THR co-ordinates RWY end co-ordinates THR Geoid undulation	THR elevation Highest elevation of TDZ of precision APP RWY
1	2	3	4	5	6
05	049.88°	1965 x 46	42/R/C/X/T Concrete	521202.06N 0000959.14E – GUND 151 ft	THR 35 ft
23	229.89°	1965 x 46	42/R/C/X/T Concrete	521235.49N 0001103.71E – GUND 151 ft	THR 47 ft
05	049.91°	899 x 35	– Grass	521211.12N 0001032.14E – GUND 151 ft	THR 36 ft
23	229.92°	899 x 35	– Grass	521229.87N 0001108.40E – GUND 151 ft	THR 36 ft
10	099.89°	699 x 35	– Grass	521211.73N 0001007.18E – GUND 151 ft	THR 30 ft
28	279.89°	699 x 35	– Grass	521207.84N 0001043.49E – GUND 151 ft	THR 35 ft

Slope of RWY/SWY	Stopway Dimensions (m)	Clearway Dimensions (m)	Strip Dimensions (m)	OFZ
7	8	9	10	11
05 – 0.14% up	0	183 x 210	2124 x 300	
23 – 0.83% down first 400 m	0	161 x 210	2124 x 300	

12	Remarks:	Threshold displaced on Concrete Runway 05 by 216 m. Threshold displaced on Concrete Runway 23 by 145 m.

Paper 1 Answers and Explanations

ENP1Q1   Answer D

Firstly, the true track is found by measuring the direction of the line between Chichester/Goodwood and Grove. It is best to place the protractor about half-way along the track line in order to average the direction (330° True).

The wind velocity (250/20) is then entered onto the flight computer and used to find the true heading (illustrated below using the wind down method):

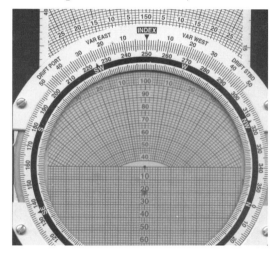

First the wind is entered onto the flight computer.

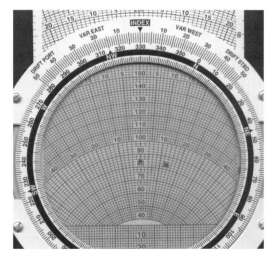

Then the centre dot is placed over the true air speed, and the heading disc rotated down to put the true track at the top.

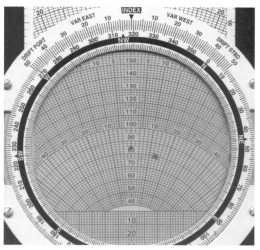

Rotate the heading dial down (turning the heading into the wind) until there is the same difference in degrees between track and heading at the wind cross and on the heading dial. At this point read off the true heading and groundspeed. Don't forget to allow for magnetic variation (given on the flight plan form); westerly variation is added to the true direction to give the magnetic direction.

The possible answers normally allow for a tolerance of up to 5°, so you may well have an answer a degree or so different to the correct answer, but still accurate enough for you to select the closest option. If your answer is very different to any of the options you should re-check your calculations, and also check that you have not accidentally used the true heading (instead of magnetic), or the track instead of heading, by mistake.

Further Reference: Flight Plan
PPL3 » Navigation » Aeronautical Maps » Measurement of Direction
PPL3 » Navigation » Navigation Principles: The Triangle of Velocities » Triangle of Velocity Calculations on the Flight Computer

ENP1Q2   Answer B

See explanation at ENP1Q1 for further information on how the groundspeed is found using the flight computer.

The possible answers normally allow for a tolerance of up to 5 knots, so you may well have an answer a few knots or so different to the correct answer, but still accurate enough for you to select the closest option. If your answer is very different to any of the options you should re-check your calculations.

Further Reference: Flight Plan; and PPL3 » Navigation » Aeronautical Maps » Scale and Distance
PPL3 » Navigation » Navigation Principles: The Triangle of Velocities » Triangle of Velocity Calculations on the Flight Computer

ENP1Q3   Answer B

Using the figures from the flight plan, and the 'wind down' method of calculation, the flight computer should end up looking like this:

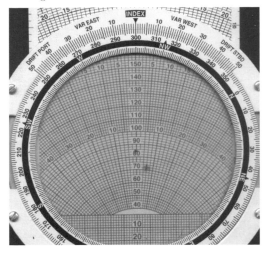

Do not forget to use the new wind velocity figures for the second leg, and do not forget to add the westerly variation in order to find the magnetic heading.

Further Reference; Flight Plan

PPL3 » Navigation » Aeronautical Maps » Measurement of Direction
PPL3 » Navigation » Navigation Principles: The Triangle of Velocities » Triangle of Velocity Calculations on the Flight Computer

ENP1Q4   Answer B

The normal tolerance in answer options is around 3 miles, so once again if your calculated answer is significantly different to all the options, re-checking your flight plan is in order. It is usual to plan distance in nautical miles, if the wind velocity and groundspeed are also in nautical miles (knots).

Further Reference; Flight Plan

PPL3 » Navigation » Aeronautical Maps » Scale and Distance
PPL3 » Navigation » Navigation Principles: The Triangle of Velocities » Triangle of Velocity Calculations on the Flight Computer
PPL3 » Navigation » Navigation Principles: Airspeed, Groundspeed Time and Distance » Time, Speed and Distance

ENP1Q5   Answer C

Using the wind down method, the flight computer set up to find this answer should look as below:

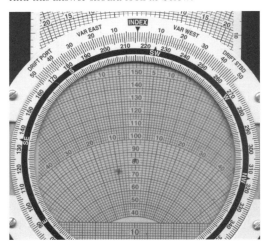

Further Reference: Flight Plan
PPL3 » Navigation » Aeronautical Maps » Measurement of Direction
PPL3 » Navigation » Navigation Principles: The Triangle of Velocities » Triangle of Velocity Calculations on the Flight Computer

ENP1Q6   Answer D

The tolerance on this question is around 2 to 3 imperial gallons. It is fairly simple to add up the given figures:

Start, taxy, power check and take-off	2
Approach, landing and/or missed approach	2
Reserve fuel	5
Sub total	9

The only flight computer calculation required is that for the flight plan time (1 hour 30 minutes plus 10 minutes diversion) = 1 hour 40 minutes. On the flight computer, 1 hour 40 minutes at 9 imperial gallons per hour = 15 imperial gallons.

9imp gal per hr

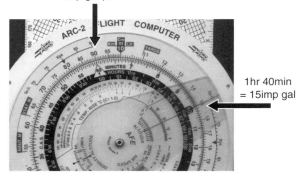

1hr 40min = 15imp gal

15 + 9 = 24 imperial gallons
Further Reference: PPL3 » Navigation » Flight Planning: Fuel Planning » Fuel Planning

ENP1Q7 Answer A

Firstly, the two weights given can be added together:

Basic (empty) weight	1200lbs
Pilot	180lbs
Sub-total	1380lbs

The weight of the fuel is calculated on a Flight Computer given the fuel volume and the specific gravity:

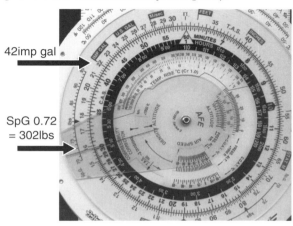

42imp gal

SpG 0.72 = 302lbs

Sub-total	302lbs

These weights total (1380 + 302) = 1682lbs.

2400 – 1682 = 718lbs

Therefore the maximum payload that can be carried, without exceeding the MTWA, is 718lbs.

Note that this calculation takes no account of balance, centre of gravity or loading restrictions.

Further Reference: PPL3 » Navigation » Flight Planning: Fuel Planning » Specific Gravity Calculation

ENP1Q8 Answer C

The maximum angle between wind direction and runway direction that can be reached before exceeding the maximum crosswind component (15 knots) is calculated on a Flight Computer as shown below:

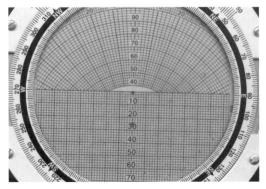

The wind speed is marked on the flight computer. To keep the calculation simple, place a direction of 000 under INDEX.

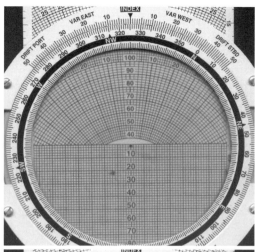

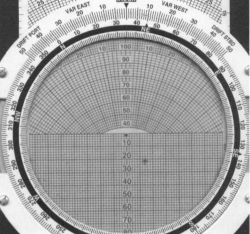

Now rotate the heading disc until the crosswind component reaches the maximum permitted (15kts). At the 15 knots crosswind component, the angle between heading and wind direction is 35°.

Further Reference: PPL3 » Navigation » Flight Planning: Performance » Crosswind Component

ENP1Q9   Answer D

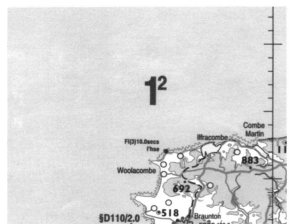

A Maximum Elevation Figure – MEF – represents the maximum possible elevation in thousands and hundreds of feet (altitude, amsl) of terrain, obstructions or unknown obstructions within the defined area. It is NOT a safety altitude, as it allows no safety margin above the highest terrain/obstruction.

Further Reference: PPL3 » Navigation » Vertical Navigation » Calculation of Minimum Safety Altitude

ENP1Q10   Answer B

Although it is not a legal requirement to obtain permission to enter a MATZ, it is clearly good airmanship to do so – the MATZ is there for a reason. Note also that crossing Odiham at 2000ft amsl would take the aircraft directly through the Odiham Aerodrome Traffic Zone (ATZ), which extends to 2000ft above the airfield – making 2405ft amsl in the case of Odiham. It IS a legal requirement to obtain permission to enter an active ATZ.

To avoid the MATZ is good airmanship, and altering heading to the left is the better option as this will take the aircraft less far off-course and into less congested airspace compared to altering heading to the right.

Further Reference: PPL3 » Navigation » Flight Planning: Summary » Radio Frequencies

PPL2 » UK Procedures » Airspace Restrictions and Hazards

UK AIM » Aeronautical Information Publication » ENR 2.2 Other Regulated Airspace – Military Aerodrome Traffic Zones

ENP1Q11   Answer C

The obstacle symbol is noted in the map key at the bottom of the chart. The bold figure below the obstruction symbol is the elevation of the obstacle Above Mean Sea Level (AMSL).

Further Reference: Study of map and map key

ENP1Q12   Answer C

Windrush is located 3nm to the right (starboard) of track after flying16nm from Grove. The Track Error (TE) that has occurred can be calculated by the formulae:

$$\frac{\text{Distance off-track}}{\text{Distance travelled}} \text{ x } 60$$

or

$$\frac{3}{16} \text{ x } 60 = 11.25°$$

Altering the heading by just the TE will only leave the aircraft flying parallel to the required heading. To reach the destination Closing Angle (CA) must be calculated:

$$\frac{\text{Distance off-track}}{\text{Distance to go}} \text{ x } 60$$

or

$$\frac{3}{48} \text{ x } 60 = 3.75°$$

TE (11.25) + CA (3.75) = total heading change required: 15°. The heading change is to port (the left) because the aircraft is currently right of track.

Further Reference: Study of map

PPL3 » Navigation » Practical Navigation: Off-Track Calculations and Track Markings » The One in Sixty Rule

ENP1Q13
Answer A

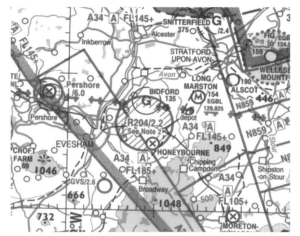

Restricted area R204 carries the notation on the chart 'See note 2'. This note, found with the key at the bottom of the chart, says that certain Restricted areas, including R204, apply only to helicopters and microlights.

Further Reference: Study of map and map key

UK AIM » Aeronautical Information Publication » ENR 1.1.5 Airspace Restrictions, Danger Areas and Hazards to Flight

ENP1Q14
Answer C

Pilots of aircraft unable to avoid an Area of Intense Aerial Activity (AIAA) are strongly advised to make use of a radar service if available. The appropriate contact frequency for the Oxford AIAA is printed on the charts and is given as 124.275. As with any other VHF communications frequency printed on a CAA chart, this frequency is in Megahertz –MHz.

Further Reference: Study of map including map key

PPL2 » Operational Procedures » Other Hazards to Flight

UK AIM » Aeronautical Information Publication » ENR 1.1.5.2 Hazards to Flight

ENP1Q15
Answer B

Flight plan time Grove to Shobdon is 55 minutes. 55 minutes at a consumption of 5 imperial gallons per hour = 4.6 imperial gallons.

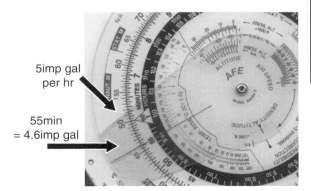

This fuel used to get to Shobdon, (4.6) is deducted from fuel on board (18) leaving 13.4 imperial gallons when overhead Shobdon.

From this figure (13.4), the fuel reserve (5 imperial gallons) is deducted, leaving 8.4 imperial gallons.

At 5 imperial gallons per hour, 8.4 imperial gallons = 1 hour and 41 minutes endurance before reaching the 5 imperial gallon reserve.

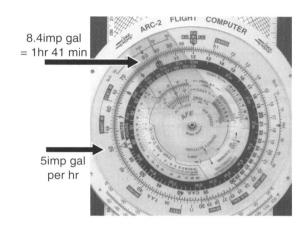

Further Reference: Flight plan

PPL3 » Navigation » Flight Planning: Fuel Planning » Fuel Planning

ENP1Q16
Answer D

The distance from Grove to Berrow is 41nm. This distance has been covered in 36 minutes, which on the flight computer equates to a groundspeed of 68 knots.

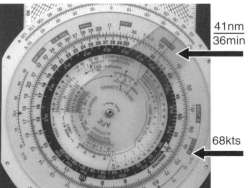

The distance remaining from Berrow to Shobdon is 24nm. At a groundspeed of 68 knots, this distance will be covered in 21 minutes.

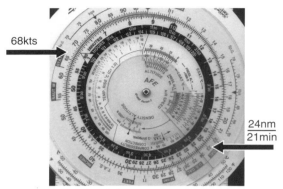

Remember, time is on the inner scale, distance is on the outer scale

Current time (14:21) + time to go (21 minutes) gives an ETA of 14:42

Further Reference: Study of map and flight plan

PPL3 » Navigation » Navigation Principles: Airspeed, Groundspeed, Time and Distance » Time, Speed and Distance

ENP1Q17   Answer C

The minimum level for flight over a 'congested area' is 1000ft above the highest fixed object within 600m or high enough to glide clear, whichever is higher.

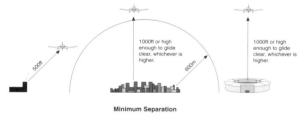

Minimum Separation

On a CAA 1:500,000 chart it is possible for there to be an obstruction 299ft above ground level that is not marked on the chart. It is further possible for there to be terrain up to 499ft above sea level that is not marked by a contour line, elevation tint or spot height. This leaves the possibility of there being an unmarked obstruction 798ft (299ft + 499ft) above mean sea level. This indicates a minimum altitude of 1800ft to comply with the '1000ft' minimum height rule, let alone any additional altitude required to glide clear of the 'congested area' of Cheltenham in the event of a powerplant failure.

Note also that the track passes close to two spot heights of almost 1000ft amsl (978 and 968) just before passing over Cheltenham.

Further reference: Study of map and map key

PPL3 » Navigation » Vertical Navigation » Calculation of Minimum Safety Altitude

UK AIM » Air Navigation Order (Rules of the Air) » Rule 5: Low flying prohibitions

ENP1Q18   Answer A

An Aerodrome Traffic Zone extends up to 2000ft above aerodrome level. Therefore, with an elevation of 101ft, Gloucestershire's ATZ extends to 2101ft amsl. It is true that at 2,700ft amsl you will be above the ATZ, but as a matter of airmanship it would be a poor decision to refuse to contact Gloucestershire when flying this close. The ATZ is active during the notified hours of watch of the ATC/AFIS unit, even if they cannot be contacted.

Further, the strong recommendation to contact Gloucestershire is based not just on its ATZ, but specifically on its Instrument Approach Procedures (IAPs) outside controlled airspace – indicated by the chevroned cones extending to the west and east of the airfield. Your track crosses one of these IAPs, and according to the map key relating to ATZs (which is usually a vertical panel on the left-hand side of the chart), pilots are strongly recommended to contact an airfield's ATSU if flying within 10nm of an airfield with an IAP outside controlled airspace.

Further Reference: PPL2 » Air Law » Rules of the Air » Aerodrome Traffic Zones and Map Key

ENP1Q19   Answer C

The elevation of Shobdon airfield is marked on the chart and, because it is an elevation (meaning a vertical distance Above Mean Sea Level – AMSL), it is measured using QNH – because when the QNH pressure setting is put on the altimeter subscale, the altimeter displays altitude above mean sea level.

In the example used in this question, the airfield elevation should not be confused with the NDB frequency (426) or the radio frequency (123·5).

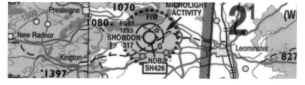

Further reference: Study of map and map key

PPL3 » Navigation » Vertical Navigation » Checking the Altimeter

ENP1Q20   Answer D

D stands for **D**anger area, there are also **R**estricted areas (**R**) and **P**rohibited areas (**P**).

216 is the danger area designator, its details can be found in the UK Aeronautical Information Publication (AIP) and some flight guides.

2.3 is the upper limit in 1000s of feet above mean sea level (amsl). All danger areas start at the surface.

OCNL/10.0 indicates that occasionally (with NOTAM notification) the danger area extends up to 10,000ft amsl.

Questions regarding map symbols can usually be answered by checking the key usually printed at the bottom, or the side, of the chart.

Further Reference: Map Key

ENP1Q21   Answer A

This can be remembered simply by knowing what the abbreviation 'VOR' stands for, namely:

VOR   VHF **O**mni-directional **R**ange

Further Reference: PPL3 » Navigation » Radio Navigation » VHF Omni-directional Range

UK AIM » Aeronautical Information Publication » GEN3.4.3.1 Radio Navigation Services

ENP1Q22   Answer C

If the aircraft is located on the 165° radial, it is on a bearing of 165° FROM the VOR station.

In order to track directly towards the VOR station the aircraft needs to fly the reciprocal course directly towards the station. 165° + 180° = 345°. For the CDI needle to operate in the correct sense (ie show correct 'fly left' or 'fly right' indications), the 'TO' flag must be showing when tracking towards the station.

345°

Further Reference: PPL3 » Navigation » Radio Navigation » VHF Omni-directional Range (VOR)

ENP1Q23   Answer B

Aircraft is too low to receive a reliable signal from the VOR station. Increasing the height of the VOR or receiving station, will increase the range.

VHF transmission accuracy and range can be affected by site and propagation error, the height of the transmitting station and the altitude and distance of the receiving station.

Errors such as coastal refraction, thunderstorm effect and night effect do not effect VHF transmissions such as those of a VOR station, but do effect lower frequency transmissions, such as those in the LF and MF bands.

Further Reference: PPL3 » Navigation » Radio Navigation » Ground Direction Finding (DF)

UK AIM » Aeronautical Information Publication » GEN3.4.3.1 Radio Navigation Services

ENP1Q24   Answer B

Radar operates at radio frequencies where the radio waves operates on the 'line of sight' principle. It follows that if the radar antenna is placed higher above the local terrain and obstacles, it will be able to 'see' further and so radar range is increased.

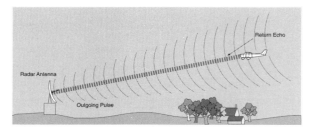

Further reference: PPL3 » Navigation » Radio Navigation » Ground Radar

ENP1Q25   Answer A

The transponder is the aircraft-based element of Secondary Surveillance Radar that returns the coded pulse sent by the ground-based system. The Plan Position Indicator (PPI) is the radar screen used by the controller, where the SSR information from the aircraft's transponder is displayed next to the aircraft's 'primary' radar return.

Further Reference: PPL3 » Navigation » Radio Navigation » Secondary Surveillance Radar (SSR)

From	To	FL/Alt	MSA	TAS	W/V	Trk (T)	Drift	Hdg (T)	Varn.	Hdg (M)	G/S	DIST	Time
Goodwood	Grove	3000	2300	85	250/20	330	11°S	319	3°W	322	80	51	38
Grove	Shobdon	3500	2700	85	270/15	306	6°S	300	3°W	303	72	65	55

Alternate

From	To	FL/Alt	MSA	TAS	W/V	Trk (T)	Drift	Hdg (T)	Varn.	Hdg (M)	G/S	DIST	Time
Shobdon	Woonton	As req	2700	85	270/15	203	10°P	213	3°W	216	76	5	4

Paper 2 Answers and Explanations

ENP2Q1   Answer D

The illustrations below show the 'wind up' method of heading/groundspeed calculation.

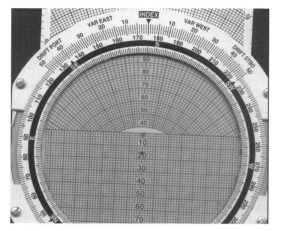

The wind direction is placed under the INDEX mark. The centre dot is placed over 15 on the wind grid and a mark is made on centreline at the top of the wind grid.

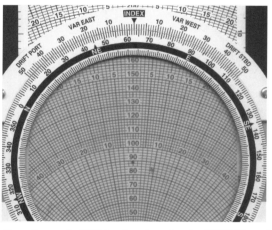

Now the track (063) is placed under the INDEX, and the wind slide moved until the wind cross is on the arc representing the TAS of 85 knots. The wind cross is 9° to the right. Looking 9° to the right from the INDEX gives a heading of 072° True.

Remember to add westerly variation to this figure (+2°W) to obtain the magnetic heading of 074°M.

The possible answers normally allow for a tolerance of up to 5°, so you may well have an answer a degree or so different to the correct answer, but still accurate enough for you to select the closest option. If your answer is very different to any of the options you should re-check your calculations, and also check that you have not accidentally used the true heading, or the track, by mistake.

Further Reference; Flight Plan
PPL3 » Navigation » Aeronautical Maps » Measurement of Direction
PPL3 » Navigation » Navigation Principles: The Triangle of Velocities » Triangle of Velocity Calculations on the Flight Computer

ENP2Q2   Answer A

At explanation ENP2Q1 the second illustration shows that the ground speed (where the centre dot is placed using the wind up method) is 89 knots.

The possible answers normally allow for a tolerance of up to 5 knots, so you may well have an answer a few knots or so different to the correct answer, but still accurate enough for you to select the closest option. If your answer is very different to any of the options you should re-check your calculations!

Further Reference; Flight Plan
PPL3 » Navigation » Aeronautical Maps » Scale and Distance
PPL3 » Navigation » Navigation Principles: The Triangle of Velocities » Triangle of Velocity Calculations on the Flight Computer

ENP2Q3   Answer C

Again using the wind-up method. First place the wind on the plotting disc. Remember that the wind of this leg is different to that on the first.

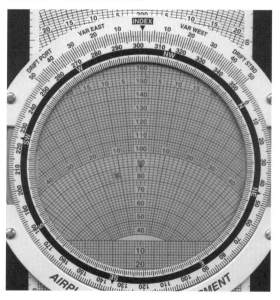

With the true tack (302) under the index, and the wind cross on the TAS (85) arc, the heading is found as 11° to the left of the INDEX mark – namely 291° True. Remember to add the westerly variation (+2°W) to this heading to obtain the magnetic heading of 293° Magnetic.

Further Reference: Flight Plan
PPL3 » Navigation » Aeronautical Maps » Measurement of Direction
PL3 » Navigation » Navigation Principles: The Triangle of Velocities » Triangle of Velocity Calculations on the Flight Computer

ENP2Q4   Answer C

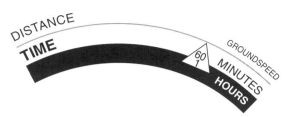

For each leg, the flight time is found by setting the groundspeed on the flight computer using the time index, then finding the distance (outer scale), and reading-off the time (inner scale) under the leg distance.

The example given below is for the first leg (distance 59nm, G/S 89 knots):

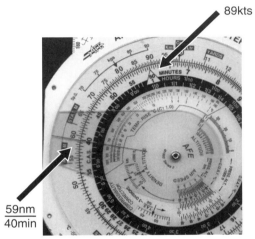

89kts

59nm
40min

The normal tolerance in answer options is around 5 minutes, so once again if your calculated answer is significantly different to all the options, re-checking your flight plan is in order.

Further Reference: Flight Plan

PPL3 » Navigation » Aeronautical Maps » Scale and Distance

PPL3 » Navigation » Navigation Principles: The Triangle of Velocities » Triangle of Velocity Calculations on the Flight Computer

PPL3 » Navigation » Navigation Principles: Airspeed, Groundspeed Time and Distance » Time, Speed and Distance

ENP2Q5   Answer D

The answer is taken from the flight plan form.

Further Reference: Flight Plan

PPL3 » Navigation » Aeronautical Maps » Measurement of Direction

PPL3 » Navigation » Navigation Principles: The Triangle of Velocities » Triangle of Velocity Calculations on the Flight Computer

ENP2Q6   Answer D

The tolerance on this question is around 2 to 3 US gallons. It is fairly simple to add up the amounts already given:

Start, taxy, power check and take-off	3
Approach, landing and/or missed approach	2
Reserve fuel	7
Sub total	12

The only flight computer calculation required is that for the flight plan time (1 hour 50 minutes plus 15 minutes diversion) = 2 hours 5 minutes. On the flight computer, 2 hours 5 minutes at 9 US gallons per hour = 18.8, which rounds up to 19

9US gal per hr

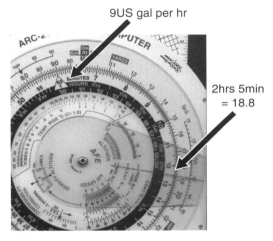

2hrs 5min
= 18.8

19 + 12 = 31 US gallons

Further Reference: PPL3 » Navigation » Flight Planning: Fuel Planning » Fuel Planning

ENP2Q7   Answer B

Firstly, the two weights given can be added together:

Basic (empty) weight	1300lbs
Pilot	170lbs
Sub-total	1470lbs

Given the volume (40 US gallons) and specific gravity (0.72), the weight of the fuel is calculated on a Flight Computer:

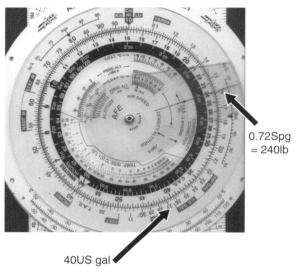

0.72Spg = 240lb

40US gal

Weight of fuel =	240lbs
These weights total (1470 + 240) =	1710lbs
2300 – 1710 = 590lbs	

Therefore the maximum payload that can be carried, without exceeding the MTWA, is 590lbs.

Note that this calculation takes no account of balance, centre of gravity or loading restrictions.

Further Reference: PPL3 » Navigation » Flight Planning: Fuel Planning » Specific Gravity Calculation

ENP2Q8   Answer A

The map symbol, at the position given can be checked against the map key, which also 'decodes' the figures denoting winch launching. It is important to appreciate that hand/para gliders may be encountered in this area both outside the marked circle and higher than the winch launch altitude. The winch launch altitude is only an indication of the maximum altitude to which cables may be encountered.

Further reference: Study of map and map key

PPL3 » Navigation » Aeronautical Maps » Depiction of Airfields

UK AIM » Aeronautical Information Publication (AIP) » ENR 5.2 Hang Gliding, Paragliding and Parascending Sites

And

UK AIM » Aeronautical Information Publication (AIP) » ENR 5.3 Cable Launching of Gliders, Hang Gliders and Parascending Parachutes

ENP2Q9   Answer C

The blue colour of the aerodrome symbol denotes that it is a civilian airfield. The red dotted circle around it denotes the ATZ - Aerodrome Traffic Zone. The blue pecked-line box around the airfield name denotes that it is a customs aerodrome.

All of this information can be gleaned by simple reference to the map key at the bottom of the chart.

Further reference: Study of map and map key
PPL3 » Navigation » Aeronautical Maps » Depiction of Airfields

ENP2Q10   Answer B

The base of controlled airspace in this area is 2500ft amsl – this is denoted on the chart as;

   'LTMA A 2500' +'

which decodes as;

LTMA	London TMA
A	Class A airspace
2500'	Base 2500ft amsl
+	Upper limit above FL245

So, flight must be carried out at an altitude not above 2400ft amsl to remain clear of controlled airspace.

Flight at an altitude is controlled by reference to QNH. When routing under a TMA, pilots are advised to use the QNH of any airfield beneath that TMA, and one of the airfields under the TMA is Gatwick

Further Reference: PPL3 » Navigation » Vertical Navigation » Calculation of Minimum Safety Altitude

ENP2Q11   Answer B

The magnetic track for the route is 065°(M) – that is the true track of 063° + variation of 2°W. In this quadrant, flight levels to comply with the Quadrantal rule are 'odd' – eg FL30, FL50 etc. Flight Levels can only be used above the Transition Altitude. In the UK, the standard Transition Altitude outside controlled airspace is 3000ft QNH.

The question states that the QNH is below standard – 1000mb as opposed to the standard 'Flight Level' setting of 1013mb. So, when standard setting (1013) is set, an aircraft at FL30 (the lowest Flight Level on this magnetic track) would actually be below the Transition Altitude of 3000ft, because at FL30 on 1013mb, the actual altitude based on the given QNH of 1000mb is 390ft lower (13mb x 30ft).

Hence on this day, FL30 is equivalent to an altitude of 2610ft (3000ft – 390ft).

It is not permitted for a Flight Level to be below the Transition Altitude, so FL 30 is not available.

The next available 'odd' flight level is FL50, which with this QNH **IS** above the Transition Altitude.

Further Reference: flight plan
and
PPL3 » Navigation » Vertical Navigation » Altimeter Settings
and
UK AIM » Air Navigation Order (Rules of the Air) » Rule 30 Quadrantal Rule and semi circular rule

ENP2Q12   Answer C

This question might best be answered by a process of elimination. It should become apparent that at least two of the options (A and B) involve flying at a level that will put the aircraft inside class A airspace. These can be dismissed.

Answer D also mentions altitude 3500ft as a possibility, as well as 'any' level. Although you have been unable to contact Lashenden/Headcorn radio, the Aerodrome Traffic Zone (ATZ) remains active during the notified hours of watch of the AGCS radio station so flight through it in these circumstances would be illegal.

Thus any option that involves possible flight inside controlled airspace or inside an active ATZ without establishing radio contact can be ruled out.

The final piece of information that should steer towards the correct answer is the parachute symbol on the airfield (meaning Free Fall Parachuting Drop Zone, active up to FL150) and the legend 'Intense Parachuting'. It should be evident that any option that involves over-flying such an area, during the notified hours of radio watch, without establishing contact, is not safe. The UK Aeronautical Information Publication (AIP), and the 'Frequency Reference Card' supplied with the CAA 1:500,000 chart both advise that if no information can be obtained regarding a FFPDZ, it should be assumed that the Drop Zone is _active_.

Further Reference: Study of the map and map key

ENP2Q13   Answer D

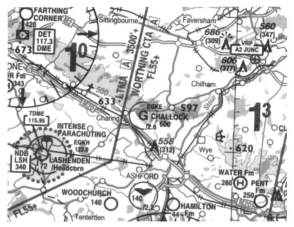

The gliding site symbol at Challock also indicates the maximum altitude of any winch launching in thousands of feet, so 2.6 indicates winch launching to a maximum altitude of 2600ft.

Further Reference: Study of the map and map key

PPL3 » Navigation » Aeronautical Maps » Depiction of Airfields

ENP2Q14   Answer B

The map symbol can be 'decoded' by reference to the map key. So far, so easy. However, in order the identify the correct symbol it is necessary to carefully plot the latitude and longitude figures given.

Further reference: Study of map and map key

PPL3 » Navigation » The Earth » Form of the Earth, Latitude and Longitude

ENP2Q15   Answer C

Flight plan time Canterbury to Stapleford is 27 minutes, plus 10 minutes to the alternate makes 37 minutes. 37 minutes at a consumption of 30 litres per hour = 18 litres (rounded up to the nearest litre).

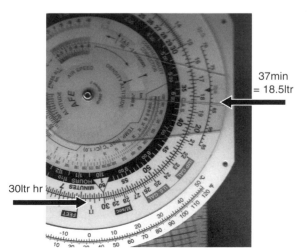

37min
= 18.5ltr

30ltr hr

The fuel used to get to the alternate, (18) is deducted from 74, leaving 56 litres.

From this, the fuel reserve (25 litres) is deducted, leaving 31 litres.

At 30 litres per hour, 31 litres = 1 hour and 2 minutes endurance before reaching the 25 litre reserve.

30ltr hr   31ltr = 1hr 2min

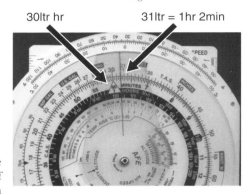

Further Reference: Flight plan and PPL3 » Navigation » Flight Planning: Fuel Planning » Fuel Planning

ENP2Q16   Answer C

Stapleford

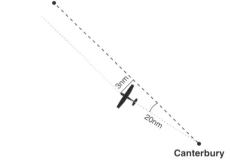

3nm

20nm

Canterbury

The power station is 3nm to the left (port) of track after flying 20nm from Grove. The Track Error (TE) that has occurred can be calculated by the formulae:

$$\frac{\text{Distance off-track}}{\text{Distance travelled}} \times 60$$

or

$$\frac{3}{20} \times 60 = 9°$$

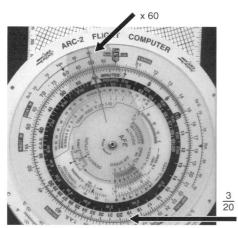

Remember, if you altering the heading by just the TE (ie by altering heading 9° to the right – starboard), the aircraft will fly parallel to the required track, in other words it would arrive 3nm to the left of Stapleford. To reach the destination, the Closing Angle (CA) must be calculated:

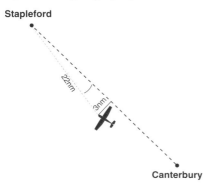

$$\frac{\text{Distance off-track}}{\text{Distance to go}} \times 60$$

or

$$\frac{3}{22} \times 60 = 8° \text{ (to the nearest degree)}$$

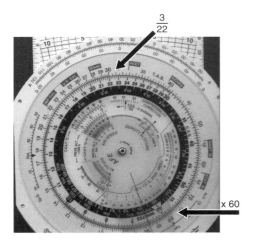

TE (9) + CA (8) = total heading change required: 17°. The heading change is to right (starboard) because the aircraft is currently left of track.

Further Reference: Study of map

PPL3 » Navigation » Practical Navigation: Off-Track Calculations and Track Markings » The One in Sixty Rule

ENP2Q17 Answer C

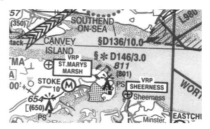

This is another question which can be answered simply by carefully reading the map and the map key. The symbols next to the danger area designation are decoded in the map key to mean that a Danger Area Activity Information Service (DAAIS) is available (<u>NOT</u> a DACS) for the danger area, and that the danger area is covered by local byelaws which prohibit entry when active

Further, the map key states that if no reply is received to calls on the nominated frequency, the danger area should be assumed to be active (and so avoided).

Further Reference: Study of map and map key

UK AIM » Aeronautical Information Publication » ENR 1.1.5 Airspace Restrictions, Danger Areas and Hazards to Flight

ENP2Q18   Answer B

The distance from St Marys Marsh VRP to where the London TMA (LTMA) base drops to 2500ft is 10nm. So the distance available to complete the descent is (10-3 =) 7nm.

At a groundspeed of 105 knots, a distance of 7nm is covered in 4 minutes (rounded down to the nearest minute).

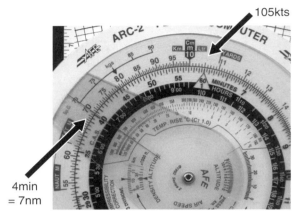

105kts

4min
= 7nm

The descent required is (3300 – 2200 =) 1100ft.

$$\frac{1100}{4} = 275\text{ft per minute}$$

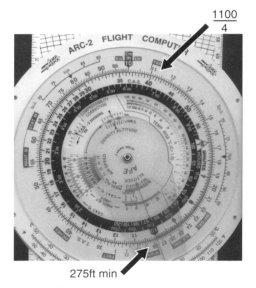

$$\frac{1100}{4}$$

275ft min

The Landing Distance Available (LDA) is given in the runway dimensions box.

Further Reference: Study of map
PPL3 » Navigation » Vertical Navigation » Vertical Navigation Calculations

ENP2Q19   Answer D

See the 'ATS AIRSPACE' and 'ATS COMMUNICATIONS FACILITIES' section of the AIP extract.

Further reference: Study of AIP extract

ENP2Q20   Answer D

See the 'ATS AIRSPACE' section of the AIP extract. Note that the abbreviation 'aal' stands for 'above aerodrome level'.
Further reference: Study of AIP extract

UK AIM » Air Navigation Order (ANO) » Article 156 Meaning of Aerodrome Traffic Zone

ENP2Q21   Answer B

A VOR ground station transmits two signals, the aircraft's VOR receiver measures the phase difference between these two signals to establish the aircraft bearing relative to the ground station.

Further reference: PPL3 » Navigation » Radio Navigation » VHF Omni-directional Range (VOR)

ENP2Q22   Answer D

VOR operates in the Very High Frequency (VHF) band (30-3200MHz) – in fact VOR stands for **V**HF **O**mni-directional **R**ange.

VHF transmissions are largely unaffected by errors (e.g. coastal refraction, thunderstorm effect, night effect etc.) that effect transmissions in the lower frequency bands. However, VHF transmissions can be affected by three particular errors:

■ Site error, if the area around the transmission area contains buildings or obstacles which can reflect or deflect signals.

■ Propagation error, (also sometimes known as 'scalloping'), caused if the signal is travelling over hilly terrain and the receiver is at low level – the signal can be deflected or scatted.

■ Duct propagation, when a strong temperature inversion causes VHF signals to travel far further at low level than the normal 'line-of-site' range limitation.

Further Reference: PPL3 » Navigation » Radio Navigation » VHF Omni-directional Range
PPL3 » Navigation » Radio Navigation » Ground Direction Finding (DF)
UK AIM » Aeronautical Information Publication » GEN3.4.3.1 Radio Navigation Services

ENP2Q23   Answer A

First consider the situation if there was no drift. The aircraft is tracking directly away from the NDB, so regardless of the QDR (radial), the needle of the Relative Bearing Indicator (RBI) will point directly behind the aircraft, ie to 180°. Remember, the question is asking about the relative bearing indication – where the NDB is located relative to the nose of the aircraft (which is taken as 000°).

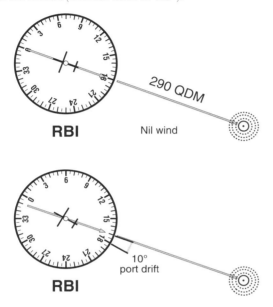

The key point then is the drift. If the aircraft is drifting port (left) by 10°, the aircraft nose must be pointing 10° to the right of track. If this situation is depicted over the RBI, you can see that the needle is pointing 10° to the right of 180°, namely 170°.

Further Reference: PPL3 » Navigation » Radio Navigation » Automatic Direction Finding (ADF)

ENP2Q24   Answer C

The aircraft is on the 150° radial – by definition a radial is a magnetic direction <u>FROM</u> a station. This situation is depicted below:

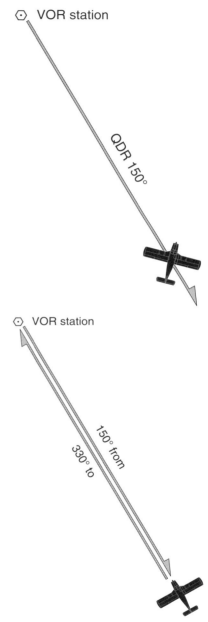

In order to fly <u>TO</u> the station, the aircraft must fly in the reciprocal (opposite) direction to the radial – in this case 330° (i.e. 150° + 180°).

On the Course Deviation Indicator (CDI) this is achieved by setting the desired track at the top of the indicator, and – most essentially – checking that the 'TO' flag is showing.

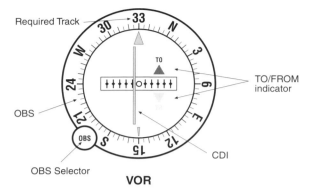

Required Track

TO/FROM indicator

OBS

OBS Selector

CDI

VOR

When using a VOR (or localiser or ILS), the recommended sequence of actions is **FIFO**:

Frequency – check and select

Ident – identify the morse code

Flags – check that the warning flag has disappeared

OBS – use the Omni Bearing Selector (OBS) to select the desired track and check that the TO/FROM flag appears in the correct sense.

Further Reference: PPL3 » Navigation » Radio Navigation » VHF Omni-directional Range

---

ENP2Q25   **Answer C**

Information from the aircraft's transponder can only be received by 'in range' Air Traffic Service Units who have the necessary Secondary Surveillance Radar (SSR) – not all radar units have SSR capability. Even then, a controller can 'deselect' transponder information in various ways to reduce Plan Position Indicator (PPI) screen clutter.

Where the controller chooses to receive an aircraft's transponder SSR information, that information is displayed on the same screen as 'primary' radar information, and next to that aircraft's 'primary' radar return.

Further Reference: PPL3 » Navigation » Radio Navigation » Secondary Surveillance Radar (SSR)

From	To	FL/Alt	MSA	TAS	W/V	Trk (T)	Drift	Hdg (T)	Varn.	Hdg (M)	G/S	DIST	Time
Shoreham	Canterbury	2400	2200	85	175/15	063	9°P	072	2°W	074	89	59	40
Canterbury	Stapleford	2400	1900	85	190/20	302	11°S	291	2°W	293	91	41	27

Alternate

Stapleford	North Weald	1400	1800	85	190/20	001	2°S	359	2°W	001	103	4.5	2.5

Paper 3 Answers and Explanations

ENP3Q1   Answer B

Using the wind down method, the flight computer set-up to calculate this heading is as below:

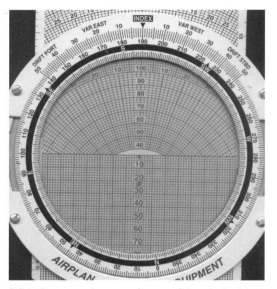

With the centre dot on at the top of the wind grid, place the wind direction (190) at the wind index and mark a wind cross 22 knots below the centre dot.

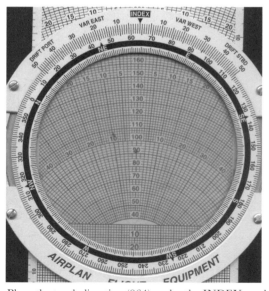

Place the track direction (064) under the INDEX, and place the centre dot on the TAS (92).

Rotate the disc into wind, bringing the wind cross down, until the angle between track (064) and heading is the same on the plotting disc and at the INDEX. At the INDEX read off the true heading (076) and at the wind cross read off the

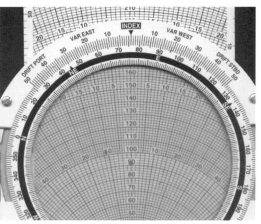

groundspeed (103kts). Remember to add the westerly variation (+3°W) to obtain the magnetic heading – 079°.

The possible answers normally allow for a tolerance of up to 5°, so you may well have an answer a degree or so different to the correct answer, but still accurate enough for you to select the closest option. If your answer is very different to any of the options you should re-check your calculations, and also check that you have not accidentally used the true heading, or the track, by mistake.

Further Reference: Flight Plan

PPL3 » Navigation » Aeronautical Maps » Measurement of Direction

PPL3 » Navigation » Navigation Principles: The Triangle of Velocities » Triangle of Velocity Calculations on the Flight Computer

ENP3Q2   Answer A

Using the flight computer calculation described in explanation ENP3Q1, the groundspeed is read off at the wind cross (wind-down method) or the centre dot (wind-up method).

The possible answers normally allow for a tolerance of up to 5 knots, so you may well have an answer a few knots or so different to the correct answer, but still accurate enough for you to select the closest option. If your answer is very different to any of the options you should re-check your calculations!

Further Reference: Flight Plan

PPL3 » Navigation » Aeronautical Maps » Scale and Distance

PPL3 » Navigation » Navigation Principles: The Triangle of Velocities » Triangle of Velocity Calculations on the Flight Computer

ENP3Q3   Answer C

Using the wind-down method, the flight computer set up that calculates the true heading on this leg is as below:

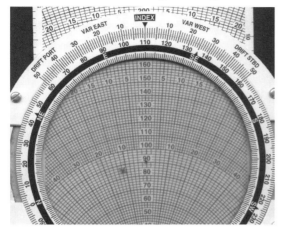

Remember to use the different w/v on this leg (180/18) and the slightly different TAS (90).

Further Reference: Flight Plan

PPL3 » Navigation » Aeronautical Maps » Measurement of Direction

PPL3 » Navigation » Navigation Principles: The Triangle of Velocities » Triangle of Velocity Calculations on the Flight Computer

ENP3Q4   Answer A

The normal tolerance in answer options is around 5 minutes, so once again if your calculated answer is significantly different to all the options, re-checking your flight plan is in order.

Further Reference: Flight Plan

PPL3 » Navigation » Aeronautical Maps » Scale and Distance

PPL3 » Navigation » Navigation Principles: The Triangle of Velocities » Triangle of Velocity Calculations on the Flight Computer

PPL3 » Navigation » Navigation Principles: Airspeed, Groundspeed Time and Distance » Time, Speed and Distance

ENP3Q5   Answer D

Further Reference: Flight Plan

PPL3 » Navigation » Aeronautical Maps » Scale and Distance

ENP3Q6   Answer D

The tolerance on this question is around 5 litres. It is fairly simple to add up the amounts given:

Start, taxy, power check and take-off	10
Approach, landing and/or missed approach	8
Reserve fuel	25
Sub total	43

The only flight computer calculation required is that for the flight plan time (1 hour 40 minutes plus 10 minutes diversion) = 1 hour 50 minutes. On the flight computer, 1 hour 50 minutes at 28 litres per hour = 51.5, which rounds up to 52 litres.

43 + 52 = 95 litres

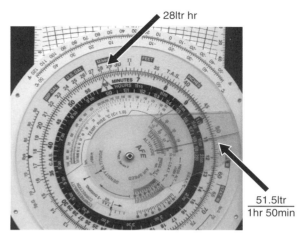

Further Reference: PPL3 » Navigation » Flight Planning: Fuel Planning » Fuel Planning

ENP3Q7   Answer B

Firstly, the two weights given can be added together:

Basic (empty) weight	1150lbs
Pilot	175lbs
Sub-total	1325lbs

The weight of the fuel is calculated on a Flight Computer:

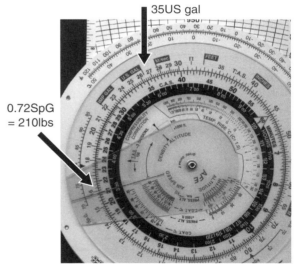

Sub-total	210lbs

These weights total (1325 + 210) = 1535lbs.

2200 – 1535 = 665lbs

Therefore the maximum payload that can be carried, without exceeding the MTWA, is 665lbs.

Note that this calculation takes no account of balance, centre of gravity or loading restrictions.

Further Reference: PPL3 » Navigation » Flight Planning: Fuel Planning » Specific Gravity Calculation

ENP3Q8   Answer C

The maximum angle between wind direction and runway direction that can be reached before exceeding the maximum crosswind component (12 knots) is calculated on a Flight Computer. Firstly 000 is set under the INDEX, and with the centre dot on the top of the wind grid, a wind cross is made 20 knots below the centre dot.

The disc is now rotated left and right until a crosswind component of 12kts is reached. This occurs at an angle of 35° (ie at 035° and 325°).

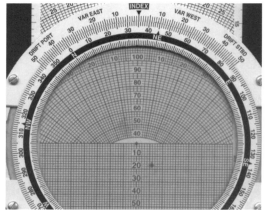

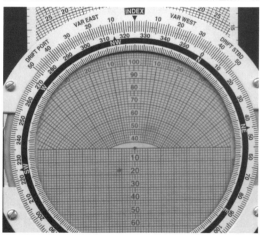

Further Reference: PPL3 » Navigation » Flight Planning: Performance » Crosswind Component

ENP3Q9   Answer D

A Maximum Elevation Figure – MEF – represents the maximum possible elevation (altitude, amsl) of terrain, obstructions or unknown obstructions within the defined area. It is NOT a safety altitude, as it builds in no safety margin above the highest terrain/obstruction.

Further Reference: PPL3 » Navigation » Vertical Navigation » Calculation of Minimum Safety Altitude

ENP3Q10   Answer B

The magnetic track for the leg from Gloucestershire to Northampton/Sywell is 067° (that is, True track 064° + variation 3°W). This puts the track in the quadrant where Odd Flight Levels are used – e.g. FL30, FL50, FL70 etc.

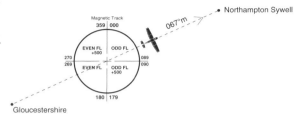

The transition altitude outside controlled airspace is 3000ft, so – depending on the pressure setting – the first available Flight level is FL30 – an Odd FL.

Because the pressure is greater than standard (which is 1013mb), this first FL is available, in other words flying at FL30 will not take the aircraft below the transition altitude. At FL30 on 1013mb, the aircraft is at altitude 3240ft – because pressure (QNH 1021) is 8mb more than standard, which at 30ft per mb = 240ft. 3000+ 240 = 3240ft.

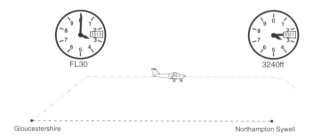

Of course, the question asks for the highest available FL along the route from Gloucestershire to Northampton/Sywell. Examination of the chart shows that the lowest controlled airspace along the route is a section of Daventry CTA (class A airspace) with a base of FL45. Therefore FL50 is not available, so the highest useable FL on the correct quadrant is FL30.

Further reference; Study of map

PPL3 » Navigation » Vertical Navigation » Altimeter Settings

UK AIM » Air Navigation Order (Rules of the Air) » Rule 30 Quadrantal rule and semi circular rule

## ENP3Q11					**Answer B**

Long Marston is located 6nm to the left (starboard) of track after flying 21nm from Gloucestershire. The Track Error (TE) that has occurred can be calculated by the formulae:

$$\frac{\text{Distance off-track}}{\text{Distance travelled}} \times 60$$

or

$$\frac{6}{21} \times 60 = 17.25° \text{ (to the nearest degree)}$$

Altering the heading by just the TE will only leave the aircraft flying parallel to the required heading. To reach the destination Closing Angle (CA) must be calculated:

$$\frac{\text{Distance off-track}}{\text{Distance to go}} \times 60$$

or

$$\frac{6}{37} \times 60 = 9.75° \text{ (to the nearest degree)}$$

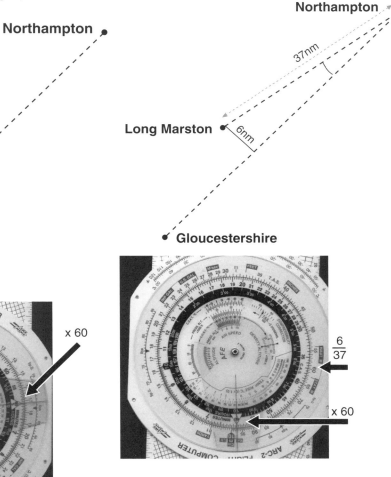

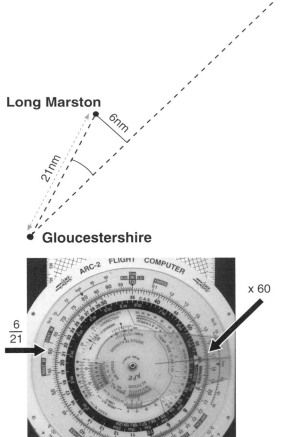

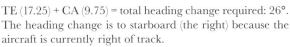

TE (17.25) + CA (9.75) = total heading change required: 26°. The heading change is to starboard (the right) because the aircraft is currently right of track.

Further Reference: Study of map
PPL3 » Navigation » Practical Navigation: Off-Track Calculations
Track Markings » The One in Sixty Rule

ENP3Q12   Answer D

The symbol shows multiple obstacles with a maximum elevation of 617ft (above mean sea level). The smaller figure in brackets is the maximum height (above ground level) of the obstacles.

Further reference: Study of map and map key

ENP3Q13   Answer D

The flight plan time from Northampton Sywell to Cambridge is 25 minutes, plus ten minutes for the diversion makes 35 minutes. 35 minutes at 30 litres per hour = 17·5 litres

So, fuel remaining on arrival at the alternate is (70 – 17·5 litres) = 52·5 litres.

52·5 litres – 25 litres reserve = 27·5 litres

At 30 litres per hour, 27·5 litres = 55 minutes.

Further Reference: Flight plan
PPL3 » Navigation » Flight Planning: Fuel Planning » Fuel Planning

ENP3Q14   Answer B

The time taken to fly the 17nm from overhead Northampton Sywell to overhead the mast is 14 minutes (11·27 – 11·13). On the flight computer, placing time (14 min) under distance (17nm) gives a ground speed of 73 knots.

The remaining distance to Cambridge is 19nm (36-17). At the actual groundspeed of 73 knots, this distance will be covered in 16 minutes (rounded to the nearest minute).

11·27 + 16 minutes = 11·43

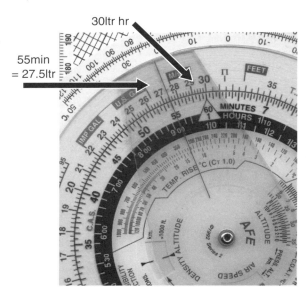

The possible range of answers given will normally allow you to select the closest response, even if it is a minute or two different to the answer you have calculated.

Further Reference: Study of map
flight plan
PPL3 » Navigation » Navigation Principles: Airspeed, Groundspeed, Time and Distance » Time, Speed and Distance

ENP3Q15   Answer A

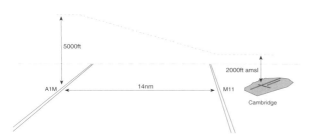

The distance of the descent is (18nm-4nm) = 14nm. At 105kt groundspeed this distance will be covered in 8 minutes.

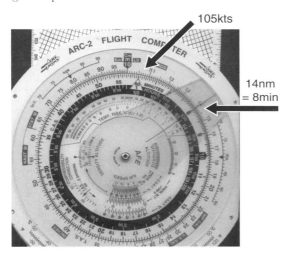

The descent is though 3000ft (i.e. 5000ft – 2000ft). 3000ft divided by 8 minutes = 375ft per minute.

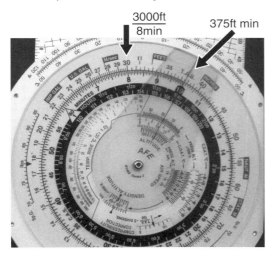

Further Reference: PPL3 » Navigation » Vertical Navigation » Vertical Navigation Calculations

ENP3Q16   Answer C

KNOWN LAND SITED OBSTACLES ABOVE 300ft AGL ARE SHOWN ON THIS CHART. A SMALL NUMBER OF OBSTACLES BELOW 300ft AGL ARE SHOWN FOR LANDMARK PURPOSES. PERMANENT OFF-SHORE OBSTACLES ARE SHOWN REGARDLESS OF HEIGHT CATEGORY. See UK AIP ENR 1-1.
WARNING: INFORMATION IS TAKEN FROM BEST AVAILABLE SOURCES BUT IS NOT GUARANTEED COMPLETE.

MILITARY AERODROME TRAFFIC ZONES (MATZs) have the following vertical limits: SFC to 3000ft AAL within the circle and 1000ft AAL to 3000ft AAL within the stub.

STANDARD MATZ WITH TWO STUBS AND LARS

Zone configuration may vary, often two or more MATZs are amalgamated to produce a Combined Zone (CMATZ). Controlling Aerodromes show the MATZ penetration frequency to be used. See UK AIP ENR 2-2.

LOWER AIRSPACE RADAR SERVICE (LARS). The abbreviation LARS has been added to the MATZ frequency to identify those participating MATZ ATS Units. Other participating Units are identified by a LARS frequency annotation. The Service, Radar Advisory (RAS) or Radar Information (RIS), is available to all aircraft in unregulated airspace up to and including FL95 within approximately 30NM of each participating ATS Unit. See UK AIP ENR 1-6-3.

Once again, simple reference to the map key will confirm the proper name for this type of airspace. The contact frequency is that for the controlling Air Traffic Service Unit for those requiring a MATZ penetration service.

Further reference: Study of map and map key

ENP3Q17   Answer C

The figure of '/3.3' on the lower right of the circle that depicts the Gransden Lodge gliding site indicates that winch launching may take place up to a maximum altitude of 3300ft amsl.

As with most map symbols, this information can be found on the map key.

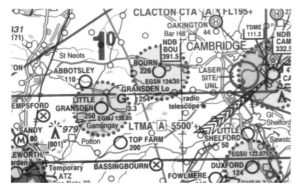

Further Reference: PPL3 » Navigation » Aeronautical Maps » Depiction of Airfields and Study of map key

ENP3Q18   Answer C
Further reference: Study of AIP extract

ENP3Q19   Answer C
Further reference: Study of AIP extract

TAXIWAYS AND CHECK LOCATIONS/POSITIONS DATA		
12:	Surface: Concrete/Asphalt	Strength: 20/R/
16 (Customs):	Surface: Concrete	Strength: 10/R/
17:	Surface: Concrete/Asphalt	Strength: 35/R/

| 05 | 049.88° | 1965 x 46 | 42/R/C/X/T Concrete | 521202.06N 0000959.14E – GUND 151 ft | THR 35 ft |
| 23 | 229.89° | 1965 x 46 | 42/R/C/X/T Concrete | 521235.49N 0001103.71E – GUND 151 ft | THR 47 ft |

ENP3Q20   Answer D

See 'Remarks' at the bottom of the page.

Slope of RWY/SWY	Stopway Dimensions (m)	Clearway Dimensions (m)	Strip Dimensions (m)	OFZ
7	8	9	10	11
05 – 0.14% up	0	183 x 210	2124 x 300	
23 – 0.83% down first 400 m	0	161 x 210	2124 x 300	
12 Remarks:			Threshold displaced on Concrete Runway 05 by 216 m. Threshold displaced on Concrete Runway 23 by 145 m.	

Further reference: Study of AIP extract

ENP3Q21   Answer D

The relevant 'Q' code definitions in relation to direction finding are:

QDM   The aircraft's **magnetic track to** the VDF station – the magnetic heading, if there was no wind, to take the aircraft to the VDF station

QDR   The aircraft's **magnetic track from** the VDF station

QUJ   The aircraft's **true track to** the VDF station.

QTE   The aircraft's **true track from** the VDF station.

Further reference: PPL3 » Navigation » Radio Navigation » Ground Direction Finding (DF)

ENP3Q22   **Answer A**

On its own, a Relative Bearing Indicator (RBI) only points to where the NDB is relative to the aircraft. This means that if an aircraft was tracking directly away from an NDB in conditions of nil drift, the needle would always point directly behind the aircraft (ie Relative Bearing 180°)

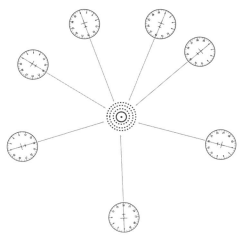

So, the aircraft's track is irrelevant to answering this question (it is already stated that the aircraft is tracking directly away from the NDB), all that counts is the drift.

Starboard (right) drift means that the aircraft's nose must be pointed to the left of track – in this case by 10°.

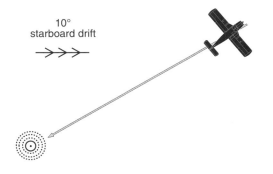

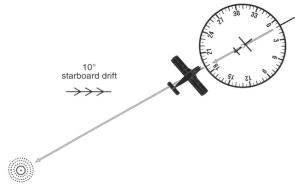

Therefore, if the aircraft is pointing 10° to the left of track while tracking away from an NDB, the needle of the RBI will be pointing 10° left of the tail – a relative bearing of 190°.

Further Reference: PPL3 » Navigation » Radio Navigation » Automatic Direction Finding (ADF)

ENP3Q23   **Answer B**

At its most simple, the aircraft's transponder transmits a four-digit number which is displayed on a radar screen, usually next to the aircraft's primary radar contact.

Although the radar controller and the ground equipment can interpret SSR information to determine ranges and bearings from airfields, or other traffic, this data is not transmitted by the aircraft's transponder.

Further Reference: PPL3 » Navigation » Radio Navigation » Secondary Surveillance Radar (SSR)

ENP3Q24   **Answer C**

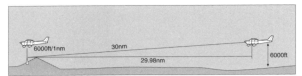

The aircraft's DME uses radar principles (measuring the time taken for a radio pulse to be sent and returned back to the aircraft) to measure the direct distance between the aircraft and the DME ground station. Anytime the aircraft is higher than the DME ground station, this distance will be the direct 'slant' range to the DME, not the exact horizontal distance to overhead the ground DME. At lower altitudes (below 10,000ft) and anything more than a few miles from the ground DME station, the difference between horizontal range and slant range is normally immaterial.

Further Reference: PPL3 » Navigation » Radio Navigation » Distance Measuring Equipment (DME)

ENP3Q25   **Answer A**

This can be remembered simply by knowing what the abbreviations 'VOR' and 'VDF' stand for, namely:

VOR   **VHF O**mni-directional **R**ange

VDF   **VHF D**irection **F**inding

For interest, SSR and DME operate in the Ultra High Frequency (UHF) band, and NDBs operate in the Low Frequency (LF) and Medium Frequency (MF) bands.

Radionavigation Aid	Frequency band
DME	UHF
NDB	LF & MF
SSR	UHF
VDF	VHF
VOR	VHF

Further Reference: PPL3 » Navigation » Radio Navigation » VHF Omni-directional Range

UK AIM » Aeronautical Information Publication » GEN3.4.3.1 Radio Navigation Services

From	To	FL/Alt	MSA	TAS	W/V	Trk (T)	Drift	Hdg (T)	Varn.	Hdg (M)	G/S	DIST	Time
Gloucestershire	Northampton Sywell	3000	2400	92	190/22	064	12°P	076	3°W	079	103	56	33
Northampton Sywell	Cambridge	3000	1800	90	180/18	098	12°P	110	3°W	113	86	36	25

Alternate

Cambridge	Duxford	2200	1800	90	180/18	195	2°S	193	3°W	196	73	7	6

Communications

Communications Essential Revision

▶ Pre-Flight

The higher an aircraft flies, the **greater the range** of VHF communications.

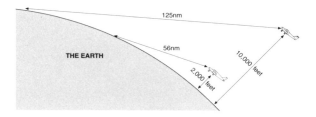

▶ General Operating Procedures

The **phonetic alphabet**:

Letter	Phonetic Word
A	Alpha
B	Bravo
C	Charlie
D	Delta
E	Echo
F	Foxtrot
G	Golf
H	Hotel
I	India
J	Juliett
K	Kilo
L	Lima
M	Mike
N	November
O	Oscar
P	Papa
Q	Quebec
R	Romeo
S	Sierra
T	Tango
U	Uniform
V	Victor
W	Whiskey
X	X-ray
Y	Yankee
Z	Zulu

Number	Pronunciation
0	ZERO
1	WUN
2	TOO
3	TREE
4	FOWER
5	FIFE
6	SIX
7	SEVEN
8	AIT
9	NINER
Decimal	DAYSEEMAL
Hundred	HUN DRED
Thousand	TOUSAND

Numbers are transmitted as separate digits in the following cases: aircraft callsigns; altimeter settings; flight levels, headings, wind speed/direction; transponder codes; radio frequencies. When a **radio frequency is transmitted**, the word 'decimal' is used. When **time is transmitted**, just the minutes past the hour are used unless there may be confusion. Time is always given in UTC, using the 24 hour clock. Numbers containing hundred or thousands are transmitted using the digits of the number together with the word HUN DRED or TOUSAND in these instances: altitude; cloud ceiling; cloud height; height.

▶ Air Traffic Service Units

The **ATSU callsigns** are:

Type of ATSU	Callsign
Air Traffic Control Unit	Approach, Control, Director, Ground, Radar, Tower
Aerodrome Flight Information Service (AFIS)	Information
Aerodrome Air/Ground Communications Service	Radio

It is normal practice to drop the name, callsign and suffix of the Air Traffic Service Unit (or ground station) once satisfactory two-way communication has been established, and where there will be no confusion.

►Callsigns, Abbreviations, General Procedures

An aircraft may only abbreviate its callsign after an ATSU has done so. The main **callsign abbreviations** are:

Callsign	Abbreviation
Aircraft registration	First and last two letters of registration
Operator Designator and registration	Operator designator and last two letters of registration
Aircraft type and registration	Aircraft type and last two letters of registration
Operator Designator and flight identification	NO ABBREVIATION PERMITTED
Aircraft type only	NO ABBREVIATION PERMITTED

The following **spoken abbreviations** are common:

Abbreviation	Meaning
ATIS*	Automatic Terminal Information Service (pronounced "Ay-tis")
ATC	Air Traffic Control (in general)
ATZ	Aerodrome Traffic Zone
CAVOK*	Visibility, cloud and present weather better than certain prescribed conditions (pronounced "Cav-okay")
CB*	Cumulo Nimbus (pronounced "Cee-bee")
DF	Direction Finding
ETA	Estimated Time of Arrival
FIR	Flight Information Region
FIS	Flight Information Service
IFR	Instrument Flight Rules
IMC	Instrument Meteorological Conditions
LARS*	Lower Airspace Radar Service
MATZ*	Military Aerodrome Traffic Zone
MET*	Meteorology or Meteorological
PAPI*	Precision Approach Path Indicator
POB	Persons On Board
QDM	A magnetic track to a point (e.g. a heading to steer assuming zero wind)
QFE	The altimeter pressure setting to indicate height (above a fixed point on the surface)
QNH	The altimeter pressure setting to indicate altitude (above mean sea level)
SSR	Secondary Surveillance Radar
TCAS	Terminal Alert and Collision Avoidance System (pronounced "Tee-Kas")
TMA	Terminal Control Area
UHF	Ultra High Frequency (used at military airfields)
UTC	Co-ordinated Universal Time
VASI*	Visual Approach Slope Indicator (pronounced "Var-Zi")
VDF	VHF Direction Finding
VFR	Visual Flight Rules
VMC	Visual Meteorological Conditions
VOLMET*	Meteorological information for aircraft in flight

* These abbreviations tend to be spoken as a single word.

The order of precedence for radio messages, starting with the most important, is:

1. Distress messages
2. Urgency messages
3. Direction Finding messages
4. Flight Safety messages
5. Meteorological messages
6. Flight Regularity messages

►Departure Procedures

The readability of aircraft transmissions can be graded as:

Readability Scale	Definition
1	Unreadable
2	Readable now and then
3	Readable but with difficulty
4	Readable
5	Perfectly readable

A **departure clearance** describes the routing to be followed after take-off. A departure clearance is not a clearance to take-off. A pilot ready to take-off should report 'ready for departure', and not use the phrase 'take-off' until, the ATSU does so.

A **conditional clearance** is given in the format:

Aircraft callsign/the condition/the instruction

►En-route Procedures

A **Radar Advisory Service** will pass information on conflicting traffic and advise on avoiding action. A **Radar Information Service** will pass information on conflicting traffic and, the pilot is left to decide on avoiding action.

A **compulsory position report** takes the following format:
 Aircraft callsign;
 Position;
 Time;
 Level;
 Next position and ETA.

A **Special VFR** (SVFR) clearance allows a flight to operate in a control zone (CTR) without complying with Instrument Flight Rules (IFR), but in weather conditions which do not meet the Visual Meteorological Conditions (VMC) criteria specified for that airspace.

MATZ penetration should be requested at least 15nm or 5 minutes flying time before reaching the zone boundary – whichever is greater.

The standard **Secondary Surveillance Radar** (SSR) transponder terminology is:

Confirm (level)	Check and confirm your level
Confirm squawk	Confirm the mode and code set on the transponder
Reset Squawk (mode and code)	Set the transponder to standby and reselect the assigned mode and code
Squawk (mode and code)	Set this mode and code on the transponder and turn it on
Squawk ident	Operate the identification feature ('ident') of the transponder
Squawk standby	Set the transponder to 'standby'

The **standard transponder codes** are:

7000	The standard conspicuity code, to be used outside controlled airspace if no other code has been allocated to the aircraft
7500	The aircraft is being subject to unlawful interference
7600	The aircraft has experienced a communications failure
7700	The aircraft is in difficulties

In **VHF Direction Finding** (**VDF**) the following 'Q codes' may be used:

QDM	The magnetic track **TO** the VDF station; the magnetic heading for the aircraft to steer to reach the VDF station, assuming no wind.
QDR	The magnetic bearing of the aircraft **FROM** the VDF station, the reciprocal of the QDM.
QTE	The true bearing FROM the VDF station – the QDR corrected for magnetic variation.

VDF information given to an aircraft will be qualified as one of the following classes:

Class A	Accuracy ±2°
Class B	Accuracy ±5°
Class C	Accuracy ±10°
Class D	Accuracy less than class C

▶ Arrival/Traffic Pattern Procedures

The standard overhead join:

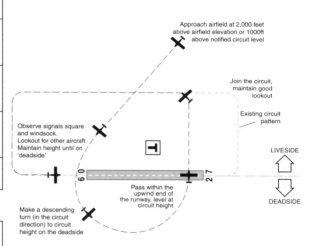

The standard circuit positions are:

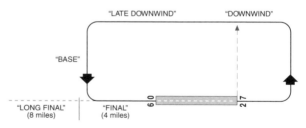

▶Emergency Procedures

Distress:	The aircraft is threatened by serious and/or imminent danger and requires immediate assistance. Spoken word **MAYDAY** A distress (Mayday) message takes priority over *all other radio messages*.
Urgency:	A condition concerning the safety of an aircraft or other vehicle, or of some person on board or in sight, but not requiring immediate assistance. Spoken word **PAN PAN** An urgency (Pan Pan) message takes priority over *all messages except a distress message*.

An emergency radio call should initially be made on the radio frequency in use. If the pilot cannot make contact, or if no frequency is currently in use, the pilot should use the international distress frequency 121.5MHz.

The standard format of an emergency message is:

1. **MAYDAY, MAYDAY, MAYDAY** for distress

   or

   PAN PAN, PAN PAN, PAN PAN for urgency
2. Name of the **station addressed**
3. Aircraft **callsign**
4. Aircraft **Type**
5. **Nature** of emergency
6. **Intentions** of pilot
7. **Position** (or last known position); Flight Level/Altitude/Height; Heading
8. **Pilot qualifications** (e.g. No instrument qualification: IMC rating etc.)
9. Any other **useful information** e.g. persons on board etc.

▶Glossary of standard words and phrases:

Word/Phrase	Meaning
Acknowledge	Confirm that you have received and understood this message
Affirm	Yes (shortened from affirmative)
Approved	Permission for proposed action is granted
Break	This is a separation between messages
Break Break	Indicates a separation between messages in a busy RTF environment
Cancel	Annul the previously transmitted clearance
Changing to	I intend to call (unit) on (frequency)
Check	Examine a system or procedure
Cleared	Authorised to proceed under the conditions specified
Climb	Climb and maintain
Confirm	I request verification of (message/information)? Did you correctly receive this message?
Confirm squawk (code)	Confirm the code and mode you have set on the transponder
Contact	Establish radio contact with (unit), (they have your details)
Correct	True or Accurate
Correction	An error has been made. The correct message is…
Descend	Descend and maintain
Disregard	Ignore
Fanstop	I am initiating a practice engine failure after take-off
Freecall	Call (ATSU), (they do not have your details)
How do you read?	What is the readability of my transmissions?
I Say Again	I will repeat (for clarity or emphasis)
Maintain	Continue in accordance with condition specified
Monitor	Listen out on (frequency)
Negative	No, or That is not correct, or Permission is not granted
Out	This exchange is ended and no response is expected
Over	This transmission is ended and I expect a response
Pass your message	Proceed with your message
Read Back	Repeat all, or a specified part, of the message; exactly as you received it
Report	Pass requested information
Request	I want to know, or I want to obtain
Roger	I have received all of your last transmission
Say Again	Repeat all, or a specified part, of your last transmission
Speak Slower	Slow down your rate of speaking
Squawk (code and mode)	Set this mode and code
Squawk Charlie	Set the transponder to mode C
Squawk ident	Operate the ident button on the transponder
Squawk standby	Set the transponder to the standby position
Standby	Wait and I will call you
Unable	I cannot comply with your request, instruction or clearance (a reason is normally given)
Wilco	I understand your message and will co-operate with it
Words Twice	As a request – please transmit each word twice As information – I will transmit each word twice

Items that must be **read back**:

1	Runway in use
2	Clearance to land/take-off/backtrack, cross, enter, or hold short of, an active runway
3	Altimeter Settings
4	Airways, route and approach clearances
5	Taxy instructions
6	Level instructions
7	Heading instructions
8	Speed instructions
9	VDF information
10	Frequency changes
11	Type of radar service
12	SSR (transponder) operating instructions
13	Transition levels

And any other message, item or instruction if an ATSU requests a read back

JAA Private Pilot Licence – Aeroplanes & Helicopters

Communications

Time allowed: 40 minutes

No. of questions: 30

Total Marks: 100

Instructions:

The paper consists of 30 multiple choice questions, each carries 3.33 marks. The pass mark is 75% (i.e. 23 questions or more must be answered correctly). Marks are not deducted for incorrect answers.

Be sure to carefully read each question and ensure that you understand it before considering the answer choices. Only one of the answers is complete and correct; the others are either incomplete, incorrect or based on a misconception.

You should indicate the correct answer by placing a cross in the appropriate box of the answer sheet. If you decide to change an answer, you should erase the original choice and put a cross in the box representing your new selection.

Each question has an average answer time of 1 minute 20 seconds. No credit is given for unanswered questions.

1. How would a radio transmission that is readable, but with difficulty, be classified?

   (a) Readability 5

   (b) Readability 2

   (c) Readability 4

   (d) Readability 3

2. In response to an ATC query "(aircraft callsign) are you visual with the field?", the correct response may use which of following phrases?

   (a) ALMOST, BUT NOT YET

   (b) ROGER

   (c) CORRECT

   (d) AFFIRM or NEGATIVE

3. An aircraft's call-sign may be abbreviated by the pilot:

   (a) Only after it has been abbreviated by the ATSU

   (b) At the pilot's discretion

   (c) In any ongoing RTF exchange

   (d) Never

4. A radio frequency of 118.6MHz should be transmitted as:

   (a) WUN WUN AIT SIX

   (b) WUN WUN AIT DAYSEEMAL SIX

   (c) WUN WUN AIT POINT SIX

   (d) EIGHTEEN DAYSEEMAL SIX

5. An ATC instruction to check and confirm the aircraft's level for the purposes of verifying the transponder's Mode C read-out will be transmitted as:

   (a) [Callsign] squawk ident

   (b) [Callsign] confirm Mode C readout

   (c) [Callsign] confirm your level

   (d) [Callsign] squawk Charlie

6. The RTF phrase which means "Wait and I will call you" is:

   (a) Read Back

   (b) Wilco

   (c) Standby

   (d) Hold

7. A time of 1500 is transmitted as, and represents,

   (a) FIFTEEN HUNDRED HOURS, 3pm local time

   (b) WUN TOUSAND FIFE HUNDRED HOURS, 5pm UTC

   (c) ZERO ZERO HOURS, 1500 local time

   (d) WUN FIFE ZERO ZERO, 1500 UTC

8. At an airfield with ATC in operation, when a pilot has completed the pre take-off checks and is ready to take-off, the pilot should report:

   (a) 'Ready for departure'

   (b) 'Ready for take-off'

   (c) 'Ready in turn'

   (d) 'Ready to Go

9. During the en-route phase of a flight, in response to the invitation to "Pass your message", the most appropriate reply would include:

   (a) Callsign and type; altitude/level; pilot qualifications; Request

   (b) Callsign and type; departure, current position; next reporting point; persons on board

   (c) Callsign; current position; altitude/level; endurance; flight plan time to destination

   (d) Callsign and type; departure and destination, current position; altitude/level; intentions and flight rules; Request

10. What is the correct ATC phrase meaning 'operate the special position identification feature of your transponder' – that is the ident button:

    (a) Squawk standby

    (b) Squawk confirmation

    (c) Squawk Charlie

    (d) Squawk ident

11. Unlike a Radar Information Service (RIS), a Radar Advisory Service (RAS) is only available to:

    (a) Flights operating under VFR

    (b) Flights operating above FL95

    (c) Flights operating within 30nm

    (d) Flights operating under IFR

12. During the en-route phase of flight, a pilot wishes to file an airborne flight plan. This is best done using which ATSU service:

    (a) ATIS

    (b) FIS

    (c) VOLMET

    (d) A/G

13. A recorded broadcast of an individual airfield's meteorological and aerodrome information is most likely to be:

(a) ASS – Aerodrome Status Service

(b) AIS – Aerodrome Information Service

(c) MIS – Meteorological Information Service

(d) ATIS – Automatic Terminal Information Service

14. A 'distress' or 'urgency' call:

(a) Should initially be made on the frequency in use

(b) Should only ever be made on 121.5MHz

(c) Should be made initially to the nearest airfield

(d) Should be made on 123.45MHz

15. Which of the following is <u>not</u> a type of aeronautical communication service?

(a) ATC

(b) ACC

(c) AFIS

(d) AGCS

16. A QFE pressure setting of 981 millibars/hectopascals should be transmitted as:

(a) Altimeter Nine Eighty One

(b) Pressure Nine Eight One

(c) QFE Nine Eight One

(d) QFE Nine Eight One millibars

17. Which of the following options best describes the correct order of priority for RTF messages?

(a) Meteorological messages take precedence over Distress messages

(b) Flight Regularity messages take precedence over Urgency messages

(c) Flight Safety messages take precedence over Direction Finding messages

(d) Meteorological messages take precedence over Flight Regularity messages

18. A recorded message broadcast to pass routine arrival/departure information for a specific airfield is known as a:

(a) Specified Airfield Transit Information Service (SATIS)

(b) Particular Airfield Promulgation Information Service (PAPIS)

(c) Automatic Terminal Information Service (ATIS)

(d) Automated Flight Information Service (AFIS)

19. Turning onto final approach at a range of 6nm from the runway threshold, the pilot should report:

(a) Final

(b) Extended Final

(c) Long Final

(d) Short Final

20. An aircraft that is in an urgency situation should prefix its emergency call with the words:

(a) Mayday

(b) Pan Pan

(c) Pan

(d) Pan Pan; Pan Pan; Pan Pan

21. When an aircraft is making a 'Standard Overhead Join', the area to the side of the active runway opposite the prevailing circuit, where the aircraft descends to circuit height, is known as the:

(a) DESCENDING SIDE

(b) DEADSIDE

(c) OFFSIDE

(d) LIVESIDE

22. If making an Urgency or Distress message, following the appropriate prefix, the pilot should then state:

(a) The words 'all stations'

(b) The aircraft callsign

(c) The name of the station addressed

(d) The nature of the emergency

23. The classifications of emergency message are:

(a) Fuel Emergency, Urgency and Full Emergency

(b) Uncertainty, Safety and Mayday

(c) Pan and Distress

(d) Urgency and Distress

24. A pilot has been passed, acknowledged and has set a QFE pressure setting. As long as this pressure setting is in use, in term should be used to refer to the aircraft's level?

(a) Altitude

(b) Flight Level

(c) Height

(d) Any of the above, at the pilot's discretion

25. A ground station at an airfield using the callsign suffix 'Radio' is offering which type of service?

(a) An Air Ground Communications Service (AGCS or A/G)

(b) An Aerodrome Flight Information Service (AFIS)

(c) A Radar Approach Service

(d) A Ground Movement Control service

26. A pilot in contact with a VDF station wishes to obtain the aircraft's true bearing from the station. The request should include the appropriate 'Q' code, which in this case will be:

(a) QDR

(b) QDM

(c) QUJ

(d) QTE

27. To request a MATZ crossing, it is recommended that the pilot should contact the relevant ATSU:

(a) 15nm or 5 minutes from the MATZ boundary (whichever is sooner)

(b) 15nm or 5 minutes from the MATZ boundary (whichever is later)

(c) At any time before reaching the MATZ boundary

(d) At the MATZ boundary

28. The correct call-sign prefix to indicate that the pilot is a student pilot flying solo is:

(a) Novice

(b) Solo

(c) Learner

(d) Student

29. Which of the following best represents an item to be given as part of an initial Urgency or Distress call?

(a) Time airborne since departure

(b) Flight plan time en-route

(c) Location in terms of bearing and distance from station addressed

(d) Location in terms of present or last known position; Flight Level, Altitude or Height; heading

30. An Aerodrome Flight Information Service primarily provides information concerning the aerodrome and guidance to assist pilots in avoiding collisions to aircraft:

(a) Within 25nm and below 4,000ft

(b) Within the Aerodrome Traffic Zone (ATZ)

(c)   In radio contact

(d) On the ground only

1. A pilot wishing to indicate that he/she has received all of the last transmission should use the phrase:

   (a) WILCO

   (b) OVER

   (c) ROGER

   (d) CORRECT

2. How should a time of ten to ten in the morning be transmitted?

   (a) Ten to Ten Alpha Mike

   (b) Niner Fifty

   (c) Fife Zero or Zero Niner Fife Zero

   (d) Ten Ten

3. If the number 4500 is used in relation to an altitude, height or cloud ceiling, it should be pronounced as:

   (a) FOWER FIFE ZERO ZERO

   (b) FOURTY FIFE HUNDRED

   (c) FOWER TOUSAND FIFE HUNDRED

   (d) FOWER FIFE HUNDRED

4. A squawk of 7600 indicates that:

   (a) The aircraft has experienced a radio failure

   (b) The aircraft is engaged in parachute dropping

   (c) The aircraft is subject to unlawful interference

   (d) The aircraft is crossing an international boundary

5. What phrase indicates to a pilot that he/she should check and confirm the aircraft's level for the purposes of verifying the transponder mode C readout as seen by ATC?

   (a) Confirm (Level)

   (b) Verify (level)

   (c) Confirm Mode C reading

   (d) Read back Mode C level

6. A pilot makes a radio call in the following format:

   Aircraft callsign/Position/Time/Level/Next position and ETA

   This call is most likely to be:

   (a) A request for MATZ penetration

   (b) A request for Airways joining

   (c) A compulsory Position Report

   (d) An Emergency call

7. If a pilot needs to file an airborne flight plan, with which particular type of ATSU is it recommended that this should be done?

   (a) APPROACH

   (b) DIRECTOR

   (c) RADAR

   (d) FIS

8. When giving a Conditional Clearance to an aircraft awaiting departure, where the subject of the condition is an aircraft on approach, which of the following statements is true?

   (a) The aircraft on approach must be of 5700kg MTOW or more

   (b) The aircraft on approach must have its landing light illuminated

   (c) The aircraft on approach must be no more than number three to land

   (d) The aircraft on approach must be the next aircraft to land

9. A radio frequency of 118.625 should be transmitted as:

   (a) One Eighteen Decimal Six Two Five

   (b) One One Eight Decimal Six Two Five

   (c) One One Eight Sixty Two Point Five

   (d) Eight Point Six Two Five

10. The three types of Air Traffic Service Unit (ATSU), or aeronautical communication service, are:

    (a) Control unit, Information unit, Alerting unit

    (b) ATC, AFIS, AGCS

    (c) Approach, Tower, Ground

    (d) ACC, Tower, Mobile Ground Communications

11. When making a standard 'overhead join' from 1000ft above the circuit height, at what point would the pilot commence the descent to circuit height and report 'descending'?

    (a) Once within the ATZ, but not within 500ft of circuit height until on the 'dead side'

    (b) Once on the dead side of the runway, which is always the right-hand side

    (c) Once on the dead side of the runway, turning in the same direction as the established circuit

    (d) Over the 'live side' of the runway, whilst turning opposite to the established circuit direction

12. The transponder code 7700 can be used to indicate:

    (a) A simulated emergency, as long as you have broadcast this intention to the ATSU

    (b) A simulated emergency, if in communication with an ATSU

    (c) A distress situation, if the pilot is not in direct communication with an ATSU

    (d) A radio failure

13. When requesting a MATZ crossing, which of the following most closely represents the information to be passed?

    (a) Position, Heading, Time en-route

    (b) Position, ETA at next waypoint, destination, POB

    (c) ETA at MATZ boundary, Flight conditions, Level, Fuel endurance

    (d) Type; Point of departure, present Position; Altitude/height/flight level; Intentions; Request

14. The correct ATC phraseology meaning 'Confirm the code and mode set on the transponder' is:

    (a) Verify Squawk (code)

    (b) Confirm Squawk (code)

    (c) Squawk (code)

    (d) Reset Squawk (mode) (code)

15. A radar service that provides information on the bearing, range and level of conflicting traffic, but does not advise on avoiding action, is a:

    (a) Radar Control Service

    (b) Radar Advisory Service

    (c) Alerting Service

    (d) Radar Information Service

16. How should location be given as part of an initial Urgency or Distress call?

    (a) Bearing and distance from station addressed

    (b) Flight plan time en-route from departure

    (c) Distance airborne since departure and departure point

    (d) Present or last known position

17. Urgency is a condition where:

    (a) The aircraft is threatened by serious and/or imminent danger, and requires immediate assistance

    (b) There is a situation concerning the safety of an aircraft or other vehicle, or of some person on board or in sight, but not requiring immediate assistance

    (c) There is uncertainty of the flight's current status

    (d) It is expected that the aircraft will require assistance in the foreseeable future

18. An aircraft that is in 'distress' is:

    (a) Aware of a situation that may effect the safety of another aircraft or vehicle

    (b) To receive priority over all other radio calls except a 'PAN PAN' call

    (c) Aware of a condition concerning the safety of an aircraft or other vehicle, or of some person on board or in sight, but not requiring immediate assistance

    (d) In serious and/or imminent danger and requires immediate assistance

19. An emergency call regarding a condition of urgency is prefixed by the word(s):

(a) 'Mayday' spoken three times

(b) 'Mayday' spoken twice

(c) 'Pan' spoken three times

(d) 'Pan Pan' spoken three times

20. Following the 'MAYDAY' or 'PAN PAN' prefix to an emergency call, the recommended message format continues:

(a) Name of station addressed/aircraft type/nature of emergency

(b) Aircraft callsign/name of station addressed/aircraft type

(c) Aircraft callsign/aircraft type/name of station addressed

(d) Name of station addressed/Aircraft callsign/aircraft type

21. Which of the following best represents the order of information to be given in an emergency call:

(a) Aircraft callsign/Name of station addressed/nature of emergency/intentions of pilot/position (inc. level and heading)/pilot qualification/other information/aircraft type

(b) Name of station addressed/nature of emergency/position (inc. level and heading)/intentions of pilot/pilot qualification/other information/ Aircraft callsign/aircraft type

(c) Aircraft callsign/aircraft type/Name of station addressed/nature of emergency/intentions of pilot/pilot qualification/position (inc. level and heading)/other information/

(d) Name of station addressed/Aircraft callsign/aircraft type/nature of emergency/intentions of pilot/position (inc. level and heading)/pilot qualification/other information

22. The correct phraseology for a pilot to use once the pre take-off checks have been completed and he or she is ready to take-off is:

(a) [Callsign] ready for take-off

(b) [Callsign] ready for departure

(c) [Callsign] take-off

(d) [Callsign] pre take-off checks complete

23. An airfield operating an Aerodrome Flight Information Service (AFIS) should use the callsign:

(a) Radio

(b) Approach or Tower as appropriate

(c) Information

(d) Zone

24. An Aerodrome Flight Information Service (AFIS) is provided primarily:

(a) To offer flight information service for all aircraft in the specified FIR

(b) To give instructions and advice for aircraft inbound to the airfield

(c) For the safe and efficient conduct of flight within the Aerodrome Traffic Zone (ATZ)

(d) To provide information to all aircraft within 10nm/3000ft of the airfield

25. Where a read back IS NOT required, the phrase to indicate that a pilot has understood a message and will co-operate with it is:

(a) Roger

(b) Affirm

(c) Wilco

(d) Confirm

26. Which of the following choices best describes the correct order of priority for RTF messages?

(a) Urgency messages take precedence over Distress messages

(b) Flight Regularity messages take precedence over Meteorological messages

(c) Flight Safety messages take precedence over Flight Regularity messages

(d) Flight Regularity messages take precedence over Direction Finding Messages

27. An ATC instruction to climb or descend to an altitude could take which of the following forms?

(a) 'G-CD, descend altitude 2500ft'

(b) 'G-CD, climb to QHN 2500ft'

(c) 'G-CD, descend 2500ft'

(d) 'G-CD, Climb to altitude 2500ft'

28. An ATC route clearance can be given as:

(a) A departure clearance, which automatically includes take-off clearance

(b) A conditional clearance

(c) A clearance to take-off, with further instructions to follow

(d) A departure clearance, this is NOT a take-off clearance

29. A pilot wishes to know the magnetic bearing of the aircraft from a VDF station. The correct 'Q' code to use to obtain this bearing is:

(a) QTE

(b) QDM

(c) QNH

(d) QDR

30. A flight wishing to enter a control zone, which is unable to comply with IFR, but where conditions do not meet VMC criteria, may request a:

(a) Specified VFR (SVFR) Clearance

(b) Special VFR (SVFR) Clearance

(c) Single VFR (SVFR) Clearance

(d) Statutory VFR (SVFR) Clearance

1. The RTF phrase for 'I have received all of your last transmission' is:

    (a) 'Roger', which also implies that any instructions will be complied with

    (b) 'Roger', which does not mean that any instructions will be complied with

    (c) 'Roger', which means that a response is required

    (d) 'Roger', which has the same meaning as 'affirm'

2. The correct classifications of emergency messages are:

    (a) Distress, Pan, Alert

    (b) Emergency, Urgency, Standby

    (c) Mayday, Emergency, Alert

    (d) Distress, Urgency

3. Pilots are recommended to make contact with the appropriate ATSU 15 miles or 5 minutes (whichever is sooner) before reaching:

    (a) A LARS area

    (b) A compulsory reporting point

    (c) A MATZ boundary

    (d) An ATZ

4. The standard format of a 'conditional clearance' is:

    (a) (Aircraft callsign)/(condition)/(instruction)

    (b) (Aircraft callsign)/(instruction)/(condition)

    (c) (Condition)/(instruction)/(aircraft callsign)

    (d) (Instruction) (aircraft callsign)/(condition)

5. A radio transmission that is classified as readability 2 is:

    (a) Readable now and then

    (b) Readable but with difficulty

    (c) Unreadable

    (d) Readable

6. Where an ATSU permits a callsign to be abbreviated, the correct abbreviation of Thurston G-ASMY would be:

    (a) Thurston MY

    (b) Thurston G-MY

    (c) Thurston G-ASMY

    (d) Thurston Y

7. In an on-going communications exchange, it is normal practice to abbreviate the aircraft callsign:

    (a) Once satisfactory two-way communications have been established, and there will be no confusion

    (b) Only after the ATSU has abbreviated the aircraft callsign

    (c) Never

    (d) Only after the pilot has made a specific request to ATSU to abbreviate the aircraft callsign

8. Which of the following calls represent the proper initial call to the Aerodrome Flight Information Service at Wolverhampton airfield by a pilot requiring a flight information service?

(a) Wolverhampton radio, G-ABCD request flight information service

(b) Wolverhampton approach, G-ABCD request flight information service

(c) Wolverhampton information, G-ABCD request radar information service

(d) Wolverhampton information, G-ABCD request flight information service

9. If a pilot wishes to indicate that the aircraft has suffered a radio communications failure, the appropriate transponder code to use is:

(a) 7500

(b) 7700

(c) 7000

(d) 7600

10. An ATIS at an airfield provides:

(a) An Aerodrome Transit Indicator Service

(b) An Alerting Traffic Information Service

(c) An Automatic Terminal Information Service

(d) An Alternative Type Indicator Service

11. An ATSU at an airfield offering at Air Traffic Control service could use the callsign:

(a) Information

(b) Radio

(c) Controller

(d) Tower

12. In response to the radio call 'G-CD final', what response would be expected from an Aerodrome Flight Information Service (AFIS)?

(a) Roger G-CD, surface wind 180/10

(b) G-CD, runway 15 cleared to land, surface wind 180/10

(c) G-CD, land at your discretion, surface wind 180/10

(d) G-CD, continue approach, surface wind 180/10

13. An ATSU that wants a pilot to set the code 7000 on the transponder and select the altitude reporting function. The correct RTF instruction would be:

(a) Set 7000, Charlie

(b) Squawk 7000 mode Charlie

(c) Send down 7000 with Charlie

(d) Set conspicuity with altitude reporting

14. A pilot is in established communication with an ATSU, who have allocated a squawk (SSR code), when an emergency situation occurs. The pilot should notify this emergency condition by:

(a) Changing to 121.5MHz and making an emergency call

(b) Changing the squawk to 7000 whilst maintaining radio silence

(c) Making an emergency call on the frequency in use and maintaining the allocated SSR code

(d) Squawking 7700 whilst changing to 121.5MHz

15. A pilot can abbreviate the aircraft callsign:

(a) Once ATC have done so, then retain that abbreviation on initial contact with all subsequent ATSUs

(b) Subject to written permission from the CAA

(c) Never

(d) Only after the ATSU has abbreviated the aircraft callsign, reverting to the full callsign on each initial contact with the next ATSU

16. Which of the following best represents ATC messages that must be read back in full?

(a) Airways or route clearances, Taxy instructions, Level instructions, Type of radar service, SSR (transponder) operating instructions, Runway state

(b) Altimeter Settings, Airways or route clearances, Transition levels, Visibility, Time checks, VDF information, Traffic information, Frequency changes

(c) Airways or route clearances, Taxy instructions, Level instructions, Speed instructions, VDF information, Frequency changes, Type of radar service, Transition levels

(d) Runway in use, Clearance to land/take-off/backtrack, cross, enter, or hold short of, an active runway, Altimeter Settings, Speed instructions, Cloud base, Surface wind

17. A pilot has a very important message concerning the safety of an aircraft or some person in it, or some person or vehicle in sight of the aircraft but not requiring immediate assistance. This is a .... situation:

(a) Urgency

(b) Difficulty

(c) Distress

(d) Safety

18. A distress message should be prefixed by:

(a) PAN PAN' repeated three times

(b) 'PAN' repeated three times

(c) 'MAYDAY MAYDAY' said once

(d) 'MAYDAY' repeated three times '

19. Which of the following is not a <u>required</u> part of an Urgency or Distress message?

(a) Number of persons on board

(b) Frequency used for emergency call

(c) Aircraft type

(d) Position

20. When making an emergency call, the name of the station addressed:

(a) Should never be given

(b) Should be given at the end of the message

(c) Should be given immediately after the 'MAYDAY' or 'PAN PAN' prefix where know and if circumstances permit

(d) Emergency calls should always be addressed to 'London D & D Cell'

21. After the prefix, an emergency message should (where circumstances permit) take what order?

(a) Nature of emergency/aircraft callsign/name of station addressed/intentions of pilot/position (inc. level and heading)/pilot qualification/other information/aircraft type

(b) Name of station addressed/aircraft callsign/aircraft type/nature of emergency/intentions of pilot/position (inc. level and heading)/pilot qualification/other information

(c) Pilot qualification/position (inc. level and heading)/other information/ aircraft callsign/aircraft type/nature of emergency/intentions of pilot/pilot qualification/position (inc. level and heading/other information)

(d) Aircraft callsign/aircraft type/intentions of pilot/pilot qualification/other information

22. When should a pilot, in communication with an ATC unit, first use the phrase 'take-off'?

(a) To indicate that the aircraft is ready for take-off

(b) When 'booking-out' by radio

(c) Only when the words 'take-off' have first been used y the ATSU, for example when giving clearance to take-off

(d) To acknowledge a departure clearance

23. Where a flight is receiving a Radar Information Service, which of the following statements is true?

(a) ATC will inform the pilot of conflicting traffic, but no avoiding action is given

(b) ATC will inform the pilot of conflicting traffic, and advise on avoiding action

(c) ATC is responsible for terrain clearance

(d) RIS will only be given to aircraft operating under IFR

24. Which of the following choices best describes the correct order of priority for radio messages?

(a) Flight Safety messages take precedence over Urgency messages

(b) Flight Regularity messages take precedence over Meteorological messages

(c) Distress messages take precedence over Flight Regularity messages

(d) Flight Regularity messages take precedence over Direction Finding Messages

25. In which of the following circumstances might it be appropriate to request a Special VFR (SVFR) clearance?

(a) To cross an ATZ in uncontrolled airspace when flying IFR

(b) To cross a Class A airway in VMC

(c) To cross a CTR, without landing at the controlling aerodrome, without contacting ATC

(d) To operate in a CTR without complying with IFR

26. A time of 2107 could be transmitted as:

(a) SEVEN

(b) SEVEN PLUS

(c) SEVEN PAST

(d) TOO WUN ZERO SEVEN

27. A flight is instructed to fly at a specified altitude. The correct pressure setting to use so that the altimeter indicates altitude is:

(a) QNH

(b) QFE

(c) QDM

(d) QSY

28. The magnetic bearing to a VDF station, or the magnetic heading to reach a VDF station assuming nil wind, is described in the 'Q' code as:

(a) QNE

(b) QDR

(c) QTE

(d) QDM

29. When can a Conditional Clearance be given by an ATC unit?

(a) Only when the aircraft/vehicles concerned are visible to the pilot and controller

(b) Only when Low Visibility Procedures (LVPs) are in operation

(c) Only in situations of high traffic density

(d) Only when the clearance relates to an aircraft and a vehicle

30. After making an initial call to an ATSU, a pilot is instructed to 'standby'. The correct response is:

(a) 'Standing By (callsign)', make a further call if more than 30 seconds elapse

(b) 'Roger standby (then pass message)'

(c) No response is expected, assume no onward clearance

(d) 'Wilco', and continue assuming onward clearance has been given

Paper 1 Answers and Explanations

ECP1Q1   Answer D

The 'readability' of a radio transmission can be classified in accordance with the table below:

Readability Scale	Definition
1	Unreadable
2	Readable now and then
3	Readable but with difficulty
4	Readable
5	Perfectly readable

Further Reference: PPL2 » Communications » Departure Procedures » Radio Check

ECP1Q2   Answer D

The essential purpose of standard phraseology in aviation communications is to avoid confusion and ambiguities. This is why so much emphasis is placed on only using recognised phraseology. In response to a query, the following responses are particularly inappropriate:

'CORRECT'   This only means 'True or accurate'

'WILCO'   This only means 'I have understood and will comply with your message'

'ROGER'   This only means 'I have received all of your last transmission'

It should be clear that using either of these replies to a question that simply require a 'yes' (AFFIRM) or 'no' (NEGATIVE) response is almost certain to generate confusion and ambiguity

Further Reference: PPL2 » Communications » Departure Procedures » Standard Phraseology

ECP1Q3   Answer A

Once satisfactory two-way communication has been established with an ATSU, it is normal practice for both parties to drop the use of the ATSU call-sign and suffix in an ongoing exchange. However, an aircraft may only abbreviate its own call-sign after the ATSU has first done so.

Further Reference: PPL2 » Communications » Callsigns, Abbreviations, General Procedures » Callsigns

ECP1Q4   Answer B

The standard protocol is that when transmitting a radio frequency, all digits are pronounced, and the decimal place is indicated using the word 'decimal' (pronounced DAYSEEMAL).

Further Reference: PPL2 » Communications » General Operating Procedures » Transmission of Numbers and Transmission of Time

ECP1Q5   Answer C

Where an aircraft's transponder is fitted with Mode C, this mode will give the aircraft's flight level (based on 1013mb/hPa) to the radar unit. Some units are able to process this read-out further and convert the screen display to show the aircraft's altitude based on the actual QNH. The ATC instruction "Confirm [level]" means that the pilot should check and confirm the aircraft's level and is used to verify that the Mode C Flight Level / Altitude read-out the controller is seeing is within acceptable tolerances.

Further Reference: PPL2 » Communications » En-route Procedures » Use of Transponder

ECP1Q6   Answer C

'Standby' means wait. No acknowledgement is required; wait and the ATSU will call the pilot back. The instruction "standby" does **not** imply that any clearance or service is given to the pilot.

PPL2 » Communications » En-route Procedures » Establishing Contact – Passing Details

ECP1Q7   Answer D

The digits of a time are normally transmitted individually, sometimes stating the minutes only, but usually all four digits if the time is 'on the hour' or where confusion might arise. In aviation time is referred to using the '24 hour' clock, which equates to the '12' hour clock as below:

0100	1am
0200	2am
0300	3am
0400	4am
0500	5am
0600	6am
0700	7am
0800	8am
0900	9am
1000	10am
1100	11am
1200	12am (midday or noon)
1300	1pm
1400	2pm
1500	3pm
1600	4pm
1700	5pm
1800	6pm
1900	7pm
2000	8pm
2100	9pm
2200	10pm
2300	11pm
2400	12pm (midnight)

The standard time reference for aviation time is 'UTC', which to all intents and purposes is the same as what used to be referred to at 'GMT'. UTC is the same all over the world, when it is 1200UTC in London, it is 1200UTC at every other place in the world, it does not vary by location or season.

Further Reference: PPL2 » Communications » General Operating Procedures » Transmission of Numbers and Transmission of Time

ECP1Q8   Answer A

When the pilot is ready for take-off, the correct phrase to use is 'Ready for departure'. The pilot should never use the phrase 'take-off' until acknowledging a clearance to take-off issued by an ATC unit.

Further Reference: PPL2 » Communications » Departure Procedures » Taxying Instructions, Holding Instructions, Take-off Instructions

ECP1Q9   Answer D

When an ATSU invites a pilot flying en-route to "Pass your message", probably the most commonly used mnemonic for passing flight details is TP AIR:

T   aircraft **T**ype
P   Point of departure and destination, present **P**osition
A   **A**ltitude/height/flight level, with altimeter setting if appropriate
I   **I**ntentions i.e. estimate, routing, destination, flight rules (VFR/IFR) etc.
R   **R**equest – type of service required etc.

This mnemonic should provide all the information the controller needs; you will be prompted if further information is required.

Further Reference: PPL2 » Communications » En-route Procedures » Establishing Contact – Passing Details

ECP1Q10   Answer D

The phrase 'squawk ident' means 'Operate the special position identification feature', this 'special identification feature' is the ident button on the transponder. When this button is pressed, the aircraft's Secondary Surveillance Radar (SSR) return on the controller's radar screen flashes. The most common SSR phrases, and their meanings, are given below:

Standard Phraseology	Meaning
Squawk (code and mode)	Set this mode and code
Squawk standby	Set the transponder to the standby position
Squawk Charlie	Set the transponder to mode C
Squawk ident	Operate the ident button on the transponder
Confirm squawk (code)	Confirm the code and mode set on the transponder
Reset Squawk (mode)(code)	Set the transponder to standby, then re-select the assigned code and mode
Confirm (level)	Check and confirm your level (used to verify the Mode C flight level/altitude read-out the controller is seeing)

(SSR operating instructions require a read back).

Further Reference: PPL2 » Communications » En-route Procedures » Use of Transponder

ECP1Q11   Answer D

A Radar Advisory Service (RAS) is an Air Traffic Radar Service which is only available to aircraft operating under IFR (Instrument Flight Rules), regardless of the in-flight conditions. When providing this service the controller will pass information on any known conflicting traffic and **advice** on avoiding action, advice which the pilot is expected to comply with. The pilot must advise the controller before changing heading or level.

PPL2 » Communications » En-route Procedures » Radar and Non-Radar Services

ECP1Q12   Answer B

The Flight Information Service (FIS) exists to give information useful to the safe and efficient conduct of a flight. In the UK, each Flight Information Region has one or more FIS contact frequencies, and these FIS are useful contact points for such services as filing an airborne flight plan, obtaining airways joining clearances, obtaining meteorological information etc.

Further Reference: PPL2 » Communications » En-route Procedures » Radar and Non-Radar Services

ECP1Q13   Answer D

At larger airfields there may be a recorded broadcast of aerodrome and current weather information, this broadcast is known as 'ATIS' (Automatic Terminal Information Service). An ATIS broadcast usually transmits on either a dedicated VHF frequency or is radiated by a VOR close to the airfield. An ATIS broadcasts the actual weather report for the airfield, together with the runway in use and any other relevant departure or arrival information. When arriving at or departing from an airfield which has ATIS, the pilot should listen to the ATIS information before establishing contact with the ATSU and confirm receipt of the ATIS in the initial call.

Further Reference: PPL2 » Communications » En-route Procedures » VOLMET and ATIS

ECP1Q14   Answer A

An emergency radio call, such as a Distress or Urgency message, should initially be made on the radio frequency in use. Only if the pilot is unsuccessful in making contact, or if no frequency is currently in use, should the pilot make the call on the international distress frequency of 121.5MHz.

Further Reference: PPL2 » Communications » Emergency Procedures » Emergency Frequencies

ECP1Q15   Answer B

There are three types of Traffic Service Unit (ATSU), or aeronautical communication service, namely:

Air Traffic Control Unit (ATC Unit);

Aerodrome Flight Information Service (AFIS);

Aerodrome Air/Ground Communication Service (AGCS).

Further Reference: PPL2 » Communications » Air Traffic Service Units » Types of ATSU

ECP1Q16   Answer C

Pressure settings should always be transmitted as separate digits – hence 'Nine Eight One" and not "Nine Eighty One". Although the word 'millibars' can be omitted when the pressure is 1000 millibars or more, it should always be used when the pressure setting being transmitted is below 1000 millibars.

Further Reference: PPL2 » Communications » General Operating Procedures » Transmission of Numbers and Transmission of Time PPL2 » Communications » Callsigns, Abbreviations, General Procedures » Omission of Words and Phrases

ECP1Q17   Answer D

The order of priority of RTF aeronautical messages, starting with the most important, is:

(1) Distress messages

(2) Urgency messages

(3) Direction Finding messages

(4) Flight Safety messages

(5) Meteorological messages

(6) Flight Regularity messages

Further Reference: PPL2 » Communications » Call Signs, Abbreviations, General Procedures » Categories of Message

ECP1Q18   Answer C

An Automatic Terminal Information Service (ATIS) broadcast usually transmits on either a dedicated VHF frequency or is radiated by a VOR close to the airfield. An ATIS broadcasts the actual weather report for the airfield, together with the runway in use and any other relevant departure or arrival information. Each broadcast is given a letter, and when arriving at or departing from an airfield which has ATIS, the pilot should listen to the ATIS information before establishing contact with the ATSU and confirm receipt of the ATIS in the initial call by quoting the letter.

Further Reference: PPL2 » Communications » En-route Procedures » VOLMET and ATIS

ECP1Q19   Answer C

Distance from Touchdown	Radio Report
8 – 4 miles	Long Final
Less than 4 miles	Final

Further Reference: PPL2 » Communications » Arrival/Traffic Pattern Procedures » Landing Clearance

ECP1Q20   Answer D

An urgency emergency message should be prefixed with the spoken words 'Pan Pan' repeated three times.

Further Reference: PPL2 » Communications » Emergency Procedures » Distress/Urgency Calls

ECP1Q21   Answer B

In the standard overhead join, the arriving aircraft maintains its altitude (often 2,000ft above aerodrome level) until it is on the side of the landing runway opposite to the active circuit. This side of the runway is known as the 'Deadside' and it is on this side of the runway that the aircraft descends to circuit height.

Further Reference: PPL2 » Communications » Arrival/Traffic-Pattern Procedures » Circuit Joining and Overhead Joins

ECP1Q22   Answer C

The correct format of an emergency message, following the prefix 'Mayday, Mayday, Mayday' or 'Pan Pan, Pan Pan, Pan Pan' as appropriate, is:

(1) Name of the station addressed

(2) Aircraft callsign

(3) Aircraft Type

(4) Nature of emergency

(5) Intentions of pilot

(6) Position (or last known position); Flight Level/Altitude/Height; Heading

(7) Pilot qualifications (e.g. No instrument qualification, student pilot, etc.)

(8) Any other useful information e.g. persons on board etc

Further Reference: PPL2 » Communications » Emergency Procedures » Distress/Urgency Calls

ECP1Q23   Answer D

The two classified states of emergency are:

URGENCY – A condition concerning the safety of an aircraft or other vehicle, or of some person on board or in sight, but not requiring immediate assistance.

DISTRESS – The aircraft is threatened by serious and/or imminent danger and requires immediate assistance.

Further Reference: PPL2 » Communications » Emergency Procedures » Priority of Messages

ECP1Q24   Answer C

The table below summarised the three altimeter settings, and the appropriate terminology. It is essential that there is no confusion between pilot and controller on this point, the pilot should always know what pressure setting is being used and how it represents the aircraft's vertical distance above the surface.

Altimeter Setting	Datum	Terminology
QFE	A fixed point on the surface	'Height'
QNH	Mean Sea Level	'Altitude'
Standard Setting	The 1013mb pressure level	'Flight Level'

Further Reference: PPL2 » Communications » En-Route Procedures » Level and Position Reporting

ECP1Q25   Answer A

The three types of Air Traffic Service Units (ATSU) at an airfield, and the appropriate callsign suffixes, are:

Type of ATSU	Callsign
Air Traffic Control Unit	Control, Radar, Approach, Director, Tower, Ground
Aerodrome Flight Information Service	Information
Aerodrome Air/Ground Communication Service	Radio

Further Reference: PPL2 » Communications » Air Traffic Service Units » Types of ATSU

ECP1Q26   Answer D

A pilot can request the aircraft's true bearing from a VDF station (in other words, the magnetic radial, corrected for variation), by using the 'Q' code QTE, or simply by requesting 'True Bearing'. The appropriate 'Q' codes to be used when requesting or confirming VDF information are:

QDM   The magnetic track **TO** the VDF station

QDR   The magnetic bearing **FROM** the VDF station

QTE   The true bearing **FROM** the VDF station

Further Reference: PPL2 » Communications » En-Route Procedures » VHF Direction Finding (VDF)

ECP1Q27   Answer A

A pilot wishing to enter a MATZ is advised to contact the controlling airfield at a range of 15nm, or a flying time of 5 minutes, from the MATZ boundary – whichever is sooner (ie further away).

Further Reference: PPL2 » Communications » En-route Procedures » MATZs

ECP1Q28   Answer D

Within the UK, student pilots who are flying solo should use the callsign prefix 'Student' on making initial contact with an ATSU, so that the Air Traffic Service can take into account the student pilot's more limited ability and experience when issuing information and/or instructions.

PPL2 » Communications » Callsigns, Abbreviations, General Procedures » Student Callsign

ECP1Q29   Answer D

The correct format of an emergency message is given at Explanation ECP1Q22.

Although there is a recommended emergency message format, in reality the pilot should include the location (present or last known) in any terms that make sense. Likewise, the current level and heading may not be relevant in all situations.

Further Reference: PPL2 » Communications » Emergency Procedures » Distress/Urgency Calls

ECP1Q30   Answer B

An Aerodrome Flight Information Service (AFIS) is provided at an aerodrome primarily for the safe and efficient conduct of flight within the Aerodrome Traffic Zone – ATZ. To aircraft about to take-off and those in flight an AFIS issues information concerning the aerodrome and guidance to assist pilots in avoiding collisions.

PPL2 » Communications » Air Traffic Service Units » Types of ATSU

Paper 2 Answers and Explanations

ECP2Q1   Answer C

The word 'ROGER' means that the speaker has received all of the last transmission – nothing more. There is no inference that the speaker has understood the message in any way, or has any intention of acting on it or complying with any instruction or clearance within it.

Further Reference: PPL2 » Communications » Departure Procedures » Roger

ECP2Q2   Answer C

A time of ten to ten in the morning is, of course, also 09:50.

Provided no confusion will arise, time is normally transmitted in minutes only. Even if the hour is included as well, each digit is transmitted separately.

Further Reference: PPL2 » Communications » General Operating Procedures » Transmission of Numbers and Transmission of Time

ECP2Q3   Answer C

When a number is given in relation to altitude, height, cloud height, cloud ceiling and visibility, it is normally pronounced in thousands (TOUSAND) and hundreds (HUN DRED) of the relevant unit.

Further Reference: PPL2 » Communications » General Operating Procedures » Transmission of Numbers and Transmission of Time

ECP2Q4   Answer A

Transponder code (squawk) 7600 is one of the 'special purpose' codes to be used in specified circumstances and when ATC have not allocated the aircraft a squawk. The special purpose codes, and their meanings, are:

Code	Meaning
7500	Unlawful interference with planned operation of flight
7600	Radio Failure
7700	Emergency Condition

Further Reference: PPL2 » Communications » En-route Procedures » Use of Transponder

ECP2Q5   Answer A

The table below summarises common Secondary Surveillance Radar (SSR) phraseology and the appropriate meaning:

Standard Phraseology	Meaning
Squawk (code)	Set this code
Squawk standby	Set the transponder to the standby position
Squawk charlie	Set the transponder to mode C (altitude reporting)
Squawk ident	Operate the ident button on the transponder (special position identification feature)
Confirm squawk (code)	Confirm the code and mode set on the transponder
Reset Squawk (mode)(code)	Set the transponder to standby, then re-select the assigned code and mode
Confirm (level)	Check and confirm your level (used to verify the Mode C flight level/altitude read-out the controller is seeing)
Stop squawk Charlie	Deselect the altitude reporting feature

All SSR operating instructions require a read back.

Further Reference: PPL2 » Communications » En-route Procedures » Use of Transponder

ECP2Q6   Answer C

A compulsory position report is fairly rare nowadays, and position reporting is normally confined to airways and advisory routes, especially where there is no radar service available. The correct format for a position report is:

> **Aircraft callsign**
> **Position**
> **Time**
> **Level**
> **Next position and ETA**

Further Reference: PPL2 » Communications » En-route Procedures » Level and Position Reports

ECP2Q7   Answer D

It is recommended that an airborne flight plan should be filed on a Flight Information Service frequency, for example 'London Information'

Further Reference: PPL2 » Communications » En-route Procedures » Radar and Non-Radar Services

ECP2Q8   Answer D

Conditional Clearances are only used when the aircraft concerned are visible to both the controller and pilot. In the case of landing traffic, the subject of the condition must be the first aircraft on approach. A Conditional Clearance is given in the format:

Callsign/the condition and identification of subject of the condition/the instruction

Further Reference: PPL2 » Communications » Departure Procedures » Conditional Clearances

ECP2Q9   Answer B

When a radio frequency is pronounced, the word "decimal" is included and every digit is transmitted.

Further Reference: PPL2 » Communications » General Operating Procedures » Transmission of Numbers and Transmission of Time

ECP2Q10   Answer B

There are three types of Traffic Service Unit (ATSU), or aeronautical communication service, namely:

Air Traffic Control Unit (ATC Unit)	A place from which instructions and advice can be issued.
Aerodrome Flight Information Service (AFIS)	An Aerodrome Flight Information Service (AFIS) is provided at an aerodrome primarily for the safe and efficient conduct of flight within the Aerodrome Traffic Zone – ATZ. An AFIS is provided by a Flight Information Service Officer (FISO).
Aerodrome Air/Ground Communication Service (AGCS)	An air/ground communication service is a rudimentary service provided by a radio operator who holds a certificate of competence.

Further Reference: PPL2 » Communications » Air Traffic Service Units » Types of ATSU

ECP2Q11   Answer C

The standard over-head join is illustrated below. The 'descending' call is made once the aircraft has commenced its descent on the 'deadside'.

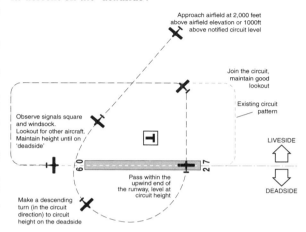

Approach airfield at 2,000 feet above airfield elevation or 1000ft above notified circuit level

Join the circuit, maintain good lookout

Existing circuit pattern

LIVESIDE

Observe signals square and windsock. Lookout for other aircraft. Maintain height until on 'deadside'

DEADSIDE

Pass within the upwind end of the runway, level at circuit height

Make a descending turn (in the circuit direction) to circuit height on the deadside

Further Reference: PPL2 » Communications » Arrival/Traffic Pattern Procedures » Circuit Joining and Overhead Joins

ECP2Q12   Answer C

The transponder code 7700 indicates an emergency, but should only be used in the first instance if the pilot is not in direct communication with an ATSU and if no other ATC-allocated squawk is in use.

If the pilot is already in communication with an ATSU when an emergency arises, the appropriate emergency call should be made, and in due course the ATSU will advise if the squawk should be changed.

Further Reference: PPL2 » Communications » En-Route Procedures » Use of Transponder

PPL2 » Communications » Emergency Procedures » Distress/Urgency Calls

ECP2Q13   Answer D

Option D represents the closest fit to the recommended MATZ penetration request, and is based around the standard 'TP AIR' message format, namely:

T	aircraft **T**ype
P	Point of departure, present **P**osition
A	**A**ltitude/height/flight level, with altimeter setting if appropriate
I	**I**ntentions i.e. estimate, routing, destination, flight rules (VFR/IFR) etc.
R	**R**equest – type of service required etc.

Further Reference: PPL2 » Communications » En-route Procedures » MATZs

ECP2Q14 — Answer B

The full set of Secondary Surveillance Radar phrases and their meaning is given at explanation ECP1Q10.

Further Reference: PPL2 » Communications » En-route Procedures » Use of Transponder

ECP2Q15 — Answer D

As the name implies, a Radar Information Service (RIS) provides information on conflicting traffic, but leaves the pilot to decided on what avoiding action (if any) to take. Information on other traffic is most often given in the form:

- the relative bearing of the conflicting traffic
- distance from the conflicting traffic
- flight direction of the conflicting traffic
- relative speed of the conflicting traffic, or aircraft type and level if known

Further Reference: PPL2 » Communications » En-route Procedures » Radar and Non-Radar Services

ECP2Q16 — Answer D

The correct format of an emergency message is given at in the 'Essential Revision' section.

Although there is a recommended emergency message format, in reality the pilot should include the location (present or last known) in any terms that make sense. Likewise, the current level and heading may not be relevant in all situations.

Further Reference: PPL2 » Communications » Emergency Procedures » Distress/Urgency Calls

ECP2Q17 — Answer B

The definitions of Urgency and Distress are given in full at the 'Essential Revision' section.

Further Reference: PPL2 » Communications » Emergency Procedures » Distress/Urgency Calls

ECP2Q18 — Answer D

The definition of 'Distress' is given in the 'Essential Revision' section, but it is given here again:

DISTRESS – The aircraft is threatened by serious and/or imminent danger and requires immediate assistance

Further Reference: PPL2 » Communications » Emergency Procedures » Priority of Messages

ECP2Q19 — Answer D

A message regarding a condition of urgency is transmitted using the prefix 'Pan Pan' repeated three times.

Further Reference: PPL2 » Communications » Emergency Procedures » Distress/Urgency Calls

ECP2Q20 — Answer D

The recommended format of an emergency call is given at the 'Essential Revision' section.

Further Reference: PPL2 » Communications » Emergency Procedures » Distress/Urgency Calls

ECP2Q21 — Answer D

The recommended format of an emergency call is given in the 'Essential Revision' section.

Further Reference: PPL2 » Communications » Emergency Procedures » Distress/Urgency Calls

ECP2Q22 — Answer B

After completing the pre-take-off checks satisfactorily, the pilot reports that he or she is ready to depart. The phraseology used is "ready for departure". The words 'take-off' are **not** used at this stage. Once a pilot has reported ready for departure, and if the ATSU knows of no reason why the aircraft should not go, the words "take-off" can be used for the first time, by the ATSU: the phrase "take-off" will first be used by the ATSU, not the pilot.

Further Reference: PPL2 » Communications » Departure Procedures » Taxying Instructions, Holding Instructions, Take-off Instructions

ECP2Q23 — Answer C

An Aerodrome Flight Information Service (AFIS) is indicated by using the word 'Information' after the airfield name. eg 'Wolverhampton Information'.

The full list of ATSU call signs is given in the 'Essential Revision' section.

Further Reference: PPL2 » Communications » Air Traffic Service Units » Types of ATSU

ECP2Q24 — Answer C

An Aerodrome Flight Information Service (AFIS) is provided at an aerodrome primarily for the safe and efficient conduct of flight within the Aerodrome Traffic Zone – ATZ.

Further Reference: PPL2 » Communications » Air Traffic Service Units » Types of ATSU

ECP2Q25 — Answer C

The meaning of 'WILCO' is 'I understand your message and will comply with it'. 'Wilco' is an abbreviation for 'will comply'.

The word 'Roger' merely means that the message has been received, it does not imply that it has been understood, nor that it will be complied with.

Further Reference: PPL2 » Communications » En-route Procedures » Standard Phraseology

ECP2Q26 — Answer C

The order of priority of RTF aeronautical messages is given in explanation ECP1Q17.

Further Reference: PPL2 » Communications » Call Signs, Abbreviations, General Procedures » Categories of Message

ECP2Q27   Answer D

When giving a climb or descent instruction in relation to an altitude or height, the word 'TO' is always used after the climb/descent instruction and before the required altitude/height. Hence the message format is:

"(aircraft callsign)/(Climb/descend) TO
ALTITUDE/HEIGHT (altitude/height in feet)"

The word 'TO' is omitted when giving climb/descent instructions in relation to a Flight Level.

Further Reference: PPL2 » Communications » En-route Procedures » Level and Position Reporting

ECP2Q28   Answer D

An ATC route clearance may often be in the format of a departure clearance, a set of instructions giving a route (and level and squawk instructions) to be followed AFTER departure. An ATC route clearance is **NOT** an instruction to take-off or enter an active runway.

Further Reference: PPL2 » Communications » Departure Procedures » Departure Clearance/Departure Instructions

ECP2Q29   Answer D

QDR is defined as the magnetic bearing of the aircraft FROM the VDF station. It is the reciprocal of the QDM – the magnetic bearing to the station, or the magnetic heading to reach the station assuming nil wind. The QDR can also be described as the radial.

The full set of 'Q' codes used in VHF Direction Finding is given in the 'Essential Revision' section.

Further Reference: PPL2 » Communications » En-route Procedures » VHF Direction Finding (VDF)

ECP2Q30   Answer B

A Special VFR (SVFR) clearance allows a flight to operate in a control zone (CTR) without complying with Instrument Flight Rules (IFR), but in weather conditions which do not meet the Visual Meteorological Conditions (VMC) criteria specified for that airspace.

Further Reference: PPL2 » Air Law » Division of Airspace and Air Traffic Services » Special VFR

Paper 3 Answers and Explanations

ECP3Q1   Answer B

The phrase 'Roger' means only 'I have received all of your last transmission'. It should not be used where the speaker wishes to indicate that an instruction will be complied with, or that a message has been understood, or in place of a required read back, or to indicate anything other than the speaker has received the other parties transmission.

Further Reference: PPL2 » Communications » Departure Procedures » Roger

ECP3Q2   Answer D

There are two classifications of emergency message: Distress and Urgency. A distress message takes priority over all other radio messages. An urgency message takes priority over all messages except a distress message.

Further Reference: PPL2 » Communications » Emergency Procedures » Priority of Messages

ECP3Q3   Answer C

It is recommended that a flight planning to enter a Military Aerodrome Traffic Zone (MATZ) should contact the controlling ATSU 15 miles or 5 minutes (whichever is sooner) before reaching the MATZ boundary.

Further Reference: PPL2 » Communications » En-route Procedures » MATZs

ECP3Q4   Answer A

A controller may offer a *conditional clearance*. To give a conditional clearance the format is:

Aircraft callsign/the condition/ the instruction.

Thus, for example:

(callsign) "G-VC…/

(the condition, and the object of the condition) …after the landing Warrior…

(the instruction/clearance) …runway 31 line-up and wait"

For a pilot to be able to accept such a clearance, he/she must be able to identify the object of the condition.

Further Reference: PPL2 » Communications » Departure Procedures » Conditional Clearances

ECP3Q5   Answer A

The table of the 'readability' of a radio transmission is given in the 'Essential Revision' section.

Further Reference: PPL2 » Communications » Departure Procedures » Radio Check

ECP3Q6   Answer A

This callsign is abbreviated in accordance with the table given at explanation ECP1Q5.

Further Reference: PPL2 » Communications » Callsigns, Abbreviations, General Procedures » Callsigns

ECP3Q7   Answer B

In the initial contact with an Air Traffic Service Unit (ATSU) or ground station, the full aircraft call sign and the full Air Traffic Service Unit (ATSU) name, call sign and suffix should be used. The pilot should only abbreviate the aircraft's call sign AFTER the ATSU has done so and use the same abbreviate given by the ATS.

Further Reference: PPL2 » Communications » Callsigns, Abbreviations, General Procedures » Callsigns

ECP3Q8   Answer D

An airfield operating an Aerodrome Flight Information Service (AFIS) has the callsign 'information'. Where a pilot requires a specific service, (eg MATZ penetration, Radar Information Service, Flight Information Service) it is an option to make that request in the initial call to the ATSU.

Further Reference: PPL2 » Communications » Air Traffic Service Units » Types of ATSU

ECP3Q9   Answer D

The main 'special purpose' transponder codes are:

7700	Emergency
7600	Radio Failure
7500	Unlawful Interference
7000	Conspicuity

Further Reference: PPL2 » Communications » En-route Procedures » Use of Transponder

ECP3Q10   Answer C

An Automatic Terminal Information Service (ATIS) is a recorded broadcast of the actual weather report for the airfield, together with the runway in use and any other relevant departure or arrival information.

Further Reference: PPL2 » Communications » En-route Procedures » VOLMET and ATIS

ECP3Q11   Answer D

An ATC unit may use various callsigns depending on the service being offered, for example Ground, Tower, Approach, Radar, Director and Zone. See the table at the 'Essential Revision' section.

Further Reference: PPL2 » Communications » Air Traffic Service Units » Types of ATSU

ECP3Q12   Answer C

An AFIS unit cannot issue clearances to an aircraft in flight. In the instance given, it can only invite the pilot to 'Land at your discretion'.

Further Reference: PPL2 » Communications » Arrival/Traffic pattern Procedures » Landing Clearance

ECP3Q13   Answer B

The full set of phraseology to be used in relation to transponders is given at explanation ECP1Q10.

Further Reference: PPL2 » Communications » En-route Procedures » Use of Transponder

ECP3Q14   Answer C

Where a pilot is already in communication with an ATSU, an emergency call should be made on the frequency in use. In the same way, if an aircraft already has an allocated SSR code (squawk), this should be retained, at least initially.

Further Reference: PPL2 » Communications » Emergency Procedures » Emergency Frequencies

PPL2 » Communications » Emergency Procedures » Distress/Urgency Calls

ECP3Q15   Answer D

In the initial contact with an Air Traffic Service Unit (ATSU) or ground station, the full aircraft callsign and the full Air Traffic Service Unit (ATSU) name, callsign and suffix should be used. The pilot should only abbreviate the aircraft's callsign AFTER the ATSU has done so and use the same abbreviate given by the ATS.

Further Reference: PPL2 » Communications » Callsigns, Abbreviations, General Procedures » Callsigns

ECP3Q16   Answer C

The full list of ATC messages that must be read back by a pilot is given in the 'Essential Revision' section.

Further Reference: PPL2 » Communications » Departure Procedures » Items Requiring Read-back

PPL2 » Communications » En-route Procedures » Items Requiring Read-back

ECP3Q17   Answer A

'URGENCY' is defined as a condition concerning the safety of an aircraft or other vehicle, or of some person on board or in sight, but not requiring immediate assistance.

For reference, the other emergency condition is:

DISTRESS – The aircraft is threatened by serious and/or imminent danger and requires immediate assistance

Further Reference: PPL2 » Communications » Emergency Procedures » Emergency Frequencies

ECP3Q18   Answer D

An emergency message is prefixed by 'MAYDAY' (for a distress call) or 'PAN PAN' (for an urgency call) repeated three times.

Further Reference: PPL2 » Communications » Emergency Procedures » Distress/Urgency Calls

ECP3Q19   Answer B

The correct format of an emergency message is given in the 'Essential Revision' section.

You should note that although there is a recommended emergency message format, in reality the pilot should include any other information that may be useful (eg fuel state), either in the initial call or in an ongoing exchange. Although the controller(s) may well ask for information they think is relevant, and the pilot should pass on any additional information he/she regards as important, the pilot's first priority is to deal with the emergency situation, not get involved in non-essential conversations with ATC.

Further Reference: PPL2 » Communications » Emergency Procedures » Distress/Urgency Calls

ECP3Q20   Answer C

An emergency message is prefixed by 'MAYDAY' (for a distress call) or 'PAN PAN' (for an urgency call) repeated three times, after which the name of the station addressed should be given, if known and if time and circumstance permit.

Further Reference: PPL2 » Communications » Emergency Procedures » Distress/Urgency Calls

ECP3Q21   Answer B

The recommended format of an emergency call is given in the 'Essential Revision' section.

Further Reference: PPL2 » Communications » Emergency Procedures » Distress/Urgency Calls

ECP3Q22   Answer C

A pilot should only use the words 'take-off' after they have first been used by an ATSU. Normally, an ATC unit will not use the words 'take-off' until it issues a take-off clearance, and the pilot first uses the words in reading-back that clearance.

Under no circumstances must a take-off clearance be confused with a departure clearance.

Take-off clearance: Clearance to taxi immediately on to the runway and commence take-off without stopping the aircraft (If the aircraft is already lined up on the runway, the pilot should take-off without delay).

Departure Clearance: This is an ATC route clearance, it is NOT an instruction to take-off.

Further Reference: PPL2 » Communications » Departure Procedures » Taxying Instructions, Holding Instructions, Take-off Instructions

ECP3Q23   Answer A

Radar Information Service (RIS) is an *Air Traffic Radar Service*, available to aircraft in VMC or IMC, operating VFR or IFR. Under a RIS ATC provide traffic information on conflicting traffic; the pilot will have to decide on what avoiding action to take. When receiving a RIS the pilot is wholly responsible for separation from other aircraft, whether or not the controller has given traffic information. The pilot remains responsible for terrain clearance.

Further Reference: PPL2 » Communications » En-route Procedures » Radar and Non-Radar Services

ECP3Q24   Answer C

The order of priority of RTF aeronautical messages is given in explanation ECP1Q17.

Further Reference: PPL2 » Communications » Call Signs, Abbreviations, General Procedures » Categories of Message

ECP3Q25   Answer D

A Special VFR (SVFR) clearance allows a flight to operate in a control zone (CTR) without complying with Instrument Flight Rules (IFR), but in weather conditions which do not meet the Visual Meteorological Conditions (VMC) criteria specified for that airspace. To obtain a SVFR clearance it is necessary to contact the appropriate ATSU before entering the CTR. Note that a class A airway is a control area (CTA), and no SVFR is permitted in a class A CTA such as an airway.

Further Reference: PPL2 » Air Law » Division of Airspace and Air Traffic Services » Special VFR

ECP3Q26   Answer D

The digits of a time are normally transmitted individually, sometimes stating the minutes only, but usually all four digits if the time is 'on the hour' or where confusion might arise. Number of less than 10 are normally prefixed with 'zero', hence a time of seven minutes past the hour might be transmitted as 'ZERO SEVEN', but not just 'SEVEN'. See also explanation ECP2Q7.

Further Reference: PPL2 » Communications » General Operating Procedures » Transmission of Numbers and Transmission of Time

ECP3Q27   Answer A

The altimeter settings and associated terminology are summarised below.

Altimeter Setting	Datum	Terminology
QFE	A fixed point on the surface	'Height'
QNH	Mean Sea Level	'Altitude'
Standard Setting	The 1013mb pressure level	'Flight Level'

Further Reference: PPL2 » Communications » En-Route Procedures » Level and Position Reporting

ECP3Q28   Answer D

In relation to VHF Direction Finding (VDF), 'QDM' is defined as the magnetic heading to be steered by the aircraft (assuming no wind) to reach the VDF station. The Q codes are explained more fully in the 'Essential Revision' section.

Further Reference: PPL2 » Communications » En-route Procedures » VHF Direction Finding (VDF)

ECP3Q29   Answer A

A Conditional Clearance is used only when the aircraft or vehicles concerned are visible to both the controller and pilot. A Conditional Clearance can only relate to one movement.

Further Reference: PPL2 » Communications » Departure Procedures » Conditional Clearances

ECP3Q30   Answer C

'Standby' – Wait and I will call you, (no onward clearance is to be assumed, 'Standby' is not an approval or a denial).

No reply to the instruction 'standby' is expected. The pilot should make no response, and wait to be called back. Most importantly, the pilot should not assume that any onward clearance has been (or will be given). This may well result in the pilot having, for example, to orbit outside controlled airspace whilst awaiting clearance to proceed.

Further Reference: PPL2 » Communications » En-route Procedures » Establishing Contact – Passing Details

Flight Performance and Planning

Flight Performance & Planning Essential Revision

▶ Mass and Balance

If an aircraft is **over weight** or **over loaded**, the probable consequences include:

Take-off and landing speeds	Increased
Take-off and landing distances	Increased
Climb performance	Degraded
Cruise speed	Reduced
Range	Reduced
Service ceiling	Reduced
Certificate of Airworthiness	Invalidated
Insurance	Invalidated

Maximum Total Weight Authorised	Maximum weight for take-off, also known as Maximum All Up Weight (MAUW) and Maximum Take-Off Weight (MTOW)
Maximum Landing Weight	Maximum weight for landing
Maximum Ramp Weight	Maximum weight of the parked aircraft
Maximum Zero Fuel Weight	Maximum weight allowable with zero fuel in the tanks

The actual weight of the loaded aircraft is sometimes referred to as the **gross weight**.

The distance from the datum to the location of each item of loading is the **lever arm**.

Weight x Lever Arm = Moment

Total Moment ÷ Total Weight = Centre of Gravity (CG) position

Aircraft may have different weight and CG limits for operations in different categories:

Normal category	Manoeuvres used in normal flight including stalls, lazy eights, chandelles and steep turns where the angle of bank does not exceed 60°. Aerobatic manoeuvres (including spins) are not permitted.
Utility category	All manoeuvres permitted in the normal category, together with spins and steep turns with an angle of bank in excess of 60°.
Aerobatic category	All the manoeuvres of the Normal and Utility category, together with the aerobatic manoeuvres stated in the POH/FM subject to the declared entry airspeeds and load factor limits.

▶ Take-Off and Climb

Using **more flap than that recommended** in the POH/FM will lengthen the take-off distance (because of the increased drag) and may even prevent the aircraft getting airborne before the end of the runway. Using the **recommended flap setting** will shorten the take-off ground run, however climb performance may be degraded compared with a 'clean' climbing configuration. A take-off **without flap** will need a longer take-off run than when using the recommended setting, but the climb after take-off may be better without flap.

To convert actual altitude into **pressure altitude**, adjust the altitude by 30ft for each millibar difference to the standard setting of 1013mb: pressure below 1013 means a higher altitude and *vice versa*.

Taking-off into wind means that the aircraft starts the take off with the benefit of some airspeed to start with and so the take-off distance is reduced.

ITEM	CHANGE	EFFECT
Aircraft weight	Increased	Take-off distance increased
Aircraft weight	Decreased	Take-off distance decreased
Surface wind	Headwind	Take-off distance decreased
Surface wind	Tailwind	Take-off distance increased
Density Altitude	Higher (increased)	Take-off distance increased
Density Altitude	Lower (decreased)	Take-off distance decreased
Runway surface	Contaminated	Take-off distance increased
Runway surface	Hard	Take-off distance decreased
Runway surface	Soft	Take-off distance increased
Runway slope	Downslope	Take-off distance decreased
Runway slope	Upslope	Take-off distance increased

The 'baseline' for take-off performance is that of a level, dry runway with a hard surface.

CAA performance factors are used to adjust calculated **take-off distance** for factors not included in the Pilot's Operating Handbook/Flight Manual (POH/FM):

Condition	Percentage increase	Factor
10% increase in aircraft weight	20	1.2
1000ft increase in runway elevation	10	1·1
10°C increase in temperature	10	1·1
Dry grass on firm soil (grass up to 20cm/8 inches)	20	1·2
Wet grass on firm soil (grass up to 20cm/8 inches)	30	1·3
Runway upslope of 2%	10	1·1
Tailwind component of 10% of lift-off speed	20	1·2
Soft ground or snow	At least 25%	At least 1·25

When calculating take-off performance, the CAA advise adding an additional 'public transport' **safety factor** of 1.33 (ie + 33%).

Take-off safety speed is never less than 1·2 x the stalling speed in the take-off configuration.

Maximum rate of climb is achieved at the airspeed where there is the maximum excess of power available over power required. Best **rate-of-climb** speed (**Vy**) gives the maximum height gain in a specific time. Best **angle-of-climb** (**Vx**) gives the maximum height gain in a specific distance.

Weight is a major factor in **climb performance**. Reducing the weight of an aircraft is a good way of improving climb performance.

Climb *angle* can be improved by flying into the wind. Note that **the *rate* of climb** remains the same regardless of whether there is a headwind or tailwind. However, the slower groundspeed caused by the headwind component means that more altitude is gained over the same ground distance – giving a steeper *climb gradient*. The faster groundspeed caused by a tailwind gives a more shallow climb angle.

▶In Flight Performance

Best range airspeed is found where a tangential line meets the power-required curve:

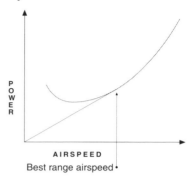

Best range airspeed

In a propeller-driven aircraft, maximum range occurs at an angle of attack very close to that at which the wing is also producing the minimum drag (which is also when the aircraft is flying at the best lift/drag ratio).

Theoretically, best range airspeed is reduced slightly when flying with a tailwind and increased slightly when flying into a headwind. Anything which distorts the shape of the aeroplane – in particular the wings – is likely to have an adverse effect on performance, for example ice will reduce lift, increase drag and increase weight (mass).

Maximum endurance is the longest possible *time* spent airborne, it is achieved at the minimum power required airspeed, which is slower than the best range airspeed. If all other factors are equal, maximum endurance is achieved at the lowest safe altitude.

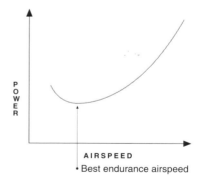

Best endurance airspeed

The greater the water content of the air (humidity), the greater the risk of **carburettor icing**. Warm air can hold more water content than cold air. A low power setting gives a greater risk of icing than a high power setting.

▶ Descent and Landing Performance

Gliding performance is defined by the aircraft's lift/drag (L/D) ratio. A L/D ratio of 10:1 means that the aircraft will travel 10 units forward for every one unit of descent. A **tailwind** increases gliding range. A **headwind** reduces gliding range. In neither case does the rate of descent (ROD) change, so the aircraft still reaches the ground in the same time. **Aircraft weight** (mass) affects best gliding airspeed, but not glide range.

Landing Performance:

ITEM	CHANGE	EFFECT
Aircraft weight	Increased	Landing distance increased
Aircraft weight	Decreased	Landing distance decreased
Surface wind	Headwind	Landing distance decreased
Surface wind	Tailwind	Landing distance increased
Density Altitude	Higher (increased)	Landing distance increased
Density Altitude	Lower (decreased)	Landing distance decreased
Runway surface	Contaminated	Landing distance increased
Runway surface	Hard	Landing distance decreased
Runway surface	Soft	Landing distance increased
Runway slope	Downslope	Landing distance increased
Runway slope	Upslope	Landing distance decreased

The 'baseline' for landing performance is that of a level, dry runway with a hard surface.

CAA performance factors to be used to adjust calculated **landing distance** for factors not included in the Pilot's Operating Handbook/Flight Manual (POH/FM):

Condition	Percentage increase	Factor
10% increase in aircraft weight	10	1·1
1000ft increase in runway elevation	5	1·05
10°C increase in temperature	5	1·05
Dry Grass on firm soil (grass up to 20cm/8in)	15	1·15
Wet Grass on firm soil (grass up to 20cm/8in)*	35	1·35
Wet paved surface	15	1·15
Runway downslope of 2%	10	1·1
Tailwind component of 10% of landing speed	20	1·2
Snow	At least 25%	At least 1·25

* If the grass is very short, the surface may become slippery and landing distance may be increased by up to 60%, giving a factor of 1·6.

When calculating landing performance, the CAA advise adding an additional 'public transport' **safety factor** of 1.43 (ie + 43%).

The final **approach airspeed** will be based on the stalling airspeed in the landing configuration, and will be approximately 1·3 x the stalling speed in the landing configuration (the exact figure will be given in the POH/FM). VAT (Velocity At Threshold), or more correctly VREF, is often very close to the approach speed.

▶ Runway Dimensions

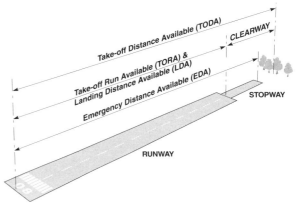

Clearway	The area beyond the TORA over which the aircraft can climb to 50ft
Emergency Distance Available (**EDA**)	The TORA plus the stopway distance
Landing Distance Available (**LDA**)	The length of runway available for the landing run
Stopway	An area where the aircraft can be safely brought to a halt
Take-Off Distance Available (**TODA**)	The TORA plus the clearway distance
Take-Off Run Available (**TORA**)	The length of runway available for the take-off run

Runway slope can be calculated by taking the altitude or elevation at each end of the runway and dividing the difference by the runway length to give a percentage.

JAA Private Pilot Licence – Aeroplanes
Flight Performance and Planning

Time allowed:	60 minutes
No. of questions:	20
Total Marks:	100

Instructions:

The paper consists of 20 multiple choice questions, each carries 5 marks. The pass mark is 75% (i.e. 15 questions or more must be answered correctly). Marks are not deducted for incorrect answers.

Be sure to carefully read each question and ensure that you understand it before considering the answer choices. Only one of the answers is complete and correct; the others are either incomplete, incorrect or based on a misconception.

You should indicate the correct answer by placing a cross in the appropriate box of the answer sheet. If you decide to change an answer, you should erase the original choice and put a cross in the box representing your new selection.

Each question has an average answer time of 3 minutes. No credit is given for unanswered questions.

Flight Performance and Planning Practice – Paper 1

1. An aircraft that is over weight (over loaded), when compared to a properly loaded aircraft, can be expected to:

(a) require a longer take-off distance, but shorter landing distance

(b) stall more slowly, but have reduced climb rate

(c) require a longer landing distance, have reduced cruise performance

(d) have the same take-off and climb performance, but cruise more slowly and require a longer landing distance

---

2. The maximum weight of aircraft with payload (e.g. passengers and cargo) allowable with zero fuel in the fuel tanks is referred to as the:

(a) Maximum Ramp Weight

(b) Maximum All Up Weight

(c) Zero Fuel Weight

(d) Zero Payload Weight

---

3. An aircraft has been loaded with 100 litres of fuel. Given a Specific Gravity (SpG) of 0.72, the weight of this fuel is:

(a) 72kg

(b) 72lbs

(c) 720kg

(d) 139kg

---

4. At take-off an aircraft has a weight of 3000lbs and a calculated Centre of Gravity (CG) position of 65.5 inches aft of datum.

In-flight, fuel consumption is planned at 50lbs per hour. The lever arm for the fuel is 61 inches aft of datum.

If the flight is planned to last 3 hours, what will be the estimated CG position on landing?

(a) 69.48 inches aft of datum

(b) 65.74 inches aft of datum

(c) 72.94 inches aft of datum

(d) 59.15inches aft of datum

5. Using the CG envelope graph below, select the combination of weight and moment acceptable for operation in the utility category:

	Weight (kg)	Moment (M.KG)
(a)	1000	1100
(b)	950	900
(c)	850	930
(d)	900	850

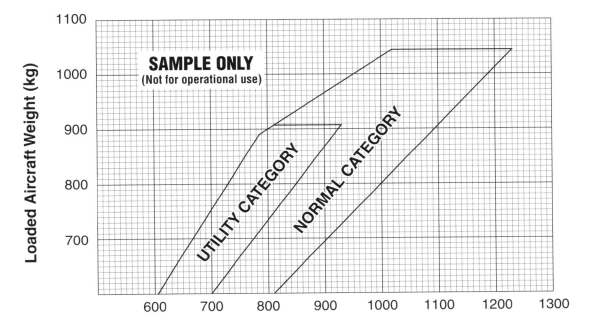

6. The length of runway available for the landing run of an aircraft is the:

(a) Landing Distance Available (LDA)

(b) Emergency Distance Available (EDA)

(c) Take-Off Distance Available (TODA)

(d) Landing Run Cleared (LRC)

7. A runway downslope can be expected to …..(i)….. take-off distance and …..(ii)….. landing distance compared with a level runway:

	(i)	(ii)
(a)	increase	increase
(b)	decrease	increase
(c)	increase	decrease
(d)	decrease	decrease

8. According to a UK CAA Aeronautical Information Circular (AIC), landing distances on a wet paved runway may increase by ….(i)…. and landing distances on very short wet grass may increase by ….(ii)…. compared with a dry, paved runway.

   Select the answers which correctly completes the above statement:

	(i)	(ii)
(a)	20%	40%
(b)	35%	60%
(c)	15%	60%
(d)	40%	50%

9. Given an airfield elevation of 945ft, and a QNH of 1002mb/hPa, what is the approximate pressure altitude?

   (a) 1275ft

   (b) 615ft

   (c) 57ft

   (d) 1947ft

10. An aircraft has a best range of airspeed of 110 knots TAS. In order to achieve the maximum range, the speed for best range could be increased slightly in conditions of:

   (a) A strong headwind

   (b) A strong crosswind

   (c) Nil wind

   (d) A strong tailwind

11. An aircraft has a stalling speed in the landing configuration of 55 knots. Its approximate approach speed can be expected to be not less than:

   (a) 61 knots

   (b) 66 knots

   (c) 68 knots

   (d) 72 knots

12. When calculating take-off and landing performance, the CAA advise adding a 'public transport' safety factor if this margin is not already included within the Pilot's Operating Handbook/Flight Manual (POH/FM) figures. This safety factor is ......(i)...... for take-off and ......(ii)...... for landing:

	(i)	(ii)
(a)	1.15	1.35
(b)	1.25	1.45
(c)	1.43	1.33
(d)	1.33	1.43

13. According to a CAA Aeronautical Information Circular (AIC), landing distance required will be increased by 10% (a factor or 1.1) by:

(a) A runway with a 2% downhill slope

(b) An increase in ambient temperature of 10°C

(c) Wet grass

(d) Snow

14. In terms of climb performance, best rate of climb can be defined as height gain in a given ....(i)...... and best angle of climb can be defined as height gain in a given .....(ii)...... :

	(i)	(ii)
(a)	time	distance
(b)	distance	gradient
(c)	power setting	time
(d)	distance	time

15. Using the table below, for a climb from 3000ft pressure altitude to 7000ft pressure altitude, assuming zero wind and standard temperature conditions, select the answer that correctly describes the:

(i) Time required

(ii) Fuel used

(iii) Distance travelled (in nm)

	(i)	(ii)	(iii)
(a)	16	8.71	27.8
(b)	12	2.3us gal	15
(c)	8	5.3l	10
(d)	8	1.6 us gal	18.5

TIME, FUEL, AND DISTANCE TO CLIMB MAXIMUM RATE OF CLIMB

CONDITIONS : Flaps up | Full throttle | Standard temperature

Weight	Pressure Altitude		Tempe-rature	Climb Speed IAS		Rate of Climb		From Sea Level				
								Time	Fuel used		Distance	
kg	ft	m	°C	km/h	kts	ft/mn	m/s	mn	US Gal	Litres	NM	km
726	Sea level		15	135	73	770	3.9	0	0	0	0	0
	1000	305	13	135	73	725	3.7	1	0.3	1.1	2	3.7
	2000	610	11	133	72	675	3.4	3	0.6	2.3	3	5.6
	3000	914	9	133	72	630	3.2	4	0.9	3.4	5	9.3
	4000	1219	7	131	71	580	2.9	6	1.2	4.5	8	14.8
	5000	1524	5	131	71	535	2.7	8	1.6	6.1	10	18.5
	6000	1829	3	130	70	485	2.5	10	1.9	7.2	12	22.2
	7000	2134	1	128	69	440	2.2	12	2.3	8.7	15	27.8
	8000	2418	-1	128	69	390	2	15	2.7	10.2	19	35.2
	9000	2743	-3	126	68	345	1.8	17	3.2	12.1	22	40.8
	10,000	3048	-5	126	68	295	1.5	21	3.7	14	27	50
	11,000	3353	-7	124	67	250	1.3	24	4.2	15.9	32	59.3
	12,000	3658	-9	124	67	200	1	29	4.9	18.5	38	70.4

NOTES :

1. Add 1.1 gallons 4.16 litres of fuel for engine start, taxi and takeoff allowance.
2. Mixture leaned above 3000 ft - 914 m for maximum RPM.
3. Increase time, fuel and distance by 10 % for each 10°C above standard temperature.
4. Distances shown are based on zero wind.

16. Using the table below, for an aircraft at 9000ft pressure altitude, select the answer that correctly describes the:
  (i) Best rate of climb airspeed
  (ii) Rate of climb

TIME, FUEL, AND DISTANCE TO CLIMB [MAXIMUM RATE OF CLIMB]

CONDITIONS :   Flaps up   Full throttle   Standard temperature

Weight	Pressure Altitude		Tempe- rature	Climb Speed IAS		Rate of Climb		From Sea Level				
								Time	Fuel used		Distance	
kg	ft	m	°C	km/h	kts	ft/mn	m/s	mn	US Gal	Litres	NM	km
726	Sea level		15	135	73	770	3.9	0	0	0	0	0
	1000	305	13	135	73	725	3.7	1	0.3	1.1	2	3.7
	2000	610	11	133	72	675	3.4	3	0.6	2.3	3	5.6
	3000	914	9	133	72	630	3.2	4	0.9	3.4	5	9.3
	4000	1219	7	131	71	580	2.9	6	1.2	4.5	8	14.8
	5000	1524	5	131	71	535	2.7	8	1.6	6.1	10	18.5
	6000	1829	3	130	70	485	2.5	10	1.9	7.2	12	22.2
	7000	2134	1	128	69	440	2.2	12	2.3	8.7	15	27.8
	8000	2418	-1	128	69	390	2	15	2.7	10.2	19	35.2
	9000	2743	-3	126	68	345	1.8	17	3.2	12.1	22	40.8
	10,000	3048	-5	126	68	295	1.5	21	3.7	14	27	50
	11,000	3353	-7	124	67	250	1.3	24	4.2	15.9	32	59.3
	12,000	3658	-9	124	67	200	1	29	4.9	18.5	38	70.4

NOTES :

1. Add 1.1 gallons 4.16 litres of fuel for engine start, taxi and takeoff allowance.
2. Mixture leaned above 3000 ft - 914 m for maximum RPM.
3. Increase time, fuel and distance by 10 % for each 10°C above standard temperature.
4. Distances shown are based on zero wind.

	(i)	(ii)
(a)	126 knots TAS	345ft/min
(b)	126 km/h IAS	345ft/min
(c)	68 knots TAS	345ft/min
(d)	73 knots IAS	17m/s

---

17. Based on a CAA-published table of conditions that affect landing performance, a 60% increase (factor 1.6) in landing distance could be caused by:

(a) A wet, paved runway

(b) Short, dry grass on firm soil

(c) Short, wet grass on firm soil

(d) A runway downslope of 2%

18. In the diagram below, the point marked as 'B' represents:

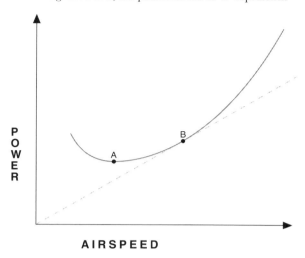

(a) The maximum endurance airspeed, the speed to fly at to cover the maximum distance

(b) The maximum endurance airspeed, the speed to fly at to remain airborne for the longest time

(c) The maximum range airspeed, the speed to fly at to cover the maximum distance

(d) The maximum range airspeed, the speed to fly at to remain airborne for the longest time

19. An aircraft has a best lift/drag (L/D) ratio of 7:1. If the aircraft flies at the angle of attack at which this L/D ratio is achieved, its approximate maximum still-air gliding distance from a height of 6000ft will be:

(a) 3nm

(b) 5nm

(c) 7nm

(d) 9nm

20. The conditions most likely to give rise to carburettor icing are:

(a) High power setting in winter

(b) Low power setting, summer day

(c) High power setting, high altitude

(d) Cruise power setting in winter

Flight Performance and Planning Practice – Paper 2

1. An aircraft that is certified in the 'Utility' category is permitted to carry-out:

    (a) All manoeuvres permitted in the normal category, as well as spins and steep turns with an angle of bank in excess of 60°.

    (b) Stalls, lazy eights, chandelles and steep turns where the angle of bank does not exceed 60°. Spins are not permitted.

    (c) All the manoeuvres of the Normal and Utility category, together with full aerobatic manoeuvres

    (d) No stalling, spinning or steep turns (angle of bank in excess of 45°)

2. An increase in aircraft weight (mass) of 10% will ....(i).... take-off speeds and ....(ii).... take-off distances by at least 20%:

	(i)	(ii)
(a)	Increase	Decrease
(b)	Decrease	Decrease
(c)	Increase	Increase
(d)	Decease	Increase

3. An airfield has an elevation of 330 feet and the QFE is 993mb. On the basis that one millibar equals 30ft, what is the pressure altitude?

    (a) 600ft

    (b) 360ft

    (c) 630ft

    (d) 830ft

4. Using the graph below, select which of the given weight/cg position combinations is permissible for operation in the utility category:

Weight	CG position
(a) 1945lbs	85.5 in. aft datum
(b) 1845lbs	88 in. aft datum
(c) 2005lbs	84.5 in. aft datum
(d) 2000lbs	92 in. aft datum

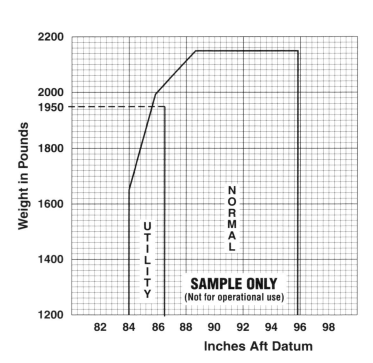

5. Select the answer which correctly completes the following statement. Assuming ISA conditions, compared with operation from a runway at sea level, operation from a runway at a high pressure altitude will require .... take-off and landing distances.

(a) Identical

(b) Shorter

(c) Longer

(d) Reduced

6. Which of the following can be expected to occur as a result of over-loading an aircraft so that it is overweight?

(a) Slower acceleration and a higher service ceiling

(b) A decreased landing and take-off speed

(c) Reduced acceleration and increased take-off run

(d) Reduced rate of climb, decreased take-off run

7. As a general rule, baseline take-off and landing performance data assumes:

(a) A grass, level runway

(b) A paved (hard), level runway

(c) The worst runway conditions permitted in the POH/FM

(d) A minimum upslope for take-off, and downslope for landing, of 2%

8. When operating on a downsloping runway, compared with a level runway, an aircraft will have a:

(a) Longer take-off distance and shorter landing distance

(b) Longer take-off distance and longer landing distance

(c) Shorter take-off distance and shorter landing distance

(d) Shorter take-off distance and longer landing distance

9. During take-off, use of the ....(i).......... flap setting will ....(ii).......... the take-off run.

Select the statement which correctly completes the above statement.

	(i)	(ii)
(a)	full	reduce
(b)	take-off	reduce
(c)	take-off	increase
(d)	take-off	have no effect on

10. Theoretically, compared to the 'still air' best-range airspeed, best range in conditions of a strong tailwind will be achieved at a:

(a) Slightly slower airspeed

(b) Slightly faster airspeed

(c) Unchanged airspeed

(d) Identical indicated airspeed, but faster true airspeed

11. An aircraft has a stalling speed in the landing configuration (Vso) of 50 knots. Its approximate approach speed – Vat (Velocity at Threshold) – can be expected to be around:

(a) 65 knots

(b) 55 knots

(c) 50 knots

(d) 100 knots

12. An aircraft is landing on runway 09 when the surface wind is reported as 260/20. It is most likely that:

(a) Groundspeed will be greater than airspeed, landing distance will be increased

(b) Groundspeed will be less than airspeed, landing distance will be increased

(c) Groundspeed will be greater than airspeed, landing distance will be decreased

(d) Groundspeed will be less than airspeed, landing distance will be decreased

13. Compared to a climb with flap retracted, climbing at the same airspeed with take-off flap extended is most likely to result in:

(a) Less lift and less drag

(b) More lift and less drag

(c) An improved rate of climb

(d) A reduced rate of climb

14. Based on a CAA-published table of conditions that affect take-off performance, a 10°C increase in temperature will …..(i)….. take-off distance by …..(ii)…..:

	(i)	(ii)
(a)	increase	10% or factor 1.1
(b)	decrease	10% or factor 1.2
(c)	decrease	10% or factor 1.1
(d)	increase	10% or factor 1

15. Maximum range is achieved at the airspeed which equates to the theoretical:

(a) lowest ratio of power to airspeed

(b) lowest lift/drag ratio

(c) minimum power required airspeed

(d) maximum power required airspeed

16. Using the table below, for an aircraft cruising at 3000ft pressure altitude, standard temperature and with 2400RPM set, select the answer that correctly describes the:
(i)   % BHP
(ii)   TAS
(iii)   Fuel burn (GPH)

RPM	PRESSURE ALTITUDE 2000 FEET											
	20°C BELOW STD. TEMP				STANDARD TEMP				20°C ABOVE STD. TEMP			
	% BHP	TAS KTS	TAS MPH	FUEL GPH	% BHP	TAS KTS	TAS MPH	FUEL GPH	% BHP	TAS KTS	TAS MPH	FUEL GPH
	−9°C (16°F)				11°C (52°F)				31°C (88°F)			
2700	92	130	150	10.7	87	129	149	10.0	82	129	148	9.5
2600	83	125	143	9.6	79	124	143	9.0	75	123	142	8.6
2500	75	119	137	8.6	71	119	136	8.1	68	118	135	7.7
2400	68	114	131	7.8	65	113	130	7.4	61	111	127	7.0
2300	61	108	124	7.0	58	106	121	6.6	55	103	118	6.3
2200	55	101	116	6.2	52	98	113	5.9	50	96	110	5.7
	PRESSURE ALTITUDE 3000 FEET											
	−11°C (12°F)				9°C (48°F)				29°C (84°F)			
2700	90	130	149	10.4	85	129	149	9.8	80	129	148	9.2
2600	82	125	143	9.4	77	124	142	8.8	73	123	142	8.4
2500	73	119	137	8.4	70	118	136	8.0	66	117	134	7.6
2400	66	113	130	7.6	63	112	129	7.2	60	110	126	6.8
2300	60	107	123	6.8	57	105	121	6.5	54	103	118	6.2
2200	54	100	115	6.1	51	97	112	5.8	50	95	108	5.6
	PRESSURE ALTITUDE 4000 FEET											
	−13°C (9°F)				7°C (45°F)				27°C (81°F)			
2700	88	129	149	10.1	83	129	149	9.6	79	129	148	9.0
2600	80	124	143	9.2	75	124	142	8.6	71	122	141	8.1
2500	72	119	137	8.2	68	118	135	7.8	65	116	133	7.4
2400	65	113	130	7.4	62	111	128	7.0	59	109	125	6.7
2300	59	106	122	6.7	56	103	119	6.3	54	102	117	6.1
2200	52	98	113	5.9	51	96	111	5.7	49	93	107	5.5

	(i)	(ii)	(iii)
(a)	66	113kts	7.6
(b)	65	130mph	7.4
(c)	62	111kts	7.0
(d)	63	129mph	7.2

17. Use the table below to answer the following question:

For an aircraft weighing 726kg, at 3500ft pressure altitude and a temperature of 8°C, the expected maximum rate of climb is:

TIME, FUEL, AND DISTANCE TO CLIMB [MAXIMUM RATE OF CLIMB]

CONDITIONS :   Flaps up   Full throttle   Standard temperature

Weight	Pressure Altitude		Temperature	Climb Speed IAS		Rate of Climb		From Sea Level				
								Time	Fuel used		Distance	
kg	ft	m	°C	km/h	kts	ft/mn	m/s	mn	US Gal	Litres	NM	km
726	Sea level		15	135	73	770	3.9	0	0	0	0	0
	1000	305	13	135	73	725	3.7	1	0.3	1.1	2	3.7
	2000	610	11	133	72	675	3.4	3	0.6	2.3	3	5.6
	3000	914	9	133	72	630	3.2	4	0.9	3.4	5	9.3
	4000	1219	7	131	71	580	2.9	6	1.2	4.5	8	14.8
	5000	1524	5	131	71	535	2.7	8	1.6	6.1	10	18.5
	6000	1829	3	130	70	485	2.5	10	1.9	7.2	12	22.2
	7000	2134	1	128	69	440	2.2	12	2.3	8.7	15	27.8
	8000	2418	-1	128	69	390	2	15	2.7	10.2	19	35.2
	9000	2743	-3	12n	68	345	1.8	17	3.2	12.1	22	40.8
	10,000	3048	-5	126	68	295	1.5	21	3.7	14	27	50
	11,000	3353	-7	124	67	250	1.3	24	4.2	15.9	32	59.3
	12,000	3658	-9	124	67	200	1	29	4.9	18.5	38	70.4

NOTES :

1. Add 1.1 gallons 4.16 litres of fuel for engine start, taxi and takeoff allowance.
2. Mixture leaned above 3000 ft - 914 m for maximum RPM.
3. Increase time, fuel and distance by 10 % for each 10°C above standard temperature.
4. Distances shown are based on zero wind.

(a) 605ft/min

(b) 557ft/min

(c) 2.8m/s

(d) 700ft/min

18. To achieve maximum endurance in a piston engine aircraft, the airspeed and altitude are likely to be:

(a) Faster than maximum range airspeed; maximum safe altitude

(b) Slower than maximum range airspeed; minimum safe altitude

(c) Slower than maximum range airspeed; maximum safe altitude

(d) Faster than maximum range airspeed; minimum safe altitude

19. In flight, a non de-iced aircraft begins to collect ice on the airframe. Which of the following statements is true?

(a) The aircraft is permitted to collect ice provided carburettor heat is selected, take no further action

(b) The aircraft should leave icing conditions immediately, by descending into warmer air if safe to do so

(c) The aircraft should be manoeuvred vigorously to shake-off the ice

(d) Icing is only a problem if cruise speed reduced by more than 10 knots

20. Two otherwise identical aircraft are gliding in still-air conditions, but one aircraft is 20% heavier than the other. Which of the following statements is true?

(a) Regardless of other factors, the heavier aircraft will have reduced gliding range

(b) The heavier aircraft should use a slower glide airspeed than the lighter one

(c) Regardless of other factors, the heavier aircraft will have reduced gliding descent rate

(d) The heavier aircraft should use a faster glide airspeed than the lighter one

1. Which of the following manoeuvres would <u>not</u> be permitted in an aircraft certified in the 'normal category':

(a) A 'lazy eight'

(b) A spin

(c) A stall

(d) A 60° angle of bank turn

2. An aircraft that is overloaded will have:

(a) A reduced endurance but unchanged range

(b) An unchanged service ceiling but reduced climb performance

(c) A reduced landing distance

(d) An increased take-off distance

3. An aircraft lands at a weight of 2000lb and a total moment of 150000 in. lb. The aircraft is then refuelled with 300 lbs of fuel which has a lever arm of 7ft 11in. aft of datum. The aircraft weight and CG is now:

(a) 2300lb   58.10 in. aft datum

(b) 2300lb   77.61 in. aft datum

(c) 2300lb   65.21 in. aft datum

(d) 1700lb   88.23 in. aft datum

4. An aircraft makes a take-off and climb at a weight of 2000lbs. For a second flight, in precisely identical conditions and using identical technique, its weight is 2500lbs. During the second take-off and climb, take-off distance will be ......(i)...... and climb performance will be .....(ii)....... than the first flight.
Select which of the following answers correctly completes the above statement:

	(i)	(ii)
(a)	longer	unchanged
(b)	shorter	degraded
(c)	longer	degraded
(d)	unchanged	increased

5. The total distance of the take-off run available (TORA), plus stopway, is known as the:

(a) Landing Distance Available (LDA)

(b) Emergency Distance Available (EDA)

(c) Take Off Distance Available (TODA)

(d) Landing Run Cleared (LRC)

6. If all other factors are equal, a lighter aircraft will have .... climb performance as opposed to a heavier one:

(a) Worse

(b) Better

(c) Unchanged

(d) Considerably worse

7. Take-off and landing performance as published in the UK is based on 'default' conditions which include:

    (a) The most adverse conditions the aircraft is certified for

    (b) The most favourable conditions the aircraft is certified for

    (c) A minimum 5 knot headwind

    (d) A dry, level runway with a hard surface

8. In order to adopt a slower approach speed and a steeper approach path at the same time, which of the following actions is the most appropriate?

    (a) Increase power

    (b) Select full flap

    (c) Select take-off flap

    (d) Select nil flap

9. In performance terms, the maximum range is achieved at the airspeed which also equates to:

    (a) The minimum power-required airspeed

    (b) The speed where the best lift/drag ratio occurs

    (c) The speed where power available equals power required

    (d) The minimum control airspeed

10. Using the latest CAA advice on light aircraft performance, published in an Aeronautical Information Circular (AIC); compared to a paved runway, the effect of operating on a grass runway is that:

    (a) landing distance is reduced (because of the drag of the grass) but take-off distance is increased for the same reason

    (b) landing distance is reduced (because of the drag of the grass) and take-off distance is reduced

    (c) landing distance is increased and take-off distance is reduced due to the reduced drag of the grass

    (d) landing distance is increased (because of the reduced braking effectiveness on grass) and take-off distance is increased due to the increased drag of the grass

11. Refer to the Pilot's Operating Handbook/Flight Manual extract below:

GROSS WEIGHT	APPROACH SPEED	AT SEA LEVEL & 15°C/59°F		AT 2500 FT. & 10°C/50°F.		AT 5000 FT. & 5°C/41°F.		AT 7500 FT. & 0°C/32°F.	
		GROUND ROLL	TOTAL TO CLEAR 50 FT. OBS.	GROUND ROLL	TOTAL TO CLEAR 50 FT. OBS.	GROUND ROLL	TOTAL TO CLEAR 50 FT. OBS.	GROUND ROLL	TOTAL TO CLEAR 50 FT. OBS.
1600	60 KIAS	445	1075	470	1135	495	1195	520	1255

LANDING DISTANCE — FLAPS LOWERED TO 40° – POWER OFF / HARD SURFACE RUNWAY – ZERO WIND

If a pilot of this aircraft uses an approach speed of 70 knots:

    (a) The stated landing distance should be achieved

    (b) The ground roll will be reduced

    (c) The landing distance is likely to be appreciably longer than stated

    (d) The landing distance available will be shorter

12. At an angle of attack/airspeed at which a piston-engine aircraft is at the minimum power required airspeed, the aircraft is likely to attain:

(a) Maximum endurance

(b) Maximum range

(c) Maximum cruise airspeed

(d) Minimum cruise airspeed

---

13. Aircraft A is taking off in still air conditions. Aircraft B is taking off in exactly the same circumstances, but with a headwind of 10 knots. Compared to aircraft A, aircraft B's lift-off will be at a ……..(i)……. groundspeed and its take-off distance will be ……..(ii)……. :

	(i)	(ii)
(a)	faster	greater
(b)	slower	greater
(c)	faster	shorter
(d)	slower	shorter

---

14. Using the graph below, given:

OAT   +15°C
Pressure Altitude   1000ft
Aircraft weight   2200lbs
Wind   5kts headwind

find the take-off distance to 50ft. Assume that the table incorporates a 33% take-off performance safety factor and so no further factor needs to be applied.

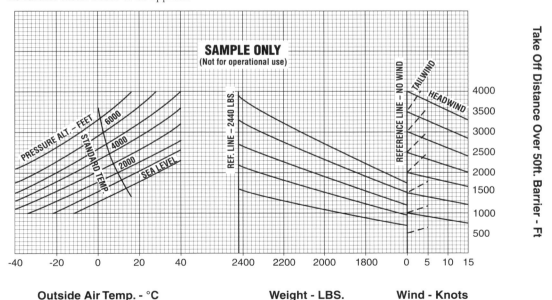

(a) 1400ft

(b) 2000ft

(c) 2500ft

(d) 2750ft

15. Using the table below, for an aircraft cruising at 4000ft pressure altitude, temperature 20°C below standard and with 2300RPM set, select the answer that correctly describes the:

(i)   BHP
(ii)   TAS
(iii)   Fuel burn (GPH)

RPM	\	\	\	\	\	\	\	\	\	\	\	\
	PRESSURE ALTITUDE 2000 FEET											
	20°C BELOW STD. TEMP				**STANDARD TEMP**				**20°C ABOVE STD. TEMP**			
	% BHP	TAS KTS	TAS MPH	FUEL GPH	% BHP	TAS KTS	TAS MPH	FUEL GPH	% BHP	TAS KTS	TAS MPH	FUEL GPH
	−9°C (16°F)				11°C (52°F)				31°C (88°F)			
2700	92	130	150	10.7	87	129	149	10.0	82	129	148	9.5
2600	83	125	143	9.6	79	124	143	9.0	75	123	142	8.6
2500	75	119	137	8.6	71	119	136	8.1	68	118	135	7.7
2400	68	114	131	7.8	65	113	130	7.4	61	111	127	7.0
2300	61	108	124	7.0	58	106	121	6.6	55	103	118	6.3
2200	55	101	116	6.2	52	98	113	5.9	50	96	110	5.7
	PRESSURE ALTITUDE 3000 FEET											
	−11°C (12°F)				9°C (48°F)				29°C (84°F)			
2700	90	130	149	10.4	85	129	149	9.8	80	129	148	9.2
2600	82	125	143	9.4	77	124	142	8.8	73	123	142	8.4
2500	73	119	137	8.4	70	118	136	8.0	66	117	134	7.6
2400	66	113	130	7.6	63	112	129	7.2	60	110	126	6.8
2300	60	107	123	6.8	57	105	121	6.5	54	103	118	6.2
2200	54	100	115	6.1	51	97	112	5.8	50	95	108	5.6
	PRESSURE ALTITUDE 4000 FEET											
	−13°C (9°F)				7°C (45°F)				27°C (81°F)			
2700	88	129	149	10.1	83	129	149	9.6	79	129	148	9.0
2600	80	124	143	9.2	75	124	142	8.6	71	122	141	8.1
2500	72	119	137	8.2	68	118	135	7.8	65	116	133	7.4
2400	65	113	130	7.4	62	111	128	7.0	59	109	125	6.7
2300	59	106	122	6.7	56	103	119	6.3	54	102	117	6.1
2200	52	98	113	5.9	51	96	111	5.7	49	93	107	5.5

	(i)	(ii)	(iii)
(a)	59	122mph	6.7
(b)	56	103kts	6.3
(c)	57	105kts	6.5
(d)	61	124mph	7.0

16. Using the table below, from engine start to 6000ft pressure altitude in standard temperature and zero wind conditions, select the answer that correctly describes the:

(i) Fuel used from engine start

(ii) Airborne distance taken

(iii) Rate of climb at 4500ft

TIME, FUEL, AND DISTANCE TO CLIMB [MAXIMUM RATE OF CLIMB]

CONDITIONS: Flaps up   Full throttle   Standard temperature

Weight	Pressure Altitude		Tempe-rature	Climb Speed IAS		Rate of Climb		From Sea Level				
								Time	Fuel used		Distance	
kg	ft	m	°C	km/h	kts	ft/mn	m/s	mn	US Gal	Litres	NM	km
726	Sea level		15	135	73	770	3.9	0	0	0	0	0
	1000	305	13	135	73	725	3.7	1	0.3	1.1	2	3.7
	2000	610	11	133	72	675	3.4	3	0.6	2.3	3	5.6
	3000	914	9	133	72	630	3.2	4	0.9	3.4	5	9.3
	4000	1219	7	131	71	580	2.9	6	1.2	4.5	8	14.8
	5000	1524	5	131	71	535	2.7	8	1.6	6.1	10	18.5
	6000	1829	3	130	70	485	2.5	10	1.9	7.2	12	22.2
	7000	2134	1	128	69	440	2.2	12	2.3	8.7	15	27.8
	8000	2438	-1	128	69	390	2	15	2.7	10.2	19	35.2
	9000	2743	-3	126	68	345	1.8	17	3.2	12.1	22	40.8
	10,000	3048	-5	126	68	295	1.5	21	3.7	14	27	50
	11,000	3353	-7	124	67	250	1.3	24	4.2	15.9	32	59.3
	12,000	3658	-9	124	67	200	1	29	4.9	18.5	38	70.4

NOTES:

1. Add 1.1 gallons 4.16 litres of fuel for engine start, taxi and takeoff allowance.
2. Mixture leaned above 3000 ft - 914 m for maximum RPM.
3. Increase time, fuel and distance by 10 % for each 10°C above standard temperature.
4. Distances shown are based on zero wind.

	(i)	(ii)	(iii)
(a)	7.2l	22.2km	605ft/min
(b)	3us gal	12nm	557ft/min
(c)	8.3l	12nm	557ft/min
(d)	7.2us gal	13.1km	485ft/min

17. Using the latest CAA advice on light aircraft performance, published an Aeronautical Information Circular (AIC), compared to a dry runway, the effect on landing distance of a wet paved runway is to ......(i)....... landing distance by ....(ii).......... :

	(i)	(ii)
(a)	increase	10% (factor 1.1)
(b)	increase	20% (factor 2.0)
(c)	decrease	20% (factor 1.2)
(d)	increase	15% (factor 1.15)

18. A 3000ft runway slopes so that the elevation at one threshold is 420ft and at the other threshold is 480ft. This slope can be calculated as:

(a) 10%

(b) 2%

(c) 20%

(d) 5%

19. In flight, an accumulation of ice on the wing is likely to result in …..(i)…… lift; …..(ii)…… drag and …..(iii)…… weight:

	(i)	(ii)	(iii)
(a)	increased	reduced	increased
(b)	reduced	increased	increased
(c)	increased	increased	unchanged
(d)	unchanged	increased	increased

20. An aircraft is gliding in 'still air' conditions. Compared with gliding with a tailwind, in still air the glide range will be …….(i)……. and rate of descent will be ………(ii)…….:

	(i)	(ii)
(a)	unchanged	unchanged
(b)	more	unchanged
(c)	less	unchanged
(d)	less	less

Paper 1 Answers and Explanations

EFPPP1Q1   Answer C

Attempting to fly an overloaded or overweight aircraft has serious performance and handling penalties, including:

- The aircraft will accelerate more slowly on take-off, and require a longer take-off distance;
- Climb performance will be degraded;
- Stall speed will be faster;
- Cruise speed, range, endurance and service ceiling will all be reduced;
- The aircraft will perform badly and is more easily overstressed;
- Approach and landing speeds will be faster and landing distances will be increased.

Further Reference: PPL4 Flight Performance and Planning » Mass and Balance » Maximum Mass Limits

UK AIM » CAA Safety Sense Leaflets 9 » Weight and Balance

EFPPP1Q2   Answer C

The Zero Fuel Weight – ZFW – is the maximum weight (aircraft + payload) permitted with zero fuel in the tanks. Put another way, any payload that takes the weight over ZFW must be fuel only.

In practical terms, ZFW represents the maximum weight of passengers and baggage that can be added to the basic aircraft weight with no fuel loaded.

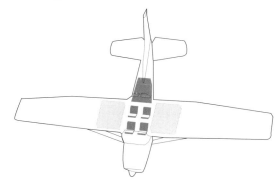

Further Reference: PPL4 Flight Performance and Planning » Mass and Balance » Maximum Mass Limits
UK AIM » CAA Safety Sense Leaflets 9 » Weight and Balance

EFPPP1Q3   Answer A

A specific gravity of 0.72 means that one litre of a liquid weighs 7.2kg.

Hence at a specific gravity of 0.72, 100 litres weighs 72kg (100 x 0.72). This calculation can be done on the Flight Computer as shown below:

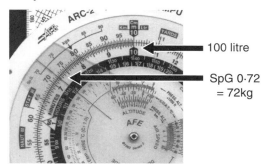

100 litre

SpG 0·72
= 72kg

A specific gravity of 0.72 also means that 1 imperial gallon of fuel weighs 7.2lbs. In this context, it is essential not to mix imperial and metric units in specific gravity calculations.

Further Reference: PPL4 Flight Performance and Planning » Mass and Balance » Maximum Mass Limits

UK AIM » CAA Safety Sense Leaflets 9 » Weight and Balance

EFPPP1Q4   Answer B

This calculation has to be done in stages:

At take-off, the total moment of the aircraft is (weight x CG) = (3000 x 65·5) = 196500.

This calculation can be done on the flight computer:

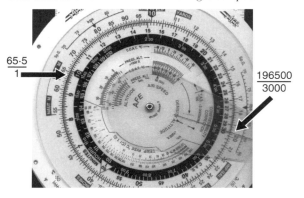

In a three hour flight, at 50lbs per hour, fuel consumed is 150lbs. Given a lever arm of 61, the fuel consumed has a moment of (61 x 150) = 9150.

So, at landing, total weight is (3000 – 150) = 2850lbs;

and total moment is (196500 – 9150) = 187350.

To find the landing CG, divide moment by weight, hence:

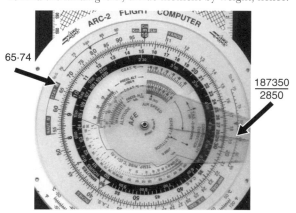

187350 ÷ 2850 = 65·74 inches aft of datum.

Note that the possible answers are sufficiently well spaced to allow a certain 'fudge factor' in the calculation for exam purposes.

Further reference: PPL4 Flight Performance and Planning » Mass and Balance » Centre of Gravity

EFPPP1Q5   Answer D

The utility part of the CG envelope is shown here shaded for clarity. Of the options given, only answer D – weight 900kg, moment 850 – falls within the shaded area.

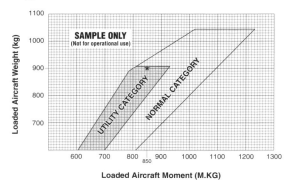

If an aircraft has defined weight or CG limitations defining a utility category (as opposed to the 'normal' category), the Pilot's Operating Handbook/Flight Manual (POH/FM) will state certain manoeuvres that can only be flown when the aircraft is loaded to be within the utility category.

Further Reference: PPL4 Flight Performance & Planning » Mass and Balance » Centre of Gravity
UK AIM » CAA Safety Sense Leaflets 9 » Weight and Balance

EFPPP1Q6   Answer A

The dimensions of a runway and its immediate

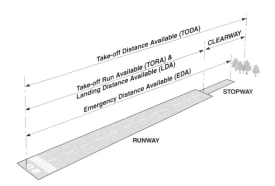

surroundings can be classified as follows:

Take-Off Distance Available (TODA)

Take-Off Run Available (TORA)

Landing Distance Available (LDA)

Emergency Distance Available (EDA)

These definitions should be memorised for exam purposes.

Further Reference: PPL4 Flight Performance & Planning » Runway Dimensions » Runway Dimensions

EFPPP1Q7   Answer B

A runway downslope will <u>decrease</u> take-off run, as the aircraft will be quicker to accelerate down the slope. However, it should also be borne in mind that in the event of an abandoned take-off, braking/stopping distance will also be increased.

A runway downslope will <u>increase</u> landing run, as the aircraft will decelerate at a reduced rate down the slope, and braking will be less effective. As a general rule of thumb, a 2% runway downslope will increase landing distance by 10%. The steeper the downslope, the greater the effect on landing distance.

Further Reference: PPL4 Flight Performance and Planning » Take-off and Climb » Calculation of Take-off Performance Calculating Landing Performance

UK AIM » CAA Safety Sense Leaflets 7 » Aeroplane Performance

EFPPP1Q8   Answer C

The relevant figures from the appropriate section of the CAA Aeronautical Information Circular (AIC) are designed to be used for making performance calculations for a factor which may not be in the aircraft's own Pilot's Operating Handbook/Flight Manual (POH/FM). If a performance factor is given in the POH/FM, that factor should be used.

The CAA table states that the following increases in calculated landing distance apply if not factored in the aircraft's POH/FM:

Wet paved runway	+15% (factor 1.15)
Wet grass	+35% (factor 1.35)

However, a note at the bottom of the table regarding landing on very short, wet grass says that landing distance may be increased by up to 60%.

For exam purposes it is necessary to memorise the CAA take-off and landing distance performance factor tables.

Further Reference: PPL4 Flight Performance & Planning » Descent and Landing Performance » Calculating Landing Performance

UK AIM » CAA Safety Sense Leaflets 7 » Aeroplane Performance

EFPPP1Q9   Answer A

Pressure altitude is the altitude indicated on an altimeter which has been set to 1013mb/hPa.

If pressure is below 1013, pressure altitude will be higher than the actual altitude.

If pressure is above 1013, pressure altitude will be lower than the actual altitude.

1mb/hPa is taken to be equivalent to 30ft.

So, in the example given the QNH (1002) is below 1013, so the pressure altitude can be expected to be higher than the current elevation (945ft). If you increase the millibar number on the altimeter sub scale, the indicated level increases (and vice versa).

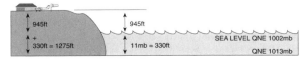

The difference between the actual pressure is (1013 – 1002) = 11mb/hPa; 11 x 30ft = 330ft.

945 + 330 = 1275. So the pressure altitude is 1275ft.

Further Reference: PPL4 Flight Performance and Planning » Take-off and Climb » Calculation of Take-off Performance

EFPPP1Q10   Answer A

The airspeed for best range airspeed is usually calculated based on 'still air' or 'zero wind' conditions. Theoretically, when flying into a strong headwind, increasing airspeed above the 'zero wind' best range airspeed will maximise range. The truth of this can be illustrated with an extreme example. If an aircraft is cruising at 110 knots into a headwind of 110 knots, its range is 0, because its groundspeed is 0. However, if airspeed is increased to 120 knots, range will increase – if only because the aircraft groundspeed is now 10 nautical miles per hour.

Conversely, when flying with a strong tailwind, reducing airspeed slightly below the 'still air' maximum range airspeed will (theoretically) increase range.

Further Reference: PPL4 Flight Performance and Planning » In-flight Performance » Cruise Performance

EFPPP1Q11   Answer D

The recommended approach speed, configuration and technique will be found in the aircraft's Pilot's Operating Handbook/Flight Manual (POH/FM). However, as an approximation the approach speed can be expected to be around 30% faster (factor 1.3) than the stalling speed in the approach configuration.

In the example given, where the stalling speed in the approach configuration is 55 knots, the approach speed could be expected to be around (55 x 1.3) = 72 knots (rounded up to the nearest knot).

Further Reference: PPL4 Flight Performance and Planning » Descent and Landing Performance » Calculating Landing Performance

EFPPP1Q12   Answer D

The CAA public transport safety factors (which are advisory for non-public transport flights, but highly recommended) are:

Take-off	1.33 (or +33%)
Landing	1.43 (or +43%)

These adjustments take account of 'real world' factors such as less-than-perfect piloting technique, engines, propellers and aircraft that are not brand new, conditions that are less than perfect, etc.

Further Reference: PPL4 Flight Performance and Planning » Take-off and Climb » Calculation of Take-off Performance

PPL4 Flight Performance and Planning » Take-off and Climb » Calculating Landing Performance

UK AIM » Aeronautical Information Circulars » AIC 67/2002 (pink 36) Take-off, climb and landing performance of light aeroplanes

UK AIM » CAA Safety Sense Leaflets 7 » Aeroplane Performance

EFPPP1Q13   Answer A

A runway downslope increases landing distance, according to the relevant CAA Aeronautical Information Circular (AIC), by about an extra 10% of the figure for a level runway. Thus, if the 'level' runway landing distance was 400m, the landing distance if the runway downslope is 2% (if all other factors are unchanged) is 440m (i.e. 400 x 1.1).

For exam purposes, it is necessary to memorise the CAA take-off and landing performance factor tables.

Further Reference: PPL4 Flight Performance and Planning » Descent and Landing Performance » Calculating Landing Performance

UK AIM » Aeronautical Information Circulars » AIC 67/2002 (pink 36) Take-off, climb and landing performance of light aeroplanes

UK AIM » CAA Safety Sense Leaflets 7 » Aeroplane Performance

EFPPP1Q14   Answer A

Best **rate-of-climb** speed is defined as attaining the maximum height gain in a specific time. This speed is sometimes referred to as **Vy**.

Best **angle-of-climb** speed is defined as attaining the maximum height gain in a specific distance. This speed is sometimes referred to as **Vx**.

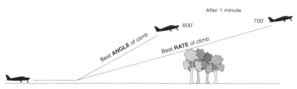

Use of the best angle of climb airspeed is normally reserved for situations when obstacle clearance is a significant factor.

Further Reference: PPL4 Flight Performance and Planning » Take-off and Climb » Principles of Climbing

EFPPP1Q15   Answer C

Weight	Pressure Altitude		Tempe-rature	Climb Speed IAS		Rate of Climb		From Sea Level				
								Time	Fuel used		Distance	
kg	ft	m	°C	km/h	kts	ft/mn	m/s	mn	US Gal.	Litres	NM	km
726	Sea level		15	135	73	770	3.9	0	0	0	0	0
	1000	305	13	135	73	725	3.7	1	0.3	1.1	2	3.7
	2000	610	11	133	72	675	3.4	3	0.6	2.3	3	5.6
	3000	914	9	133	72	630	3.2	4	0.9	3.4	5	9.3
	4000	1219	7	131	71	580	2.9	6	1.2	4.5	8	14.8
	5000	1524	5	131	71	535	2.7	8	1.6	6.1	10	18.5
	6000	1829	3	130	70	485	2.5	10	1.9	7.2	12	22.2
	7000	2134	1	128	69	440	2.2	12	2.3	8.7	15	27.8
	8000	2418	-1	128	69	390	2	15	2.7	10.2	19	35.2

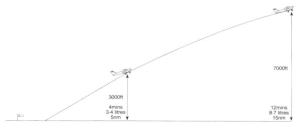

To answer this question, it is necessary to first find the relevant figures for the higher altitude. These figures represent the total time, fuel required and distance travelled to climb from sea level to 7000ft. To find the figures for the climb between 3000ft to 7000ft, subtract the relevant figures for 3000ft from the 7000ft figures. Hence:

	Sea Level to 7000ft (A)	Sea Level to 3000ft (B)	(A-B)
Time required	12 mins	4 mins	8 mins
Fuel used	8.7l	3.4l	5.3l
Distance travelled	15nm	5nm	10nm

Further Reference: PPL4 Flight Performance and Planning » Take-off and Climb » Calculation of Climb Performance

EFPPP1Q16   Answer B

TIME, FUEL, AND DISTANCE TO CLIMB [MAXIMUM RATE OF CLIMB]												
CONDITIONS :			Flaps up		Full throttle		Standard temperature					
Weight	Pressure Altitude		Tempe-rature	Climb Speed IAS		Rate of Climb		From Sea Level				
								Time	Fuel used		Distance	
kg	ft	m	°C	km/h	kts	ft/mn	m/s	mn	US Gal.	Litres	NM	km
726	Sea level		15	135	73	770	3.9	0	0	0	0	0
	1000	305	13	135	73	725	3.7	1	0.3	1.1	2	3.7
	2000	610	11	133	72	675	3.4	3	0.6	2.3	3	5.6
	3000	914	9	133	72	630	3.2	4	0.9	3.4	5	9.3
	4000	1219	7	131	71	580	2.9	6	1.2	4.5	8	14.8
	5000	1524	5	131	71	535	2.7	8	1.6	6.1	10	18.5
	6000	1829	3	130	70	485	2.5	10	1.9	7.2	12	22.2
	7000	2134	1	128	69	440	2.2	12	2.3	8.7	15	27.8
	8000	2418	-1	128	69	390	2	15	2.7	10.2	19	35.2
	9000	2743	-3	126	68	345	1.8	17	3.2	12.1	22	40.8
	10,000	3048	-5	126	68	295	1.5	21	3.7	14	27	50

The answer is found by simply reading along the line at 9000ft, and selecting the answers (and the correct units). Note that the Climb Speed table makes it clear that the airspeeds given are Indicated Air Speed (IAS) and not True Air Speed (TAS).

Further Reference: PPL4 Flight Performance and Planning » Take-off and Climb » Calculation of Climb Performance

EFPPP1Q17   Answer C

The CAA publish tables of conditions that affect take-off and landing performance, these can be found, amongst other places, in the current Aeronautical Information Circular (AIC) on light aircraft performance.

These factors are to be used only for conditions that are not allowed for in the aircraft's Pilots Operating Handbook / Flight Manual (POH/FM). In real-life, it is recommended that you refer to these tables if you wish to use these factors for calculating take-off or landing performance.

For exam purposes, it is necessary to memorise the tables.

According to the landing distance table, very short wet grass can lead to a very slippery runway surface, increasing landing distance by up to 60%

Further Reference: PPL4 Flight Performance and Planning » Descent and Landing Performance » Calculation of Landing Performance

UK AIM » Aeronautical Information Circulars » AIC 67/2002 (Pink 36) Take-off, climb and landing performance of light aeroplanes

UK AIM » CAA Safety Sense Leaflets 7 » Aeroplane Performance

EFPPP1Q18   Answer C

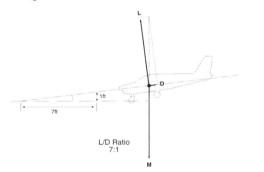

The point marked on the graph as 'B' represents the airspeed at which the aircraft will attain the maximum range. At the best range airspeed, the aircraft will cover the maximum distance for a given fuel load.

The point marked as 'A' represents the minimum power required airspeed, at which the aircraft has maximum endurance – it can stay airborne for the longest period with a given fuel load.

Further Reference: PPL4 Flight Performance and Planning » In-flight Performance » Cruise Performance

EFPPP1Q19   Answer C

A lift/drag (L/D) ratio of 7:1 indicates that the aircraft is producing 7 units of lift for one unit of drag. This converts into a gliding performance of 7 units forward for 1 unit down.

The aircraft is at a height of 6000ft. Multiplying this vertical distance (6000) by 7 (the L/D ratio) gives a glide range of (7 x 6000ft) = 42000ft.

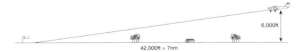

Conveniently enough, there are approximately 6000ft in a nautical mile (nm); so $42000 \div 6 = 7nm$.

For your interest, the L/D given (7:1) is fairly typical for many single engine training aircraft. For a modern competition glider, a L/D ratio of nearer 40:1 would be the norm.

Further Reference: PPL4 Flight Performance and Planning » Descent and Landing Performance » Gliding Performance

EFPPP1Q20   Answer B

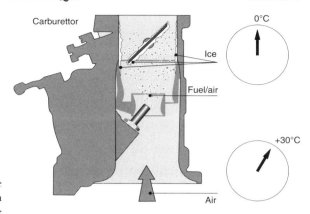

If all other factors are equal, a lower power setting (when the throttle valve is almost closed and the engine may be cooler) gives a greater risk of icing than a higher power setting.

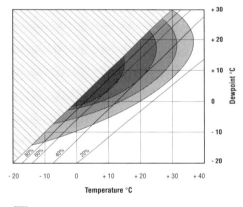

100% Relative humidity

Serious icing – any power

Moderate icing – cruise power
Serious icing – descent power

Serious icing – descent power

Light icing – cruise or descent power

In terms of atmospheric conditions, the greater the water content of the air (humidity), the greater the risk of carburettor icing. Warm air can hold more water content than cold air, and so a warm, humid summer day may well give a greater risk of carburettor icing than a cold, dry, winter night.

Further Reference: PPL4 Flight Performance and Planning » In-flight Performance » Cruise Performance

PPL4 Aircraft General Knowledge » The Induction System » Carburettor Icing

UK AIM » CAA Safety Sense Leaflets 14 » Piston Engine Icing

Paper 2 Answers and Explanations

EFPPP2Q1   Answer A

The aircraft's Pilot's Operating Handbook/Flight Manual (POH/FM) will state what manoeuvres the aircraft is permitted to perform, with recommended speeds, configurations and techniques. Sometimes, an aircraft will be permitted to do certain manoeuvres (e.g. those classified in the 'Normal' category), with extra manoeuvres (e.g. those specified in the 'Utility' category) only allowed subject to additional mass/weight and CG position limits.

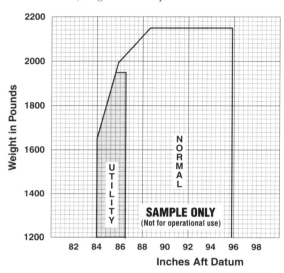

Although permitted manoeuvres will be stated in the POH/FM, in general terms those allowed for each category are:

Normal category	Manoeuvres used in normal flight including stalls, lazy eights, chandelles and steep turns where the angle of bank does not exceed 60°. Aerobatic manoeuvres (including spins) are not permitted.
Utility category	All manoeuvres permitted in the normal category, together with spins and steep turns with an angle of bank in excess of 60°.
Aerobatic category	All the manoeuvres of the Normal and Utility category, together with the aerobatic manoeuvres stated in the POH/FM subject to the declared entry airspeeds and load factor limits.

Further Reference: PPL4 Flight Performance and Planning » Mass and Balance » Centre of Gravity
UK AIM » CAA Safety Sense Leaflets 9 » Weight and Balance

EFPPP2Q2   Answer C

Increased aircraft mass (weight) means faster take-off and climb speeds than for a lighter aircraft. Some aircraft with a wide range of take-off weights may list different take-off speeds for different take-off weights. A heavier aircraft will take longer to accelerate to a faster take-off speed, and it follows that take-off distances will increase as a result. As an approximate rule of thumb, a 10% increase in aircraft weight leads to a 20% increase in take-off distance.

Further Reference: PPL4 Flight Performance & Planning » Take-off and Climb » Calculation of Take-Off Performance
UK AIM » Aeronautical Information Circulars » AIC 67/2002 (Pink 36) Take-off, climb and landing performance of light aeroplanes
UK AIM » CAA Safety Sense Leaflets 7 » Aeroplane Performance

EFPPP2Q3   Answer A

This calculation is best started by finding the QNH (ie the altimeter setting required for the altimeter to read altitude, that is elevation above sea level). The airfield is 330 feet above sea level. 330 divided by 30 = 11. So the difference between QFE and QNH is 11 millibars. On the ground at the airfield, an altimeter setting of 993mb (the QFE) causes the altimeter to read zero. Therefore, increasing the altimeter setting by 11 millibars to 1004mb (the QNH) will cause the altimeter to read altitude (or elevation) above sea level.

However, Pressure Altitude (as required in the question) is found when the altimeter is set to 1013. The difference between the current QNH (1004) and the 'standard' setting (1013) is 9mb. 9mb x 30ft = 270ft, and adding 270ft to the altitude of 330ft (because as pressure setting increases the indicated altitude increases) = 600ft.

Therefore, on the day in question, the pressure altitude at the airfield is 600ft.

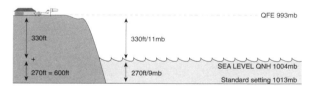

Further Reference: PPL4 Flight Performance and Planning » Take-Off and Climb » Calculation of Take-Off Performance

EFPPP2Q4

Answer A

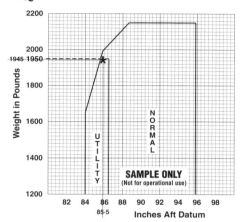

Of the possible answers given, only option A (1945lbs, 85.5 in. aft datum) falls within the utility area of the CG envelope, as required by the question.

Further Reference: PPL4 Flight Performance and Planning » Mass and Balance » Centre of Gravity

UK AIM » CAA Safety Sense Leaflets 9 » Weight and Balance

EFPPP2Q5

Answer C

A high pressure altitude, in all but the most unusual conditions, means a reduced air density (high altitude = reduced pressure = reduced air density) compared with sea level conditions. As a general rule, reduced air density means reduced aircraft performance. In the case of take-off and landing performance, the less dense the air, the longer the take-off and landing distances required by an aircraft.

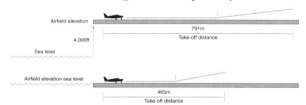

Further Reference: PPL4 Flight Performance & Planning » Take-off and Climb » Calculation of Take-Off Performance

PPL4 » Flight Performance & Planning » Descent and Landing Performance » Calculating Landing Performance

EFPPP2Q6

Answer C

Attempting to fly an over-loaded (overweight) aircraft has several serious performance penalties, including:

■ take-off and landing speeds increased
■ take-off and landing distances increased
■ climb performance reduced
■ cruise speed, range endurance and service ceiling all reduced

Further Reference: PPL4 Flight Performance & Planning » Mass and Balance » Maximum Mass Limits

UK AIM » CAA Safety Sense Leaflets 9 » Weight and Balance

EFPPP2Q7

Answer B

A paved (hard) runway that is level and dry is most often considered to be the 'baseline' runway condition for take-off and landing performance calculations. Any deviation from these conditions (wet runways, grass, sloping runways etc.) will require factoring of the take-off and landing performance, using factors given in the performance graphs/tables, or using the CAA-recommended factors if no POH/FM adjustments exist.

Further Reference: PPL4 Flight Performance and Planning » Take-off and Climb » Calculation of Take-off Performance

UK AIM » Aeronautical Information Circulars » AIC 67/2002 (Pink 36) Take-off, climb and landing performance of light aeroplanes

UK AIM » CAA Safety Sense Leaflets 7 » Aeroplane Performance

EFPPP2Q8

Answer D

A runway downslope will lead to a shorter take-off distance, as the aircraft will accelerate more quickly to its take-off speed (a component of weight acts in the same direction as thrust/power during the take-off run). Conversely, on landing the aircraft will be slower to decelerate whilst travelling down the slope as a component of weight counters the deceleration of friction and braking.

Further Reference: PPL4 Flight Performance & Planning » Take-off and Climb » Calculation of Take-Off Performance

PPL4 Flight Performance & Planning » Descent and Landing Performance » Calculating Landing Performance

UK AIM » Aeronautical Information Circulars » AIC 67/2002 (Pink 36) Take-off, climb and landing performance of light aeroplanes

UK AIM » CAA Safety Sense Leaflets 7 » Aeroplane Performance

EFPPP2Q9

Answer B

Where the aircraft's Pilot's Operating Handbook/Flight Manual (POH/FM) states a recommended flap setting for take-off, the use of this flap setting can be expected to reduce the take-off run, because the aircraft can take-off at a slower speed than for a take-off without flap.

The use of a flap setting greater than that recommended in the POH/FM is likely to significantly increase the take-off run, because of the considerable extra drag generated by the flaps when they are extended beyond the recommended take-off setting.

Further Reference: PPL4 Flight Performance & Planning » Take-off and Climb » Forces in the Take-Off Run

UK AIM » CAA Safety Sense Leaflets 7 » Aeroplane Performance

EFPPP2Q10   Answer A

The cruise performance figures in an aircraft's POH/FM rarely make any correction for headwind or tailwind. However, in theory at least, compared to a 'still air' best range airspeed, range is increased by reducing speed slightly if flying with a tailwind, and by increasing speed slightly if flying into a headwind.

Further Reference: PPL4 Flight Performance and Planning » In-flight Performance » Cruise Performance

EFPPP2Q11   Answer A

The recommended approach speed, configuration and technique will be found in the aircraft's Pilot's Operating Handbook/Flight Manual (POH/FM). However, as an approximation the approach speed can be expected to be around 30% faster (factor 1.3) than the stalling speed in the approach configuration – Vso.

In the example given, where the Vso is 50 knots, the approach speed could be expected to be around (50 x 1.3) = 65 knots.

Further Reference: PPL4 Flight Performance and Planning » Descent and Landing Performance » Calculating Landing Performance

EFPPP2Q12   Answer A

The reported wind (remembering that wind direction is the direction that the wind is coming <u>from</u>) is giving a significant tailwind component. When flying with a tailwind, whatever the stage of flight, groundspeed will be greater than the airspeed.

Landing with a tailwind is particularly hazardous not just because of the optical illusion caused by the faster-than-normal groundspeed (possibly leading the unwary pilot to reduce airspeed below the recommended approach airspeed), but also because of the very significant increase in landing distance than even a small tailwind component will cause. Even a tailwind of just 10% of landing speed (ie a tailwind component of only 5-6 knots for many light aircraft) can increase landing distance by 20%.

Further Reference: PPL4 Flight Performance and Planning » Descent and Landing Performance » Calculating Landing Performance
UK AIM » Aeronautical Information Circulars » AIC 67/2002 (Pink 36) Take-off, climb and landing performance of light aeroplanes
UK AIM » CAA Safety Sense Leaflets 7 » Aeroplane Performance

EFPPP2Q13   Answer D

In general terms, extending any amount of flap will reduce rate of climb. This occurs not least because extending flap will increase drag, and hence increase the power required at any particular airspeed. This means that there is a reduced excess of power available over power required, and reduced excess power means reduced rate of climb.

Further Reference: PPL4 Flight Performance and Planning » Take-off and Climb » Climb Performance

EFPPP2Q14   Answer A

The CAA publish tables of conditions that affect take-off and landing performance, these can be found, amongst other places, in the current Aeronautical Information Circular (AIC) on light aircraft performance.

These factors are to be used only for conditions that are not allowed for in the aircraft's Pilots Operating Handbook / Flight Manual (POH/FM). In real-life, it is recommended that you refer to these tables if you wish to use these factors for calculating take-off or landing performance, rather than trying to recall the details. However, for exam purposes, it is necessary to memorise the tables.

According to the relevant table, an increase of 10°C in temperature leads to an increase in take-off distance of 10% – a factor of 1.1.

Further Reference: PPL4 » Flight Performance and Planning » Take-off and Climb » Calculation of Take-off Performance
UK AIM » Aeronautical Information Circulars » AIC 67/2002 (pink 36) Take-off, climb and landing performance of light aeroplanes
UK AIM » CAA Safety Sense Leaflets 7 » Aeroplane Performance

EFPPP2Q15   Answer A

A graph of power required against airspeed reveals that when there is the lowest ratio of power to airspeed, the best range airspeed has been achieved. This point is found where a tangential line meets the power-required curve.

On a more practical note, maximum range is achieved at the angle of attack (and hence airspeed) at which there is the greatest ratio of lift to drag – i.e. the maximum amount of lift for the minimum amount of drag. This airspeed is also that at which the aircraft will achieve the shallowest gliding angle and so the best glide range.

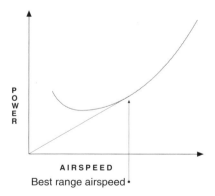

Further Reference: PPL4 Flight Performance and Planning » In-flight Performance » Cruise Performance

EFPPP2Q16   Answer D

RPM	PRESSURE ALTITUDE 2000 FEET											
	20°C BELOW STD. TEMP				STANDARD TEMP				20°C ABOVE STD. TEMP			
	% BHP	TAS KTS	TAS MPH	FUEL GPH	% BHP	TAS KTS	TAS MPH	FUEL GPH	% BHP	TAS KTS	TAS MPH	FUEL GPH
	–9°C (16°F)				11°C (52°F)				31°C (88°F)			
2700	92	130	150	10.7	87	129	149	10.0	82	129	148	9.5
2600	83	125	143	9.6	79	124	143	9.0	75	123	142	8.6
2500	75	119	137	8.6	71	119	136	8.1	68	118	135	7.7
2400	68	114	131	7.8	65	113	130	7.4	61	111	127	7.0
2300	61	108	124	7.0	58	106	121	6.6	55	103	118	6.3
2200	55	101	116	6.2	52	98	113	5.9	50	96	110	5.7
	PRESSURE ALTITUDE 3000 FEET											
	–11°C (12°F)				9°C (48°F)				29°C (84°F)			
2700	90	130	149	10.4	85	129	149	9.8	80	129	148	9.2
2600	82	125	143	9.4	77	124	142	8.8	73	123	142	8.4
2500	73	119	137	8.4	70	118	136	8.0	66	117	134	7.6
2400	66	113	130	7.6	63	112	129	7.2	60	110	126	6.8
2300	80	107	123	6.8	57	106	121	6.5	54	103	118	6.2
2200	54	100	115	6.1	51	97	112	5.8	50	95	108	5.6
	PRESSURE ALTITUDE 4000 FEET											
	–13°C (9°F)				7°C (45°F)				27°C (81°F)			
2700	88	129	149	10.1	83	129	149	9.6	79	129	148	9.0
2600	80	124	143	9.2	75	124	142	8.6	71	122	141	8.1
2500	72	119	137	8.2	68	118	135	7.8	65	116	133	7.4
2400	65	113	130	7.4	62	111	128	7.0	59	109	125	6.9
2300	59	106	122	6.7	56	103	119	6.3	54	102	117	6.1
2200	52	98	113	5.9	51	96	111	5.7	49	93	107	5.5

Answering this question should not be difficult provided you take care to locate the correct parameters on the table. They are tinted on the table above for clarity. In the exam, as in the real world, it pays to check and double check that you have followed the correct parameters to obtain the correct figures.

Check also to see if there any notes to the table which include further factors to be taken into account when calculating performance.

Further Reference: PPL4 Flight Performance and Planning » In-flight Performance » Cruise Performance

EFPPP2Q17   Answer A

Conveniently enough, the quoted temperature is exactly the ISA standard temperature, and the weight is the gross weight as stated in the table. The only calculation required is to interpolate between the rate of climb figures given for 3000ft and 4000ft to find the figure for 3500ft.

	TIME, FUEL, AND DISTANCE TO CLIMB					MAXIMUM RATE OF CLIMB						
CONDITIONS :			Flaps up		Full throttle			Standard temperature				
Weight	Pressure Altitude		Tempe-rature	Climb Speed IAS		Rate of Climb		From Sea Level				
								Time	Fuel used		Distance	
kg	ft	m	°C	km/h	kts	ft/mn	m/s	mn	US Gal.	Litres	NM	km
726	Sea level		15	135	73	770	3.9	0	0	0	0	0
	1000	305	13	135	73	725	3.7	1	0.3	1.1	2	3.7
	2000	610	11	133	72	675	3.4	3	0.6	2.3	3	5.6
	3000	914	9	133	72	630	3.2	4	0.9	3.4	5	9.3
	4000	1219	7	131	71	580	2.9	6	1.2	4.5	8	14.8
	5000	1524	5	131	71	535	2.7	8	1.6	6.1	10	18.5
	6000	1829	3	130	70	485	2.5	10	1.9	7.2	12	22.2
	7000	2134	1	128	69	440	2.2	12	2.3	8.7	15	27.8
	8000	2418	- 1	128	69	390	2	15	2.7	10.2	19	35.2
	9000	2743	- 3	12n	68	345	1.8	17	3.2	12.1	22	40.8
	10,000	3048	- 5	126	68	295	1.5	21	3.7	14	27	50
	11,000	3353	- 7	124	67	250	1.3	24	4.2	15.9	32	59.3
	12,000	3658	- 9	124	67	200	1	29	4.9	18.5	38	70.4

NOTES :
1. Add 1.1 gallons 4.16 litres of fuel for engine start, taxi and takeoff allowance.
2. Mixture leaned above 3000 ft - 914 m for maximum RPM.
3. Increase time, fuel and distance by 10 % for each 10°C above standard temperature.
4. Distances shown are based on zero wind.

There are two methods for making this calculation, each gives the same answer so which to use is a matter of personal preference:

(1) Add together the rate of climb figures for 3000ft (630) and for 4000ft (580) and divide by two.
630 + 580 = 1210. 1210 ÷ 2 = 605.

(2) Find the difference between the 3000ft (630) and 4000ft (580) figures.
630 – 580 = 50. Halve the difference (50 ÷ 2 = 25). Add this figure to the 3000ft figure (580 + 25) or subtract from the 4000ft figure (630 – 25).

In either case the answer is 605ft/min.

Further Reference: PPL4 Flight Performance and Planning » Take-off and Climb » Calculation of Climb Performance

EFPPP2Q18   Answer B

A piston-engine aircraft will attain maximum endurance when flying at the <u>minimum power required</u> airspeed. This is often around 25% slower than the airspeed for maximum range.

Remember, maximum endurance means staying airborne the longest possible <u>time</u>; maximum range means travelling the longest possible <u>distance</u>.

If all other factors are equal, maximum endurance is achieved at the lowest altitude.

Further Reference: PPL4 Flight Performance and Planning » In-flight Performance » Cruise Performance

EFPPP2Q19   Answer B

A non de-iced aircraft is not permitted to fly in conditions of known icing – which given that ice is collecting on the airframe is clearly the case.

<u>Any</u> icing is potentially very dangerous and it is imperative that the aircraft leave icing conditions immediately. If it is safe to do so, the preferred option is to descend into warmer air, where the accumulated ice will melt away. Ignoring ice is not an option.

Further Reference: PPL4 Flight Performance and Planning » In-flight Performance » Cruise Performance

UK AIM » Aeronautical Information Circulars » AIC 106/2004 (Pink 74) Frost, ice and snow on aircraft

EFPPP2Q20   Answer D

Contrary to what you might expect, both aircraft are capable of achieving the same glide range, provided each is flown at the correct airspeed for maximum lift/drag ratio. A heavier aircraft will obtain the best L/D ratio at a faster airspeed than a lighter one.

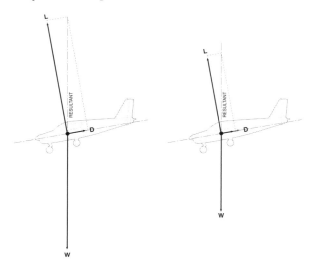

Competition gliders use this aerodynamic feature to their advantage, by carrying ballast (often in the form of water) to make them heavier, and thus able to glide around a course more quickly than a lighter glider of the same design.

Further Reference: PPL4 Flight Performance and Planning »
Descent and Landing Performance » Gliding Performance

Paper 3 Answers and Explanations

EFPPP3Q1   Answer B

The manoeuvres permitted for an aircraft certified in the normal category are covered in EFPPP2Q1. Many light aircraft are certified in more than one category, but must be loaded to different mass/CG position limits for operating in different categories.

Further Reference: PPL4 Flight Performance & Planning » Mass and Balance » Centre of Gravity

UK AIM » CAA Safety Sense Leaflets 9 » Weight and Balance

EFPPP3Q2   Answer D

The overloading of an aircraft can have very serious consequences. On take-off the aircraft will have reduced acceleration, need to reach a faster speed to fly and so have an increased take-off distance. Climb performance will be degraded and maximum altitude capability (service ceiling and absolute ceiling) will be lower. The aircraft will also be more easily overstressed. The stall speed will be increased, approach and landing speeds will be faster and landing distance will be increased.

Further Reference: PPL4 Flight Performance and Planning » Mass and Balance » Maximum Mass Limits

UK AIM » CAA Safety Sense Leaflets 9 » Weight and Balance

EFPPP3Q3   Answer B

The new weight of the aircraft found simply by adding the weight of the fuel loaded (300lb) to the weight of the aircraft as it landed (2000lb) making at total of 2300lbs.

To calculate the new CG position the new total moment must first be found. The fuel loaded (300lb) is multiplied by the fuel lever arm to give the fuel moment. Note that the total aircraft moment is given in lb inches, so the lever arm of 7ft 11in must be converted into inches: (7 x 12) + 11 = 95 inches.

300 x 95 = 28500. This can be done using the flight computer:

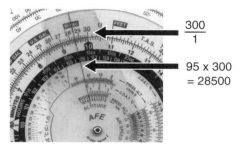

So the new total aircraft moment is
150000 + 28500 = 178500in lb.

To find the CG position, the total aircraft moment (178500) is divided by weight (2300), to give a CG position of 77.61 inches aft of datum.

This can be done on the flight computer:

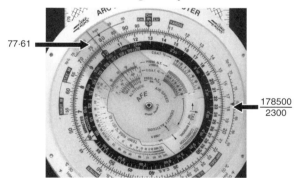

Further Reference: PPL4 Flight Performance and Planning » Mass and Balance » Centre of Gravity

EFPPP3Q4   Answer C

If all other factors are equal, a heavier aircraft (the aircraft is 500lbs heavier during the second flight) will have a longer take-off distance than a lighter one, and its climb performance will be degraded in comparison with the lighter aircraft.

Further Reference: PPL4 Flight Performance & Planning » Take-off and Climb » Calculation of Take-off Performance

PPL4 Flight Performance & Planning » Take-off and Climb » Climb Performance

UK AIM » CAA Safety Sense Leaflets 7 » Aeroplane Performance

EFPPP3Q5   Answer B

The runway and its immediate surroundings can be classified as in EFPP1Q6.

These definitions must be memorised for exam purposes.
Further Reference: PPL4 Flight Performance & Planning » Runway Dimensions » Runway Dimensions

EFPPP3Q6   Answer B

Climb performance is inextricably linked to aircraft weight – if all other factors are equal the lighter aircraft will have better climb performance than a heavier one.
Further Reference: PPL4 Flight Performance & Planning » Take-off and Climb » Climb Performance

EFPPP3Q7   Answer D

Take-off and landing performance is often based on a 'default' of a level, dry runway with a hard surface. Many of the performance 'factors' published by the UK CAA are used to allow for deviations from this 'standard' runway.
Further Reference: PPL4 Flight Performance & Planning » Take-off and Climb » Calculation of Take-Off Performance
UK AIM » CAA Safety Sense Leaflets 7 » Aeroplane Performance

EFPPP3Q8   Answer B

The use of flap allows the aircraft to fly more slowly (because stall airspeed is reduced). Furthermore, because the use of flap also increases drag the approach path can be made steeper (e.g. by selecting a lower nose attitude) without increasing airspeed. The more flap is selected, the slower the stall speed and the greater the drag. This demonstrates one of the primary advantages of flaps. They allow an aircraft to make a slower and steeper descent than would be the case if no flap was lowered.

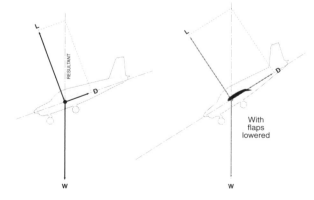

Further Reference: PPL4 Flight Performance and Planning » Descent and Landing Performance » Gliding Performance

EFPPP3Q9   Answer B

At the airspeed (and therefore angle of attack) at which the best ratio of lift to drag is achieved, the aircraft is at, or very close to, the maximum range airspeed. This means that most light aircraft will achieve their best gliding range, and their best cruise range, at the same airspeed.
Further Reference: PPL4 Flight Performance and Planning » In-flight Performance » Cruise Performance

EFPPP3Q10   Answer D

When landing on grass, the reducing braking effectiveness (compared to a paved runway) leads to an increase in landing run, and so an increase in landing distance, of up to 15% even on dry grass (and potentially up to 60% on very short, wet grass).

Take-off run on grass is also longer on grass than on a paved surface (increasing take-off distance by up to 20% on dry grass).

These tables must be memorised for exam purposes.
Further Reference: PPL4 Flight Performance and Planning » Descent and Landing Performance » Calculating Landing Performance
PPL4 Flight Performance and Planning » Take-off and Climb » Calculation of Take-Off Performance
UK AIM » Aeronautical Information Circulars » AIC 67/2002 (Pink 36) Take-off, climb and landing performance of light aeroplanes
UK AIM » CAA Safety Sense Leaflets 7 » Aeroplane Performance

EFPPP3Q11   Answer C

The POH/FM extract gives the recommended landing technique to achieve the stated landing performance, including an approach speed of 60 knots. By approaching at a faster speed, the landing distance required will be increased. As an approximate rule of thumb, a 10% increase in approach speed will increase landing distance by at least 20%. To achieve the stated landing performance, it is necessary to use the stated landing technique.
Further Reference: PPL4 Flight Performance and Planning » Descent and Landing Performance » Calculating Landing Performance

EFPPP3Q12   Answer A

The aircraft will attain maximum endurance when flying at, or very close to, the angle of attack (and therefore airspeed) for the minimum power required to sustain level flight.

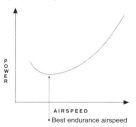

Further Reference: PPL4 Flight Performance and Planning » In-flight Performance » Cruise Performance

EFPPP3Q13   Answer D

Both aircraft are accelerating to the same lift-off airspeed, however aircraft B, with the benefit of a headwind, will reach that lift-off <u>airspeed</u> at a <u>ground</u>speed which is 10 knots slower than aircraft B. For example, if the lift-off airspeed is 60 knots, at lift-off aircraft A (still air) will have a groundspeed of 60 knots, whereas aircraft B (experiencing 10 knots headwind) will have a groundspeed of 50 knots (60-10).

Because aircraft B lifts off at a slower groundspeed, its take-off distance is shorter than for aircraft A.

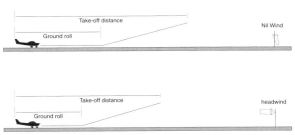

Further Reference: PPL4 Flight Performance & Planning » Take-off and Climb » Calculation of Take-Off Performance

UK AIM » CAA Safety Sense Leaflets 7 » Aeroplane Performance

EFPPP3Q14   Answer A

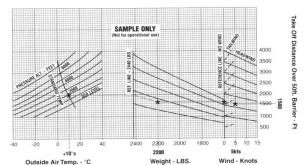

Answering this question should not be difficult provided you take care to locate the correct parameters on the graph. The line to follow is shown above tinted on the table above for clarity. Note that from each parameter (eg temperature/pressure altitude), the line goes horizontally to the next reference line, then parallels the guide lines until over the next parameter (eg weight).

Further Reference: PPL4 Flight Performance and Planning » Take-off and Climb » Calculation of Take-off Performance

UK AIM » CAA Safety Sense Leaflets 7 » Aeroplane Performance

EFPPP3Q15   Answer A

RPM	PRESSURE ALTITUDE 2000 FEET											
	20°C BELOW STD. TEMP				STANDARD TEMP				20°C ABOVE STD. TEMP			
	% BHP	TAS KTS	TAS MPH	FUEL GPH		% BHP	TAS KTS	TAS MPH	FUEL GPH	% BHP	TAS KTS	TAS MPH	FUEL GPH
	−9°C (16°F)					11°C (52°F)				31°C (88°F)			
2700	92	130	150	10.7		87	129	149	10.0	82	129	148	9.5
2600	83	125	143	9.6		79	124	143	9.0	75	123	142	8.6
2500	75	119	137	8.6		71	119	136	8.1	68	118	135	7.7
2400	68	114	131	7.8		65	113	130	7.4	61	111	127	7.0
2300	61	108	124	7.0		58	106	121	6.6	55	103	118	6.3
2200	55	101	116	6.2		52	98	113	5.9	50	96	110	5.7
	PRESSURE ALTITUDE 3000 FEET											
	−11°C (12°F)					9°C (48°F)				29°C (84°F)			
2700	90	130	149	10.4		85	129	149	9.8	80	129	148	9.2
2600	82	125	143	9.4		77	124	142	8.8	73	123	142	8.4
2500	73	119	137	8.4		70	118	136	8.0	66	117	134	7.6
2400	66	113	130	7.6		63	112	129	7.2	60	110	126	6.8
2300	60	107	123	6.8		57	105	121	6.5	54	103	118	6.2
2200	54	100	115	6.1		51	97	112	5.8	50	95	108	5.6
	PRESSURE ALTITUDE 4000 FEET											
	−13°C (9°F)					7°C (45°F)				27°C (81°F)			
2700	88	129	149	10.1		83	129	149	9.6	79	129	148	9.0
2600	80	124	143	9.2		75	124	142	8.6	71	122	141	8.1
2500	72	119	137	8.2		68	118	135	7.8	65	116	133	7.4
2400	65	113	130	7.4		62	111	128	7.0	59	109	125	6.7
2300	59	106	122	6.7		56	103	119	6.3	54	102	117	6.1
2200	52	98	113	5.9		51	96	111	5.7	49	93	107	5.5

Answering this question should not be difficult provided you take care to locate the correct parameters on the table. They are tinted on the table above for clarity. In the exam, as in the real world, it pays to check and double check that you have followed the correct parameters to obtain the correct figures.

Remember to check for any additional conditions in the notes to the table (such as speed fairings or 'wheel pants' as some manufacturers like to call them) which may affect the performance figures.

Further Reference: PPL4 Flight Performance and Planning » In-flight Performance » Cruise Performance

EFPPP3Q16   Answer B

Weight	Pressure Altitude		Tempe-rature	Climb Speed IAS		Rate of Climb		From Sea Level				
								Time	Fuel used		Distance	
kg	ft	m	°C	km/h	kts	ft/mn	m/s	mn	US Gal.	Litres	NM	km
726	Sea level		15	135	73	770	3.9	0	0	0	0	0
	1000	305	13	135	73	725	3.7	1	0.3	1.1	2	3.7
	2000	610	11	133	72	675	3.4	3	0.6	2.3	3	5.6
	3000	914	9	133	72	630	3.2	4	0.9	3.4	5	9.3
	4000	1219	7	131	71	580	2.9	6	1.2	4.5	8	14.8
	5000	1524	5	131	71	535	2.7	8	1.6	6.1	10	18.5
	6000	1829	3	130	70	485	2.5	10	1.9	7.2	12	22.2
	7000	2134	1	128	69	440	2.2	12	2.3	8.7	15	27.8
	8000	2418	- 1	128	69	390	2	15	2.7	10.2	19	35.2
	9000	2743	- 1	126	68	345	1.8	17	3.2	12.1	22	40.8
	10,000	3048	- 5	126	68	295	1.5	21	3.7	14	27	50
	11,000	3353	- 7	124	67	250	1.3	24	4.2	15.9	32	59.3
	12,000	3658	- 9	124	67	200	1	29	4.9	18.5	38	70.4

TIME, FUEL, AND DISTANCE TO CLIMB [MAXIMUM RATE OF CLIMB]

CONDITIONS : Flaps up   Full throttle   Standard temperature

NOTES :
1. Add 1.1 gallons 4.16 litres of fuel for engine start, taxi and takeoff allowance.
2. Mixture leaned above 3000 ft - 914 m for maximum RPM.
3. Increase time, fuel and distance by 10 % for each 10°C above standard temperature.
4. Distances shown are based on zero wind.

The basic figures for the climb to 6000ft are found by reading across the 6000ft line. However, note 1 states that 1.1 gallons (or 4.16 litres) or fuel burn should be added for start, taxi and take-off. Thus the 'basic' fuel burn of 1.9us gal/7.2litres becomes 3us gal/11.36 litres.

The rate of climb is found by interpolating between the ROC figures at 4000ft (580ft/min) and at 5000ft (535ft/min).
Further Reference: PPL4 Flight Performance and Planning » Take-off and Climb » Calculation of Climb Performance

EFPPP3Q17   Answer D

A wet runway increases landing distance due to the reduced braking effectiveness, leading to reduced deceleration and an increased landing run. The magnitude of this increase on a paved runway is calculated by the CAA as being 15% – a factor of 1.15. In other words, a calculated 'dry' landing distance of 500m would become (500 x 1.15) = 575m.

For the purposes of the exam, it is necessary to memorise the take-off and landing distance factor tables.

When calculating aircraft performance in real life, any factors included in the aircraft's Pilot's Operating Handbook/Flight Manual (POH/FM) over-ride the CAA advice, and the CAA factors are only used for conditions not allowed for in the POH/FM calculations.
Further Reference: PPL4 Flight Performance and Planning » Descent and Landing Performance » Calculating Landing Performance
UK AIM » Aeronautical Information Circulars » AIC 67/2002 (Pink 36) Take-off, climb and landing performance of light aeroplanes

EFPPP3Q18   Answer B

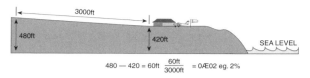

$$480 - 420 = 60ft \quad \frac{60ft}{3000ft} = 0 \cancel{E}02 \ eg. \ 2\%$$

The total change in elevation along the runway is 60ft (480 – 420). Dividing this height change by the runway length gives the elevation.

Hence 60 ÷ 3000 = 0.02 or 2%

(This calculation can be done on the flight computer as shown below)

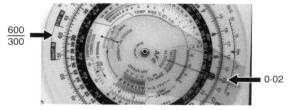

$\frac{600}{300}$ 0·02

Further Reference: PPL4 Flight Performance and Planning » Runway Dimensions » Runway Dimensions
UK AIM » Aeronautical Information Circulars » AIC 67/2002 (Pink 36) Take-off, climb and landing performance of light aeroplanes

EFPPP3Q19   Answer B

Anything that distorts the shape of the wing will have an adverse affect on performance. Ice in particular will reduce lift, increase drag and increase weight. Any of these factors singly can significantly reduce performance, and in combination their adverse influence can quickly overcome the performance capabilities of a light aircraft.
Further Reference: PPL4 Flight Performance and Planning » In-flight Performance » Cruise Performance
UK AIM » Aeronautical Information Circulars » AIC 106/2004 (Pink 74) Frost, ice and snow on aircraft

EFPPP3Q20   Answer C

A headwind or tailwind will affect gliding range, but have no affect at all on rate of descent. An aircraft gliding with a tailwind will glide further than an aircraft gliding in still air, but both will reach the ground in the same time. An aircraft gliding into a headwind will not glide as far as an aircraft gliding in still air, but once again both aircraft will descend at the same rate and reach the ground in the same time.

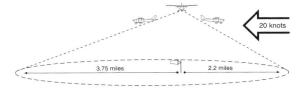

**Further Reference: PPL4 Flight Performance and Planning »
Descent and Landing Performance » Gliding Performance**

Aircraft General and Principles of Flight

Principles of Flight

▶ THE ATMOSPHERE AND PROPERTIES OF AIR

The **International Standard Atmosphere**:

Sea-level temperature	+15°C
Sea-level pressure	1013·25mb/hPa
Sea-level density	1·225kg m3
Temperature lapse rate	1·98°C per 1000ft up to 36,090ft

As altitude increases, temperature, pressure and density all decrease.

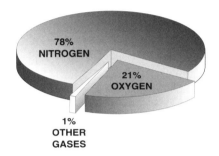

Static pressure + dynamic pressure = constant. So, as dynamic pressure increases, static pressure decreases.

▶ The Four Forces Acting on an Aircraft in Flight

In straight and level flight at a constant airspeed:

$$Lift = Weight \text{ and } Thrust = Drag$$

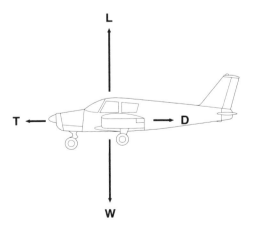

Angle of attack is the angle between the wing's chord line and the relative airflow.

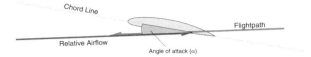

As angle of attack increases, **coefficient of lift** increases until reaching a maximum at the stalling angle, when the wing stalls. Air flowing above the wing has a faster airflow speed and lower static pressure, air flowing beneath the wing has a slower airflow speed and higher static pressure.

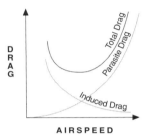

Total Drag
(eg. Parasite Drag + Induced Drag)

Induced drag decreases with increasing airspeed; **parasite drag** increases with increasing airspeed.

A 'conventional' aircraft has a download on the tailplane in level flight, to balance the nose-down pitching effect of the lift/weight forces.

▶ STABILITY AND CONTROL

An aircraft can rotate around **three axes**:

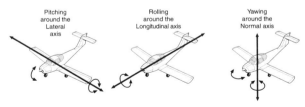

The **primary and further effects** of the main flying controls are:

Flying Control	Elevator	Aileron	Rudder
Primary effect	Pitch	Roll	Yaw
Secondary Effect	-	Yaw	Roll

'**Flutter**' is the rapid oscillation of a flying control surface, and can be countered by adding a mass balance to the control.

►TRIMMING CONTROLS

An external **trim tab** is set independently of the flying control it is attached to, and maintains the same angle relative to the flying control. A **balance tab** moves in the opposite direction to the flying control, to aid the movement of the control. An **anti-balance tab** moves in the same direction as the flying control, to damp down the movement and make the flying control feel 'heavier'.

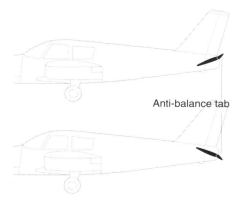

Anti-balance tab

►FLAPS AND SLATS

Trailing edge flap reduces stall speed and increases both lift and drag. A wing stalls at a shallower stalling angle of attack when flaps are extended. A leading edge **slot or slat** re-energises airflow over the wing.

►THE STALL

A **wing stalls at a set angle of attack**. The airspeed at which that angle of attack is reached varies with several factors.

Stall airspeed increases by the square root of the load factor. At a load factor of 2, stall speed increases by 41% (a factor of 1.41). In a 60° angle of bank turn, the load factor is 2.

►AVOIDANCE OF SPINS

For an aircraft to spin, it first must stall: Avoid the stall to avoid the spin. The '**autorotation**' of a spin is caused by less lift and more drag on the down-going wing than on the up-going wing.

►LOAD FACTOR AND MANOEUVRING FLIGHT

An aircraft's **load factors** are absolute limits. Exceeding a load factor limit, no matter how slightly or how momentarily, is a very serious matter, requiring the aircraft to be grounded pending an engineering inspection.

The **airspeed indicator** (ASI) has colour markings to indicate limiting airspeeds:

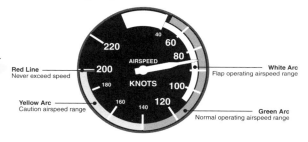

AIRCRAFT GENERAL KNOWLEDGE

►THE AIRFRAME

A stressed skin construction carries some of the loads otherwise borne by the internal structure is a **monocoque structure**. If the stressed skin is supported by a light framework, it is a **semi-monocoque** structure.

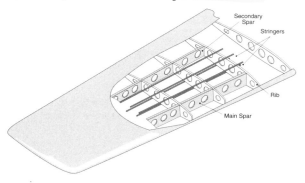

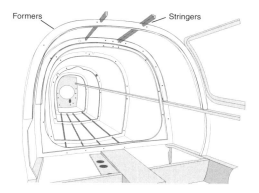

►AERO ENGINES

The four stroke cycle is also called the **Otto cycle**.

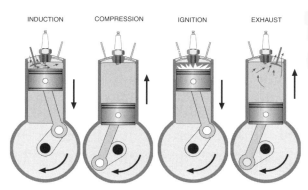

The camshaft, running at half the speed of the crankshaft, controls the opening and closing of the valves. Each **valve** opens once per complete cycle. The ratio of total cylinder volume to clearance volume is the **compression ratio**. The linear (in/out or up/down) motion of the piston is converted to rotary motion by the crankshaft.

►THE FUEL SYSTEM

100LL AVGAS is coloured blue. The use of MOGAS in UK aircraft is notified by a CAA Airworthiness Notice.

►THE INDUCTION SYSTEM

The mixture control is used to control the **ratio of fuel/air** entering the engine. As altitude increases, air becomes less dense and so mixture will become 'richer' unless the mixture is leaned. As a general rule, making the mixture richer reduces engine operating temperatures. At low power settings, the throttle valve within the carburettor is almost closed and the risk of power loss due to **carburettor icing** increases.

►THE IGNITION SYSTEM

Magnetos provide the high voltage spark to the spark plugs. Magnetos are driven by engine rotation and operate independently of the aircraft's electrical system. The **ignition switch** 'earths' the primary coil when turned off. If the switch is broken the earthing may fail and the magnetos remain 'live' even though the switch appears to be off.

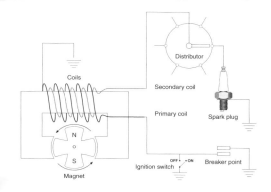

►THE COOLING SYSTEM

Most modern aero engines are **air cooled**. The **cowlings** around the engine and **baffles** within the engine compartment help to direct air flow around the cylinders, which are 'finned' to aid cooling. Increasing airspeed increases the cooling airflow over the engine.

►THE OIL SYSTEM

Most smaller aero engines have a '**wet sump**' (reservoir) under the engine, oil flows back here by gravity after flowing around the engine. A **pressure relief valve** allows oil to bypass the oil cooler if oil pressure is too high. Oil temperature is usually measured after the oil has passed through the cooler. High oil temperature and low oil pressure indicates a serious problem and a diversion to the nearest suitable airfield should be made.

►THE PROPELLER

The **propeller blade** is twisted along its length to maintain the same angle of attack along the blade when it is turning. If the propeller is 'fixed pitch', increasing airspeed will increase RPM at a set throttle position. Increasing RPM and increasing airspeed will increase power.

Torque reaction means that the aircraft will tend to rotate in the opposite direction to the rotation of the propeller.

►ENGINE HANDLING

Before starting, fuel can be pumped to the induction manifold using the **primer**. The starter warning light should extinguish once the engine has started. Oil pressure should indicate within 30 seconds of engine start.

High power and low airspeed in the climb may lead to high engine temperatures. Reducing power and increasing airspeed will help cool the engine.

In the cruise, the **mixture** can be 'leaned' to attain maximum power (max power range) or best fuel economy (best economy range).

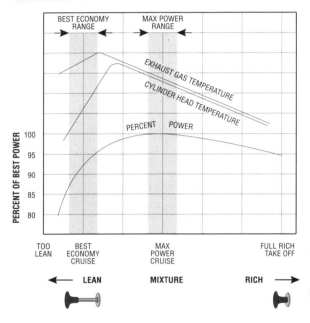

There is an increased risk of **carburettor icing** in a low power descent.

►AIRCRAFT SYSTEMS

The **alternator** normally provides electrical energy; if it fails the **battery** provides all electrical power, but for a limited period. If a fuse blows or circuit breaker pops, it can be re-set once only. A **'zero-centre' ammeter** indicates the charging rate of the battery. A **'left-centre' ammeter** indicates the current from the alternator.

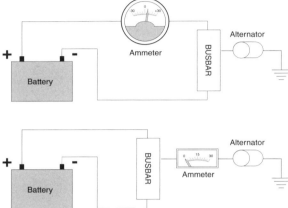

The **suction** (or **vacuum**) **system** is driven by the engine and usually provides suction for the Attitude Indicator and Heading Indicator.

The **pitot/static system** supplies static pressure to the altimeter and vertical speed indicator, and both static and pitot pressure to the airspeed indicator.

The **alternate static source** takes static pressure from within the cockpit, which will usually be at a lower pressure than that outside the aircraft.

▶ INSTRUMENTS

The **Altimeter** measures static pressure and converts this into an indication of vertical distance. The three-pointer altimeter display is very common, but easy to misinterpret with regard to altitudes above 10,000ft.

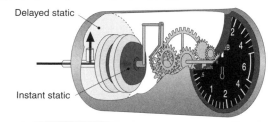

Delayed static

Instant static

The **Vertical Speed Indicator** (VSI) measures the rate of change of static pressure and converts this into a display normally in terms of feet per minute.

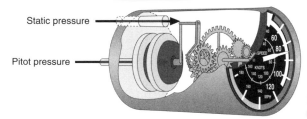

Static pressure

Pitot pressure

The **Airspeed Indicator** (ASI) measures both static and pitot pressure. It displays the pressure entering the pitot tube in terms of airspeed.

The **turn indicator** and **turn co-ordinator** use a rate gyro to measure rate of turn. They are normally electrically powered.

The **Attitude Indicator** (or artificial horizon or gyro horizon) uses an earth gyro to indicate attitude.

The **Heading Indicator** (or direction indicator or directional gyro) uses a directional gyro to indicate direction. It is set by reference to the compass, but aligns itself with a fixed point in space, not a point on the earth. As the earth rotates, the gyro will appear to wander off heading – apparent wander or apparent drift.

The **compass** is normally constructed of a number of magnets suspended in fluid. The compass assembly tends to 'dip' towards the nearest pole as it tries to align with the earth's magnetic field. This leads to turning and acceleration/deceleration errors.

▶ AIRWORTHINESS

The Pilot's Operating Handbook/Flight Manual (POH/FM) contains limitations, procedures and operational data for the operation of the individual aircraft. Any CAA supplement in a POH/FM over-rules the relevant POH/FM section. The POH/FM forms part of the aircraft's **Certificate of Airworthiness** (C of A).

The C of A is invalidated if the aircraft is repaired, modified or maintained in a way not approved by the CAA. This covers the unapproved addition (or removal) of almost anything permanently fitted to the aircraft.

Any **work carried out** on an aircraft must be recorded in the aircraft's logbooks, dated and signed for. A pilot who is also the owner of a private category C of A can also carry out certain maintenance operations. A pilot who is qualified to fly an aircraft type can also carry-out a **duplicate control system inspection'** on that type.

▶ AEROPLANE FLIGHT SAFETY

Different types of fire extinguishers are used on different types of fire:

Type of Extinguisher Type of Fire	Water	Carbon Foam	Dry Dioxide	Powder	BCF
Wood, paper cloth	X	X			X
Flammable liquid		X	X	X	X
Electrical			X	X	X
Gas				X	X
Wheel and Brake				X	X

When flying over water in a single-engine aircraft, **lifejackets** should be worn but not inflated. Lifejackets and liferafts use CO_2 (**Carbon Dioxide**) under pressure to inflate.

Carbon Monoxide (CO) is a by-product of combustion and is found in exhaust gases and fumes. CO itself is colourless, odourless and highly toxic.

AVGAS (100LL) fuel installations have predominantly red markings, AVTUR (Jet A-1) fuel installations have predominantly black markings.

▶ OPERATIONAL FLIGHT SAFETY

Windshear is caused by a sudden change in wind velocity, leading to sudden changes in airspeed. **Wake turbulence** is caused by the movement of the aircraft through the air, leaving rotating vortices in its wake. The larger and slower the aircraft, the stronger its wake turbulence. Helicopters create stronger wake turbulence than fixed wing aircraft of the same weight.

JAA Private Pilot Licence – Aeroplanes

Aircraft General and Principles of Flight

Time allowed: 90 minutes

No. of questions: 50

Total Marks: 100

Instructions:

The paper consists of 50 multiple choice questions, each carries 2 marks. The pass mark is 75% (i.e. 38 questions or more must be answered correctly). Marks are not deducted for incorrect answers.

Be sure to carefully read each question and ensure that you understand it before considering the answer choices. Only one of the answers is complete and correct; the others are either incomplete, incorrect or based on a misconception.

You should indicate the correct answer by placing a cross in the appropriate box of the answer sheet. If you decide to change an answer, you should erase the original choice and put a cross in the box representing your new selection.

Each question has an average answer time of 1 minute 48 seconds. No credit is given for unanswered questions.

Airframe

1. In the diagram below, the item arrowed is a:

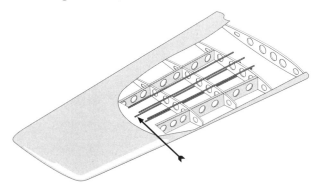

   (a) former

   (b) rib

   (c) longeron

   (d) stringer

2. Which of the following best describes items to be checked during a pilot's pre-flight inspection of an aircraft tyre?

   (a) Tyre inflation, creep, 'bulging', cuts and flat spots

   (b) Tyre inflation, colour, 'bulging', size

   (c) Tyre type, creep, tracking, cuts and flat spots

   (d) Tyre inflation, creep, type of tread pattern

3. Failure of the nosewheel torque link can lead to:

   (a) 'Spring leaf' undercarriage leg failure

   (b) Brake failure

   (c) Nosewheel shimmy

   (d) Tyre creep

4. A light aircraft with 'direct' nosewheel steering usually has:

   (a) Rods linking the rudder pedals and the nosewheel steering mechanism

   (b) No need for differential braking

   (c) A 'free-castoring' nosewheel

   (d) A nosewheel steered by the ailerons

Powerplant

5. Compression ratio is:

(a) The rate at which air ignites in a diesel engine

(b) The ratio of cylinder volume with the piston at Bottom Dead Centre, to the cylinder volume with the piston at Top Dead Centre

(c) The ratio of the volume of one cylinder to the volume of all that engine's cylinders

(d) The ratio of pressure inside the cylinder during the compression stroke to the pressure during the exhaust stroke

6. Within the engine's oil system, oil is routed via an oil cooler. The bypass valve that can allow oil to bypass the oil cooler in the event of a blockage is:

(a) Temperature-activated

(b) Pressure-activated

(c) Time-switch activated

(d) Pilot controlled

7. Within a four stroke engine the opening and closing of valves during the 'Otto' cycle is controlled by a camshaft turning at half the speed of the engine. During a complete 'Otto' cycle:

(a) The inlet valve opens once, the exhaust valve opens twice

(b) The inlet valve opens once, the exhaust valve opens once

(c) The inlet valve opens twice, the exhaust valve opens once

(d) The inlet and outlet valves both open twice

8. An engine system where a scavenge pump takes oil from the sump and returns it to a separate oil tank is a:

(a) Wet-sump oil system

(b) Wet oil tank system

(c) Dry-sump oil system

(d) Gravity feed oil tank system

9. During flight, the cylinder head temperatures of an air-cooled engine increase to their maximum limit. An appropriate response by the pilot would be to:

(a) Lean the mixture

(b) Reduce airspeed

(c) Close the cowl flaps (if fitted)

(d) Make the mixture richer

10. High oil temperature and low oil pressure should be taken as indicating:

(a) Faulty gauges, which can be ignored

(b) A serious emergency, necessitation an immediate forced landing and Mayday call

(c) A possible serious engine problem, necessitating a landing at the nearest airfield to have the problem investigated

(d) An electrical problem

11. If the magnetos become disconnected from the cockpit magneto switch:

(a) They can be stopped by turning off the Master Switch

(b) They will stop working

(c) They will remain live, even if the magneto switch is selected 'off'

(d) Their operation will not be affected

12. When air is flowing through the narrowest point of a venturi:

(a) Airflow speed will increase, static pressure will increase

(b) Airflow speed will increase, static pressure will decrease

(c) Airflow speed will decrease, static pressure will decrease

(d) Airflow speed will decrease, static pressure will increase

13. Within the engine compartment of an air-cooled engine, airflow is directed over the hottest parts of the engine by:

(a) Baffles and seals

(b) The oil system

(c) Electrically powered pumps

(d) The mixture control

14. Why is a propeller blade twisted along its length?

(a) To reduce centrifugal stress

(b) To reduce propeller torque

(c) To maintain a constant angle of attack along the blade

(d) To permit different RPM settings

15. On an aviation refuelling installation, what colour labels would you expect to indicate AVGAS 100LL and AVTUR Jet A-1 respectively?

(a) Blue; Black

(b) Red; Blue

(c) Black, Blue

(d) Red; Black

16. Oil temperature as displayed on the cockpit oil temperature gauge is measured:

(a) In the oil sump

(b) After passing through the oil cooler

(c) Over the course of several flights and averaged

(d) Referenced to the Outside Air Temperature (OAT)

17. The ideal fuel/air mixture for efficient aero engine operation is:

(a) 12 parts air to 15 parts fuel (12:15)

(b) 15 parts fuel to 1 part air (15:1)

(c) 1 part fuel to 12 parts air (1:12)

(d) 1 part fuel to 1 part air (1:1)

18. The mixture control can be used:

(a) Only above 5,000ft agl

(b) To stop the engine when Idle Cut Off (ICO) is selected

(c) To increase the amount of air entering the engine

(d) Only if carburettor icing is suspected

SYSTEMS

19. A fully charged 30 amp hour battery of an average light aircraft is (in theory) capable of supplying:

(a) 15 amps for 2 hours

(b) 30 amps for 30 hours

(c) 30 amps for 30 minutes

(d) 1 amp for 30 flights

20. If a fuse blows during flight:

(a) It should not be replaced until the aircraft has landed

(b) It should be replaced with one of a higher rating to ensure it will not blow again

(c) It can be replaced in the air with one of the same rating, but only once

(d) It can be held in

21. A suction (vacuum) pump operates the suction (vacuum)-driven instruments by:

(a) Drawing air through the instruments to the gyro rotors

(b) Blowing air through the instruments to the gyro rotors

(c) Sucking against diaphragms in the associated instruments

(d) Providing electrical power to the gyro via an air-driven generator

22. If the alternator fails during flight:

(a) Electrical loads should be reduced to the bare minimum and a landing made as soon as practical

(b) The master switch should be turned off, and the flight continued as planned

(c) The battery will supply all the electrical loads for as long as required, so the flight can continue as planned

(d) All electrical services should be switched on to stop the battery going 'flat'

INSTRUMENTS

23. The pitot tube of a moving aircraft senses:

(a) Static pressure

(b) Dynamic pressure

(c) Static and Dynamic pressure

(d) Either, depending on pilot selection

24. During a descent the static source becomes blocked. Which of the following statements correctly describes the likely effect on (i) the airspeed indicator; (ii) the altimeter and (iii) the vertical speed indicator if the descent continues at a constant rate:

(i)	(ii)	(iii)
(a) under-read	over-read	read correctly
(b) over-read	under-read	over-read
(c) under-read	under-read	show zero
(d) over-read	over-read	show zero

25. The effect of magnetic deviation on the compass can be allowed for if the pilot refers to:

(a) Isogonals on an aeronautical chart

(b) The compass deviation card

(c) The POH/FM

(d) The certificate of airworthiness

26. Static pressure drawn from an alternate static source in the cockpit of an average light aircraft will be:

(a) Exactly the same as the outside 'ambient' pressure

(b) Less than the outside 'ambient' pressure

(c) The same as pitot pressure

(d) The pressure indicated on the altimeter sub-scale

27. The normal operating range airspeed is denoted by:

(a) A red line on the airspeed indicator

(b) A yellow arc on the airspeed indicator

(c) A blue line on the airspeed indicator

(d) A green arc on the airspeed indicator

28. The Heading Indicator should be checked during cruising flight:

(a) Only following an event such as a lightning strike or electrical failure

(b) At any time against a GPS reading

(c) Against a compass at any time the wings are level

(d) Regularly against the compass during straight and level, balanced and steady airspeed flight

29. Which of the following aircraft instruments does NOT incorporate a gyroscope?

(a) Heading Indicator (also known a Direction Indicator or Directional Gyro Indicator)

(b) The Compass

(c) Attitude Indicator (also known as an artificial horizon)

(d) The Turn Co-ordinator

AIRWORTHINESS

30. A duplicate inspection on a control system may be carried out by:

(a) The aircraft's owner and another PPL holder

(b) The aircraft's owner and a licensed engineer

(c) Two licensed engineers

(d) Any two pilots

31. Which of the following statements regarding a certificate of airworthiness is correct?

(a) It is invalidated if a new aircraft owner is not notified to the authority within 28 days of change of ownership

(b) It is valid for the same period as the certificate of registration

(c) It is invalidated unless the aircraft also has a valid certificate of insurance

(d) Its period of validity is stated on the certificate

GENERAL FLIGHT SAFETY

32. Carbon Monoxide:

(a) Can be identified by its black colour

(b) May be identified by its strong smell

(c) Is not easy to identify because it is colourless and odourless

(d) Cannot enter the cockpit

33. Unless the POH/FM specifies otherwise, the correct action in the event of an engine fire in the air would be to:

(a) Open the cockpit heater controls fully and operate the fire extinguisher into the vents

(b) Shut down the engine immediately and close the cockpit heater controls

(c) Keep running the engine at full throttle to draw the fire into the cylinders

(d) Climb at full throttle to gain more height

34. A dry powder fire extinguisher can be used on which types of fire?

(a) Brake and wheel fires

(b) Wood, paper or cloth fires only

(c) Flammable liquids only

(d) Electrical fires only

PRINCIPLES OF FLIGHT

35. The force that acts perpendicular to the wings in a balanced turn is:

(a) The centrifugal force

(b) The total lift force

(c) The centripetal force

(d) The mass

36. Increasing the load carried by an aircraft:

(a) Increases stall speed at the same rate as the increase in load factor

(b) Decreases stall speed by the square root of the load factor

(c) Increases stall speed by the square root of the load factor

(d) Does not affect load factor

37. Controls are mass balanced in order to:

(a) Aerodynamically assist the pilot in moving the controls

(b) Prevent control flutter

(c) Provide equal control forces on all the controls

(d) Remove the requirement for a trimmer

38. Aerodynamic balances designed to assist a pilot in deflecting a flight control surface may be:

(a) A balance tab that moves in the opposite direction to the main control surface

(b) A trim tab on the flying control surface that moves in the same direction as the control surface

(c) A mass placed forward of the hinge line

(d) A spring in the control linkages

39. The angle of attack is:

(a) The angle between the chord and the longitudinal axis

(b) The angle between the wing and lateral axis

(c) The angle between the chord line and the relative airflow

(d) The angle between the lateral axis and the longitudinal axis

40. In decreasing order of percentage, the major components of the atmosphere are:

(a) Nitrogen, Oxygen, Water Vapour

(b) Oxygen, Carbon Dioxide, Nitrogen

(c) Oxygen, Water Vapour, Carbon Dioxide

(d) Nitrogen, Carbon Dioxide, Oxygen

41. If the temperature of a parcel of air is increased, but pressure remains constant, the density will:

(a) Remain constant

(b) Increase

(c) Decrease

(d) Only be affected by a change in pressure

42. If the outside air temperature at 10,000ft is -15°C, the deviation from International Standard Atmosphere is:

(a) ISA +10°C

(b) ISA -30°C

(c) ISA -15°C

(d) ISA -10°C

43. A slot or slat in the leading edge of a wing will:

  (a) Re-energise the airflow over the wing's upper surface, delaying airflow separation

  (b) Move the centre of gravity rearwards, thus reducing stall airspeed

  (c) Reduce drag at the cruise airspeed

  (d) Reduce lift at high angles of attack

44. A fixed 'bendable' trim tab, such as might be used on a rudder or aileron, is:

  (a) Set by the authority when the initial C of A is issued, and is not to be adjusted

  (b) Designed to be ground adjustable

  (c) Set by the manufacturer, and not to be adjusted by any other person or organisation

  (d) For training purposes only

45. Washout on an aeroplane wing means that there is a:

  (a) Reduction of angle of incidence from the wing root towards the wing tip

  (b) Reduction of angle of incidence from the wing tip towards the wing root

  (c) Tendency for the wing tips to stall first to increase stability in the stall and during slow flight

  (d) Increase in downwash at the outer wing

46. Yawing is a rotation about the:

  (a) Normal axis

  (b) Lateral axis

  (c) Longitudinal axis

  (d) Perpendicular axis

47. Adverse yaw can be minimised by:

  (a) A butterfly tail

  (b) Differential ailerons

  (c) An aileron trim tab

  (d) Mass balance

48. When an aircraft is in equilibrium in straight and level, un-accelerated flight:

  (a) Lift, weight, thrust and drag are all equal

  (b) Weight equals drag

  (c) Drag is greater than lift

  (d) Lift is greater than thrust

49. The fin on an aeroplane:

  (a) Helps to turn the aeroplane

  (b) Balances the weight of the engine

  (c) Increases directional stability

  (d) Reduces directional stability

50. The primary purpose of an anti-balance (anti-servo) tab is to:

(a) Aid movement of the flying control by reducing loads

(b) Increase flying control forces

(c) Prevent flutter

(d) Reduce adverse yaw

Airframe

1. An aircraft design where a stressed metal skin gives the structure its strength, and the skin is supported on a framework of formers and stringers is called a:

   (a) A fabric construction

   (b) A semi-monocoque structure

   (c) A cantilever structure

   (d) A solid-state construction

2. An aircraft certified in the aerobatic category can be expected to have:

   (a) A slower stalling speed than an aircraft certified in the normal category

   (b) A higher limiting load factor limit than an aircraft certified in the utility category

   (c) A higher VNE than an aircraft certified in the normal category

   (d) A slower VFR than an aircraft certified in the utility category

3. In the diagram below, the items labelled (i) and (ii) are:

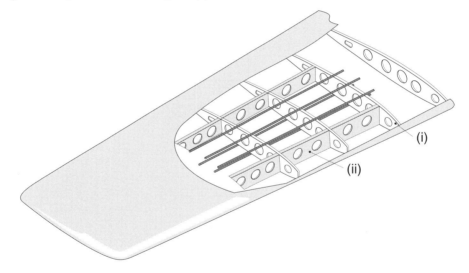

	(i)	(ii)
(a)	stringer	former
(b)	spar	rib
(c)	rib	spar
(d)	stringer	spar

4. A control lock is used:

   (a) To lock the trimmers in a fixed position

   (b) To lock the controls in steady straight and level flight

   (c) To lock the controls when the aircraft is parked

   (d) To lock the controls in the event of turbulence

Powerplant

5. During flight you notice that oil temperature is increasing and oil pressure is reducing towards the bottom of the 'green' arc. An appropriate response is to

(a) Report faulty gauges after the flight

(b) Make an immediate forced landing

(c) Divert to the nearest suitable airfield

(d) Turn the Mater Switch off, then on again

6. In relation to the cockpit magneto switch:

(a) The magnetos will not work if they become disconnected from the magneto switch

(b) The magnetos cannot work if the Master Switch is turned off

(c) The magnetos may remain 'live' if they become disconnected from the magneto switch

(d) The magnetos are not normally connected to the magneto switch

7. Operating an engine at low RPM for long periods whilst taxying is most likely to lead to:

(a) Excessive taxying speed

(b) Spark plug fouling

(c) Engine overheating

(d) Over-charging of the alternator

8. At the narrowest point of a carburettor venturi, it can be expected that:

(a) Static pressure will increase, airflow speed will increase,

(b) Static pressure will increase, airflow speed will decrease

(c) Static pressure will decrease, airflow speed will decrease

(d) Static pressure will decrease, airflow speed will increase

9. A common design feature of an air-cooled engine is:

(a) An electrically-driven cooling fan

(b) A coolant radiator

(c) 'Fins' on the engine cylinders

(d) A water jacket around the engine

10. Oil temperature as displayed in the cockpit is often measured:

(a) Just before entering the 'hot sections' of the engine

(b) Inside the oil sump

(c) Inside the oil pump

(d) Only when the engine is not running

11. Sometimes, if the throttle of an engine with a carburettor is advanced too quickly, the engine can 'hesitate' and falter due to a weak cut. A common design feature to prevent this happening is:

    (a) An electrically-driven fuel pump

    (b) An accelerator pump in the carburettor

    (c) A spring retarding throttle movement

    (d) The throttle friction control

12. The oil pressure relief valve is operated by:

    (a) Oil pressure

    (b) An electrical oil temperature sensor

    (c) A pilot-selected control

    (d) Throttle position

13. During a complete 'four stroke' cycle:

    (a) The intake valve is fixed open, the exhaust valves opens twice

    (b) The intake valve opens twice, exhaust valves open once

    (c) Both the intake and exhaust valves open once

    (d) The intake and exhaust valves open twice

14. The high tension voltage of a magneto is produced by:

    (a) Boosting the supply from the aircraft's electrical system

    (b) The aircraft battery

    (c) An airflow-powered generator

    (d) Inducing a current between the primary and secondary windings of a coil

15. The ratio of total cylinder volume to clearance volume is the:

    (a) Volumetric ratio

    (b) Compression ratio

    (c) Cylindric efficiency ratio

    (d) Otto ratio

16. If the cylinder head temperatures (CHT) of an air-cooled engine increase to their maximum limit, the CHT may be reduced by:

    (a) Making the mixture richer and increasing airspeed

    (b) Reducing airspeed, closing cowl flaps

    (c) On the ground, facing downwind

    (d) Increasing power

17. Carburettor icing is most likely in conditions of:

    (a) Temperature 0°C, relative humidity 10%, climb power

    (b) Temperature -5°C, relative humidity 30%, cruise power

    (c) Temperature +12°C, relative humidity 65%, descent power

    (d) Temperature +20°C, relative humidity 45%, climb power

18. In order to operate a UK-registered aircraft on MOGAS, where will authoritative information concerning such operation be found?

(a) In the AIP

(b) In an AIC

(c) In an aviation magazine

(d) In a CAA Airworthiness Notice

Systems

19. Theoretically, a 25 ampere hours battery can supply which of the following?

(a) 25 amps for 25 hours

(b) 5 amps for 5 hours

(c) Any given current for at least 25 hours

(d) 25 amps for over one hour

20. In the event of a suction-pump failure in vacuum system, the vacuum driven instruments (i) and the suction gauge (ii) can be expected to;

	(i)	(ii)
(a)	Revert to electrical back-up	Indicate atmospheric pressure
(b)	Start to give erroneous indications	Indicate zero
(c)	Give obviously false readings	Go to maximum pressure
(d)	Operate at reduced speed	Be unaltered

21. An aircraft is fitted with a 'centre-zero' reading ammeter (illustrated). The ammeter is presently indicating:

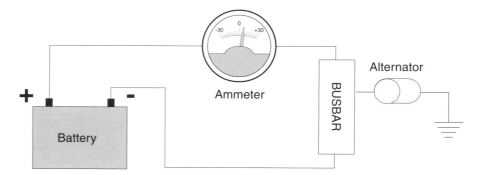

(a) A discharge, the battery is supplying all electrical power

(b) A discharge, the alternator is supplying all electrical power

(c) A positive charge, the battery is being charged by the alternator at about 5 ampere/hours

(d) A positive charge, the alternator is being charged by the battery at about 5 ampere/hours

22. An aircraft has two batteries, each of 12 volts and 30 ampere-hour capacity. To connect these batteries to provide a capacity of 60 ampere hours and 12 volts, the batteries should be connected:

(a) In series

(b) In parallel

(c) In conjunction

(d) In opposition

INSTRUMENTS

23. Which of the following statements is true regarding the Heading Indicator (HI)?

(a) Any HI will automatically synchronise with the cockpit compass

(b) Provided the suction reading is within limits, the HI will not require re-setting

(c) The 'caging' knob can be used to set the HI with reference to the compass

(d) The HI should be set to true north after adjusting the compass reading for variation

24. Which of the following statements best describes the operation of the vertical speed indicator?

(a) Two capsules within the VSI measure instantaneous dynamic pressure, and dynamic pressure from 5 seconds previously. Any difference is displayed on the instrument

(b) There are two capsules within the VSI – one measures dynamic pressure, the other static pressure. The difference between the two is displayed on the instrument

(c) An earth gyro measures vertical accelerations and displays this information as a rate of climb or rate of descent

(d) A capsule measures static pressure, this capsule is surrounded by 'delayed' static pressure. Any expansion or contraction of the capsule is displayed as a rate of climb of descent, usually in terms of feet per minute

25. Which of the following combinations contains only instruments that utilise a gyroscope?

(a) Turn co-ordinator, attitude indicator, airspeed indicator

(b) Heading indicator, turn indicator, attitude indicator

(c) Attitude indicator, heading indicator, oil pressure gauge

(d) Turn coordinator, RPM gauge, altimeter

26. An earth gyro is utilised in which particular flight instrument?

(a) Attitude Indicator (also known as an artificial horizon)

(b) Heading Indicator (also known a Direction Indicator or Directional Gyro Indicator)

(c) Turn Indicator

(d) Airspeed Indicator

27. The 'caution' airspeed range, indicating a speed range that should only be permitted in smooth flying conditions, is marked on the airspeed indicator by:

(a) The yellow arc

(b) The red line

(c) The green arc

(d) The whiter arc

28. Which combination of statements correctly describes the common compass errors?

    (i)   Acceleration and deceleration error

    (ii) Turning error

    (iii) Apparent wander

    (iv) Density error

    (v) Variation and deviation

    (a) (i), (iii) and (v)

    (b) (ii), (iii) and (v)

    (c) (i), (ii) and (v)

    (d) (i), (iv) and (v)

29. During a climb the pitot source becomes blocked. Which of the following statements correctly describes the likely effect on (i) the airspeed indicator; (ii) the altimeter and (iii) the vertical speed indicator if the climb continues at a constant rate:

	(i)	(ii)	(iii)
(a)	under-read	over-read	read correctly
(b)	over-read	read correctly	read correctly
(c)	over-read	read correctly	show zero
(d)	read correctly	under-read	show zero

AIRWORTHINESS

30. An aircraft's certificate of airworthiness:

    (a) Has an indefinite life

    (b) Has no defined life

    (c) Is valid provided the aircraft is listed on a state's registry

    (d) Is renewed subject to a specified maintenance schedule and is valid for the period stated on the certificate

31. If an aircraft with a Maximum Total Weight Authorised (MTWA) of less than 2730kg and a private category Certificate of Airworthiness (C of A) has not been maintained in accordance with the approved maintenance schedule quoted on the C of A:

    (a) The C of A is valid provided the unapproved work is signed-off by a licensed engineer at the next inspection

    (b) The C of A is now invalid

    (c) The C of A is valid provided the approved maintenance schedule is observed at the next inspection

    (d) The C of A is valid until the CAA issue a letter revoking it

GENERAL FLIGHT SAFETY

32. If a BCF extinguisher is used within the cockpit:

    (a) It must not be used on an electrical fire

    (b) The cockpit should be ventilated once the fire is out

    (c) A BCF extinguisher must never be used in the cockpit

    (d) It should only be used on wood, paper or cloth fires

33. On which types of fire may a water-based extinguisher be used?

(a) Brake and wheel fires

(b) Wood, paper or cloth fires only

(c) Flammable liquids only

(d) Electrical fires only

34. Carbon Monoxide, a colourless and odourless toxic gas, is most likely to enter the average light aircraft cockpit due to:

(a) A heating/exhaust system defect

(b) A lifejacket or liferaft inflation system leak

(c) An oxygen system failure

(d) Flight at high altitude

PRINCIPLES OF FLIGHT

35. To prevent 'flutter', the control surfaces can be fitted with:

(a) Inset hinges

(b) A mass balance

(c) Spring tabs

(d) Simple trim tabs

36. For an aircraft to maintain level flight, if the wing centre of pressure is AFT of the centre of gravity and there is no thrust/drag couple, the tailplane load must be:

(a) Upward

(b) Rearwards

(c) Zero

(d) Downward

37. In general, as airspeed is increased:

(a) All types of drag increase

(b) Parasite drag decreases, induced drag increases

(c) Parasite drag increases, induced drag decreases

(d) All types of drag decrease

38. If the angle of attack of an aerofoil is increased, the coefficient of lift will:

(a) Increase until the stalling angle of attack is reached

(b) Decrease until the stalling angle of attack is reached

(c) Remain constant

(d) Form a 'U' shape

39. In the dry atmosphere there is:

(a) Approximately twice as much oxygen as other gases

(b) Approximately three times as much nitrogen as oxygen

(c) Approximately equal proportions of nitrogen and oxygen

(d) Approximately three times as much oxygen as nitrogen

40. If the air temperature at 5,000ft amsl is +10°C, this deviation from ISA can be described as:

(a) ISA +5°C

(b) ISA -5°C

(c) ISA compliant

(d) ISA +10°C

41. If all other factors are equal, the shortest take-off run will be achieved by:

(a) Using full flap

(b) Using the recommended take-off flap setting

(c) Delaying rotation to 1·3 x stall speed

(d) Rotating as soon as the elevators are capable of pitching the aircraft nose-up

42. If all other factors are equal, an aircraft will require the greatest elevator forces during landing when:

(a) The centre of gravity is at the forward limit

(b) The centre of gravity is at the rearward limit

(c) The aircraft is loaded to its maximum landing weight

(d) The aircraft is loaded to its maximum zero fuel weight

43. The stalling angle of attack can be reduced by:

(a) Reducing angle of bank

(b) Reducing aircraft weight (mass)

(c) Extending leading edge slats

(d) Lowering trailing edge flaps

44. Disregarding the effect of humidity, if the temperature of a set parcel of air is decreased:

(a) Pressure will decrease

(b) Density will decrease

(c) Density will increase

(d) Pressure will remain constant

45. Regarding airflow in the immediate vicinity of an aircraft's wing in normal cruising flight, which of the following statements is correct?

(a) Airflow over the wing will be slower than airflow under the wing

(b) Airflow below the wing will be faster than the 'free' airflow

(c) Airflow below the wing will be at the same speed as the 'free' airflow

(d) Airflow above the wing will be faster than the 'free' airflow

46. During a level, balanced turn, total lift acts:

(a) Vertically upwards, in direct opposition to weight

(b) At 90° to the aircraft's vertical axis

(c) In the same direction as the aircraft's vertical axis

(d) At an angle to the vertical which is the square root of the load factor

47. Yaw is the secondary effect of:

(a) Application of aileron

(b) Application of rudder

(c) Application of elevator

(d) Application of slots

48. If an aircraft is disturbed from its trimmed attitude and then remains at the new attitude without input from the pilot, it can be said to have:

(a) Neutral stability

(b) Positive instability

(c) Negative instability

(d) Positive stability

49. When an elevator is moved up, the attached simple trim tab will move:

(a) In the same direction as the elevator

(b) In the opposite direction to the elevator

(c) Remain at a constant angle relative to the elevator

(d) Remain at the same angle relative to the aircraft's longitudinal axis

50. An aircraft wing will stall at a fixed:

(a) Angle of attack

(b) Indicated airspeed

(c) Calibrated airspeed

(d) Load factor

Airfame

1. The part of a wing's construction, designed to carry upwards bending loads caused by lift during flight, is labelled below as:

   (a) B, the ribs

   (b) A, the ribs

   (c) B, the spar

   (d) A, the ribs

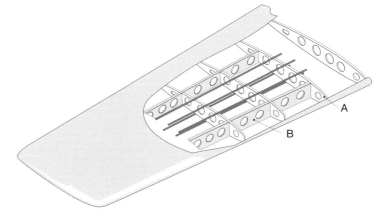

2. Painted squares on the tyre wall and adjacent wheel hub are:

   (a) Tyre wear marks, the tyre is serviceable as long as they are visible

   (b) Tyre creep marks, and should be aligned

   (c) Tyre pressure indicators, which should not line-up

   (d) Oleo alignment marks, they should be at the top of the tyre

3. A structure where all stresses are carried by the external skin is a:

   (a) Monocoque structure

   (b) A semi-monocoque structure

   (c) A semi-cantilever structure

   (d) A monoplane structure

4. In the diagram below of a typical fuselage construction, the item labelled 'A' is a:

   (a) Rib

   (b) Spar

   (c) Stringer

   (d) Former

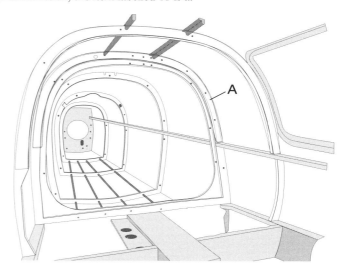

Powerplant

5. An aircraft has a right-hand propeller (a propeller that rotates clockwise when viewed from behind). With an increase in power, how will propeller torque affect the aircraft?

(a) It will roll the aircraft to the left

(b) It will roll the aircraft to the right

(c) It will reduce slipstream effect

(d) None of the above are true

6. An aircraft with an air-cooled engine regulates engine temperature in part by:

(a) Utilising a water-proof jacket around the engine

(b) Utilising a radiator on the exhaust system

(c) A cowling which directs air flow around the cylinders

(d) Flying into wind

7. An engine oil system in which oil is stored in a sump under the engine is:

(a) A wet sump system

(b) A dry sump system

(c) A semi-cantilever system

(d) A liquid cooling system

8. A piston-engine aircraft is climbing without the pilot adjusting the fuel/air mixture control. As air density decreases, the fuel/air mixture entering the engine will:

(a) Be unchanged

(b) Become leaner

(c) Become richer

(d) Depend on the altimeter setting

9. To prevent an excessively lean mixture when the throttle is opened, a carburettor may be fitted with …(i)… which …(ii)…

	(i)	(ii)
(a)	An accelerator pump	Is a plunger assembly operated by the throttle
(b)	An accelerator pump	Is a fuel jet operated by the mixture control
(c)	A slow running jet	Independent of the throttle
(d)	A pressure diaphragm	Is a plunger assembly operated by airspeed

10. What is the normal position of the switch connected to the primary magneto circuit when the magnetos are turned off?

(a) The switch is closed and the primary magneto circuit is grounded

(b) The switch is open and the primary magneto circuit is grounded

(c) The switch is closed and the primary magneto circuit is un-earthed

(d) The switch is open and the primary magneto circuit is un-earthed

11. The electrical power within a magneto is supplied by:

(a) The aircraft's electrical system

(b) The aircraft battery only

(c) Solar power

(d) A self-contained system driven by engine crankshaft rotation

12. If an aircraft with a fixed-pitch propeller is accelerated to a faster airspeed:

(a) RPM will increase even if the throttle setting is not changed

(b) RPM will be totally dependent on throttle setting

(c) The throttle setting will automatically reduce to maintain a constant RPM

(d) RPM will decrease

13. Any water in the fuel system is most likely to cause:

(a) Fuel contamination, leading to power loss

(b) An over-rich mixture

(c) An increase in Cylinder Head Temperature (CHT)

(d) A dangerous and un-commanded increase in engine power

14. After engine start the starter warning light remains lit, this means:

(a) There is a risk of imminent and serious electrical system damage

(b) The light is faulty and should be reported after the flight

(c) The starter system is faulty; it should be checked before the next start

(d) The engine starter battery is being charged

15. After engine start the oil pressure should register within the green arc within a certain time, or the engine must be shut down immediately. The time allowed is normally:

(a) 10 seconds

(b) 30 seconds

(c) 2 minutes

(d) 1 minute

16. To achieve best power setting at altitude, the mixture control of an engine fitted with a fixed-pitch propeller can be 'leaned' to achieve:

(a) A drop of 50 RPM from the 'full rich' RPM

(b) The peak RPM

(c) The lowest RPM without the engine stopping

(d) The lowest RPM before the engine starts to run 'rough'

17. Before engine starting, fuel can be delivered directly to the induction manifold by:

(a) The starter switch

(b) The primer

(c) The fuel selector

(d) The throttle

18. Given constant ambient atmospheric conditions, in which scenario is carburettor icing most likely?

  (a) High airspeed and high power setting

  (b) Cruise airspeed and cruise power setting

  (c) High airspeed, descent power setting

  (d) Low airspeed, climb power setting

19. An explosive and uncontrolled combustion within a cylinder is called:

  (a) Pre-ignition, caused by the early burning of the fuel/air mixture

  (b) Detonation, which can be caused by a fuel/air mixture too lean for the power setting selected

  (c) Plug fouling, caused by the build-up of lead or oil deposits on the spark plugs

  (d) Compression ignition, as used in diesel engines

20. To keep the engine running when the throttle is fully closed, the carburettor may be fitted with:

  (a) An idling jet

  (b) An accelerator pump

  (c) An electric fuel pump

  (d) A timing spark

21. When the cockpit magneto (ignition) switch is turned off:

  (a) It can be guaranteed that the engine will not run

  (b) The battery supply to the magnetos is cut-off

  (c) The primary coil should be earthed if the switch is operating correctly

  (d) The magnetos are disconnected from the secondary coil

22. An aircraft carburettor may incorporate a float chamber: Within this float chamber:

  (a) Fuel is held in a small reservoir, with air above at a greater pressure than the air within the carburettor venturi

  (b) Fuel is held in a small reservoir, with air above at a lower pressure than the air within the carburettor venturi

  (c) Air is held waiting to be introduced to the carburettor venturi

  (d) Oil is held in a small reservoir with air above at a lower pressure than the air within the carburettor venturi

23. When air is flowing through a constriction (such as the narrowest point of a venturi), static pressure will fall and:

  (a) Airflow speed will increase

  (b) Airflow speed will decrease

  (c) Airflow speed will remain the same

  (d) Airflow speed will be dictated by temperature

24. The propeller blade angle:

  (a) Is normally fixed from hub to tip

  (b) Is the ratio of blade length to blade cord

  (c) Becomes smaller from hub to tip to maintain an efficient angle of attack

  (d) Becomes larger from hub to tip to maintain an efficient angle of attack

Systems

25. An aircraft is fitted with a 'left-zero' reading ammeter (illustrated). The ammeter is currently indicating that:

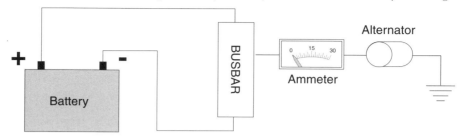

(a) The alternator is supplying zero output

(b) The battery is fully charged

(c) The battery is below normal operating temperature

(d) Current is flowing from the alternator to the battery

26. If two 12 volt, 20 ampere hour batteries are connected in series, they will act as:

(a) A 24 volt, 20 ampere hour battery

(b) A 12 volt, 40 ampere hour battery

(c) A 24 volt, 40 ampere hour battery

(d) A 12 volt, 20 ampere hour battery

INSTRUMENTS

27. Which combination of statements best describes the construction and features of a standard aircraft compass and the characteristic of magnetic direction?
(i)   It utilises a set of magnets, suspended in a liquid, to reduce friction and damp movements
(ii) It can be adjusted to minimise deviation
(iii) It can be adjusted to minimise variation
(iv) A magnetic direction adjusted for variation gives a true direction
(v)   A magnetic direction adjusted for deviation gives a compass direction

(a) (i), (ii), (iv) & (v)

(b) (i), (ii), (iii) & (v)

(c) (ii), (iii) & (iv)

(d) (i), (iii), (iv) & (v)

28. During a descent, the static vent becomes blocked, subsequently the Vertical Speed Indicator (VSI) will indicate:

(a) The correct rate of descent

(b) Zero

(c) A climb

(d) An increased rate of descent

29. The following statements best describe the construction and features of which standard aircraft instrument?
It incorporates a sealed aneroid capsule, surrounded by static air from a static source.
A linkage connects the sealed aneroid capsule to a pointer which rotates around a scale.

(a) A Vertical Speed Indicator (VSI)

(b) An altimeter

(c) An AirSpeed Indicator (ASI)

(d) A suction guage

30. The following statements best describe the construction and features of which standard aircraft instrument?

It incorporates a capsule into which static air is fed, surrounded by delayed static air from a static source.

(a) A Vertical Speed Indicator (VSI)

(b) An Altimeter

(c) An AirSpeed Indicator (ASI)

(d) A cabin altitude indicator

31. In relation to a Heading Indicator (or Directional Gyro Indicator – DGI), apparent wander (or apparent drift) is:

(a) The apparent change in heading caused by worn bearings, wear and tear, incorrect gyro spin speed etc.

(b) The apparent difference between the aircraft's heading and track

(c) The errors in indicated heading caused by acceleration and deceleration

(d) The rigidity of the gyroscope, maintaining a constant axis in relation to a point in space

Airworthiness

32. A pilot who is both owner and qualified pilot on type of an aircraft may:

(a) Carry out certain minor repairs to the aircraft without recording details in the aircraft's logbooks

(b) Carry out any repairs to the aircraft provided details are recorded in the aircraft's logbooks

(c) Carry out a duplicate inspection on a control system away from base

(d) Carry out a duplicate control inspection at any time

33. A pilot may carry-out certain minor aircraft maintenance provided that:

(a) The work is recorded in the aircraft's logbooks and certified by a CAA surveyor

(b) The work is recorded in the aircraft's logbooks and certified by an aircraft engineer

(c) The work is recorded in the aircraft's logbooks and certified by the pilot

(d) The work is not recorded in the aircraft's logooks

General Flight Safety

34. Which of the following types of fire extinguisher can be safely used for extinguishing the greatest number of different types of fire?

(a) Water

(b) Carbon Dioxide

(c) Foam

(d) BCF

35. In the light aircraft context, a colourless, odourless gas formed in the combustion process, which is a highly toxic and deadly poison, is most likely to be:

(a) Carbon Monoxide

(b) Carbon Dioxide

(c) Nitrogen

(d) Haemoglobin

36. For an over-water flight in a single-engine aircraft, it is recommended that lifejackets are:

(a) Carried in an accessible baggage area

(b) Stored in a locked, water-tight compartment

(c) Worn but not inflated

(d) Worn and inflated

Principles of Flight

37. After being disturbed from a trimmed attitude an aircraft returns to its original attitude without pilot input. This aircraft can be said to be:

(a) Positively unstable

(b) Possessing neutral stability

(c) Possessing positive stability

(d) Displaying divergent instability

38. At the stalling angle of attack:

(a) The maximum coefficient of lift is obtained

(b) The minimum coefficient of lift is obtained

(c) The maximum lift/drag ratio is obtained

(d) The minimum coefficient of drag is obtained

39. If an aircraft is disturbed from its trimmed attitude, and without input from the pilot it returns back towards its original attitude, it can be said to be displaying:

(a) Dynamic stability

(b) Static stability

(c) Divergent stability

(d) Instability

40. Which of the following best describes 'typical' atmospheric conditions in the troposphere?

(a) There is a steady increase in temperature with increasing altitude

(b) Temperature maintains a constant -56.5°C regardless of altitude

(c) There is a steady decrease in temperature with increasing altitude

(d) Altitude has no effect on temperature

41. If air pressure is decreased, but temperature is maintained constant, what will the effect be on density?

(a) Density will increase

(b) Density will decrease

(c) There will be no change of density

(d) Density is not dependant on pressure or temperature

42. When the rudder pedals are operated in-flight, the initial effect is:

(a) Roll around the vertical (normal) axis

(b) Pitch around the lateral axis

(c) Yaw around the lateral axis

(d) Yaw around the vertical (normal) axis

43. In general terms, induced drag:

(a) Increases with increasing airspeed

(b) Increases with decreasing airspeed

(c) Decreases with decreasing airspeed

(d) Is not affected by airspeed

44. In flight, total lift force:

(a) Acts approximately vertically in relation to the earth

(b) Acts approximately vertically in relation to the wings

(c) Always acts directly opposite to weight

(d) Acts along the aircraft's lateral axis

45. The secondary effect of yaw is:

(a) Roll in the opposite direction to yaw

(b) Roll in the same direction as yaw

(c) Pitch up

(d) Pitch down

46. To prevent ......(i)...... – a high speed vibration which can destroy an aircraft, flying controls may be fitted with a ....(ii)........ . The missing words are:

	(i)	(ii)
(a)	flutter	anti-balance tab
(b)	detonation	yaw damper
(c)	dutch roll	balance tab
(d)	flutter	mass balance

47. The use of the recommended flap setting for take-off should have the effect of:

(a) Improving rate of climb

(b) Reducing take-off distance

(c) Giving better take-off acceleration

(d) Causing a higher lift-off speed

48. Compared with a zero flap setting, the use of trailing edge flap leads to a:

(a) Reduced stalling angle of attack

(b) Increased stalling angle of attack

(c) Higher stall airspeed

(d) Has no effect on stalling angle of attack

49. In level flight an aircraft stalls at 60 knots. In a 60° angle of bank turn what would you expect the stalling speed to be?

(a) 60 knots

(b) 42 knots

(c) 62 knots

(d) 85 knots

50. The aircraft design feature known as 'differential ailerons' means that:

(a) One of the ailerons is larger than the other

(b) The downgoing aileron moves through a greater angle than the upgoing aileron

(c) The upgoing aileron moves through a greater angle than the downgoing aileron

(d) Only the aileron on the 'outside' of a turn is activated

Paper 1 Answers and Explanations

EAGP1Q1   Answer D

The principle features of a 'traditionally' constructed aircraft wing are depicted below. The stringers run across the ribs, parallel to the spar(s).

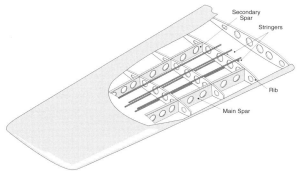

Further Reference: PPL4 » Aircraft General Knowledge » The Airframe » Wing Construction

EAGP1Q2   Answer A

The following represents the items most commonly checked during a pilot's 'pre-flight' inspection of an aircraft tyre:

Tyre inflation	Is the tyre over or under inflated?
Tyre creep	Is the tyre rotating around the wheel (best judged using the 'creep' marks)?
Tyre Bulging	Are there any bulges in the tyre, in particular the sidewall?
Cuts	Are there any cuts, splits or embedded objects in the tyre?
Tread	Is there sufficient tread depth around the tyre?
Flat Spots	Are there any 'flat spots' on the tyre – for example where the tyre has locked?

Further Reference: PPL4 » Aircraft General Knowledge » The Airframe » Undercarriage Serviceability Checks and Handling

EAGP1Q3   Answer C

The torque link helps to maintain the correct alignment of the wheel attached to a 'oleo' design undercarriage leg. In the case of the nosewheel undercarriage, failure of the torque links can lead to 'shimmy' – a high-frequency vibration, often felt as a 'shuddering' through the airframe and rudder pedals.

Further Reference: PPL4 » Aircraft General Knowledge » The Airframe » The Undercarriage

EAGP1Q4   Answer A

Light aircraft with direct nosewheel steering usually have rods linking the rudder pedals to the steerable nosewheel. Nosewheel steering is achieved simply by applying rudder in the desired direction of turn. The aircraft may well also have differential braking to allow tighter turning to be achieved.

One feature of 'direct' nosewheel steering is that if excessive force is used on the rudder pedals when the aircraft is stationary (ie the nosewheel is not turning), it is possible to damage the steering mechanism – in particular the rods. In the same way, attempting to steer the nosewheel when the aircraft is stationary and without using the proper equipment – eg a towbar – can also damage the steering rods.

Further Reference: PPL4 » Aircraft General Knowledge » The Airframe » The Undercarriage

EAGP1Q5   Answer B

Compression ratio is the ratio of total cylinder volume to clearance volume.

Total cylinder volume is the volume of the cylinder (most often expressed in cubic centimetres – cc) when the piston is right at the bottom of its travel – bottom dead centre.

Clearance volume is the volume of the cylinder when the piston is right at the top of its travel – top dead centre.

Further Reference: PPL4 » Aircraft General Knowledge » Aero Engines » The Four Stroke Cycle

EAGP1Q6   Answer B

The valve that allows oil to bypass the oil cooler in the event of a blockage of the oil cooler is a pressure-activated valve.

Further Reference: PPL4 » Aircraft General Knowledge » The Oil System » The Oil System

EAGP1Q7   Answer B

A basic knowledge of the four stroke 'Otto' cycle makes it clear that in each complete cycle the inlet valve opens once (to allow the fuel/air mixture to enter the cylinder) and the exhaust valve also opens once (to allow the burnt exhaust gases to exit the cylinder).

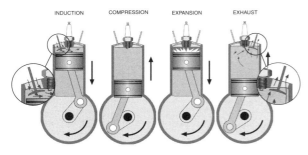

The opening and closing of the valves is controlled by a camshaft which is driven by the rotation of the crankshaft. However, the camshaft is geared to run at half the speed of the engine (that is, half the speed of the crankshaft), so that the appropriate valve only opens once for every two rotations of the crankshaft.

Further Reference: PPL4 » Aircraft General Knowledge » Aero Engines » The Four Stroke Cycle

EAGP1Q8   Answer C

In a dry-sump oil system, a scavenge pump takes oil from the sump under the engine and returns it to a separate oil tank. Thus the sump is almost 'dry' – the oil does not stay there once it has trickled down from the engine.

Further Reference: PPL4 » Aircraft General Knowledge » The Oil System

EAGP1Q9   Answer D

Making the fuel/air mixture richer increases the proportion of fuel entering the engine cylinders. A rich mixture implies that a proportion of the fuel is passing through the cylinder unburnt – in other words some fuel is merely spraying into the cylinder and helping to cool it. All the other options given (leaning the mixture, closing cowl flaps or reducing airspeed) are likely to make the engine hotter.

As a general rule of thumb, at more than 75% power the mixture should be fully rich so that excess fuel passes through the cylinders and aids cooling.

Further Reference: PPL4 » Aircraft General Knowledge » The Cooling System » The Cooling System
PPL4 » Aircraft General Knowledge » Engine Handling » In The Cruise

EAGP1Q10   Answer C

The scenario of high oil temperature and low oil pressure indicates that the engine is overheating, or that oil is being lost from the engine – or quite possibly both. In any event, this combination infers that major engine damage is imminent. A diversion to the nearest suitable airfield, whilst remaining alert to the possibility of engine failure, is usually the best course of action.

Further Reference: PPL4 » Aircraft General Knowledge » The Oil System » The Oil System

EAGP1Q11   Answer C

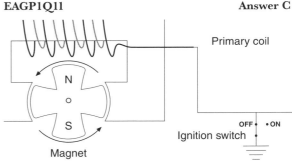

The magnetos are controlled by the cockpit magneto switches. With the magneto switches in the 'off' position, the primary circuit of the magnetos is earthed, which effectively means that the magnetos cannot produce an electrical current.

If the magnetos become disconnected from the cockpit magneto switches, they are unearthed and so 'live' – just as if the cockpit magneto switches were selected on. This is one reason for checking the magnetos just before closing down the engine. If there is no RPM drop when either magneto is selected, the magnetos may be unearthed and so be permanently 'live'.

Further Reference: PPL4 » Aircraft General Knowledge » The Ignition System » The Ignition System

EAGP1Q12   Answer B

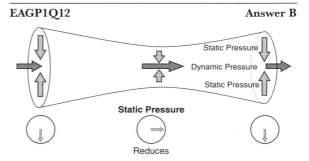

At the narrowest point of a venturi, airflow speed increases and static pressure decreases. The faster the airflow speed, the lower the static pressure. This phenomenon is an example of 'Bernoulli's theorem', and is the essence of lift.

Further Reference: PPL4 » Principles of Flight » Properties of the Atmosphere » Air in Motion

EAGP1Q13 Answer A

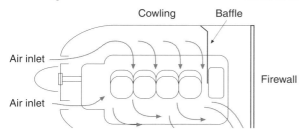

Under the cowlings and within the engine compartment of an air-cooled engine, the airflow is directed by baffles (plates) and seals to flow evenly over the hottest parts of the engine. For this reason it is important that, where possible, the condition and security of the baffles is checked during the pre-flight inspection.

Further Reference: PPL4 » Aircraft General Knowledge » The Cooling System » The Cooling System

EAGP1Q14 Answer C

Viewed from the side, the average aircraft propeller blade is 'twisted', so that the outer sections have a smaller blade angle than the inner.

When the propeller blade is rotating, the outer sections travel through a greater distance than the inner in a given time, so they are travelling faster. If the blade angle was constant along its whole length, this would mean that the outer section would have a much greater angle of attack than the inner. For this reason, the outer sections of the blade have a reduced blade angle, so that when rotating all sections of the propeller blade have approximately the same angle of attack.

Further Reference: PPL4 » Aircraft General Knowledge » The Propeller » Principles of Propellers

EAGP1Q15 Answer D

Aviation refuelling installations are 'colour coded' to differentiate between different fuels. AVGAS installations and refuelling points have RED placards, JET A1 installations and refuelling points have BLACK placards. Traditional aircraft piston engines are designed to run on AVGAS 100LL, whereas jet engines run on AVTUR Jet A-1. However, the new generation of aircraft diesel engines can run on Jet A-1.

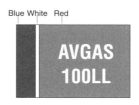 

Knowing what types of fuel your engine is permitted to use, and ensuring that only that type of fuel is uplifted to the aircraft, is of vital importance.

Further Reference: PPL4 » Aircraft General Knowledge » Aeroplane Flight Safety » Refuelling Precautions

EAGP1Q16 Answer B

Oil temperature is usually measured just before the oil enters the hot sections of the engine, most often just 'downstream' of the oil cooler and on the outlet side of the oil pump.

Further Reference: PPL4 » Aircraft General Knowledge » The Oil System » The Oil System

EAGP1Q17 Answer C

The theoretical ideal fuel/air mixture is taken to be somewhere between 1:12 to 1:15, and is sometimes known as the 'stoichiometric' mixture. In theory a fuel/air mixture in the theoretically ideal proportion will ensure that all the fuel/air mixture is burnt within the cylinder.

A mixture with a greater proportion of fuel (eg 1:9) is richer than the stoichiometric. A mixture with a lesser proportion of fuel (eg 1:18) is leaner.

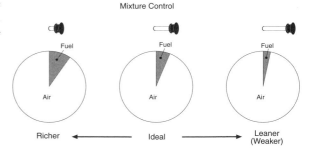

Further Reference: PPL4 » Aircraft General Knowledge » The Induction System » The Induction System

EAGP1Q18   Answer B

Contrary to popular myth, there are few universal rules as to the minimum altitude, or maximum power setting, for using the mixture control. As in most matters concerning aircraft operation, it is the aircraft's POH/FM that will give reliable information on operating procedures, limitations etc. for that aircraft.

The Idle Cut Off (ICO) position for the mixture control – in other words the fully lean selection – stops all fuel from entering the engine. It is the preferred method of shutting down a piston aero engine as it leaves no fuel in the engine. This reduces the risk of corrosion and also makes it less likely that the engine can accidentally start if, for example, the propeller is moved.

Further Reference: PPL4 » Aircraft General Knowledge » Engine Handling » After-landing and Shut Down

EAGP1Q19   Answer A

A 30 amp hour rating infers that the battery is capable (in theory, anyway) of supplying 30 amps for one hour, or 1 amp for 30 hours, or any combination of amps and time that adds up to 30 (eg 15 amps x 2 hours, 10 amps x 3 hours etc.)

This theoretical capacity is dependant on a number of factors – not least the battery being fully charged and in perfect condition, and so is best treated as a theoretical guideline rather than a realistic capacity.

Further Reference: PPL4 » Aircraft General Knowledge » Aircraft Systems » Aircraft Batteries

EAGP1Q20   Answer C

It is imperative that a blown fuse is only replaced with a fuse of the same rating. Using a fuse of a higher rating may allow excessive current to flow to the component that the fuse is meant to protect – possibly causing component failure or even the risk of an electrical fire.

A fuse should only be replaced once in flight. If it 'blows' again this is a sign of a persistent electrical problem in that circuit, and the fuse should not be replaced a second time.

Note that a fuse is not the same as the circuit breaker (CB) used in most modern aircraft electrical circuits.

Further Reference: PPL4 » Aircraft General Knowledge » Aircraft Systems » Aircraft Electrical Systems

EAGP1Q21   Answer A

As the name implies, the suction (or vacuum) pump works by drawing air through a filter at one end of the system, through the connected instruments (pulling a jet of air over the gyro rotors, making them spin) and to the engine-driven suction pump itself, from where it is expelled 'overboard'.

Further Reference: PPL4 » Aircraft General Knowledge » Aircraft Systems » The Suction System

EAGP1Q22   Answer A

If the aircraft alternator or generator fails, the battery is supplying all electrical power. The length of time that the battery will last depends on a number of variables, including its rated capacity, its state of charge, its general condition, temperature, the electrical load etc.

The safest course of action in this scenario is to reduce electrical load to a minimum (by turning off non-essential lights, radios etc.) and planning to make a landing at the nearest suitable airfield.

Further Reference: PPL4 » Aircraft General Knowledge » Aircraft Systems » Electrical Failure

EAGP1Q23   Answer C

In motion – pitot senses static pressure + dynamic pressure

Stationary – pitot senses static pressure

When the aircraft is at rest, the pitot tube will sense static pressure – the pressure of the air all around it. Once the aircraft starts to move, the pitot tube will sense both the static pressure and also the dynamic pressure – the pressure caused by moving through the air. This combined pressure being sensed in the pitot tube of a moving aircraft is sometimes called 'pitot' pressure or 'stagnation' pressure.

Further Reference: PPL4 » Aircraft General Knowledge » Instruments » The Airspeed Indicator (ASI)

EAGP1Q24   **Answer D**

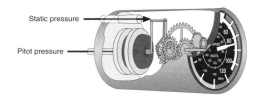

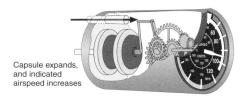

Questions of this type can often be approached by knowing how the various instruments utilise static pressure.

The Altimeter reading will be 'frozen' – it is sensing the static pressure trapped in the system, therefore it will read the level at which the static blockage occurred. If the aircraft is descending, this means that altimeter will over-read. It is indicating that the aircraft is higher than it really is.

The Vertical Speed Indicator (VSI) reading will quickly fall to zero in the event of static blockage as there will be no change of static pressure.

In the descent, the static air trapped inside the AirSpeed Indicator (ASI) will soon be less dense than the static pressure which forms part of the pitot pressure entering the ASI's capsules. Hence, even without any increase in airspeed, the capsules will tend to expand, showing an increasing indicated airspeed even if actual airspeed remains constant.

Further Reference: PPL4 » Aircraft General Knowledge » Instruments » Altimeters Errors

The Vertical Speed Indicator (VSI)/Airspeed Indicator Errors

EAGP1Q25   **Answer B**

For	N	30	60	E	120	150
Steer	359	032	061	090	119	151
For	S	210	240	W	300	330
Steer	184	213	241	269	299	332
DATE						AIRPATH

Deviation is the effect of the aircraft's own magnetic field, which will have an influence on the aircraft compass. The compass can be adjusted to minimise the effect of deviation, but some errors are likely to remain. To compensate for this residual deviation, the aircraft will have a compass deviation card, on which corrections for selected headings are noted.

The compass deviation card is updated periodically on scheduled maintenance inspections, and the compass may also be checked in the event of an occurrence that could alter the aircraft's magnetic field – such as the fitting of new equipment, a lightning strike etc.

Further Reference: PPL4 » Aircraft General Knowledge » Instruments » The Magnetic Compass

EAGP1Q26   **Answer B**

The alternate static source draws static air from inside the cockpit in the event that the external static source becomes blocked or unusable. As a general rule, static air within the cockpit of an un-pressurised aircraft will be at a lower pressure than the outside 'ambient' static pressure. The difference is usually small, but may indicate – for example – that the aircraft is slightly higher than it actually is.

Further Reference: PPL4 » Aircraft General Knowledge » Aircraft Systems » The Static Source

EAGP1Q27   **Answer D**

Most airspeed indicators are 'colour coded' to indicate specific limiting speeds and speed operating ranges. The common AirSpeed Indicator (ASI) markings are shown below:

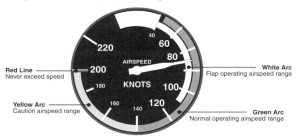

White Arc Flap operating airspeed range

Green Arc Normal operating airspeed range

Yellow Arc Caution airspeed range

Red Line Never exceed speed

So the green arc represents the range of normal operating airspeeds.

Further Reference: PPL4 » Aircraft General Knowledge » Instruments » The Airspeed Indicator (ASI)

EAGP1Q28   **Answer D**

The Heading Indicator is set by reference to the compass, which in the average light aircraft is the only other instrument capable of displaying heading (GPS units can easily display the aircraft's track, but not heading). The Heading Indicator needs to be regularly checked against the compass. Because the compass can be subject to a number of errors (turning error, acceleration/deceleration errors etc.) the aircraft should be in settled straight and level, un-accelerated flight, and in balance, for a proper compass reading to be taken.

Further Reference: PPL4 » Aircraft General Knowledge » Instruments » The Heading Indicator

EAGP1Q29   Answer B

Gyroscopes are commonly utilised in:

■ the Heading Indicator (HI) or Directional Gyro Indicator (DGI);

■ the Attitude Indicator (AI) or Artificial Horizon;

■ the Turn Co-ordinator or Turn Indicator.

Further Reference: PPL4 » Aircraft General Knowledge » Instruments » Turn Co-ordinator Serviceability Checks

EAGP1Q30   Answer C

A duplicate control system inspection is carried out if any of the aircraft's control systems has undergone maintenance or adjustment. The inspection must be carried-out by two people, and the norm is for those two people to be licensed engineers. If a duplicate control system inspection has to be carried out away from the aircraft's base, its is permitted for the inspection to be done by a licensed engineer and a pilot qualified on type.

Note that the aircraft owner is not permitted to carry out the second part of the duplicate control system inspection unless that owner is also a pilot licenced on type – which is not one of the options specified in the question.

Further Reference: PPL4 » Aircraft General Knowledge » Airworthiness » Pilot Maintenance

EAGP1Q31   Answer D

The period of validity of a Certificate of Airworthiness is often, but not always, stated on the certificate itself. The validity of the C of A is not dependant on issues such as the certificate of registration or aircraft insurance.

Further Reference: PPL4 » Aircraft General Knowledge » Airworthiness » Aircraft Documents

EAGP1Q32   Answer C

Carbon Monoxide (CO) is a colourless, odourless gas which is highly toxic and a deadly poison. CO poisoning can cause the rapid impairment of mental functions and ultimately unconsciousness and death.

CO can be formed in the combustion process, and may enter the cockpit through a leaky exhaust or heating system. Most aircraft are fitted with some form of CO detector to warn of dangerous concentrations of CO in the cockpit.

Further Reference: PPL4 » Aircraft General Knowledge » Aeroplane Flight Safety » Cabin Heating and Ventilation Systems

EAGP1Q33   Answer B

The aircraft's POH/FM is the authoritative source of information for emergency procedures. However, it is highly unlikely that an authoritative document will recommend anything other than immediately closing down the engine in the event of an engine fire. Closing the cockpit heater controls is done to seal the firewall and to prevent a fire in the engine compartment spreading into the cockpit.

Further Reference: PPL4 » Aircraft General Knowledge » Engine Handling » Engine Problem Troubleshooting

EAGP1Q34   Answer A

The table below is useful in deciding how to answer this question.

Type of Fire	Type of Extinguisher				
	Water	Foam	Carbon Dioxide	Dry Powder	BCF
Wood, paper cloth	X	X			X
Flammable liquid		X	X	X	X
Electrical			X	X	X
Gas				X	X
Wheel and Brake				X	X

Further Reference: PPL4 » Aircraft General Knowledge » Aeroplane Flight Safety » Fire Extinguishers

EAGP1Q35   Answer B

In a balanced turn, the aircraft produces a total lift force that acts at a 90° angle to (ie is perpendicular to) the wings. This total lift force provides both the vertical component of lift to balance weight, and the horizontal component into the turn.

The more steeply the aircraft banks, the greater the total lift it must generate.

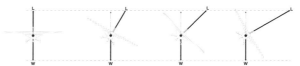

Further Reference: PPL4 » Flight Performance and Planning » In-flight Performance » Principles of Manoeuvring Flight

EAGP1Q36

Answer C

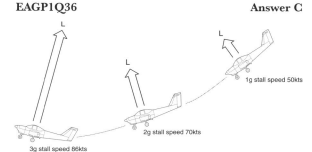

Increased load factor means increased stall airspeed – because the stalling angle of attack is reached at a faster airspeed when load factor is increased.

Stall airspeed increases by the square root of the load factor. So, if load factor is 2, stall airspeed is 1.41 x the stall airspeed when the load factor is 1 (because the square root of 2 is 1.41).

For example, if the stall speed at a load factor of 1 is 50 knots, the stall speed when the load factor is 2 will be 1.41 x 50 = 70·5 knots.

Further Reference: PPL4 » Principles of Flight » The Stall » Factors Affecting Stalling Airspeed

EAGP1Q37

Answer B

A flying control surface may be fitted with a mass balance, which moves the control surface's centre of gravity (cg) forward towards the hinge line, making the control surface less liable to flutter. Flutter is a very serious condition that may occur at high speed and can have very serious consequences.

Further Reference: PPL4 » Principles of Flight » Stability and Control » Mass and Aerodynamic Balance of the Flying Controls

EAGP1Q38

Answer A

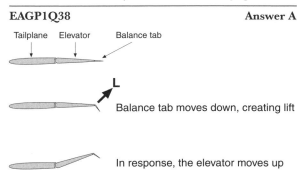

Of the options given, only A describes an aerodynamic surface that assists the movement of the flying control. By moving in the opposite direction to the flying control, the balance tab (which is located at the rear of the flying control) creates is own lift force, acting in the sense necessary to assist the movement of the main control surface. The balance tab is usually found on larger and faster aircraft to provide assistance in overcoming heavy flying control loads.

Further Reference: PPL4 » Principles of Flight » Trimming Controls » Types of Trimmer

EAGP1Q39

Answer C

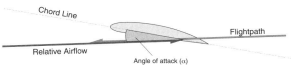

The chord line is a line drawn through the cross section of an aerofoil (eg a wing), from the leading edge through to the trailing edge. The angle between the chord line and the relative airflow is the angle of attack (also described by the Greek symbol for alpha – α).

Further Reference: PPL4 » Principles of Flight » The Four Forces » Lift

EAGP1Q40

Answer A

The basic components of the 'dry' atmosphere are as below:

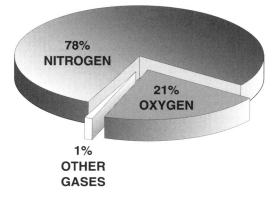

It is often overlooked that the 'dry' atmosphere does not exist outside the laboratory, and in the earth's atmosphere there is always a significant percentage of water vapour – usually in the order of 4%.

Further Reference: PPL4 » Principles of Flight » Properties of the Atmosphere » The Atmosphere

EAGP1Q41

Answer C

Air density is inversely proportional to temperature: as temperature increases, density decreases. If all other factors are equal, the warmer the air, the less dense it is. This effect becomes noticeable when comparing, for example, aircraft performance on a hot summer day as opposed to a cold winter day. Even if all other factors are equal, the aircraft taking off on a summer day will require a longer take-off distance, climb at a reduced rate and have a reduced service ceiling compared to the colder day.

Further Reference: PPL4 » Principles of Flight » Properties of the Atmosphere » The Atmosphere

EAGP1Q42   Answer D

In the International Standard Atmosphere (ISA), the standard temperature at sea level is +15°C, and this standard temperature reduces at a rate of 2°C with each 1,000ft increase in altitude.

Therefore, at 10,000ft, the ISA temperature has reduced by (10 x 2°C) = 20°C.

In the ISA, sea level temperature (+15°C), less 10,000ft of temperature reduction (20°C), = -5°C.

So, at 10,000ft the ISA temperature is -5°C. The actual temperature at 10,000ft is given in the question as -15°C, thus the actual temperature is 10°C less than the ISA temperature.

This can be described as ISA -10°C.

Further Reference: PPL4 » Principles of Flight » Properties of the Atmosphere » The Atmosphere

EAGP1Q43   Answer A

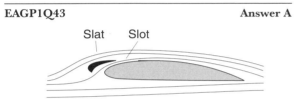

A slot or slat in the wing's leading edge will allow higher pressure air from beneath the wing to flow over the wing's upper surface. This airflow has the effect of adding energy to the air flowing over the wing, thus encouraging the airflow to follow the contours of the upper wing surface. Slots or slats mean that a wing can produce a greater maximum amount of lift, and attain a higher angle of attack than a 'clean' wing.

Further Reference: PPL4 » Principles of Flight » Flaps and Slats » Slats, Slots and Air Brakes

EAGP1Q44   Answer B

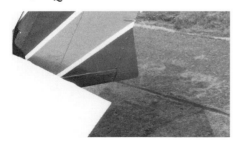

A bendable trim tab attached to a control surface is designed to be adjusted on the ground to achieve aerodynamic balance in the air. As such, its adjustment is for practical purposes a matter of trial and error, and it is recommended that the ground adjustment is done under the supervision of a licenced engineer.

Further Reference: PPL4 » Principles of Flight » Trimming Controls » Types of Trimmer

EAGP1Q45   Answer A

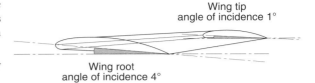

The angle of incidence is the angle between the wing's chordline and the fuselage. Washout is essentially a twist in the wing section, so that the angle of incidence at the wing root is greater than the angle of incidence at the wing tip.

Washout means that the wing root flies at a greater angle of attack than the wing tip. This means that approaching the stall, the wing root is likely to reach the stalling angle of attack before the wing tip and so the inner wing will stall before the outer. The result is that the aircraft is less likely to roll (ie 'drop a wing') at the stall and the ailerons (nearer the wing tips) are more likely to remain effective near the stall.

Further Reference: PPL4 » Aircraft General Knowledge » The Airframe » Wing Design

EAGP1Q46   Answer A

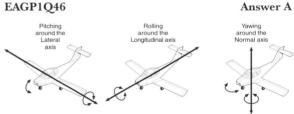

The normal axis is also sometimes called the vertical axis. It runs vertically through the aircraft's centre of gravity (CG).

When an aircraft yaws, it rotates around the normal (vertical) axis.

Further Reference: PPL4 » Principles of Flight » Stability and Control » The Three Planes of Movement

EAGP1Q47   **Answer B**

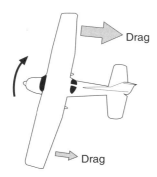

Adverse yaw is the yawing force that acts when the ailerons are deflected and the aircraft is rolling. The downgoing aileron (on the upgoing wing) produces more drag than on the upgoing aileron.

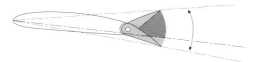

One way to reduce adverse yaw is differential ailerons, where the upgoing aileron moves through a greater angle than the downgoing aileron, thus more closely balancing the drag produced at each wing.

Further Reference: PPL4 » Principles of Flight » Stability and Control » Control in Roll

---

EAGP1Q48   **Answer D**

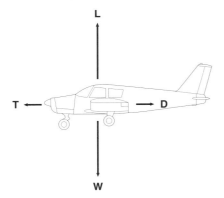

When an aircraft is in equilibrium in straight and level, un-accelerated flight;

   Lift = Weight

   Thrust = Drag

However, these forces are not all equal to each other. For example, a typical light aircraft with a weight of 700kg will be generating 700kg of lift in this situation, whereas it may be generating just 70kg of thrust to balance 70kg of drag.

Further Reference: PPL4 » Principles of Flight » The Four Forces » The Four Forces Acting on an Aircraft in Flight

EAGP1Q49   **Answer C**

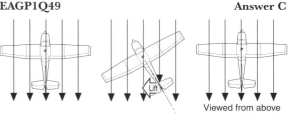

Viewed from above

The primary function of the aircraft fin (or vertical stabiliser) is to give the aircraft directional stability. If the aircraft is yawing or skidding, the affect of the airflow hitting the fin at an angle (an angle of attack) will create a lift force, rotating the aircraft around the CG so that it is facing into the airflow once more.

In essence the fin acts rather like a weather vane, rotating the aircraft so that it points into the relative airflow.

Further Reference: PPL4 » Principles of Flight » Stability and Control » Stability in Yaw

---

EAGP1Q50   **Answer B**

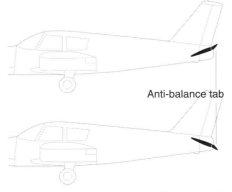

Anti-balance tab

A balance tab is fitted to the trailing edge of a flying control and moves in the opposite direction to the flying control, to aid the movement of the control (the pilot feels lighter control forces). It follows that an anti-balance tab moves in the same direction as the flying control, increasing the control forces the pilot feels (the control seems 'heavier') and so making it less likely that the pilot will move the control too far and too fast.

An anti-balance tab may be used to 'dampen' the movement of a flying control that would otherwise be too 'light'.

Further Reference: PPL4 » Principles of Flight » Trimming Controls » Types of Trimmer

Paper 2 Answers and Explanation

EAGP2Q1   Answer B

A structure in which the outside skin provides all or most of the structural strength in a monocoque structure. Where the stressed skin is supported by a light framework, the result is a semi-monocoque structure.

Further Reference: PPL4 » Aircraft General Knowledge » The Airframe » Wing Construction

EAGP2Q2   Answer B

An aircraft can be certified in one or more 'categories'; namely Normal, Utility and Aerobatic. Normal category is normally taken to have the lowest load factor limitations, and Aerobatic category the highest, with Utility category in between. It is not unusual for an aircraft to be certified in more than one category, with different weight or cg limitations applying to flight in each category.

Further Reference: PPL4 » Flight Performance and Planning » Mass and Balance » Centre of Gravity

EAGP2Q3   Answer C

The principle features of a 'traditionally' constructed aircraft wing are depicted in explanation EAGP1Q1. The ribs lie across the width of the wing and help give the structure its aerofoil cross-section. The spar(s) run the length of the wing and act as a 'spine' or 'backbone' to the wing.

Further Reference: PPL4 » Aircraft General Knowledge » The Airframe » Wing Construction

EAGP2Q4   Answer C

Control locks, whether fitted in the cockpit or fitted to the flying control surface, are designed to stop the flying controls being damaged by excessive movement when the aircraft is parked (eg by strong winds or propeller blast from other aircraft).

Although it may seem too obvious to need stating, all control locks must be removed before flight. Cockpit control locks often have a warning feature (such as an attached plate covering the magneto switches) to make it more difficult to miss them, but the best guard is to properly complete the aircraft checklist.

Further Reference: PPL4 » Aircraft General Knowledge » The Airframe » Control Locks

EAGP2Q5   Answer C

Indications of increasing oil temperature and reducing oil pressure both indicate a problem with the engine oil system – quite possibly that there is insufficient oil in the engine. Such a situation may preclude an engine failure and a diversion to the nearest suitable airfield, whilst remaining alert to the possibility of engine failure, is the safest best course of action.

Further Reference: PPL4 » Aircraft General Knowledge » The Oil System » The Oil System

EAGP2Q6   Answer C

With the cockpit magneto switch in the 'off' position, the primary circuit of the magnetos is earthed, which means that the magnetos cannot produce an electrical current.

If the magnetos become disconnected from the cockpit magneto switch, they are unearthed and so 'live' – as if the cockpit magneto switches were selected on. The position of the Master Switch has no bearing on the operation of the magnetos.

For further information see explanation EAGP1Q11.

Further Reference: PPL4 » Aircraft General Knowledge » The Ignition System » The Ignition System

EAGP2Q7   Answer B

Spark plugs are susceptible to 'fouling', which occurs when oil or lead deposits build up on the electrodes of the spark plug. This fouling can reduce engine power and make the engine run less smoothly. Spark plug fouling can occur when an engine is allowed to idle at low RPM for prolonged periods.

Further Reference: PPL4 » Aircraft General Knowledge » The Ignition System » The Ignition System

EAGP2Q8   Answer D

At the narrowest point of a venturi, airflow speed increases and static pressure decreases.

For more information see explanation EAGP1Q12

Further Reference: PPL4 » Principles of Flight » Properties of the Atmosphere » Air in Motion

EAGP2Q9   Answer C

Almost all air-cooled aircraft engines have cylinders which are covered in 'fins'. These fins increase the surface area of the cylinders to allow the greatest possible heat dissipation to the air flowing over them. This airflow is directed into the engine compartment by the cowlings and the air inlets, directed around the engine compartment by baffles and seals, and usually exits the engine compartment underneath the aircraft, sometimes via cowl flaps.

Further Reference: PPL4 » Aircraft General Knowledge » The Cooling System » The Cooling System

EAGP2Q10   Answer A

Although individual systems vary, as a general rule oil temperature is measured from the oil system just before oil enters the 'hot sections' of the engine. This point is often also just downstream of the oil cooler.

Further Reference: PPL4 » Aircraft General Knowledge » The Oil System » The Oil System

EAGP2Q11   Answer B

When the throttle of an engine with a carburettor is advanced too quickly, say from idle to full power in less than a second or two, there may well be a lag between the 'butterfly' valve in the carburettor opening and sufficient fuel entering the venturi of the carburettor to maintain the correct the fuel-air mixture. The lack of fuel can lead to a 'weak cut'. This possibility is guarded against in some engines by fitting the carburettor with an 'accelerator pump' which, when the throttle is opening rapidly, injects a shot of fuel into the venturi.

Further Reference: PPL4 » Aircraft General Knowledge » The Induction System » The Induction System

EAGP2Q12   Answer A

The oil pressure relief valve incorporates a spring which allows the valve to open in the event that oil pressure exceeds a set value. The oil pressure relief valve is often located just ahead of the oil cooler, and opens if the oil cooler becomes blocked, allowing oil to bypass the cooler.

Further Reference: PPL4 » Aircraft General Knowledge » The Oil System » The Oil System

EAGP2Q13   Answer C

The opening and closing of the valves is controlled by a camshaft which is driven by the rotation of the crankshaft. It is geared to run at half the speed of the engine (that is, half the speed of the crankshaft), so that each valve only opens once for every two rotations of the crankshaft.

For more information see explanation EAGP1Q7

Further Reference: PPL4 » Aircraft General Knowledge » Aero Engines » The Four Stroke Cycle

EAGP2Q14   Answer D

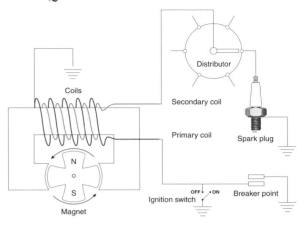

The heart of a magneto is a magnet that rotates between primary and secondary coil windings. As the magnet rotates, the magnetic field produces an electrical current in the primary coil. At a set moment the circuit is broken, inducing a very high voltage in the secondary coil. This very high voltage then travels to the distributor from where it travels down leads to the spark plugs. The whole process is totally remote from the aircraft battery or any other elements of the aircraft's electrical system.

Further Reference: PPL4 » Aircraft General Knowledge » The Ignition System » The Ignition System

EAGP2Q15   Answer B

The ratio of total cylinder volume to clearance volume is the compression ratio.

For more information see explanation AGP1Q5

Further Reference: PPL4 » Aircraft General Knowledge » Aero Engines » The Four Stroke Cycle

EAGP2Q16   Answer A

If the fuel/air mixture is made richer, cylinder head temperature (CHT) should reduce, as the excess of fuel passes unburnt through the cylinder, acting as a coolant. Increasing the airflow over the cylinders (by increasing airspeed in the air, or facing into wind on the ground) will also help cool the engine, as will reducing power.

Further Reference: PPL4 » Aircraft General Knowledge » The Cooling System » The Cooling System

Further Reference: PPL4 » Aircraft General Knowledge » Engine Handling » In The Cruise

EAGP2Q17   Answer C

In general terms, the higher the relative humidity (in other words the greater the moisture content of the air), the greater the risk of carburettor icing. It is important to note that warm air is capable of holding more moisture than cold air, so a cold temperature does not necessarily increase the risk of carburettor icing – it is the relative humidity than counts. Of course, the closer together the temperature and the dewpoint, the higher the relative humidity.

In any given conditions of relative humidity, carburettor icing will always be more likely at a low power setting (such as used in the descent) than a higher power setting.

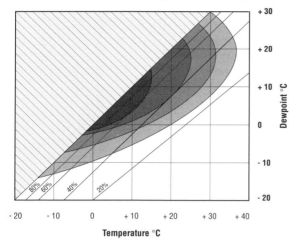

100% Relative humidity

Serious icing – any power

Moderate icing – cruise power
Serious icing – descent power

Serious icing – descent power

Light icing – cruise or descent power

Further Reference: PPL4 » Aircraft General Knowledge » The Induction System » Carburettor Icing

EAGP2Q18   Answer D

MOGAS is MOtor GASoline – in other words leaded car petrol. The CAA have drawn-up a list of aircraft which may use MOGAS, and this listing is found in a CAA Airworthiness Notice.

Further Reference: PPL4 » Aircraft General Knowledge » The Fuel System » Fuel Grades
UK AIM » CAA Safety Sense Leaflets 4 » Use of MOGAS

EAGP2Q19   Answer B

The capacity of a battery is commonly rated in terms of ampere hours, with a figure of 25-30 ampere hours being typical for a single engine light aircraft. An ampere hour is equivalent to a current of 1 amp for one hour. Therefore, in theory at least, a battery with a capacity of 25 ampere hours can supply 25 amps for one hour, or 1 amp for 25 hours, or any other combination of current and time that adds up to 25.

Further Reference: PPL4 » Aircraft General Knowledge » Aircraft Systems » Aircraft Batteries

EAGP2Q20   Answer B

If the suction pump (also known as the vacuum pump) fails, the gyros within the instruments normally driven by the vacuum system (Attitude Indicator and Heading Indicator) can be expected to run-down over a period of a few minutes, during which time these instruments will start to give increasingly erroneous readings. The danger is that during this period the subtle deterioration of these readings may not be immediately apparent, and in the absence of an additional reference – such as the visual horizon or the turn co-ordinator – the pilot may trust and rely on these false-reading instruments.

However, in the event of a suction pump failure, the suction gauge should indicate the failure almost instantly – hence the importance of regularly monitoring the suction gauge when relying of the vacuum-driven instruments.

Further Reference: PPL4 » Aircraft General Knowledge » Aircraft Systems » The Suction System

EAGP2Q21   Answer C

The Zero-Centre ammeter is fitted between the battery and the main busbar to show the charging rate of the battery. If the alternator is supplying power to the electrical system and charging the battery, the zero-centre ammeter will show a positive charge. If the alternator fails or is off-line, the battery is supplying all electrical power to the electrical system and the zero-centre ammeter will show a negative discharge.

Further Reference: PPL4 » Aircraft General Knowledge » Aircraft Systems » Aircraft Electrical Systems

EAGP2Q22   Answer B

As a general rule, aircraft batteries are connected in parallel in order to provide the maximum capacity – in other words they will keep the electrical system going for the longest time. Where two or more batteries are connected in parallel, they will have the same voltage as each individual battery, but the total capacity (in amp hours) of the two batteries combined.

Further Reference: PPL4 » Aircraft General Knowledge » Aircraft Systems » Aircraft Batteries

EAGP2Q23   Answer C

The Heading Indicator, also sometimes known quaintly as the Directional Gyro Indicator (DGI), is set by reference to the magnetic compass. In most single engine light aircraft, the adjustment is done by the pilot using the caging/adjustment knob. It is necessary to regularly check, and if required adjust, the HI against the magnetic compass. In flight this checking and adjustment should only be done during steady, balanced, straight and level flight at a constant airspeed.

Further Reference: PPL4 » Aircraft General Knowledge » Instruments » The Heading Indicator

EAGP2Q24   Answer D

Delayed static

Instant static

The Vertical Speed Indicator (VSI) consists of a capsule within the sealed instrument. The current static pressure is fed into the capsule. Static pressure which has been 'delayed' by a few seconds is fed into the sealed chamber surrounding the capsule. Any difference between the 'current' static pressure and the 'delayed' static pressure will cause the capsule to expand or contract, and this movement of the capsule is transmitted to the instrument needle by a series of linkages to be displayed as a rate of climb or descent indication usually in units of hundreds of feet per minute.

Further Reference: PPL4 » Aircraft General Knowledge » Instruments » The Vertical Speed Indicator (VSI)

EAGP2Q25   Answer B

Gyroscopes are most commonly utilised in the following flight instruments:

■ Turn Co-ordinator (also the turn and slip indicator or turn indicator);

■ Heading Indicator (also sometimes referred to as the Direction Indicator or Directional Gyro Indicator);

■ Attitude Indicator (also known as the Artificial Horizon or Gyro Horizon).

Further Reference: PPL4 » Aircraft General Knowledge » Instruments » The Turn Indicator
The Turn Co-ordinator/The Attitude Indicator (AI)/The Heading Indicator

EAGP2Q26   Answer A

It is the Attitude Indicator (AI) which utilises an 'earth' gyro which has freedom of movement in all three planes. This can be remembered by the fact that the Attitude Indicator display shows a representation of the earth – namely the horizon line.

Further Reference: PPL4 » Aircraft General Knowledge » Instruments » The Attitude Indicator (AI)

EAGP2Q27   Answer A

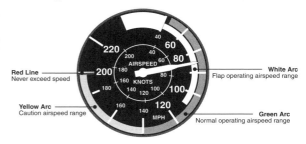

The yellow arc of the airspeed indicator lies between the green arc (normal operating speed range) and the red line (never exceed speed). The yellow 'caution' speed range denotes the speed range to be used only when flying in smooth conditions.

For further information see EAGP1Q27

Further Reference: PPL4 » Aircraft General Knowledge » Instruments » The Airspeed Indicator (ASI)

EAGP2Q28   Answer C

The compass is subject to the following errors:

Variation – the difference between the true north pole and the magnetic north pole.

Deviation – the effect of the aircraft's magnetic field on the compass.

Dip – the effect of the magnets within the compass trying to align with the earth's magnetic field.

Acceleration and deceleration errors – false compass readings during a change in speed.

Turning error – false compass readings when turning, in particular when turning through Northerly or Southerly headings.

Further Reference: PPL4 » Aircraft General Knowledge » Instruments » The Magnetic Compass

EAGP2Q29 — Answer B

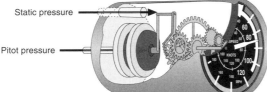

Static pressure

Pitot pressure

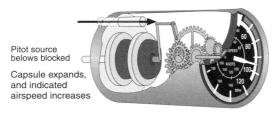

Pitot source belows blocked

Capsule expands, and indicated airspeed increases

Questions of this type can often be approached by knowing how the various instruments utilise static and pitot pressure.

The altimeter reading will not be affected – it senses only static pressure.

The Vertical Speed Indicator (VSI) reading will not be affected – it senses only static pressure.

In the climb, the static air in the AirSpeed Indicator (ASI) will soon be less dense than the static pressure and pitot pressure trapped in the ASI's capsules. Hence, even at a constant airspeed, the capsules will tend to expand, indicating an increasing airspeed – the ASI will over-read.

Further Reference: PPL4 » Aircraft General Knowledge » Instruments » Altimeters Errors
The Vertical Speed Indicator (VSI)/Airspeed Indicator Errors

EAGP2Q30 — Answer D

The period of validity of a Certificate of Airworthiness is often, but not always, stated on the certificate itself. The validity of the C of A is not dependant on issues such as the certificate of registration or aircraft insurance, however the aircraft must be maintained in accordance with the approved maintenance schedule for the C of A to remain valid.

Further Reference: PPL4 » Aircraft General Knowledge » Airworthiness » Aircraft Documents

EAGP2Q31 — Answer B

Any aircraft that has a Certificate of Airworthiness (C of A) must be maintained in accordance with the specified maintenance procedures. Failure to maintain the aircraft in accordance with these specified procedures will automatically invalidate the C of A – no specific action is necessary. Any owner/pilot faced with this situation should consult a licenced engineer and/or the CAA. It likely that the C of A will remain invalid at least until the aircraft has been inspected.

Further Reference: PPL4 » Aircraft General Knowledge » Airworthiness » Aircraft Documents

EAGP2Q32 — Answer B

A BCF fire extinguisher is suitable for use on any type of fire – this is the main reason why BCF extinguishers are found in most aircraft cockpits.

If a BCF extinguisher is used in the cockpit in flight, it is recommended that all vents and windows should be closed before using the extinguisher, and once the fire is out the cockpit should be fully ventilated to clear any fumes.

Further Reference: PPL4 » Aircraft General Knowledge » Aeroplane Flight Safety » Fire Extinguishers

EAGP2Q33 — Answer B

The table at explanation EAGP1Q34 can be used to answer this question.

The limited range of fire types which can be safely extinguished using a water-based fire extinguisher is one reason why they are rare in the aviation environment.

Further Reference: PPL4 » Aircraft General Knowledge » Aeroplane Flight Safety » Fire Extinguishers

EAGP2Q34 — Answer A

Carbon Monoxide is a colourless, odourless gas which is highly toxic and potentially lethal. It is formed as a by product of the combustion process. Most light aircraft heating systems incorporate a 'heat exchanger' which takes heat from the aircraft's exhaust system, therefore it is a defect in the exhaust and/or heater system that is most likely to lead to carbon monoxide entering a light aircraft cockpit.

Further Reference: PPL4 » Aircraft General Knowledge » Aeroplane Flight Safety » cabin heating and ventilation Systems

EAGP2Q35 — Answer B

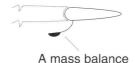

A mass balance

'Flutter' is the high-frequency vibration of a flying control, felt as a 'buzz' through the control column. Flutter is a very serious condition that may occur at high speed and can have very serious consequences.

To prevent flutter, a flying control surface may be fitted with a mass balance ahead of the control's hinge line, which moves the control's centre of gravity (cg) forward, making the control less liable to flutter.

Further Reference: PPL4 » Principles of Flight » Stability and Control » Mass and Aerodynamic Balance of the Flying Controls

EAGP2Q36   Answer D

An aircraft's weight and lift forces are usually arranged so that weight acts through a point (the centre of gravity – cg) which is ahead of the point through which lift is acting – the centre of pressure (CP). This couple between the lift and weight forces produces a force to rotate the aircraft nose-down around the cg – in other words a nose-down pitching moment.

This nose-down pitching force is balanced by the tailplane (behind the cg) producing a downward force which creates a force to pitch the aircraft nose-up.

Further Reference: PPL4 » Principles of Flight » The Four Forces » Balance and Couples

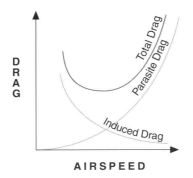

Total Drag
(eg. Parasite Drag + Induced Drag)

EAGP2Q37   Answer C

The total drag experienced by an aircraft can be broken down into two elements: parasite drag and induced drag.

Parasite drag covers all the elements of drag that are not related to the production of lift – form drag, skin friction, interference drag etc. As airspeed increases, parasite drag increases.

Induced drag (sometimes called lift-dependent drag) is a by-product of the production of lift. As a general rule, as airspeed increases, induced drag decreases.

Further Reference: PPL4 » Principles of Flight » The Four Forces » Drag

EAGP2Q38   Answer A

A typical graph of angle of attack v coefficient of lift will look as below:

It can be seen that as angle of attack (α) increases, so coefficient of lift (CL) increases – up to a certain point. This point is the 'critical' or 'stalling' angle of attack. Beyond this point, any further increase in α will actually lead to a decrease in CL.

Further Reference: PPL4 » Principles of Flight » The Four Forces » Lift

EAGP2Q39   Answer B

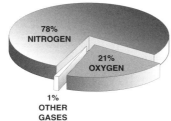

The approximate proportion of nitrogen to oxygen is 3:1. The figure may not be exact, but it is the closest answer that represents the following percentages of gases in the dry atmosphere.

Further Reference: PPL4 » Principles of Flight » Properties of the Atmosphere » The Atmosphere

EAGP2Q40   Answer A

Based on the ISA parameters of a sea-level temperature of +15°C, and a temperature lapse rate of 2°C per 1000ft, it is possible to calculate the 'ISA' temperature for any given altitude below 36,090ft.

Thus, at 5,000ft, the ISA reduction in temperature is 5 x 2°C, = 10°C.

Sea level temperature (+15°C), subtract 10°C, = +5°C. So the ISA temperature at 5,000ft is +5°C.

The actual temperature at 5,000ft is +10°C. This is 5°C more than the ISA temperature, and so can be described as ISA +5°C

This way of describing temperature is often used in aircraft performance calculations.

Further Reference: PPL4 » Principles of Flight » Properties of the Atmosphere » The Atmosphere

EAGP2Q41   Answer B

An aircraft that has flaps will have a recommended flap setting for take-off. The use of this setting will allow the aircraft to get airborne after the shortest attainable ground run (take-off run).

Further Reference: PPL4 » Principles of Flight » The Airframe » Flaps

EAGP2Q42   Answer A

As the Centre of Gravity (CG) moves forward, so the aircraft will feel increasingly 'nose-heavy' to the pilot, and require increasing 'up' elevator to prevent the aircraft pitching nose down.

On landing, the pilot applies 'up' elevator during the landing flare and hold-off. It follows that it is with a forward CG position that the pilot will have to apply the greatest force to the elevator during landing. In this context, the mass (weight) of the aircraft is not a factor, it is the CG position that counts.

Further Reference: PPL4 » Principles of Flight » Stability and Control » Stability in Pitch

EAGP2Q43   Answer D

The stalling angle of attack does NOT depend on factors such as weight (mass), angle of bank, load factor etc. – although all these factors will affect the speed at which the stalling angle of attack is reached. However, the stalling angle of attack is altered by the wing configuration, and in particular if trailing edge flaps are lowered, the stalling angle of attack is reduced.

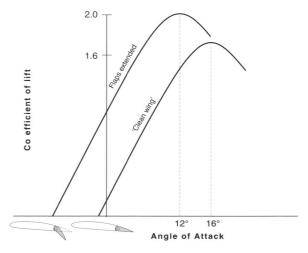

Further Reference: PPL4 » Principles of Flight » The Stall » Factors Affecting Stalling Airspeed

EAGP2Q44   Answer C

Density is inversely proportional to temperature: in other words, if air temperature decreases, air density increases. Cold air is more dense than warm air.

Air density is a major factor in aircraft performance. As a general rule, aircraft can take-off and land in shorter distances in dense air than in less dense air, so there may be a noticeable increase in take-off distance on a hot summer day as opposed to a cool winter day, even if all other factors are equal.

Further Reference: PPL4 » Principles of Flight » Properties of the Atmosphere » The Atmosphere

EAGP2Q45   Answer D

The 'free' airflow is taken to be the airflow outside the influence of the aircraft's wing. The air that is close to the wing is accelerated as it passes over the top surface of the wing – the airflow here is faster than the 'free' airflow.

Faster airflow speed implies lower air pressure – the effect is similar to airflow through the narrow throat of a venturi – and this is a major factor in the production of lift.

Further Reference: PPL4 » Principles of Flight » The Four Forces » Lift

EAGP2Q46   Answer C

Lift acts at around 90° to the lifting surface –ie the wing. Thus, when viewed from directly ahead (or directly behind) lift is acting in line with the aircraft's vertical axis. This is why an aircraft is banked to make a turn – the total lift acts in the direction of the turn, providing not just the force keeping the aircraft airborne, but also providing a force to turn the aircraft. The more lift force the pilot puts in the direction of the turn, the faster the rate of turn.

Further Reference: PPL4 » Flight Performance and Planning » In-flight Performance » Principles of Manoeuvring Flight

EAGP2Q47   Answer A

The primary effect of aileron is roll. However, as the ailerons are deflected, and the aircraft rolls, the wing producing the most lift (i.e. the rising wing) also produces more drag than the downgoing wing. The effect of this drag differential is yaw – in this case adverse yaw acting against the direction of the turn.

It is also worth noting that once the aircraft has rolled and the wings are no longer level, the aircraft will tend to slip towards the lower wing. The effect of a sideways airflow on the vertical fin and rudder will, rather like a weathervane, cause the aircraft to yaw into the direction of the slip – in other words in the same direction as the turn.

The table below summarises the primary and secondary effect of the principle flying controls.

Flying Control	Elevator	Aileron	Rudder
Primary effect	Pitch	Roll	Yaw
Secondary Effect	–	Yaw	Roll

Further Reference: PPL4 » Principles of Flight » Stability and Control » Control in Roll

EAGP2Q48   Answer A

The situation described is one where the aircraft, once disturbed from its original attitude, holds the new attitude without pilot input.

There is no tendency for the aircraft to return to its original attitude – which would be positive static stability.

There is no tendency for the aircraft to diverge further from the original attitude – which would be negative (divergent) static stability.

Because the aircraft is holding the new attitude, it is displaying neutral static stability.

Further Reference: PPL4 » Principles of Flight » Stability and Control » Static and Dynamic Stability

EAGP2Q49   Answer C

A simple trim tab maintains its position relative to the control surface it is attached to, irrespective of any movement of the control surface. It may help to remember that the trim tab is applying an aerodynamic force to the control surface, it does this by being set at an angle to the control surface. Left to fly 'hands-off', the control surface will set itself at an angle dictated by the trim tab setting (provided other factors such as airspeed, power setting and balance are constant).

Further Reference: PPL4 » Principles of Flight » Trimming Controls » Types of Trimmer

EAGP2Q50   Answer A

This is an often-confused issue, because stalling is nearly always referred to in terms of speed. Nevertheless, the fact is that an aerodynamic surface (such as a wing) stalls at a specific angle of attack. The angle of attack is the angle between the surface (ie the wing) and the relative airflow. The 'stalling airspeed' referred to is the speed at which that angle of attack will be reached under a specific set of circumstances (such as weight, load factor, aircraft configuration etc).

Aerobatic pilots are prone to say that an aircraft can be stalled at almost any speed, and this can be done by altering the factors that dictate stall speed (in particular load factor), because the higher the load factor, the faster the speed at which the stalling angle of attack will be reached. However, in untrained hands and/or a non-aerobatic aircraft, this is NOT a principle that can be safely tested out.

Further Reference: PPL4 » Principles of Flight » The Stall » Principles of the Stall

Paper 3 Answers and Explanations

EAGP3Q1   Answer C

The wing spar, labelled as 'B' in the diagram accompanying the question, can be thought of as the 'spine' or backbone of the structure that makes up the wing's construction. In flight, under positive load factors, the spar usually carries an upwards bending load due to the generation of lift. On the ground, the spar usually carries a downwards bending load under the weight of the wing and, for example, fuel in wing fuel tanks. These bending loads can be particularly noticeable on the long wings of larger airliners.

Further Reference: PPL4 » Aircraft General Knowledge » The Airframe » Wing Construction

EAGP3Q2   Answer B

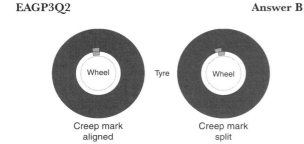

Tyre creep marks are painted across the tyre sidewall and onto the wheel – when they are first painted the creep marks line-up. If the tyre begins to slip around the wheel, the two halves of the creep mark will start to split. If the split exceeds half the width of the creep mark, the tyre should be considered as unserviceable.

Further Reference: PPL4 » Aircraft General Knowledge » The Airframe » Undercarriage Serviceability Checks and Handling

EAGP3Q3   Answer A

A structure where all or most of the stresses are carried by the skin or covering of the structure is a 'monocoque' structure. An aircraft of monocoque structure allows the designer to reduce or do away with the heavy internal structure incorporated in some aircraft designs.

Further Reference: PPL4 » Aircraft General Knowledge » The Airframe » Wing Construction

EAGP3Q4   Answer D

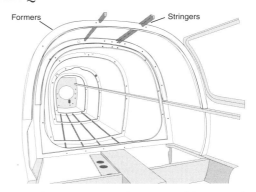

A 'typical' fuselage construction, as used in most aircraft, consists if a series of 'formers' which give the fuselage its shape. These are connected by stringers that run the length of the fuselage, and the metal skin is attached to this structure.

Further Reference: PPL4 » Aircraft General Knowledge » The Airframe » Fuselage Construction

EAGP3Q5   Answer A

Torque is the tendency of an aircraft to roll in the opposite direction to the propeller rotation. If the propeller is rotating clockwise, the aircraft will try to roll anti-clockwise. As seen from behind, this anti-clockwise torque reaction will roll the aircraft to the left.

In aircraft with very powerful engines and large propellers (such as the piston-engines 'warbirds', torque can be a serious consideration, especially during take-off.

Further Reference: PPL4 » Aircraft General Knowledge » The Propeller » The Fixed-Pitch Propeller

EAGP3Q6   Answer C

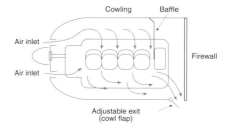

Water-proof jackets and radiators are found in water-cooled engines (such as the vast majority of car engines) – not an air-cooled engine. The cowlings that surround most aircraft piston engines help to direct airflow over and around the engine and, in conjunction with baffles, ensure a fairly even cooling of all the engine. Note that the reference to flying into wind is based on a false premise. Flying into wind (or downwind, or crosswind) does not in general affect the aircraft's airspeed, and hence does not alter the airflow over the engine.

Further Reference: PPL4 » Aircraft General Knowledge » The Cooling System » The Cooling System

EAGP3Q7 Answer A

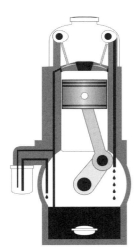

In a wet sump oil system, oil returns by gravity to a reservoir, or sump, at the bottom of the engine after flowing around the engine. The majority of non-aerobatic light aircraft piston engines have a 'wet sump' oil system.

Further Reference: PPL4 » Aircraft General Knowledge » The Oil System » The Oil System

EAGP3Q8 Answer C

If air density decreases (as happens with increasing altitude), and the quantity of fuel entering the fuel/air mixture is unchanged, the mixture will become richer – that is there is an increasing proportion of fuel and a reducing proportion of air in the mixture. Engine power is sensitive to the fuel/air ratio, and an engine being fed with an excessively rich mixture will not be able to develop full power.

Further Reference: PPL4 » Aircraft General Knowledge » The Induction System » The Induction System

EAGP3Q9 Answer A

An accelerator pump may be connected to the throttle by a linkage, so that when the throttle is 'opened' (that is, power is increased), a 'shot' of fuel is injected into the carburettor venturi, to prevent the fuel/air mixture becoming excessively lean, so reducing engine power.

Further Reference: PPL4 » Aircraft General Knowledge » The Induction System » The Induction System

EAGP3Q10 Answer A

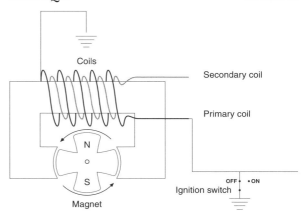

When the magneto is turned off, the switch is in the closed position and so the primary circuit should be grounded (earthed). This means that any current induced by the rotor magnet (for example if the propeller is rotated) should flow continuously around the primary coil and **not** induce a high voltage in the secondary coil – it is that voltage that travels to the spark plugs.

Further Reference: PPL4 » Aircraft General Knowledge » The Ignition System » The Ignition System

EAGP3Q11 Answer D

Within a magneto is a small magnet that rotates between the primary and secondary coils. The rotation of the magnet produces a fluxing magnetic field which induces an electrical current. The rotation of the magnet is driven by a mechanical linkage, ultimately to the engine crankshaft. So, when the engine is rotating, the magneto should be producing an electrical current.

It is important to appreciate that the magneto operates independently of the aircraft's electrical system. As long as the engine is turning, the magneto should be producing electrical current.

Further Reference: PPL4 » Aircraft General Knowledge » The Ignition System » The Ignition System

EAGP3Q12 Answer A

An aircraft with a fixed-pitch propeller can be likened to a car stuck in one gear. If the car starts to motor down a hill it will accelerate, and as a result the engine RPM will increase.

The fixed-pitch propeller of an aircraft will work in just the same way. Even if the throttle position is unchanged, as the aircraft accelerates the RPM will increase – and vice versa.

Further Reference: PPL4 » Aircraft General Knowledge » The Propeller » The Fixed-Pitch Propeller

EAGP3Q13   Answer A

As with any other contamination, water in the fuel system is very dangerous and can lead to partial or total power loss.

Water is more dense than aviation fuel and so tends to pool at the lowest point in a fuel tank or fuel system. For this reason drains are fitted at these lowest points allowing a fuel sample to be taken before flight to check for contamination. Water appears as clear bubbles at the bottom of the fuel sample.

Further Reference: PPL4 » Aircraft General Knowledge » The Fuel System » The Fuel System

EAGP3Q14   Answer A

If the starter warning light remains lit after engine start, this indicates that the starter motor is still engaged. A starter motor being turned by the engine will quickly become a generator which can cause serious damage to the electrical system. In this situation the engine should be shut down immediately.

Further Reference: PPL4 » Aircraft General Knowledge » Engine Handling » Starting Procedure

EAGP3Q15   Answer B

The normally stated period for oil pressure to start rising after engine start is 30 seconds. As a general rule, in a cold engine oil pressure will take longer to register than in a warm engine. If oil pressure does not register within 30 seconds of starting the engine should be shut down without delay. Running the engine with insufficient oil pressure can quickly lead to serious damage.

Further Reference: PPL4 » Aircraft General Knowledge » Engine Handling » Starting Procedure

EAGP3Q16   Answer B

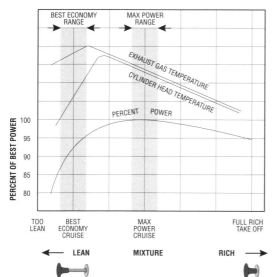

By definition, the highest (or peak) RPM infers the maximum power. So leaning the mixture to the point of maximum RPM also achieves the best power.

Mixture leaning procedures are normally given in the aircraft's POH/FM, together with the associated fuel consumption figures. As well as maximum power, and engine can be leaned to best economy – which usually means sacrificing some speed in exchange for a lower fuel consumption.

If there is no specific POH/FM leaning procedure, a compromise procedure is to lean the mixture until maximum RPM is achieved, then move the mixture back towards rich until the RPM drops by 50RPM. This will give a power setting slightly less than maximum power, but the fuel consumption will be greater than either the maximum power or best economy settings.

Further Reference: PPL4 » Aircraft General Knowledge » Engine Handling » In The Cruise

EAGP3Q17   Answer B

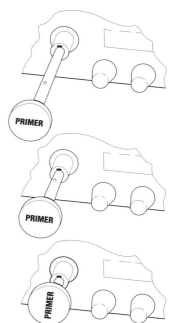

Some light aircraft engines incorporate a manual primer to aid starting. The primer is simply a plunger assembly plumbed into the fuel system, which delivers a 'shot' of fuel directly into the induction manifold, close to the intake valves of the cylinders. In this way the engine is 'primed' with neat fuel to ensure that there is plenty of fuel in the cylinders when trying to start to engine.

Further Reference: PPL4 » Aircraft General Knowledge » Engine Handling » Starting Procedure

EAGP3Q18   Answer C

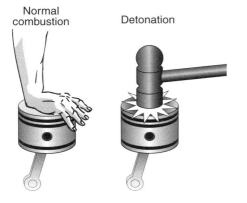

The key in this question is the power setting. In any given set of conditions, carburettor icing will always be more likely at a lower power setting. When the engine is set to a low power setting (such as may be used in the descent), the throttle valve is nearly closed – meaning that any ice has a much smaller gap to obstruct. Moreover, at the lower power setting there will be less residual heat in the engine, and even the 'hot' air supplied when carburettor heat is selected is likely to be cooler than during, say, cruising flight at a higher power setting.

Further Reference: PPL4 » Aircraft General Knowledge » The Induction System » Carburettor Icing

EAGP3Q19   Answer B

During normal operation, the fuel/air mixture in the cylinder does <u>not</u> explode – it burns in a controlled way that pushes the piston down the cylinder, rather than hitting it like a hammer blow. If the fuel/air mixture does explode (usually due to using an excessively lean mixture at a high power setting), the pilot may be able to hear a 'pinking' sound. If detonation does occur, very serious damage can be caused to the engine very quickly.

Further Reference: PPL4 » Aircraft General Knowledge » Aero Engines » Basic Engine Design
Further Reference: PPL4 » Aircraft General Knowledge » Engine Handling » In The Cruise

EAGP3Q20   Answer A

When the throttle is at idle, the butterfly valve is nearly closed, and there may be insufficient velocity of airflow through the venturi to draw through the required fuel. To maintain sufficient fuel inflow when the throttle is closed, the carburettor may be fitted with an 'idling' or 'slow running' fuel jet which sprays fuel into the venture when the throttle is closed or nearly so.

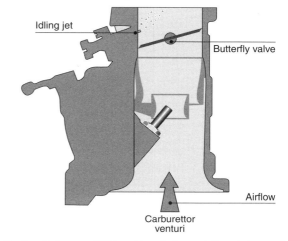

Further Reference: PPL4 » Aircraft General Knowledge » The Induction System » The Induction System

EAGP3Q21   Answer C

The magnetos are controlled by the cockpit magneto (ignition) switches. When the magneto switch is in the 'off' position, the primary coil of the magnetos should be earthed, meaning that the magnetos cannot produce an electrical current. However, if the magnetos become disconnected from the cockpit magneto switches, they are unearthed and so still 'live'.

For further information see explanation EAGP1Q11

Further Reference: PPL4 » Aircraft General Knowledge » The Ignition System » The Ignition System

EAGP3Q22   Answer A

The float chamber of a carburettor contains a small reservoir of fuel that has been drawn from the fuel system, from here the fuel is drawn into the carburettor venturi.

In order for the fuel to flow from the float chamber to the venturi, it is vital that the air pressure above the fuel in the float chamber is at a higher pressure than the static air pressure within the venture. If the reverse was true (if the air pressure over the fuel was at a lower pressure than that within the venturi), a suction would form over the fuel, holding it in the float chamber.

Further Reference: PPL4 » Aircraft General Knowledge » The Induction System » The Induction System

EAGP3Q23   **Answer A**

At an airflow constriction, such as the narrowest point of a venturi, static pressure decreases and airflow speed increases.

For further information see explanation EAGP1Q12

Further Reference: PPL4 » Principles of Flight » Properties of the Atmosphere » Air in Motion

---

EAGP3Q24   **Answer C**

In order to maintain an efficient angle of attack across the length of the propeller blade, the inner sections of the blade, near the propeller hub, are set at a greater blade angle than the outer sections near the tip. This is done because in each rotation, the inner sections move a shorter distance than the outer in the same time, meaning that the inner section (near the hub) is travelling more slowly than the outer section (near the tip).

For further information see explanation EAGP1Q14

Further Reference: PPL4 » Aircraft General Knowledge » The Propeller » Principles of Propellers

---

EAGP3Q25   **Answer A**

A left-centre ammeter is installed between the alternator and the main bus bar and indicates the flow of current from the alternator to the electrical system.

In the example illustrated (repeated below), the ammeter is showing zero output. Therefore the alternator is not supplying any output to the electrical system.

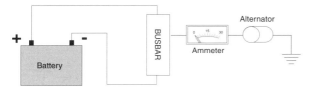

Further Reference: PPL4 » Aircraft General Knowledge » Aircraft Systems » Aircraft Electrical Systems

---

EAGP3Q26   **Answer A**

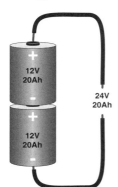

If two batteries are connected in series, the result is effectively a battery with the same capacity (in ampere hours) as a single battery but double the voltage.

If the two batteries are connected in parallel, they will have double the capacity (in ampere hours) but the same voltage. Where an aircraft has more than one battery, they are usually connected in parallel.

Further Reference: PPL4 » Aircraft General Knowledge » Aircraft Systems » Aircraft Batteries

---

EAGP3Q27   **Answer A**

The key features of the compass and characteristics of magnetic direction are:

■ The compass utilises a set of magnets, which are suspended in a liquid to reduce friction and damp out movements.

■ These magnets attempt to align with the earth's magnetic field, causing the compass to point towards magnetic north.

■ Variation is the difference between true north and magnetic north. The compass is not adjusted for variation.

■ Deviation is caused by the effect of the aircraft's own magnetic field upon the compass. The compass will be adjusted to minimise deviation.

Further Reference: PPL4 » Aircraft General Knowledge » Instruments » The Magnetic Compass

---

EAGP3Q28   **Answer B**

The Vertical Speed Indicator (VSI) works by comparing the current static pressure with that from a few moments previously. Any difference between the two is measured and displayed as a rate of climb or a rate of descent.

If the static vent becomes blocked, the 'pressure differential' measured by the VSI will soon become zero, and so the VSI will indicate zero (that is no climb or descent) regardless of what the aircraft is actually doing.

Further Reference: PPL4 » Aircraft General Knowledge » Instruments » The Vertical Speed Indicator (VSI)

EAGP3Q29   **Answer B**

The Altimeter has a case which is connected to the static pressure source. Inside this case is a sealed aneroid capsule which, through a series of linkages, is connected to the pointer on the altimeter face. The action of the static pressure inside the altimeter case on the sealed aneroid capsule causes the capsule to contract or expand, and this is displayed in the form of altitude by the altimeter reading.

Further Reference: PPL4 » Aircraft General Knowledge » Instruments » The Altimeter

---

EAGP3Q30   **Answer A**

The Vertical Speed Indicator (VSI) has a capsule which is connected to the static pressure source. Around this capsule is static air from the same source, but which has been delayed. A series of linkages connect the static air capsule to the pointer on the VSI face. Any change of static pressure causes the capsule to contract or expand, and the rate of change of static pressure is displayed in the form of a rate of climb or rate of descent.

Further Reference: PPL4 » Aircraft General Knowledge » Instruments » The Vertical Speed Indicator (VSI)

EAGP3Q31   Answer D

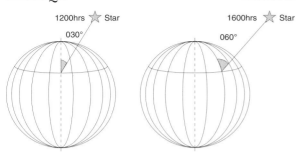

When a heading indicator is set against the compass, in essence its gyro is being aligned with a fixed point in space, not a point on the earth. As the earth rotates, the gyro will appear to 'wander' away from its pre-set alignment as it continues to point towards a fixed point in space. This effect is known as apparent drift or apparent wander.

Further Reference: PPL4 » Aircraft General Knowledge » Instruments » The Heading Indicator

EAGP3Q32   Answer C

Under normal circumstances, if any of an aircraft's control systems has undergone maintenance or adjustment, it must be checked in duplicate, with the two inspections done by separate engineers. However, if the aircraft is away from base when such a duplicate inspection is required, it is permissible that the second part of the inspection is carried out by a pilot qualified on type.

Further Reference: PPL4 » Aircraft General Knowledge » Airworthiness » Pilot Maintenance

EAGP3Q33   Answer C

Any permitted aircraft maintenance work carried out by a pilot must be entered into the aircraft's logbooks, and this entry must be dated and signed by the person who carried out the work – which in this case is the pilot in question.

Further Reference: PPL4 » Aircraft General Knowledge » Airworthiness » Pilot Maintenance

EAGP3Q34   Answer D

It is the BCF extinguisher – using an extinguishing agent called Halon 1211 that is the most common type of fire extinguisher found in light aircraft.

For more information refer to the table at explanation EAGP1Q34.

Further Reference: PPL4 » Aircraft General Knowledge » Aeroplane Flight Safety » Fire Extinguishers

EAGP3Q35   Answer A

Carbon Monoxide (CO) is a colourless, odourless gas which is highly toxic and a deadly poison. CO poisoning can cause the rapid impairment of mental functions and ultimately unconsciousness and death.

CO can be formed in the combustion process, and may enter the cockpit through a leaky exhaust or heating system.

Further Reference: PPL4 » Aircraft General Knowledge » Aeroplane Flight Safety » Cabin Heating and Ventilation Systems

EAGP3Q36   Answer C

For over-water flight in a single-engine aircraft, it is recommended that lifejackets are worn but not inflated.

Lifejackets can be very difficult to put on in the cabin of an average single-engine aircraft, and such an action is not a practical proposition for a pilot who is also trying to fly an aircraft to an imminent ditching. So, lifejackets must be worn.

It is important that the lifejackets are not inflated whilst the wearer is inside the aircraft. At the very least doing so increases the risk that the lifejacket will get punctured. At the worst, the bulk of the inflated lifejacket will impede exit from the aircraft – and if the cabin fills with water the lifejacket's buoyancy may prevent the wearer from escaping the aircraft. This has happened in ditching accidents.

Further Reference: PPL4 » Aircraft General Knowledge » Aeroplane Flight Safety » Survival Equipment

EAGP3Q37   Answer C

In general terms, stability is positive when it tends to return the aircraft to the original state (in this case the trimmed attitude). The element of stability that makes an aircraft tend to return back towards its original state is 'static' stability. The element of stability that damps out that movement until the aircraft has settled back at the original state is 'dynamic' stability.

Further Reference: PPL4 » Principles of Flight » Stability and Control » Static and Dynamic Stability

EAGP3Q38   Answer A

As angle of attack increases, the value of coefficient of lift also increases, until it reaches its maximum value at around the stalling angle of attack. At this point the wing is producing the greatest coefficient of lift, but also a very high coefficient of drag.

If angle of attack is increased beyond the stalling angle, coefficient of lift will reduce sharply.

For more information see explanation EAGP2Q38.

Further Reference: PPL4 » Principles of Flight » The Four Forces » Lift

EAGP3Q39   **Answer B**

Static stability is a measure of how readily an aircraft tends to return back towards its original condition if disturbed from steady, trimmed, flight. An aircraft with strong static stability will quickly move back towards its original condition, one with weak static stability will be much slower to react.

Further Reference: PPL4 » Principles of Flight » Stability and Control » Static and Dynamic Stability

EAGP3Q40   **Answer C**

The troposphere is the layer of the atmosphere closest to the earth and in contact with the surface. It is a feature of the troposphere that with increasing altitude, temperature tends to decrease. In the International Standard Atmosphere (ISA), this temperature decrease – lapse rate – is defined as being approximately 2°C per 1000ft, up to 36,000ft.

Further Reference: PPL4 » Principles of Flight » The Atmosphere and Properties of the Air » The Atmosphere

EAGP3Q41   **Answer B**

Density is proportional to pressure: if pressure decreases, density will decrease and vice versa (assuming all other factors remain constant).

Further Reference: PPL4 » Principles of Flight » The Atmosphere and Properties of the Air » The Atmosphere

EAGP3Q42   **Answer D**

Each of the three primary flight controls rotates the aircraft around one of the three axis, as below:

Flight Control	Primary Effect	Axis
Rudder	Yaw	Vertical (normal)
Aileron	Roll	Lateral
Elevator	Pitch	Longitudinal

See also explanation EAGP1Q46

Further Reference: PPL4 » Principles of Flight » Stability and Control » The Three Planes of Movement

EAGP3Q43   **Answer B**

Induced drag can be considered as inversely proportional to airspeed – induced drag increases as speed decreases, and decreases as airspeed increases.

To be strictly correct, induced drag is proportional to coefficient of lift (CL) – a high CL value means a high induced drag. High CL is associated with a high angle of attack, and in 'normal' flight conditions a high angle of attack is associated with slow airspeeds.

Further Reference: PPL4 » Principles of Flight » The Four Forces » Drag

EAGP3Q44   **Answer B**

In flight, an aircraft produces a total lift force that acts at a 90° angle to (ie it is perpendicular to) the wings. This total lift force provides both the vertical component of lift to balance weight, and in a turn it also produces the horizontal component into the turn. See EAGP2Q46.

Further Reference: PPL4 » Flight Performance and Planning » In-flight Performance » Principles of Manoeuvring Flight

EAGP3Q45   **Answer B**

The key primary and secondary effects of aileron and rudder are:

Control	Primary Effect	Secondary Effect
Aileron	Roll	Yaw
Rudder	Yaw	Roll

In respect of this specific question, when an aircraft yaws, the wing on the 'outside' of the yaw (eg the right wing if the aircraft is yawing to the left) will be travelling faster than the 'inner' wing. This increase in speed means that the 'outer' wing is generating more lift than the inner, causing roll in the same direction as the yaw. The effect of dihedral will also aid this roll.

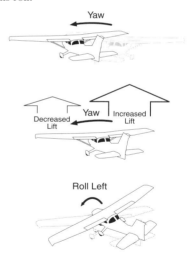

Further Reference: PPL4 » Principles of Flight » Stability and Control » Stability in Yaw

EAGP3Q46   **Answer D**

'Flutter' is the high-frequency vibration of a flying control, felt as a 'buzz'. Flutter is a very serious condition that may occur at high speed and can have very serious consequences.

To prevent flutter, a flying control surface may be fitted with a mass balance.

Further Reference: PPL4 » Principles of Flight » Stability and Control » Mass and Aerodynamic Balance of the Flying Controls

EAGP3Q47   Answer B

The use of the recommended flap setting will reduce the aircraft's stalling speed, this means it can get airborne at a slower speed, and therefore take-off run is reduced as the aircraft only has to accelerate to a slower speed than when taking off without flaps.

It is worth remembering that the use of flap will lead to a reduced rate of climb after take-off (because of the increased drag). The increased drag will also lead to a slower acceleration on take-off, although the effect is unlikely to be noticeable.

Further Reference: PPL4 » Flight Performance and Planning » Take-off and Climb » Forces in the Take-off Run

EAGP3Q48   Answer A

When trailing edge flap is lowered, the stall is reached at a reduced angle of attack compared to a 'clean' wing. The use of flap still leads to a slower stall but the fact that this happens at a reduced angle of attack means, for example, that on landing an aircraft does not have to achieve an excessively nose-high attitude on landing.

See also EAGP2Q43.

Further Reference: PPL4 » Principles of Flight » The Stall » Factors Affecting Stalling Airspeed

EAGP3Q49   Answer D

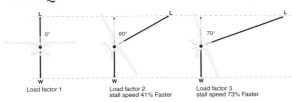

Stalling speed increases by the square root of the load factor, and in a 60° angle of bank the aircraft is assumed to be experiencing a load factor of 2. Therefore, at a load factor of 2, stall speed is 1.41 x the 'normal' stall speed at a load factor of 1 (because the square root of 2 is 1.41).

So, the stall speed in a 60° angle of bank turn is 1.41 x the wings level stall speed.

1.41 x 60 knots is 85 knots (to the nearest knot).

Further Reference: PPL4 » Principles of Flight » The Stall » Factors Affecting Stalling Airspeed

EAGP3Q50   Answer C

Differential ailerons operate so that when the control column is moved to roll the aircraft, the upgoing aileron moves up through a great angle than the downgoing aileron moves down. This is done to minimise 'adverse yaw' – the tendency of the aircraft to yaw against the direction of roll when the ailerons are deflected (because the downgoing aileron produces more drag than the upgoing aileron).

For more information see EAGP1Q47.

Further Reference: PPL4 » Principles of Flight » Stability and Control » Control in Roll

Human Performance and Limitations

Human Performance and Limitations Essential Revision

▶ The Functions of the Body (Basic Physiology)

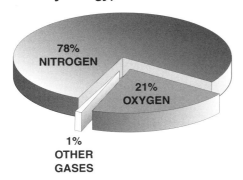

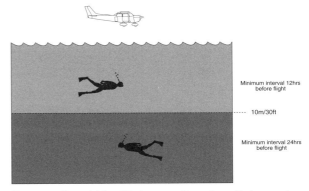

The **proportions of gases** in the atmosphere remain fairly constant with increasing altitude although pressure reduces with increasing altitude.

Blood is moved around the body by the **circulatory system**, which transports nutrients, water and oxygen to body cells and carries away wastes such as carbon dioxide. The body's store of **Carbon Dioxide** (CO_2) regulates the breathing rate.

Hypoxia is the situation where there is insufficient oxygen to meet the needs of the body, it is generally considered to become a problem once flying above 10,000ft. The symptoms of hypoxia (beginning with the first signs) can include:

- *Personality changes and impaired judgement*
- *Confusion and difficulty concentrating*
- *Loss of co-ordination*
- *Drowsiness*
- *Headaches, dizziness and nausea*
- *Blue/grey skin colour*
- *Hyperventilation*
- *Loss of basic senses*
- *Unconsciousness*

The problems associated with hypoxia become more severe with increasing altitude, and the time available for the pilot to perform useful tasks without any supplementary oxygen – the **time of 'useful consciousness'** – is reduced.

Hyperventilation is 'over-breathing' which can be caused intense stress or anxiety, certain levels of vibration and turbulence, high *g*, hypoxia, pain or motion sickness. Symptoms include:

- *Dizziness, light-headedness*
- *Tingling sensations in the extremities*
- *Vision impairment*
- *Hot and cold feelings*
- *Unconsciousness*

Do not fly within 24 hours of **scuba diving** using compressed air (12 hours if diving depth does not exceed 10m/30ft). **Decompression Sickness** is the situation where nitrogen comes out of solution in the blood, causing possible severe pain especially in the joints.

The air cavity of the middle **ear** is connected to the nose and throat via the *Eustachian tube*. Air pressure within the middle ear is equalised to the external pressure via the Eustachian tube. However, if due to illness or infection, the Eustachian tube becomes swollen or blocked, this pressure equalisation may not take place and the result can be severe pain and ultimately bleeding into the middle ear or perforation of the eardrum. A pilot or passenger with a **cold,** the **flu** or any other condition that may lead to a blocked nose or sinuses is strongly advised to **not fly.**

The basic components of the **eye** are:

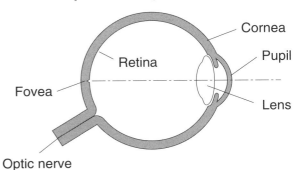

To see a faintly-lit image in **poor light**, look slightly (10°) to one side of it.

▶ Health and Flying

2 units of alcohol =   or   or

Alcohol leaves the body at the rate of one unit per hour. One unit is approximately equivalent to one small measure of wine or spirit or half a pint of beer. Hypoxia will occur at a lower altitude in a **smoker** than in a non-smoker. Do not fly within 24 hours of **donating blood**. **Carbon Monoxide (CO)** is colourless, odourless and very toxic. It is a by-product of the combustion process and may enter the cockpit via a leaky exhaust/heating system.

The most common cause of **in-flight pilot incapacitation** is gastroenteritis.

▶ The Functions of the Mind (Basic Psychology)

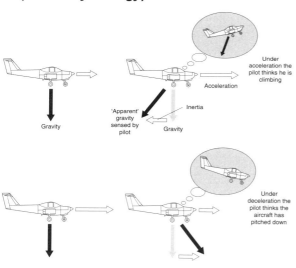

To avoid **spatial disorientation** in IMC or poor visual conditions, trust the flight instruments rather than 'seat of the pants' sensations. Flying over a sloping cloud bank can lead the pilot to bank to aircraft away from wings level flight in order to align with the cloud bank rather than the horizon.

A downsloping runway will make the approach seem low, an upsloping runway will make the approach seem high.

A wide runway will make the approach seem too low, a narrow runway will make the approach seem too high.

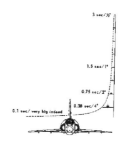

Aircraft on collision course stay on a constant bearing to each other. The image of an aircraft approaching head-on grows very slowly until the last few seconds, when the image size grows very rapidly. The eyes can only 'see' when at rest, not when moving.

Situational awareness means that a pilot is considering all available information to exercise safe and accurate judgement.

▶ Stress and Managing Stress

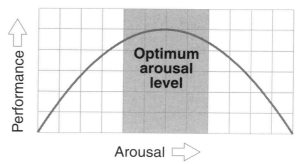

▶ Personalities and Cockpit (or Crew) Resource Management

In a 'two crew' cockpit, even the more junior or less experienced pilot should always **openly express any doubts**, concerns or misgivings.

▶Cockpit Design and Procedures

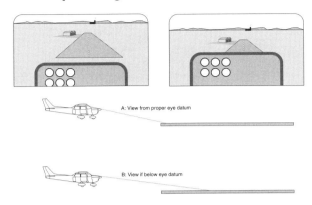

A: View from proper eye datum

B: View if below eye datum

A pilot seated below the **Design Eye Position** (eye line reference) will have a poor view ahead of and below the aircraft, especially on approach.

The 'three needle' altimeter display is very common, but open to misinterpretation as the levels above 10,000ft may not be immediately obvious.

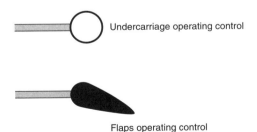

Undercarriage operating control

Flaps operating control

Cockpit controls used to operate different systems should look and feel different to each other.

▶Safety and Survival Equipment

Motion sickness occurs because of conflicting information being received from the eyes, the vestibular apparatus of the ears and the other sensory organs.

JAA Private Pilot Licence – Aeroplanes & Helicopters

Human Performance and Limitations

Time allowed:	30 minutes
No. of questions:	20
Total Marks:	100

Instructions:

The paper consists of 20 multiple choice questions, each carries 5 marks. The pass mark is 75% (i.e. 15 questions or more must be answered correctly). Marks are not deducted for incorrect answers.

Be sure to carefully read each question and ensure that you understand it before considering the answer choices. Only one of the answers is complete and correct; the others are either incomplete, incorrect or based on a misconception.

You should indicate the correct answer by placing a cross in the appropriate box of the answer sheet. If you decide to change an answer, you should erase the original choice and put a cross in the box representing your new selection.

Each question has an average answer time of 1 minute 30 seconds. No credit is given for unanswered questions.

Human Performance and Limitations Practice – Paper 1

1. If a pilot experiences "spatial disorientation" whilst flying on instruments, the best solution is to:

(a) Trust the senses

(b) Request ATC assistance

(c) Refer to, and believe in, the flight instruments

(d) Close the eyes and fly by 'feel'

---

2. The breathing rate is regulated largely by chemical balance within the body, and in particular the level of stored ....(i)......... . Select the word(s) that correctly complete this statement:

(i)

(a) Oxygen

(b) Nitrogen

(c) Carbon dioxide

(d) Carbon monoxide

---

3. Decompression Sickness (DCS) or 'the bends' can occur in particular after scuba or sub-aqua diving when:

(a) Nitrogen forms into bubbles in the body as atmospheric pressure is reduced

(b) Oxygen forms into bubbles in the body as atmospheric pressure is reduced

(c) Carbon Dioxide forms into bubbles in the body as atmospheric pressure is reduced

(d) Carbon Monoxide forms into bubbles in the body as atmospheric pressure is reduced

---

4. The effects of hypoxia (insufficient oxygen) are likely to occur differently in a smoker than in a non-smoker. A heavy smoker is likely to experience the onset of hypoxia:

(a) Less severely than a non-smoker

(b) At a slower rate than a non-smoker

(c) At a higher altitude than a non-smoker

(d) At a lower altitude than a non-smoker

5. In the diagrams below, the left-hand diagram (A) represents an approach to a level runway. In the right-hand diagram (B), an aircraft at the same height and distance from a runway with exactly the same dimensions, is likely to be approaching a runway that is:

(a) upsloping

(b) downsloping

(c) level but with a transverse slope

(d) contaminated

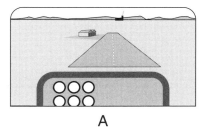
A

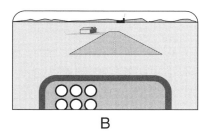
B

6. As altitude increases:

(a) The proportion of oxygen in the air reduces and the proportion of nitrogen increases

(b) The proportion of oxygen and other gases in the air remains largely unchanged

(c) The partial pressure of gases increases

(d) The proportion of oxygen in the air increases and the proportion of nitrogen decreases

7. If a pilot considers that he or she has been exposed to exhaust fumes during a flight, the possibility of ......(i)..... should be considered, which may preclude flying for .....(ii)...... .

	(i)	(ii)
(a)	Hypoxia	about an hour
(b)	Carbon Monoxide Poisoning	at least a number of days
(c)	Carbon Monoxide Poisoning	no more than 30 minutes
(d)	Hyperventilation	12 hours

8. Which if the following options best describes the body's nervous systems?

(a) Central, Peripheral, Autonomic

(b) Core, exterior, extra-sensory

(c) Peripheral, Internal, Hyperactive

(d) Autonomic, Automatic, Laundromatic

9. Many medicines can be bought 'over-the-counter' (OTC) – that is without the need for a prescription. In relation to such 'self-medication', the UK CAA recommend that:

(a) Any 'OTC' medicine will have no significant side-effects

(b) Any side-effects will not be effective at altitude

(c) Any pilot considering such 'self-medication' should consult an Authorised Medical Examiner (AME)

(d) Medicines bought from a pharmacy are guaranteed free from side-effects

10. The time available for the pilot to perform useful tasks without any supplementary oxygen is generally referred to as the:

(a) Hyperventilation period

(b) Hypoxic allowance

(c) Time of Diminished Responsibility

(d) Time of Useful Consciousness

11. The desirable condition for a pilot of good situational awareness is best achieved by:

(a) Using all available information to make safe decisions and exercise good judgement

(b) Being aware of the 'majority view' in a group and conforming with it

(c) Disregarding data that does not fit with a previously formed opinion

(d) Focussing on a single instrument indication

12. Four units of alcohol should be eliminated from the blood in approximately what time?

(a) One hour

(b) Eight hours

(c) Two hours

(d) Four Hours

13. Following an abrupt deceleration manoeuvre, a pilot flying in poor visibility might experience a strong sensation of pitching nose-down. The best response is to:

(a) Reduce power

(b) Trim nose-up

(c) Trust, and act according to, the flight instruments

(d) Pitch nose down

14. When flying in poor visibility conditions, such as haze, obstructions and obstacles may appear to be:

(a) Higher than they actually are

(b) Closer than they actually are

(c) More numerous than they actually are

(d) More distant than they actually are

15. Where two pilots are flying together and acting as flight crew, one of the pilots should feel able to openly express any doubts about a course of action chosen by the other:

(a) Regardless of the relative experience of the two pilots

(b) Only if the aircraft is in grave or imminent danger

(c) Only if a protocol has been agreed with the aircraft operator

(d) Only if the 'questioning' pilot is the more experienced

16. A light aircraft flying at 90 knots is conflicting head-on with a military jet flying at 420 knots. At what rate (approximately) are they closing in terms of seconds per mile?

(a) 15 seconds per mile

(b) 10 seconds per mile

(c) 20 seconds per mile

(d) 7 seconds per mile

17. The circulatory system is responsible for:

(a) Respiration

(b) Transmitting nerve signals to the brain

(c) The sense of vision

(d) Moving blood around the body

18. When the eyes are at rest and with no distant object to focus on, they tend to focus:

(a) At a point about 10km away

(b) At infinity

(c) At a point about 1km away

(d) At a point about 1-2m away

19. Hyperventilation is caused by ….. (i) ….. and can be treated by ….. (ii) …..:

	(i)	(ii)
(a)	over-breathing	breathing 100% oygen
(b)	insufficient oxygen	breathing 100% oygen
(c)	insufficient food	eating sugary food
(d)	over-breathing	calming the victim to restore a normal breathing rate

20. To reduce the possibility of suffering from Decompression Sickness ('the bends'), it is recommended that a minimum period of ….. is allowed between scuba diving to depths in excess of 30ft and flying. The missing figure is:

(a) 6 hours

(b) 12 hours

(c) 24 hours

(d) 48 hours

1. A heavy smoker is likely to experience the symptoms and effects of hypoxia at .... than a non-smoker. Select the phrase which correctly complete this statement.

   (a) the same altitude

   (b) a higher altitude

   (c) a slower rate

   (d) a lower altitude

2. After drinking a pint of average strength beer or lager (taken to be two units of alcohol), how long will be required to eliminate this amount of alcohol from the blood?

   (a) Two hours

   (b) One Hour

   (c) 30 minutes

   (d) The alcohol level is too low to be eliminated from the blood

3. A pilot suffering from spatial disorientation during flight in poor visibility is recommended to:

   (a) Close the eyes and rely on balance sensations

   (b) Orientate the aircraft with any visual reference, no matter how vague

   (c) Assess the balance and acceleration sensations to decide on control inputs

   (d) Assess, and rely upon, the flight instruments

4. A pilot flying in straight and level flight, but decelerating, may experience a sensation of:

   (a) Rolling and turning

   (b) Skidding

   (c) Pitching nose-down

   (d) Pitching nose-up

5. A pilot making a visual approach to a down-sloping runway may well make an approach that is ......(i)...... than intended:

   (a) slower

   (b) more shallow

   (c) steeper

   (d) closer

6. You are flying with a more-experienced pilot, who is acting as Pilot in Command and has selected a course of action that you consider to be dangerous.

   The safest course of action is to:

   (a) Note the matter and report it to the relevant authorities after the flight

   (b) Make a report to ATC

   (c) Seek clarification from the pilot after the flight

   (d) Openly express your views.

7. An altimeter incorporating a 'three needle' display is best described as:

(a) Reliable but inaccurate, difficult to misinterpret

(b) Unreliable, inaccurate but easy to interpret

(c) Easy to misinterpret, but reliable and accurate

(d) Rarely reliable or accurate but easy to interpret

8. A light aircraft flying at an airspeed of 90 knots is approaching a military jet head-on. The jet is flying at 390 knots. If one of the pilots spots the other aircraft at a range of 3nm, how long is left to avoid a collision?

(a) About 20 seconds

(b) About 30 seconds

(c) About 40 seconds

(d) About 50 seconds

9. Ideally, cockpit controls which operate different systems should:

(a) Look and feel different

(b) Be differentiated by colour alone

(c) Look and feel the same

(d) Be placed close to each other

10. Good situational awareness is an invaluable attribute in any pilot. How can situational awareness best be maintained?

(a) By relying on data which reinforces your existing perceptions

(b) By focusing on a limited number of factors, to avoid confusion

(c) By disregarding information which conflicts with your established perception

(d) By making use of all available information in the decision-making process

11. Hyperventilation should be suspected if a victim is suffering from:

(a) Dizziness, blurred vision and anxiety below FL100

(b) Confusion and drowsiness above FL100

(c) Headache and nausea above FL100

(d) Skin irritation and pains in the joints above FL180

12. Pressure between the middle ear and outside air cannot be equalised if:

(a) Due to a cold the Eustachain tube is blocked

(b) Due to hypoxia the ear drum is perforated

(c) Due to excessive noise the rods and cones are damaged

(d) Due to motion sickness the vestibular apparatus is blocked

13. Which of the following is <u>least</u> likely to cause hyperventilation?

(a) Intense stress or anxiety

(b) Certain levels of vibration and turbulence

(c) Tiredness

(d) Motion sickness

14. The medical condition of gastro-enteritis:

(a) Is the commonest cause of in-flight pilot incapacitation and renders a pilot unfit to fly

(b) Does not preclude the pilot from flying provided it is treated with medication

(c) Does not prevent the pilot flying as a co-pilot

(d) Is acceptable in a pilot if treated with 'over the counter' medicines only

15. A pilot may experience a false sensation of pitching nose down if an aircraft that is actually in straight and level flight:

(a) Accelerates

(b) Yaws

(c) Decelerates

(d) Rolls

16. When approaching a runway wider than the pilot is used to, the aircraft will appear to be:

(a) At too fast an airspeed

(b) Low on the approach

(c) On the correct approach slope

(d) High on the approach

17. When a person is deprived of the oxygen that the body needs, they are said to be suffering from:

(a) Hyperventilation

(b) Hypothermia

(c) Hysteresis

(d) Hypoxia

18. During a night flight, you are advised of conflicting traffic in the 12 o'clock position. For the best chance of spotting the traffic you should look:

(a) About 10 degrees either side of dead-ahead

(b) Dead-ahead

(c) It depends on the aircraft's heading

(d) Directly above the aircraft

19. Within the eye, the retina:

(a) Focuses light rays on the optic disc

(b) Focuses light rays passing through the lens

(c) Protects the cornea

(d) Contains two types of light-sensitive cells

20. What is the generally recognised minimum period for eyes to adapt from bright light to full night vision?

(a) 5 minutes

(b) 30 minutes

(c) 50 minutes

(d) 10 minutes

1. During flight you have been trained to consider all input, to constantly up-date your situation and to plan ahead. This desirable action is known as:

   (a) Situational awareness

   (b) Conformality

   (c) Convergence

   (d) Confirmation Bias

2. The eye datum of the Design Eye Position or Eye Line Reference is established:

   (a) To enable the pilot to see all his flight instruments with minimum scan movement of the head.

   (b) To determine the eventual size of the flight deck and where window frames will be positioned so as not to interfere with the pilot's field of view.

   (c) So that the pilot can maintain an optimal view of all the important displays in the cockpit, and of the world outside.

   (d) To create the datum for aircraft cabin measurements

3. If flying over a cloud layer when the real horizon is obscured:

   (a) The pilot can be sure of wings level flight through visual reference alone

   (b) To the pilot, the aircraft may appear higher than it actually is

   (c) A sloping cloud bank may cause the pilot to bank

   (d) The pilot can be assured of maintaining the correct attitude

4. A pilot may suffer a visual illusion that the aircraft is too low when approaching a runway that is …… than normal.

   (a) softer

   (b) more narrow

   (c) wider

   (d) longer

5. After diving with scuba equipment if a depth of 30ft has not been exceeded, the recommended time interval before flying is:

   (a) 6 hrs.

   (b) 24 hrs.

   (c) 48 hrs.

   (d) 12 hrs.

6. If a pilot is suffering from a cold, a likely consequence is:

   (a) The Eustachian tubes may become blocked meaning that the pilot is unable to equalise pressure between the middle ear and the atmosphere

   (b) The inner ear may become blocked, meaning that the pilot is unable to equalise pressure between the inner ear and the middle ear

   (c) The middle ear may become blocked, meaning that the pilot is unable to equalise pressure between the Eustachian tubes and the inner ear

   (d) The outer ear may become blocked, meaning that the Eustachian tube is unable to equalise pressure with the inner ear

7. Successful treatment for hyperventilation is likely to include:

    (a) Increasing the heart rate

    (b) Reducing altitude

    (c) Slowing to a normal breathing rate, by re-breathing exhaled air if necessary

    (d) Increasing the breathing rate

8. A key feature of decompression sickness (DCS), which is a particular danger following scuba diving, is:

    (a) The body has insufficient oxygen to meet its needs

    (b) Nitrogen forms bubbles in the body as pressure is increased

    (c) Nitrogen forms bubbles in the body as pressure is reduced

    (d) An imbalance of Carbon Dioxide affects the breathing rate

9. If a pilot considers that he or she may have been exposed to exhaust fumes in flight, he or she should expect to be fit to fly:

    (a) Once signed off as fit by an instructor

    (b) Within an hour of breathing uncontaminated air

    (c) No more than six hours after last exposure to Carbon Monoxide

    (d) After at least several days

10. When on a head-on collision course with another aircraft, that aircraft will appear to:

    (a) Grow bigger at a constant rate

    (b) Grow bigger slowly, and then grow bigger rapidly at close range

    (c) Remain at a constant image size

    (d) Grow in size more slowly as range decreases

11. To spot a distant and faint object at night, it is best to:

    (a) Look directly at the object

    (b) Close one eye

    (c) Squint

    (d) Look about 10° to one side of the object

12. A military jet flying at 480 knots is approaching 'head-on' to a light aircraft which is flying at 120 knots. If the light aircraft pilot spots the approaching military jet at a range of 2nm, what period of time is available to avoid collision?

    (a) Around 12 seconds

    (b) Around 30 seconds

    (c) Around 25 seconds

    (d) Around 50 seconds

13. Breathing too rapidly, apprehension or motion sickness, can cause:

(a) Hyperventilation

(b) Hypoxia

(c) Hydroxia

(d) Hypoglycaemia

14. The <u>initial</u> effects of hypoxia (ie insufficient oxygen to meet the body's needs) are:

(a) Dizziness, nausea

(b) Impaired judgement, loss of inhibitions, confusion, difficulty in concentrating

(c) Loss of consciousness

(d) Loss of muscular co-ordination

15. The period available for a pilot to perform useful tasks without supplemental oxygen and before the onset of hypoxia is best described as:

(a) The Time of Useful Consciousness, which reduces with increasing altitude

(b) The Time of Useful Consciousness, which is unchanged with increasing altitude

(c) The Time of Useful Consciousness, which increases with increasing altitude

(d) The Time of Total Consciousness, which increases with increasing altitude

16. The most common cause of sudden in-flight incapacitation in pilots is:

(a) A heart attack

(b) A blood clot

(c) Lack of caffeine

(d) Acute gastroenteritis

17. In the cockpit of a 'complex' single engine aircraft:

(a) The undercarriage and flap controls should look and feel the same

(b) The undercarriage and flap controls should look and feel different

(c) The undercarriage and flap controls should be next to each other

(d) The undercarriage and flap controls should only be accessible from the right hand seat

18. In the diagrams below, assuming that in all views the aircraft is on the correct approach angle to land, the runway that is most likely to be downsloping is:

(a) Runway A

(b) Runways A or C

(c) Runway C

(d) Runway B

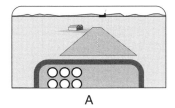
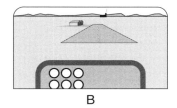
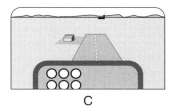

        A   B   C

19. As altitude increases, hypoxia becomes a risk because:

(a) The proportion of oxygen in the air reduces

(b) The proportion of oxygen in the air increases

(c) The proportion of nitrogen in the air increases

(d) The partial pressure of oxygen in the air decreases

20. The auditory range of the average human is in the region of:

(a) 20,000Hz – 20,000,000Hz

(b) 2MHz – 20MHz

(c) 2Hz – 20Hz

(d) 20Hz – 20,000Hz

Paper 1 Answers and Explanations

EHFP1Q1   Answer C

It is not uncommon for pilots – even those with considerable flying experience – to receive conflicting signals about the aircraft's attitude when flying in poor or zero flight visibility. In these circumstances, the recommended response is to rely on, and trust, the aircraft instruments, as in the absence of a visual horizon these are far more likely to be giving an accurate representation of the aircraft's attitude and performance than the balance senses.

Further Reference: PPL5 » Human Factors » The Functions of the Mind (Basic Psychology) » Spatial Disorientation and Visual Illusions

EHFP1Q2   Answer C

Breathing rate (respiration) is largely controlled by the level of Carbon Dioxide stored in the body. It happens that the level of Carbon Dioxide stored within the body is much greater than the level of oxygen stored.

The role of Carbon Dioxide in regulating breathing rate is the reason why one method of treating hyperventilation (over-breathing) is to breathe into a bag held over the nose and mouth. Re-breathing exhaled air (which contains high levels of Carbon Dioxide) helps to restore the body's Carbon Dioxide levels, so returning breathing rate to normal.

Further Reference: PPL5 » Human Factors » The Functions of the Body (Basic Physiology) » Breathing Problems and Flight at High Altitude

EHFP1Q3   Answer A

Reduced pressure affects the store of nitrogen within the body. At sea-level pressure, nitrogen exists within the body in solution. During a climb to high altitude, the reduced atmospheric pressure allows nitrogen to come out of solution and form into bubbles. These are carried around the bloodstream and tend to congregate in the joints – shoulder, elbow, wrists, knees and ankles. The result can vary from mild discomfort to severe pain which may cause collapse. This pain is known in diving circles as "the bends" and is the most common symptom of decompression sickness ('DCS').

Further Reference: PPL5 » Human Factors » The Functions of the Body (Basic Physiology) » Breathing Problems and Flight at High Altitude

EHFP1Q4   Answer D

A smoker will suffer more than a non-smoker from any degree of hypoxia and so it is likely that the symptoms of hypoxia may manifest themselves at a lower altitude in a heavy smoker than in a non-smoker.

Further Reference: PPL5 » Human Factors » The Functions of the Body (Basic Physiology) » Breathing Problems and Flight at High Altitude

EHFP1Q5   Answer B

Level runway   Downsloping runway   Upsloping runway

During a visual approach, pilots tend to rely on the appearance of the runway to judge the approach angle. On approach to a down-sloping runway, the aircraft often appears to the pilot to be too low. Approaching an up-sloping runway, the aircraft may well appear to the pilot to be too high. This may well result in too shallow an approach. In addition, an up-sloping runway will appear to be longer than it really is whilst a down-sloping runway will appear to be shorter.

Further Reference: PPL5 » Human Factors » The Functions of the Mind (Basic Psychology) » Spatial Disorientation and Visual Illusions

EHFP1Q6   Answer B

The *proportion* of gases within the air stays largely unchanged with increasing altitude, however the *amount* of air, including its proportion of oxygen, taken in during each breath reduces markedly with the decreasing pressure (as altitude increases, pressure decreases).

Further Reference: PPL5 » Human Factors » The Functions of the Body (Basic Physiology) » Composition of the Atmosphere

EHFP1Q7   Answer B

If Carbon Monoxide poisoning is suspected at any time, such as when exhaust fumes have entered the cockpit, the pilot should land at the earliest available opportunity and have the aircraft (and him/herself and any passengers) properly examined. After exposure to exhaust gases in the cockpit, it may be several days before a pilot is fit to fly and in any event it is important to seek proper medical advice before flying again.

Further Reference: PPL5 » Human Factors » Health and Flying » Toxic Hazards

EHFP1Q8   Answer A

The body has a number of nervous systems, and text books do not all agree on what they are called. The consensus is that there is a Central Nervous System (consisting of the spinal cord and brain) and a Peripheral Nervous System. This is sub-divided into the sensory-somatic nervous system (the sense of sight, hearing, smell etc) and the autonomic nervous system that runs between the central nervous system and internal organs such as the heart and lungs.

Further Reference: PPL5 » Human Factors » Health and Flying » Alcohol and Drugs

EHFP1Q9   Answer C

Many very common medicines that are available without prescription (ie Over-The-Counter) can have very serious side-effects. For example, there have been documented cases of total in-flight incapacitation caused by a well-known non-prescription painkiller.

As a general rule, it is worth working on the principle that if you are ill enough to need medication, you're probably too ill to fly. In any case, it is recommended that the advice of an Authorised Medical Examiner is sought before mixing medication with flying.

Further Reference: PPL5 » Human Factors » Health and Flying » Common Ailments and Medication

EHFP1Q10   Answer D

An ability to recognise the onset of hypoxia is vital to any pilot flying at high levels. The risk of hypoxia becomes more severe with increasing altitude, and the time available for the pilot to perform useful tasks without any supplementary oxygen – the time of 'useful consciousness' – is reduced.

Further Reference: PPL5 » Human Factors » The Functions of the Body (Basic Physiology) » Breathing Problems and Flight at High Altitude

EHFP1Q11   Answer A

To say that a pilot has good situational awareness is to say that he or she knows what is going on both in the aircraft and around it, and thus can make safe and accurate decisions and exercise good judgment based on **all available information.**

Further Reference: PPL5 » Human Factors » The Functions of the Mind (Basic Psychology) » Situational Awareness, Confirmation Bias

EHFP1Q12   Answer D

Although this advice is subject to a great many caveats, and you wouldn't want to bet your licence on it, for the purposes of answering this question it is assumed that one unit of alcohol takes one hour to be eliminated from the blood; hence four units would take four hours.

Further Reference: PPL5 » Human Factors » Health and Flying » Alcohol and Drugs

EHFP1Q13   Answer C

In conditions of limited or zero outside visual reference, it is quite possible for the pilot to sense changes of attitude that are false. In good visibility, these sensations are over-ruled by the strong visual cues of the aircraft's true attitude. When these visual cues are missing, it is imperative that the pilot uses, and trusts, the interpretation of the flight instruments to control the aircraft.

It is to all intents and purposes impossible to fly an aircraft by 'seat-of-the-pants' sensations without reference to the view outside or the flight instruments. Further, without proper training even flying 'on instruments' may not be possible. Studies have shown that a pilot without instrument flying training will lose control of the aircraft once outside visual references are removed in an average of three minutes.

Further Reference: PPL5 » Human Factors » The Functions of the Mind (Basic Psychology) » Spatial Disorientation and Visual Illusions

EHFP1Q14   Answer B

When flying in hazy conditions, objects at the limit of visible detection, perhaps partly clouded by haze, will appear further away than they really are. So mountains or obstructions can apparently suddenly loom up out of the haze when the pilot thought at first glance that they were a safe distance away.

Further Reference: PPL5 » Human Factors » The Functions of the Mind (Basic Psychology) » Spatial Disorientation and Visual Illusions

EHFP1Q15   Answer A

Regardless of the relative experience of the pilots, as flight crew any pilot should openly express any doubts or concerns about the operation of the flight, including the actions and decisions of a more experienced crew member.

Creating an atmosphere in the cockpit where such doubts or concerns can be expressed is an important part of Crew (or Cockpit) Resource Management – CRM.

Further Reference: PPL5 » Human Factors » Personalities and Cockpit (or Crew) Resource Management » Group Decision Making

EHFP1Q16   Answer D

The closing speed of the aircraft is found by adding their two speeds together. 90 + 420 = 510 knots – or 510 nautical miles (nm) per hour.

At 60 knots, an aircraft covers 60nm per hour, or 1nm per minute (there being 60 minutes in an hour). Therefore dividing 510kts by 60mins gives a speed of 8·5 miles per minute.

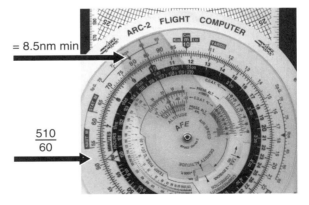

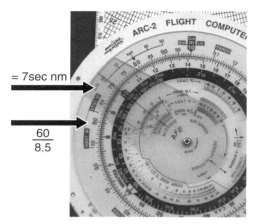

= 7sec nm

$\frac{60}{8.5}$

To convert this figure into seconds per mile, divide 60 by 8·5

The answer is slightly over seven seconds per mile.

This calculation can be done mentally if the speeds involved are multiples of 60; for example 420 knots = seven miles per minute (420/60). 90 knots = one and a half miles per minute (90/60) etc.

Further Reference: PPL5 » Human Factors » The Functions of the Mind (Basic Psychology) » Lookout

---

EHFP1Q17   Answer D

Blood is moved around the body by the circulatory system, which transports nutrients, water and oxygen to body cells and carries away wastes such as carbon dioxide.

Further Reference: PPL5 » Human Factors » The Functions of the Body (Basic Physiology) » The Breathing Machine

---

EHFP1Q18   Answer D

Unless an effort is made to focus on distant objects, when at rest the eyes tend to focus on a point just 1-2 metres ahead. This, it must be said, is not the ideal place to spot an oncoming aircraft!

To improve your chances of spotting conflicting traffic, make a conscious effort to focus on a distant object (such as the horizon, clouds etc.) during your lookout scan.

Further Reference: PPL5 » Human Factors » The Functions of the Mind (Basic Psychology) » Lookout

---

EHFP1Q19   Answer D

Hyperventilation is a condition of over-breathing – that is breathing deeper and more rapidly than is necessary. Because the symptoms of hyperventilation can be quite similar to those for hypoxia, it is generally considered that when flying at a cabin altitude (ie the effective altitude inside the aircraft) of below FL100 – pressure altitude 10,000ft – breathing problems are more likely to be caused by hyperventilation than hypoxia.

The key to treatment of hyperventilation is to return the breathing rate to normal, if possible by helping the victim to become calm enough to return to a normal breathing rate.

Further Reference: PPL5 » Human Factors » The Functions of the Body (Basic Physiology) » Breathing Problems and Flight at High Altitude

---

EHFP1Q20   Answer C

The general advice is not to fly within 24 hours of scuba diving (or 12 hours if a depth of 30ft / 10 metres has not been exceeded). This figure is, of course, a minimum and in some circumstances a longer interval may be prudent.

Minimum interval 12hrs
before flight

10m/30ft

Minimum interval 24hrs
before flight

Further Reference: PPL5 » Human Factors » The Functions of the Body (Basic Physiology) » Breathing Problems and Flight at High Altitude

Paper 2 Answers and Explanations

EHFP2Q1   Answer D

A smoker will suffer more than a non-smoker from any degree of hypoxia and it is likely that the symptoms of hypoxia will occur at a lower altitude in a heavy smoker than in a non-smoker.

Further Reference: PPL5 » Human Factors » The Functions of the Body (Basic Physiology) » Breathing Problems and Flight at High Altitude

EHFP2Q2   Answer A

The CAA guidance is that alcohol leaves the bloodstream at the rate of one unit per hour. Therefore, in the example given the two units of alcohol will take two hours to leave the body.

It is worth noting that the general assumption that one unit of alcohol is equivalent to half a pint of beer, or one glass or wine, or one measure of spirits, may be becoming outdated. 'Premium' strength beers and lagers, and larger measures of wine and spirits, make it more likely that more units of alcohol may be consumed than the standard guidance recognises.

Further Reference: PPL5 » Human Factors » Health and Flying » Alcohol and Drugs

EHFP2Q3   Answer D

It is a well-known phenomena in pilots without proper instrument flying training (and occasionally, even those with considerable instrument flying experience), that in conditions of poor or completely removed visual references, the balance and acceleration senses from the inner ear mechanisms can be over-powering. This can lead the pilot into losing control of the aircraft as these senses give the pilot a false picture of the aircraft's attitude.

Some years ago, it was common practice as part of the PPL course to place the pilot in conditions where there was no visual reference, and then invite him/her to attempt to maintain straight and level flight by balance senses alone. The result was nearly always a quick entry into a spiral dive.

In some cases a very limited visual reference (a brief glimpse of the ground, an ill-defined horizon on a very hazy day over water, flight between shallow cloud layers) can be just as disorientating.

In all cases, the only real answer is to trust, and act upon, the information from the flight instruments. And also, of course, not to get into these conditions unless you are properly trained and prepared.

Further Reference: PPL5 » Human Factors » The Functions of the Mind (Basic Psychology) » Spatial Disorientation and Visual Illusions

EHFP2Q4   Answer C

In general terms, under deceleration there is a sensation of pitching nose-down; under acceleration there is a sensation of pitching nose-up.

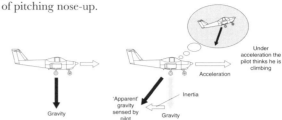

These false perceptions are common causes of spatial disorientation.

Further Reference: PPL5 » Human Factors » The Functions of the Mind (Basic Psychology) » Spatial Disorientation and Visual Illusions

EHFP2Q5   Answer C

Sloping runways are a common cause of visual illusions. Approaching a down-sloping runway, the aircraft will appear to be lower (on a more shallow approach) than it really is. As a result the pilot may eventually approach higher, and consequently make a steeper approach, than intended.

Conversely, approaching an up-sloping runway the pilot may well perceive that the aircraft is higher than it actually is, leading to a more shallow approach than intended.

For further detail, see explanation HFP1Q5

Further Reference: PPL5 » Human Factors » The Functions of the Mind (Basic Psychology) » Spatial Disorientation and Visual Illusions

EHFP2Q6   Answer D

The prime advantage of having two (or more) pilots in the cockpit is for each crew member to act as a series of checks and balances. Gross errors and mistakes are, in general, less likely to occur where both pilots are actively involved in the decision making process and are able to express their views openly.

Fatal accidents involving professional aircrew have occurred where at least one crew member has recognised a dangerous situation, but failed to make his views known openly enough to influence events.

Further Reference: PPL5 » Human Factors » Personalities and Cockpit (or Crew) Resource Management » Group Decision-Making

EHFP2Q7   Answer C

Although the three-needle altimeter is generally considered reliable and accurate, the three needle display can be misinterpreted. Although most pilots soon learn to be able to assimilate the 'hundreds' and 'thousands' needles at a glance, pilots who rarely fly above 10,000 feet may not immediately grasp the significance of the third 'tens of thousands' needle.

For this reason, many three-needle altimeters have a 'striped area' which is visible when the aircraft is below 10,000ft and gradually covered up by a central disc as the aircraft climbs above 10,000ft.

Further Reference: PPL5 » Human Factors » Cockpit Design and Procedures » Flight Instrument Displays

EHFP2Q8   Answer A

The two aircraft have a closing speed of 480 knots (90 + 390). At this speed, the aircraft are closing at a rate of 480nm per hour, which is (480/60) 8 miles per minute, or (60/8) a mile every 7.5 seconds.

Thus, at three miles the aircraft have about (3 x 7.5) = 22.5 seconds before collision, so realistically no more than 20 seconds to react.

For further information, see the explanation HFP1Q16

Further Reference: PPL5 » Human Factors » The Functions of the Mind (Basic Psychology) » Lookout

EHFP2Q9   Answer A

Ideally cockpit controls which operate different systems should look and feel different from each other. In the case of flap and undercarriage controls, one really useful design feature is to shape the cockpit controls so that they look and feel like the item they operate; the undercarriage control looks like a wheel, the flap control resembles a flap.

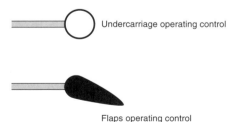

Undercarriage operating control

Flaps operating control

Further Reference: PPL5 » Human Factors » Cockpit Design and Procedures » Controls

EHFP2Q10   Answer D

Good situational awareness is an attribute which many pilots feel comes with experience. In reality it is more a mind set, but one that is easier to attain as the pilot reaches the stage where there is enough 'spare' mental capacity to consider and process the mass of information available to a pilot at any one time (and not just whilst actually flying the aircraft).

The opposite of good situational awareness is where a pilot either disregards information that conflicts with his pre-conceived idea of what is happening, or chooses to give undue weight to information favourable to that perception (ie one favourable weather report in a mass of bad ones).

It is the processing of all available information, and a willingness to consider even information that does not fit with your pre-conceived model of what is happening, that forms the basis of good situational awareness. And good situational awareness is the foundation of sound judgement.

Further Reference: PPL5 » Human Factors » The Functions of the Mind (Basic Psychology) » Situational Awareness, Confirmation Bias

EHFP2Q11   Answer A

Hyperventilation or over-breathing is a condition where breathing is both deeper and more rapid than necessary. It is a condition most often associated with intense stress or anxiety, although it can also be caused by certain levels of vibration and turbulence, high g, hypoxia, pain or motion sickness. The symptoms of hyperventilation are:

- Dizziness, light-headed feelings and a sense of 'unreality'
- Tingling sensations, particularly in the fingers and hands, toes and feet
- Vision impairment such as blurring, tunnel vision or clouded vision
- Hot and cold feelings around the body
- Unconsciousness

The symptoms of hyperventilation and hypoxia are quite similar, but in general if above 10,000ft, assume hypoxia and act accordingly. If significantly below that altitude, hyperventilation is more likely.

Further Reference: PPL5 » Human Factors » The Functions of the Body (Basic Physiology) » Breathing Problems and Flight at High Altitude

EHFP2Q12   Answer A

If, due to illness or infection, the Eustachian tubes become swollen or blocked (this most often happens if suffering from a cold, sore throat, rhinitis, sinusitis or hay fever), the result can be severe pain and ultimately bleeding into the middle ear or perforation of the eardrum. Not surprisingly, a pilot suffering from a cold or similar ailment is advised not to fly.

Further Reference: PPL5 » Human Factors » The Functions of the Body (Basic Physiology) » The Ears

EHFP2Q13   Answer C

Hyperventilation is often associated with intense stress or anxiety, although it can also be caused by certain levels of vibration and turbulence, high *g*, hypoxia, pain or motion sickness

Further Reference: PPL5 » Human Factors » The Functions of the Body (Basic Physiology) » Breathing Problems and Flight at High Altitude

EHFP2Q14   Answer A

Gastro-enteritis is a general term for an infection of the stomach or intestines, which can cause acute abdominal pain, nausea, vomiting and diarrhoea. Although total incapacitation through gastroenteritis is rare, it is a serious condition in the context of flying an aircraft and renders the sufferer unfit to act as a pilot.

Further Reference: PPL5 » Human Factors » Health and Flying » Incapacitation

EHFP2Q15   Answer C

A general description of any false perception of the aircraft's attitude is *spatial disorientation*. If an aircraft is flying straight and level at a constant speed, the force of gravity acts straight down. However, a deceleration can lead to the sensation of pitching down, leading to a reaction of pitching nose-up. So the airspeed decays further, leading to further deceleration and the temptation to pitch more nose-up. Clearly there is the danger of a stall in this scenario.

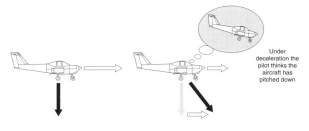

Under deceleration the pilot thinks the aircraft has pitched down

Further Reference: PPL5 » Human Factors » The Functions of the Mind (Basic Psychology) » Spatial Disorientation and Visual Illusions

EHFP2Q16   Answer B

The shape of a runway will affect the pilot's perception of the approach angle. A pilot on approach to a wider-than-normal runway might believe that he is too low. The pilot on approach to the narrower-than-normal runway might believe that he is too high. In much the same way, a runway (or other object) that is smaller than expected will be perceived as being further away than it actually is and *vice versa*.

'Normal' width runway   Wide runway   Narrow runway

Further Reference: PPL5 » Human Factors » The Functions of the Mind (Basic Psychology) » Spatial Disorientation and Visual Illusions

EHFP2Q17   Answer D

A situation where there is insufficient oxygen to meet the body's needs is known as hypoxia, and it is most commonly associated with flight above 10,000ft (Flight Level 100).

Further Reference: PPL5 » Human Factors » The Functions of the Body (Basic Physiology) » Breathing Problems and Flight at High Altitude

EHFP2Q18   Answer A

The 'clock' code is used in reporting directions to an aircraft. Based on a traditional clock face, 12 o'clock is dead ahead and 6 o'clock is directly behind. Three o'clock is on the right wing tip, 9 o'clock is on the left wing tip.

Thus the reported traffic is directly ahead, and at the same level unless otherwise reported.

The question starts by stating 'During a night flight...' At night, it is recommended that to view a faintly lit object, it is best to look slightly to one side of it rather than directly at it. Therefore, in these circumstances, it is best to look slightly to one side of 'dead ahead' to give the best chance of spotting traffic reported as '12 o'clock'.

Further Reference: PPL5 » Human Factors » The Functions of the Mind (Basic Psychology) » Lookout

EHFP2Q19   **Answer D**

The outer covering of the front of the eyeball is the *cornea*, and this helps to focus light rays that then pass via the *pupil* to the *lens*. The lens further focuses the light rays on to a point on the back of the eyeball (*retina*). The retina has two types of light-sensitive cells – *rods* and *cones*. The part of the retina on to which the lens focuses light rays is the *fovea*, and the cones are concentrated at this central point.

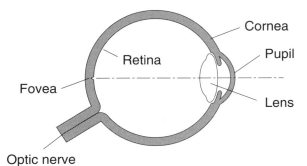

Further Reference: PPL5 » Human Factors » The Functions of the Body (Basic Physiology) » The Eyes

EHFP2Q20   **Answer B**

The eye can take up to 30 minutes to adapt fully to low-light conditions. So, if a pilot goes straight from a brightly-lit room to an aircraft directly outside at night, that person might be taking-off well before the eyes have fully adjusted to the dark conditions.

Further Reference: PPL5 » Human Factors » The Functions of the Body (Basic Physiology) » The Eyes

Paper 3 Answers and Explanations

EHFP3Q1   Answer A

Good situational awareness means that a pilot knows what is going on both in the aircraft and around it, and thus can make safe and accurate decisions and exercise good judgment based on <u>all available information</u>. Updating this information, and using it to plan ahead, is the foundation of sound pilot judgement.

Further Reference: PPL5 » Human Factors » The Functions of the Mind (Basic Psychology) » Situational Awareness, Confirmation Bias

EHFP3Q2   Answer C

With the seat height adjusted so that the eyes are as close as possible to the Design Eye Position or Eye Line Reference, the pilot will have the optimum view of both the flight instruments and cockpit controls, and also the outside view. Sitting with the eyes significantly below the recommended eye datum will reduce view forward and down, which can be a particular problem during approach and landing.

Further Reference: PPL5 » Human Factors » Cockpit Design and Procedures » Eye Datum

EHFP3Q3   Answer C

If an aircraft is flying over a cloud bank that is sloping (which is by no means a rare phenomenon) and the true

horizon is obscured, if the wings are kept level to the cloud bank the aircraft will actually be banked; and the pilot will no doubt be wondering why the aircraft keeps wandering off heading! Similarly, if an aircraft is flying low over sloping terrain and the distant horizon is not in view, the aircraft may be banked when thought to be level.

Further Reference: PPL5 » Human Factors » The Functions of the Mind (Basic Psychology) » Spatial Disorientation and Visual Illusions

EHFP3Q4   Answer C

The shape of the runway can alter the pilot's perspective of an aircraft's position relative to a 'normal' glideslope. See also EHFP2Q16

Further Reference: PPL5 » Human Factors » The Functions of the Mind (Basic Psychology) » Spatial Disorientation and Visual Illusions

EHFP3Q5   Answer D

The general advice is that you should not fly at all with 24 hours of diving using compressed air (or **12 hours if diving did not exceed 10m/30ft**).

Further Reference: PPL5 » Human Factors » The Functions of the Body (Basic Physiology) » Breathing Problems and Flight at High Altitude

EHFP3Q6   Answer A

The air cavity of the middle ear is connected to the nose and throat (and so atmospheric pressure) via the *Eustachian tube*. In other words, pressure within the middle ear is equalised to atmospheric pressure via the Eustachian tube. If due to illness or infection (such as a cold), the Eustachian tube becomes swollen or blocked, this pressure equalisation may not take place.

Further Reference: PPL5 » Human Factors » The Functions of the Body (Basic Physiology) » The Ears

EHFP3Q7   Answer C

Hyperventilation or over-breathing is a condition where breathing is both deeper and more rapid than necessary.

The treatment for hyperventilation is to return the breathing rate to normal. The victim may be able to do this unaided by consciously slowing down the breathing rate or by re-breathing exhaled air (eg by breathing into and from a bag held over the nose and mouth).

Further Reference: PPL5 » Human Factors » The Functions of the Body (Basic Physiology) » Breathing Problems and Flight at High Altitude

EHFP3Q8   Answer C

Decompression Sickness (DCS) is the situation where nitrogen comes out of solution in the blood, causing possible severe pain especially in the joints. This tends to happen as pressure is reduced either as the diver surfaces, or if the diver enters a low pressure environment (eg flying in an aircraft) too soon after diving.

Further Reference: PPL5 » Human Factors » The Functions of the Body (Basic Physiology) » Breathing Problems and Flight at High Altitude

EHFP3Q9   Answer D

The real danger of exhaust fumes or gases is that they are certain to contain the deadly gas Carbon Monoxide. The general advice is that after exposure to Carbon Monoxide, a pilot should expect to have to wait at least a number of days before being fit for flight. In addition, a medical examination is also strongly recommended.

Further Reference: PPL5 » Human Factors » Health and Flying » Toxic Hazards

EHFP3Q10   Answer B

It is a feature of an aircraft approaching head-on that its image size appears to grow very slowly for some time, then grows very rapidly as the range closes down.

Further Reference: PPL5 » Human Factors » The Functions of the Mind (Basic Psychology) » Lookout

EHFP3Q11   Answer D

Because of the construction of the eye, to spot a faint object at night it is best to look slightly to one side (about 10°) of it.

If you're not convinced, wait for the next clear night, then spend some time under the stars allowing your eyes to adjust to the darkness. With a little experimentation you should soon find that you can spot the dimmest stars better by looking slightly to one side of them.

Further Reference: PPL5 » Human Factors » The Functions of the Body (Basic Physiology) » The Eyes

EHFP3Q12   Answer A

The aircraft have a closing speed of 600 knots (480 knots + 120 knots). At 600 knots (ie 600nm an hour), the aircraft are closing at 10nm per minute (ie 600/60) or 1nm every six seconds (10/60).

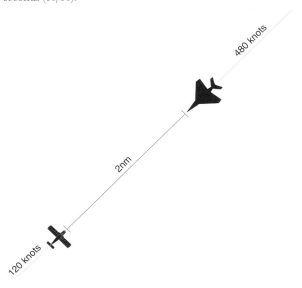

Thus a distance of 2nm will be closed in 12 seconds.

Further Reference: PPL5 » Human Factors » The Functions of the Mind (Basic Psychology) » Lookout

EHFP3Q13   Answer A

Hyperventilation, or over-breathing, is a condition where breathing is both deeper and more rapid than necessary. It is a condition most often associated with intense stress or anxiety, although it can also be caused by certain levels of vibration and turbulence, high *g*, hypoxia, pain or motion sickness, as well as by a lack of oxygen. The symptoms of hyperventilation are:

- ■ *Dizziness, light-headed feelings and a sense of 'unreality'*
- ■ *Tingling sensations, particularly in the fingers and hands, toes and feet*
- ■ *Vision impairment such as blurring, tunnel vision or clouded vision*
- ■ *Hot and cold feelings around the body*
- ■ *Unconsciousness*

Many of these symptoms are similar to those for hypoxia. The key to determining the cause of such symptoms is whether the sufferer is high enough to be likely to be experiencing hypoxia (typically FL100 +).

Further Reference: PPL5 » Human Factors » The Functions of the Body (Basic Physiology) » Breathing Problems and Flight at High Altitude

EHFP3Q14   Answer B

Although the precise way individuals are affected by hypoxia varies, in general terms the symptoms progress in the same sequence and many of them are similar to the effects of getting increasing drunk or high.

Starting first with the initial effects, the symptoms of hypoxia are:

- *Personality changes and impaired judgement*
- *Confusion and difficulty concentrating*
- *Loss of co-ordination*
- *Drowsiness*
- *Headaches, dizziness and nausea*
- *Blue/grey skin colour (cyanosis)*
- *Hyperventilation ('over-breathing')*
- *Loss of basic senses*
- *Unconsciousness*

Further Reference: PPL5 » Human Factors » The Functions of the Body (Basic Physiology) » Breathing Problems and Flight at High Altitude

EHFP3Q15   Answer A

An ability to recognise the onset of hypoxia is vital to any pilot flying at high levels. The problems of hypoxia become more severe with increasing altitude and the time available for the pilot to perform useful tasks without supplemental oxygen – the time of 'useful consciousness' – is reduced.

Further Reference: PPL5 » Human Factors » The Functions of the Body (Basic Physiology) » Breathing Problems and Flight at High Altitude

EHFP3Q16   Answer D

The most common cause of in-flight pilot incapacitation is gastroenteritis. Gastroenteritis is a general term for an infection of the stomach or intestines, which can cause acute abdominal pain, nausea, vomiting and diarrhoea. Any pilot suffering from, or suspected of developing, gastroenteritis is unfit to fly.

With regard to medication, it should be remembered that as a general rule, a pilot ill enough to require medication is too ill to fly.

Further Reference: PPL5 » Human Factors » Health and Flying » Incapacitation

EHFP3Q17   Answer B

Any cockpit controls that operate different systems should, ideally, look and feel different to avoid the inadvertent use of the wrong control.

Undercarriage operating control

Flaps operating control

Probably the best example is the undercarriage and flap controls, which are usually kept apart from each other (often on different sides of the throttle quadrant) and designed to look and feel different to each other. This is done to differentiate them so that, for example, a pilot is less likely to raise the undercarriage, as opposed to the flaps, during the after-landing checks.

Further Reference: PPL5 » Human Factors » Cockpit Design and Procedures » Controls

EHFP3Q18   Answer D

During a visual approach, pilots tend to rely on the appearance of the runway to judge the approach angle. On approach to a down-sloping runway, the aircraft appears to the pilot to be low. Approaching an up-sloping runway, the aircraft may well appear to the pilot to be high.

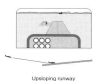

Level runway   Downsloping runway   Upsloping runway

Further Reference: PPL5 » Human Factors » The Functions of the Mind (Basic Psychology) » Spatial Disorientation and Visual Illusions

EHFP3Q19   Answer D

The *proportion* of oxygen within the air stays largely unchanged with increasing altitude, however the *amount* of oxygen taken in reduces markedly with the decreasing pressure and as altitude increases, pressure decreases. The amount of oxygen within the air can be expressed by the term *partial pressure*. At sea level the partial pressure of oxygen is around 212mb (i.e. 21% of 1013mb – the standard sea level pressure). At 20,000ft the partial pressure of oxygen is closer to 105mb.

Further Reference: PPL5 » Human Factors » The Functions of the Body (Basic Physiology) » Composition of the Atmosphere

EHFP3Q20   Answer D

Sound travels as waves through the air and these waves pass the ear flap (pinna) and travel along the outer ear canal, causing the eardrum to vibrate. This motion is transmitted by the small bones of the middle ear to the cochlea of the inner ear. Here the resulting movements stimulate the minute hair cells by deforming them; in response they originate electrical signals which pass up the fibres of the auditory nerve to the brain. The auditory range of the average human is in the region of 20Hz – 20,000Hz.

Further Reference: PPL5 » Human Factors » The Functions of the Body (Basic Physiology) » The Ears

Answers

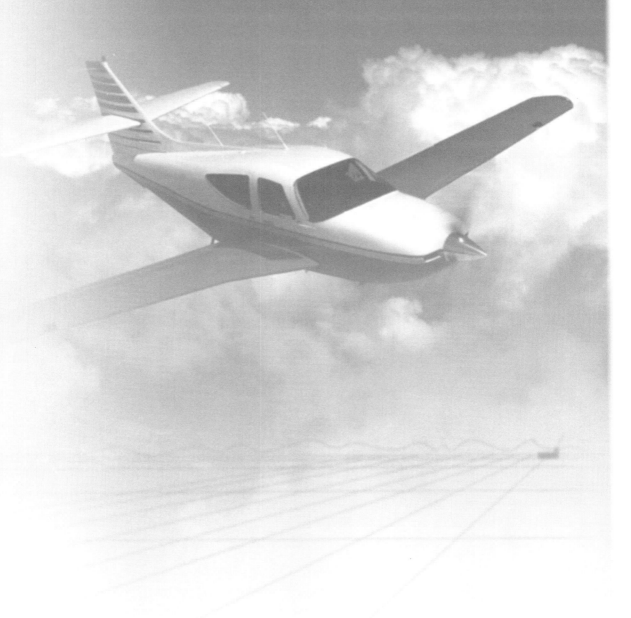

	A	B	C	D
1	X			
2			X	
3		X		
4				X
5	X			
6	X			
7			X	
8		X		
9		X		
10			X	
11	X			
12			X	
13		X		
14		X		
15	X			
16			X	
17		X		
18				X
19		X		
20				X
21			X	
22	X			
23			X	
24	X			
25			X	
26				X
27			X	
28	X			
29		X		
30			X	

	A	B	C	D
31	X			
32				X
33		X		
34	X			
35	X			
36	X			
37	X			
38		X		
39				X
40				X

	A	B	C	D
1		X		
2		X		
3		X		
4		X		
5				X
6				X
7			X	
8				X
9	X			
10				X
11				X
12	X			
13	X			
14		X		
15		X		
16			X	
17				X
18	X			
19			X	
20			X	
21			X	
22		X		
23				X
24				X
25			X	
26		X		
27			X	
28				X
29		X		
30			X	

	A	B	C	D
31		X		
32	X			
33				X
34				X
35			X	
36	X			
37		X		
38		X		
39				X
40	X			

	A	B	C	D
1			☒	
2		☒		
3				☒
4		☒		
5	☒			
6			☒	
7	☒			
8		☒		
9	☒			
10			☒	
11				☒
12				☒
13	☒			
14		☒		
15			☒	
16			☒	
17			☒	
18	☒			
19		☒		
20	☒			
21				☒
22			☒	
23				☒
24				☒
25		☒		
26				☒
27			☒	
28				☒
29			☒	
30		☒		

	A	B	C	D
31		☒		
32		☒		
33			☒	
34		☒		
35		☒		
36			☒	
37	☒			
38			☒	
39			☒	
40	☒			

	A	B	C	D
1				X
2		X		
3				X
4			X	
5	X			
6	X			
7				X
8			X	
9	X			
10		X		
11			X	
12				X
13			X	
14	X			
15		X		
16	X			
17			X	
18		X		
19			X	
20			X	

	A	B	C	D
1	X			
2				X
3			X	
4	X			
5		X		
6	X			
7				X
8				X
9				X
10		X		
11		X		
12	X			
13		X		
14				X
15				X
16	X			
17				X
18			X	
19		X		
20			X	

	A	B	C	D
1				X
2				X
3	X			
4				X
5			X	
6				X
7		X		
8				X
9			X	
10			X	
11			X	
12			X	
13		X		
14				X
15			X	
16		X		
17			X	
18		X		
19				X
20			X	

Q	Paper 1	Paper 2	Paper 3
1	D	D	B
2	B	A	A
3	B	C	C
4	B	C	A
5	C	D	D
6	D	D	D
7	A	B	B
8	C	A	C
9	D	C	D
10	B	B	B
11	C	B	B
12	C	C	D
13	A	D	D
14	C	B	B
15	B	C	A
16	D	C	C
17	C	C	C
18	A	B	C
19	C	D	C
20	D	D	D
21	A	B	D
22	C	D	A
23	B	A	B
24	B	C	C
25	A	C	A

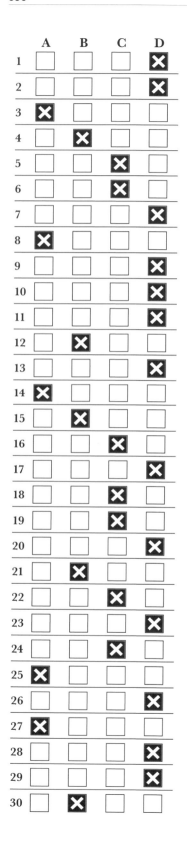

#	Paper 1	Paper 2	Paper 3
1	D	C	B
2	D	C	D
3	A	C	C
4	B	A	A
5	C	A	A
6	C	C	A
7	D	D	B
8	A	D	D
9	D	B	D
10	D	B	C
11	D	C	D
12	B	C	C
13	D	D	B
14	A	B	C
15	B	D	D
16	C	D	C
17	D	A	A
18	C	D	D
19	C	D	B
20	D	D	C
21	B	D	B
22	C	B	C
23	D	C	A
24	C	C	C
25	A	C	D
26	D	C	D
27	A	D	A
28	D	D	D
29	D	D	A
30	B	B	C

	A	B	C	D
1			X	
2			X	
3	X			
4		X		
5				X
6	X			
7		X		
8			X	
9	X			
10	X			
11				X
12				X
13	X			
14	X			
15			X	
16		X		
17			X	
18			X	
19			X	
20		X		

	A	B	C	D
1	X			
2			X	
3	X			
4	X			
5			X	
6			X	
7		X		
8				X
9		X		
10	X			
11	X			
12	X			
13				X
14	X			
15	X			
16				X
17	X			
18		X		
19		X		
20				X

	A	B	C	D
1		X		
2				X
3		X		
4			X	
5		X		
6		X		
7				X
8		X		
9		X		
10				X
11			X	
12	X			
13				X
14	X			
15	X			
16		X		
17				X
18		X		
19		X		
20			X	

	A	B	C	D
1				☒
2	☒			
3			☒	
4	☒			
5		☒		
6		☒		
7		☒		
8			☒	
9				☒
10			☒	
11			☒	
12		☒		
13	☒			
14			☒	
15				☒
16		☒		
17			☒	
18		☒		
19	☒			
20			☒	
21	☒			
22	☒			
23			☒	
24				☒
25		☒		
26		☒		
27				☒
28				☒
29		☒		
30			☒	

	A	B	C	D
31				☒
32			☒	
33		☒		
34	☒			
35		☒		
36			☒	
37		☒		
38	☒			
39			☒	
40	☒			
41			☒	
42				☒
43	☒			
44		☒		
45	☒			
46	☒			
47		☒		
48				☒
49			☒	
50		☒		

	A	B	C	D
1		X		
2		X		
3			X	
4			X	
5			X	
6			X	
7		X		
8				X
9			X	
10	X			
11		X		
12	X			
13			X	
14				X
15		X		
16	X			
17			X	
18				X
19		X		
20		X		
21			X	
22		X		
23			X	
24				X
25		X		
26	X			
27	X			
28			X	
29		X		
30				X

	A	B	C	D
31		X		
32		X		
33		X		
34	X			
35		X		
36				X
37			X	
38	X			
39		X		
40	X			
41		X		
42	X			
43				X
44			X	
45				X
46			X	
47	X			
48	X			
49			X	
50	X			

#	A	B	C	D
1			X	
2		X		
3	X			
4				X
5	X			
6			X	
7	X			
8			X	
9	X			
10	X			
11				X
12	X			
13	X			
14	X			
15		X		
16		X		
17		X		
18			X	
19		X		
20	X			
21			X	
22	X			
23	X			
24			X	
25	X			
26	X			
27	X			
28		X		
29		X		
30	X			

#	A	B	C	D
31				X
32			X	
33			X	
34				X
35	X			
36			X	
37			X	
38	X			
39		X		
40			X	
41		X		
42				X
43		X		
44		X		
45		X		
46				X
47		X		
48	X			
49				X
50			X	

	A	B	C	D
1			X	
2			X	
3	X			
4				X
5		X		
6		X		
7		X		
8	X			
9			X	
10				X
11	X			
12				X
13			X	
14		X		
15	X			
16				X
17				X
18				X
19				X
20			X	

	A	B	C	D
1				X
2	X			
3				X
4			X	
5			X	
6				X
7			X	
8	X			
9	X			
10				X
11	X			
12	X			
13			X	
14	X			
15			X	
16		X		
17				X
18	X			
19				X
20		X		

	A	B	C	D
1	X			
2			X	
3			X	
4			X	
5				X
6	X			
7			X	
8			X	
9				X
10		X		
11				X
12	X			
13	X			
14		X		
15	X			
16				X
17		X		
18				X
19				X
20				X